Edited by
Nigel C. Gibson

RETHINKING FANON

The Continuing Dialogue

HB

Humanity
Books

an imprint of Prometheus Books
59 John Glenn Drive, Amherst, New York 14228-2197

Published 1999 by Humanity Books, an imprint of Prometheus Books

03 02 01 00 99   5 4 3 2 1

Library of Congress Cataloging-in-Publication Data

Rethinking Fanon : the continuing dialogue / edited by Nigel C. Gibson.
       p.   cm.
    Includes bibliographical references and index.
    ISBN 1–57392–708–2 (alk. paper). — ISBN 1–57392–709–0 (pbk. : alk. paper)
       1. Fanon, Frantz, 1925–1961—Contributions in political science.
    2. Fanon, Frantz, 1925–1961—Contributions in social sciences. I. Gibson, Nigel C.
    JC273.F36R47   1999
    325'.3'092—dc21   99–13601
                                                                    CIP

Printed in the United States of America on acid-free paper

Contents

Introduction
Nigel Gibson   9

I. POLITICS AND REVOLUTION

1. Frantz Fanon: Portrait of a Revolutionary
   Emmanuel Hansen   49

2. Rescuing Fanon from the Critics
   Tony Martin   83

3. Frantz Fanon, World Revolutionary
   Lou Turner and John Alan   103

4. Fanon as a Democratic Theorist
   Hussein M. Adam   119

5. Revolutionary Psychiatry of Fanon
   Hussein A. Bulhan   141

5

II. CULTURAL CRITICISM

6. Remembering Fanon: Self, Psyche,
   and the Colonial Condition
   Homi Bhabha   179

7. Travelling Theory Reconsidered
   Edward W. Said   197

8. Resistance Theory/Theorizing Resistance
   or Two Cheers of Nativism
   Benita Parry   215

9. Critical Fanonism
   Henry Louis Gates Jr.   251

III. FANON, GENDER, AND NATIONAL CONSCIOUSNESS

10. Women, Nationalism, and Religion in the
    Algerian Liberation Struggle
    Marie-Aimée Helie-Lucas   271

11. Fanon and Gender Agency
    Anne McClintock   283

12. Interior Colonies: Frantz Fanon
    and the Politics of Identification
    Diana Fuss   294

13. Fanon's Feminist Consciousness and
    Algerian Women's Liberation: Colonialism,
    Nationalism, and Fundamentalism
    T. Denean Sharpley-Whiting   329

14. Challenging the Social Order:
    Women's Liberation in Contemporary Algeria
    Zouligha   354

IV. FANON'S QUEST FOR A NEW HUMANISM

15. Fanon and the FLN: Dialectics of
    Organization and the Algerian Revolution
        Lou Turner   369

16. Radical Mutations: Fanon's Untidy Dialectic of History
        Nigel Gibson   408

Bibliography   447

About the Contributors   465

Introduction

Nigel Gibson

FANONIAN TRAVELING

The consciousness of self is not the closing of the door to communication. Philosophic thought teaches us, on the contrary, that it is its guarantee.

Fanon

Fanon was at the center: to the left, Sekyi-Otu's *Dialectic of Experience*; to the right, Homi Bhabha's *Location of Culture*; and below Gordon, Sharpley-Whiting, and White's *Fanon: A Critical Reader*. This was the window of my local bookstore this past summer— with the African-style multicolored covers of the new editions of Fanon's *The Wretched of the Earth* and *Toward the African Revolution* on one level, and *Black Skin, White Masks* on another. Though it only stayed that way for a couple of weeks, and the bookstore later closed down, it was long enough to give notice of Fanon's status in the late 1990s.

Reading Edward W. Said's essay "Travelling Theory," and his essay in this volume "Travelling Theory Revisited," might lead one to ask what has been lost now that Fanon, removed from his own cultural context, is heard mainly in English and in the university setting. Does Fanon have relevance beyond the Anglo-American academy?

Whereas Fanon's own traveling from Martinique to France to Algeria and abandonment of his French citizenship were marks of his development as a revolutionary, and his trip to Washington marked his death, it is in the United States that the most vocal rebirth of Fanonism is evident. The twenty-five or so years of the discussion about Fanon in the English-speaking world represented in this volume should be contrasted with the relative lack of discussion of Fanon in French.[1] Yet, wherever studied, Fanon demands an active engagement, and as Edouard Glissant put it in *Caribbean Discourse*, this is perhaps his enduring quality and challenge, and perhaps also one reason why he has been forgotten closer to "home":

> It is difficult for a French Caribbean individual to be the brother, the friend, or simply the associate of a fellow countryman of Fanon. Because, of all the French Caribbean intellectuals, he is the only one to have *acted on his ideas* . . . to take full responsibility for *a complete break*.

Rethinking Fanon represents different ways this responsibility has been manifested across various fields of inquiry and the ways in which a complete break has been interpreted and resisted. The first essays of part one represent a period of Fanon studies close to Fanon's life and provide an important basis for understanding Fanon. Emmanuel Hansen (chapter 1) and Tony Martin (chapter 2) are concerned with setting the record straight and correcting fallacious assertions about Fanon's life. Readers interested in a political biography of Fanon's fascinating but short life will find Hansen's chapter particularly illuminating. Both chapters also situate Fanon in Marxism, négritude, Pan-Africanism, and the historical context of postwar decolonization, specifically the Algerian revolution. Placing Fanon in these contexts helps provide a framework for better understanding the questions Fanon was asking in the decade of the 1950s. Whether considered a revolutionary humanist (Hansen), a revolutionary psychiatrist (Bulhan, whose *Frantz Fanon and the Psychology of Oppression* helped widen the field), or a radical democrat (Adam, chapter 4), Fanon's originality depends on a grasp of his historical and intellectual contexts.

The character of Fanon's Marxism is questioned in a number of essays in part one.[2] The critique of Fanon 1960s and 1970s by an array of Trotskyists, Stalinists, and Maoists as well as the debates about the orthodoxy of his class concepts might be less compelling today, yet Fanon's engagement with Marx remains important for Fanon's analysis of racism and colonialism. Not merely phenomenological, racism has a material structure, and from Fanon's point of view is a product of a specific conjuncture, which requires uprooting (Fanon 1967a, 82).* In "Racism and Culture" (presented at the First Congress of Negro Writers and Artists in Paris, 1956), Fanon insists on a dialectical approach. He reminds us that it is not simply the material base but the relation of "stages" of production and subjective resistance which forces bourgeois society to evolve more and more subtle and sophisticated forms of racism. The old "material basis of the doctrine," biologism, is replaced by a more "democratic and humane" system of culturalism:

> The perfecting of the means of production inevitably brings about the camouflage of the techniques by which man is exploited, hence forms of racism. . . . In the very heart of the "civilized nations" the workers finally discover that the exploitation of man, at the root of a system, assumes different faces. At this stage racism no longer dares appear without disguise. (Fanon 1967b, 35–36)

"True liberation" puts an end to racism because it "puts into the people's hands all the material means which make possible the radical transformation of society" (1968, 310). This redevelopment of a subject-object dialectic entails "rethinking" Marx's categories in the colonial context and "working out new concepts" for period of independence.

---

*Complete publication information for all references can be found in the bibliography located at the end of this volume.

Like Marx, who famously said that he was "not a Marxist," Fanon was critical of the parties associated with Marxism, which paid little serious attention to the "National Question." "His concern [was] with what the masses do and say and think," argued Adolfo Gilly. Gilly caught something of Fanon's Marxism in his introduction to the American edition of *A Dying Colonialism* when he wrote Fanon's "belief [was] that it is the masses, and not leaders nor systems, who in the final analysis make and determine history" (Fanon 1967c, 2). Sensitivity to Fanon's Marxism is ably demonstrated in Tony Martin's essay "Rescuing Fanon from the Critics." Martin grounds Fanon's thought in Marx's famous phrase from *The Eighteenth Brumaire* that people make history but not in circumstances of their own choosing. Martin calls it the "leitmotif" of Fanon's philosophy.

Lou Turner and John Alan (chapter 3) also recognize that an affinity between Fanon and their Marxist-Humanist philosophy requires a "complete break" with much of what is considered Marxism. For Turner and Alan, Fanon's philosophy came alive again in the revolutionary movement of Black Consciousness in South Africa. According to Turner and Alan philosophies of liberation "travel" subterraneously and along noninstitutional lines: Just as the white rulers "denuded a continent via the infamous triangular trade in *slave, rum, and molasses*, the [Africans, Afro-Caribbeans, and Black-Americans] were exchanging ideas—the ideas of freedom, the experiences of Black masses in action, and their aspirations for *a new world*."

Fanon was essentially out of print in early 1970s Britain. In fact, one port of entry for Fanon's ideas was the post-Soweto (1976) arrival of South African exiles, especially the Black Consciousness Movement (BCM), who set up office in London in the late 1970s and published the journal *Solidarity*. The BCM community engendered a new interest in Fanon that had also been displayed in Steve Biko's book *I Write What I Like*.

Nevertheless, while Fanon remained decidedly marginal in Britain, he continued to be discussed by both African-American and African intellectuals in the United States inside and outside the academy (i.e., Adam, who was one of the few to reconsider Fanon in the light of the African democracy movements of the early 1990s, Hussein A. Bulhan [chapter 5], Hansen, and Turner and Alan). During the 1980s he was added to "Contemporary Civilization" curricula in America's elite colleges but mostly as a foil to the "dead white male" canon and almost always reduced to a theorist of therapeutic violence gleaned from the wildly misunderstood "Concerning Violence" chapter in *The Wretched of the Earth*.

Fanonian journeys in the academy and in radical movements have not been only geographical. Each voyage has reacted to previous engagements and is also a product of its own historical context. This contextualization is also apparent in Homi K. Bhabha's seminal "Remembering Fanon" (chapter 6). Though reprinted in various edited versions in the United States, the essay, originally written for the 1986 British edition of *Black Skin, White Masks*, takes as one of its points of departure the status (or non status) of Fanon and of blacks in British left politics. The essay is situated in the politics of the British black movement that had come of age in the late 1970s, and came under a nationwide spotlight during the summer of rebellion in 1981. For Kobena Mercer the context included attempts "to rethink questions of black peoples' experience of the psychiatric system in contemporary Britain." As Mercer puts it, "given the marginalization and exclusion of the subject of 'race' from the concerns of white left politics of psychiatry, Fanon's work may still yield . . . conceptual resources" (1986, 140). On the other hand, it was Hussein Bulhan's work in the United States that followed through most rigorously the politics of psychoanalysis and psychiatry. In Britain, however, it was cultural studies that brought Fanon center stage despite Mercer's warning that "Fanon's starting point was not 'cultural differences' . . . but . . . questions of 'real power,' created by history and social relations" (1986, 140). Paradoxically, questions of cultural difference, not "real power," still determine reference to Fanon, who remains a marginal figure for the British Left.[3]

Though Bhabha's transatlantic journey might fit with the domestication identified in Said's initial conception of traveling theory as it became the property of American cultural studies (see Gibson, 1999), an enduring aspect of Bhabha's essay—which creatively applies Lacanian psychoanalytic concepts to *Black Skin, White Masks*—is the upsetting of binaries and unsettling preconceived ideas. Bhabha's essay represents an important divide from the "Fanonians" of part one. After Bhabha's Lacanian reading we cannot read Fanon as we had, though it is a mistake of cultural theorists to begin here, eliding the important scholarship of part one, mostly by African and African-American radicals.

To those who recognize Fanon as a voice of the 1960s Black Power movement, or even see him relevant to discussions of an American racism which he called "dialectical gangrene" (the dialectic referring to the constant determination to fight it [1967b, 36]), the 1980s Anglo-American stage of Fanon studies remains somewhat anemic. Nevertheless, it would not be an exaggeration to maintain that Bhabha is central to the creation of a new interest in Fanon. For Bhabha the title "Black Skins, White Masks" caught a "grotesque mimicry or doubling that threatens to split the soul and whole undifferentiated skin of the ego." Bhabha's understanding of Fanon's construction of the colonial subject, "a triple person" (Fanon 1967a, 79), is best understood through Freud's "Fetishism" where the possibility of embracing multiple contradictory beliefs is expressed. Unlike Bulhan and Fanon, however, Bhabha does not question the institution of psychiatry in the colonial system.

Inside the academy one might wonder how there could have been life for Fanon before Bhabha. Of course others in the academy in the United States, notably Edward W. Said, had been working on Fanon during the same period, but Bhabha's work remains paradigmatic.

The importance of the debates in cultural and literary studies in the late 1980s and early 1990s is reflected in part two with essays from Bhabha, Edward W. Said (chapter 7), Benita Parry (chapter 8), and Henry Louis Gates (chapter 9). An overview of the late 1980s "debate," dubbed "Critical Fanonism" is found in Gates's essay though it is placed at the end of this section, as an opinion rather than as an introduction. Gates notes that Fanon has been reinstated as a "global theorist"; not as earlier radicals had viewed him—a theorist of "Third World" revolution—but as a global theorist of texts, and of literary critical criticism. An irresistible figure, Gates argues, who is seen "as both oppositional and postmodern," Fanon is readily (and ironically[4]) employed in English literature as a critic of British Romanticism and William Blake, Shakespeare and the Renaissance, and even Ezra Pound. Gates's concern is not with these appropriations but with the theory behind them, namely, "colonial discourse theory"—his is a reading of the readings of Fanon. His comparison and critique of five key postcolonial theorists (even if they might not identify themselves as such)—Edward W. Said, Benita Parry, Gayatri C. Spivak, Homi Bhabha, and Abdul JanMohammed—is included here as a useful overview and foray into the field of postcolonial studies. Gates's essay is important, not only because in its synthesis of a new stage of reading readings, but also because it represents an academic domestication of "Fanon" who is represented as "Rashomon-like" and "wide open to interpretation." In the end, perhaps paradoxically, for Gates, it is his under-reading of Memmi's anti-Fanon, not his reading of Said's, Bhabha's, or Parry's "Fanon" who comes out ahead.

Benita Parry reacts in part to the decontextualization of Fanon in postcolonial studies, and to a knee-jerk anti-essentialism, which almost becomes a parody of the essentialism it wishes to avoid. She quotes approvingly Stuart Hall's adage that "all knowledge is contextual." Parry argues that postcolonial analysis often abstracts resistance from its moment of performance and she reinvestigates whether the whole project of African nationalism can simply be discarded as a reverse ethnocentrism which simply mirrors existing categories, performing an identical function and producing the same effects as the system it contests. Her route of inquiry to Fanon is via négritude. By re-articulating the question "what in négritude was liberating," Parry sheds new light on Fanon's own arguments and questions of identity and agency. In contrast to the simplistic model of Black Nationalism that often associates Fanon with Manichean thinking (of which he issued a deep critique), or simply following Sartre's dismal of blackness as

a "minor" term in the dialectic, Parry argues that Fanon understands an intellectual apprehension of blackness as both a construct and as a visceral attachment to the powerful fiction of black
identity. Fanon marks négritude, or cultural affirmation, Parry
argues, "as a necessary moment in the realization of a combative
position." She quotes Fanon:

> This rediscovery, this absolute valorization almost in defiance of
> reality, objectively indefensible, assumes an incomparable and
> subjective importance. . . . [T]he plunge into the chasm of the
> past is the condition and source of freedom. (1967b, 43).

Parry concludes that Fanon's writings on "National Culture"
marked a "disenchantment with the official cultural nationalism of
the newly independent African states." But she also shows that his
concept of "cultural" is a product of a critique of political positions
held by intellectuals who held political power, i.e., Senghor of
Senegal, who had withheld support for the Algerian struggle, or
Césaire, who had supported a referendum to make Martinique an
overseas department of France, or Rabemananjara of Madagascar,
who voted against the Algerian people at the United Nations. In
contrast to Albert Memmi, Parry contends that Fanon's call for a
new humanism, and his turning away from Europe as a source
and model of meanings and aspirations, holds in place the vision
of the anticolonial struggle as a global emancipatory project while
projecting the radical hope of an "oppositional humanism."

In *Culture and Imperialism*, Edward W. Said wrote of Césaire's
influence on Fanon's humanism, in his essay here he investigates
the impact of Georg Lukács's *History of Class Consciousness* on
Fanon's *The Wretched of the Earth*. The traveling of Lukács's theory of
reification (through the Frankfurt School and beyond) provided
Said with his original example of how, when taken out of their cultural contexts, theories lose some of their original power and rebelliousness. Such an assumption is challenged via Fanon. In the colonial context, Lukács's subject-object dialectic, argues Said, is rede-
ployed by Fanon with devastating intellectual and political force in

The Wretched of the Earth. Though Lukács resonates from the first page, Said argues that this is not a simple inscription of the Lukácsian dialectic. Said's essay raises many questions about the redeployment of "European" thought, as well as the openings and limitations of thinking about thought in spatial parameters. Rather than simply applying theory (and the limitation of this method partly explains theory's loss of power out of context), Fanon's *reworking* of the dialectic (what Said calls *reinscription*) results in recreating it.

Said criticizes Lukács for the absence of the *national* element in *History and Class Consciousness*,[5] but Said reminds us, it is not until the chapter titled "The Pitfalls of National Consciousness" that Fanon makes clear what he has intended all along. Far from guaranteeing real independence, the nationalist elite will perpetuate colonialism in a new form. Said claims that Fanon's radical humanism, too easily avoided by antihumanist poststructuralists, is the great challenge to post-colonial states.

The intellectual re-evaluations engendered by postmodern literary studies (deconstruction and poststructuralism) with their emphasis on the discursive and textual are important to these later appreciations of Fanon. Newly envisioned, he has emerged as an important forerunner of discussions of "postcoloniality." For Said, traveling theory, and here he is speaking of Adorno, remains "transgressive"—"tougher, harder, more recalcitrant"—when it offers no redemptive quality, or synthesis, and is likely to be expressed in the most difficult language. At the same time, theory's geographical dispersion also depends on the exercise of "reigniting" its fiery core. This is what thwarts it from "growing old." Nevertheless, reigniting this fiery core does not exist outside of a political context, and this applies to Fanon as well as to ourselves—in other words, we are speaking of refashioning a subject-object dialectic. The power of *The Wretched* comes from Fanon's ability to synthesize, yet the work is very much grounded in his involvement and analysis of the Algerian revolution. Indeed, it is this praxis that provides him the capability to redevelop the subject-object dialectic.

Everyone will take what they need from Fanon, but are decontextualized generalizations about Fanon (and here I am thinking of a dehistoricized and deterritorized postcolonial theory) valuable? Or do we, by returning to the revolutionary problematic, and the different ways he spoke of it in *The Wretched*, in *A Dying Colonialism*, and in his political journalism, find new ways to reconnect with Fanon, new ways to reignite the fire? One example of alternative routes of traveling theory has been the ways in which Fanon's works have been discussed by feminist theorists, especially as it had reconsidered the problematic of women's liberation and national liberation.

Earlier feminist theorists, who emphasized the place of violence in Fanon's thought, and who focused on the gendering of the "native" protagonist, tended to mistakenly view Fanon as simply a conservative, an upholder of the veil and of women's subordination in Algerian society. In contrast, part three, "Fanon, Gender, and National Consciousness" is representative of the more sophisticated and nuanced discussions that have been taking place of late.

Marie-Aimée Helie-Lucas (chapter 10) writes from within the Algerian national liberation struggle. A socialist-feminist who silenced her feminist criticism for the sake of "unity," she implicates Fanon in the all-too-quick degeneration of the Algerian "socialist" project. She accuses him of myth making, of exaggerating the degree of women's involvement and agency in the Algerian revolution and thereby papering over real gender inequities that arose during the liberation struggle. The myth of women's participation, she maintains, justified putting off women's liberation. Yet Helie-Lucas falls into the trap of equating Fanon with the politics of the post-colonial regime. If we reject this equation, her arguments about Algerian state capitalism and her invocations for a true liberation for all have a strongly Fanonian ring.

Stimulated by Bhabha's reading of Fanon (even though he had avoided the issue of gender), Anne McClintock (chapter 11) and Diana Fuss (chapter 12) give us two important readings of Fanon's essay "Algeria Unveiled" from *A Dying Colonialism*. *Identification Papers*, the title of Fuss's book, gives the impression of political and geographical boundaries, pass-laws, and I.D.s, but Fanon's reference to "an identification paper" in *The Wretched of the Earth* (if it is from Fanon and not Freud that Fuss takes the title) is to another register, namely the libido at the level of a group and within the context of "tradition." For instance, Fanon wonders,

> [T]he so-called prehistoric societies attach great importance to the unconscious. The atmosphere of myth and magic frightens me and so takes on an undoubted reality. By terrifying me, it integrates me in the traditions and the history of my district or of my tribe, as it was an identification paper. (1968, 55)

Fuss exemplifies the position that psychoanalysis provided Fanon with a vocabulary and an intellectual framework for diagnosing and for treating the neurotic structure of colonialism. We can see from the preceding quote how such a structure is distorted in the colonial situation, because, though it is a world that "belongs to me," it is entirely unreal, and even more terrifying than the world dominated by the settlers. For Fanon it is not only the context but the discourse itself which is intimately connected to the colonial situation. Like Bulhan, Fuss's *reading* of Fanon (from the field of literary criticism) suggests that colonialism shapes "the very terms in which psychoanalysis comes to understand the process of identification." For Fuss, Fanon asks questions about identification that Freud and Lacan fail to ask. Fuss also makes a particularly arresting and original discussion of Fanon's remarks on homosexuality in *Black Skin, White Masks* which have often been hastily dismissed as simply homophobic.

By exploring the "multiple fissure" of gender through Fanon's work, McClintock further explores areas of Bhabha's observations of the "palpable pressure of division and displacement" in Fanon's *Black Skin, White Masks* that Bhabha himself has declined doing. McClintock finds two types of nationalism in Fanon, a "mechanical nationalism" sanctioned by "structural logic," and a more open-ended and strategically difficult and unpredictable view of national agency. With this latter national "subject" in mind, McClintock (like Helie-Lucas) criticizes Fanon for crediting women's liberation entirely to national liberation and giving women almost no agency prior to nationalism. Fanon had "brilliantly" raised the question of women's agency, McClintock avers, only to foreclose it. In contrast to T. Denean Sharpley-Whiting's writing (chapter 13) of Fanon's concept of a "new woman" and to Lou Turner (chapter 15) seeing a "birth of a new dialectic" in Fanon's articulation of "woman as revolutionary," McClintock concludes with the acute observation that women's liberation is "not raised as one of the 'pitfalls' of national consciousness."

Reading Fanon psychoanalytically has been enormously fruitful. But Fanon always reminds us of the shortcomings of such an approach. In his essay on the radio in *A Dying Colonialism*, for example, Fanon speaks of the parallel between the victim of hallucinations and "the hallucinatory psychoses" of colonial society. After 1956, he writes, "[T]he radio voices became protective, friendly. . . . The foreign technique, which has been 'digested' in connection with the national struggle, had become a fighting instrument for the people and a protective organ against anxiety" (1967c, 89). Fanon then describes a parallel between the victim of hallucinations and "its counterpart in the disintegrating colonial situation," reminding us that the dehumanized reality produced by the social reality informs and limits the practice of psychology. By 1956, as the Battle of Algiers heated up, Fanon's situation at Blida-Joinville hospital was unworkable. He resigned from his post and officially joined the revolution.

Sharpley-Whiting provides an alternative and much more fully contextualized reading of Fanon and women's liberation. Her discussion takes us from Helie-Lucas's critique to a many-sided discussion of the veil touching on Islamic fundamentalism and women in Algeria today. In contrast to Helie-Lucas's mythical Fanon (and to Fuss and McClintock, whom she discusses), Sharpley-Whiting wants feminists to put Fanon to use practically and creatively. Silenced by the official nationalist discourse, she argues, Fanon offered another view to challenge women's marginalization. His account of the creation of "the new woman" who assumes an individual responsibility for self and action has been blocked, but it is a history that should not be allowed to rewritten. Fanon is too often misread, she declares, and inscribed in myths that are grounded in "historico-textual revisionisms." A "defense" of Fanon is needed, and Sharpley-Whiting offers one.

The section ends with the chapter, "Challenging the Social Order: Women's Liberation in Contemporary Algeria," an interview with feminist activist Zouligha. When one of the interviewers gave me a draft of the interview in June 1998, I immediately thought that it would be a good way to conclude this section. Though she does not discuss Fanon, Zouligha brings the dehumanization, depersonalization, and "nonviability" of contemporary Algeria into focus, echoing Fanon's description of colonial totalitarianism. The increasingly repressive society, a result of the war between armed Islamic fundamentalist groups, the FIS (Islamic Salvation Front) and the GIA (Groupes Islamiques Armée), and the government, has fundamentally silenced the people. The picture Zouligha draws of relations at the school where she works is particularly striking. Of the murders, "it is impossible to mourn." Of life in Algeria, "we cannot talk, everything is repressed, we keep everything inside. . . . It is a sick society." In Fanon's words, it is a nonviable society and one that needs to be replaced.

RE-READING FANON'S IDEA OF LIBERATION IN THE FACE OF ISLAMIC FUNDAMENTALISM IN ALGERIA

Colonialism and its derivatives do not, as a matter of fact, constitute the present enemies of Africa. For my part, the deeper I enter into the culture and political circles the surer I am that the great danger that threatens Africa is the absence of ideology.

Fanon

The leader . . . uses every means to put [the people] to sleep.

Fanon

In the following section a brief analysis of some of the tendencies inherent in the Algerian revolution will help provide a basis for understanding the politics of religion in post-colonial Algeria. It will also provide another context for Fanon's political practice—Fanon's dialectical approach to understanding of the Algerian revolution—as well as a way to view the vicissitudes of Fanon as traveling theory.

To argue that the rise of contemporary Islamic fundamentalism in Algeria proves Fanon's theorization of the Algerian revolution is flawed is neither correct nor original. The position is based on the mistaken assumption that Fanon misunderstood Algerian politics and culture, that he was overconfident in the ability of the revolution to create a "new person," and that he was not critical of conservative aspects of culture.[6] This position mirrors the Manicheanism Fanon criticizes and thus fails to understand Fanon or to fully grasp the politics of Islamic fundamentalism.

Many contemporary perceptions of Algeria are dominated by the rise of Islamic fundamentalism. The reality is far more complex. "Islamic fundamentalism" (which is itself contested) does not exhaust Islam. Indeed, Islam (by "Islam" I mean practices and cultures, not doctrines in the Koran) has a myriad of expressions, factions as well as adaptations to local belief systems. Islam in Algeria is no exception. No matter what claims to orthodoxy are made, each Islamic movement should be studied in its own economic, political, and social context, as well as in light of the failure of a post-colonial regime,[7] like Algeria's, to map out a liberatory ideology and to address fundamental socioeconomic problems.

Islamic observance in Algeria at independence was fairly weak in the urban areas and far from "orthodox" in the countryside. The construction of the equation Algeria = Islam was formulated before the war of liberation by Ulama (Association of Reformist Ulama, which officially joined the FLN [Front de Libération Nationale] in 1956) as a cultural claim, which it advocated alongside political assimilation with France. The latter was based on the assumption that the Algerian masses were "weak" and "needed to be under the protective wing of a strong and civilized nation." At independence, the claim to Islamic orthodoxy became important for some FLN leaders in the struggle to establish political hegemony within the party/state organization.

Reading today's Islamic fundamentalism back into Algerian history (and one could find a history of pronouncements for the "return to a pure Islam" going back a thousand years), means that one forgets that the current fundamentalism is the result of a number of factors, among them the numerous pragmatic political decisions of FLN leaders (including making Islam the state religion in 1976) made so as to hold onto state power. In other words, one needs to consider the contested ideas (and lack of ideas) behind this hybrid, and the failure to open national liberation along the lines Fanon suggested.[8]

Despite all the rhetoric about "Islam and Socialism," about proving the "Islamic roots of socialism," about "Arabization" and "Islamization," at independence the FLN lacked coherence on the question of Islam, as it did on ideology in general. Whereas the FLN leaders' references to Islam were for factional and pragmatic reasons, conservatives used their alliance with the clerics to attack dissent and individual rights. Among the first victims were women.

The FLN's Soummam Platform (1956) had encouraged an open society although it was limited in its idea of women's role in the revolution. Even before gaining independence FLN conservatives sought to close down that openness. One expression of this can be seen in the FLN response to the 1959 French family law as a "Koranic issue," and so bespeaking the degeneration of national liberation. After independence, Islamic reformists encouraged attacks on unveiled women on the streets of Algiers, while the nationalist leadership called for the abolition of an autonomous trade union movement. Both clerics and nationalists saw the usefulness of each other in strangling Revolutionary Algeria.

While "orthodox" reformist Islam, and a modernizing nationalism using socialist language, found an elective affinity, Fanon attempted to provide an alternative direction. Forty years later, in the face of fundamentalism, Fanon's critique of national chauvinism and his vision of a new humanism remain cogent.

With the advent of the Soummam Platform the division

between a national and religious chauvinism on one side and a national liberation on the other began to be articulated. It was the latter, Fanon argued in *The Wretched of the Earth*, that had to develop into a "consciousness of social and political needs, in other words into humanism" (1968, 204). However, under Ramdane Abane's[9] leadership at Soummam Conference (which Ben Bella and the external leadership did not attend), the FLN was as "humanist" as it would get, explicitly criticizing "theocracy" and making almost no positive statement about Islam. Increasingly the FLN publicly identified with Islam for popularization purposes, which also had the effect of obscuring the class differences between the centralizing, "modernizing," and elite Islam of the Sunni clerical Ulama (who became part of the FLN leadership after 1958), and the decentralized Sufi Islam (which Ulama considered its enemy) influential among the rural Muslims.[10] Fanon would stridently address this incipient class division between the nationalist elite (divided among clerical, military, and politico) and the rural masses, in the "Pitfalls of National Consciousness."

Sufi Islam had been broadly anticolonial and the Sufi religious brotherhoods had successfully mobilized local resistance during the early years of French colonialism. In the 1830s, the great hero of Algerian anticolonial resistance, the Marabout Abd al Qadir, had fought the French and developed the basis for an egalitarian state based on Islamic principles.[11] During the early period of colonialism (1830–1870) the rural masses had maintained a significant degree of autonomy from colonial rule which was concentrated in towns. After the defeat of the French in the Franco-Prussian war the *colons* assumed civilian control of the colony, causing the last substantial armed revolt by the Algerians. Defeated by French reinforcements the *colons* demanded "a holocaust of marabouts" (Ruedy 1992, 79). In a sense they got what they wanted.

Colon control of over the territory expanded under the Third Republic. France had given Alsace to Germany, and many families wishing to remain French migrated to Algeria.[12] One hundred thousand hectares of Kabyle land were allocated to them and as a consequence old forms of property, cultural practices, and labor processes were destroyed. The best lands expropriated, the rural masses became pauperized, landless peasants, many drifting to the towns or abroad to France.[13] The material basis for cultural autonomy, and the Marabouts' power, was broken. By the 1950s the settler population had grown to one million and the Marabouts had long ceased to be an actively anticolonial force.

Fanon had been critical of Sufi practices—for example, "ecstatic" all night dances—not because he found them unorthodox, but because of their otherworldliness. What he condemned were pacifying influences over the peasantry. Because practices like dance and possession provided an outlet for the native's anger, they became spheres in which the community could be seemingly free and liberated while still under colonial rule. For Fanon the future heaven would be not granted through such action but gained through genuinely anticolonial self-activity (1968, 55–57). Nonetheless, Fanon appreciated the cultural resistance of those peoples who had been able to keep their culture even partly intact, even if he regarded much of this culture as broken down and petrifying.[14]

Into the void left by the destruction of the decentralized rural Sufi brotherhoods stepped the reformist centralized urban Ulama about whom Fanon was surprisingly unspecific in his criticism. For him, however, Islam was not *the* rallying call. If the development of rural revolutionary subjectivity depended on a growing confidence about the possibility of self-determination, then the greatest organized ideological threat to national consciousness evolving into a new humanism was the urban intellectual elite. Schooled either by Ulama or by colonial institutions, Fanon criticized the urban intellectual's elitist attitudes toward the rural masses in *The Wretched*, calling it an intellectual "laziness." However, the painstaking process of systematically separating his conception of national liberation from others was not yet finished in *The Wretched of the Earth*.

For Fanon Islam's role in Algerian nationalism was symbolic, reflecting the long period of resistance to colonialism, even if some "traditional" authorities had collaborated with the colonialist.

Though it is unclear whether Sufi Marabouts collaborated with the French as Ulama claimed, the FLN dealt harshly with those it considered collaborators, not in the name of a fundamentalist Islam, or even Pan-Arabism, but in the name of national, namely Algerian, liberation. On the other hand, the conservative nationalist leaders of the FLN and ALN (Armée Libération Nationale) wished to systematize a cultural credo with the old Ulama slogan, "Islam is our religion, Arabic our language, Algeria our fatherland" to put a break on the "irreversible change" that Fanon argued was taking place in the country. There lies a certain irony in the use of such slogans about Islam when Sufism, the Islam of the rural masses, was considered by Ulama to be heretical and in need of being destroyed.

In contrast to Fanon naming the Algerian peasant as revolutionary subject in *The Wretched of the Earth*, Ulama regarded the Algerian masses as ideologically backward. An urban/rural and a class division lay behind these opposing attitudes. Moreover, rather than following a stageist conception of revolution, where colonized countries would have to first go through a "bourgeois stage" before moving to "socialism" (as advocated by the Communists), Fanon's conception of continuous revolution was constructed on the "movement from below" providing a basis for upsetting preconceived ideas of nationalism and national boundaries. He wrote in *The Wretched of the Earth* that "the intellectual forgets, that the forms of thought and what it feeds on, together with modern techniques of information, language, and dress have dialectically reorganized the people's intelligence and that the constant principles which acted as safeguards during the colonial period are now undergoing extremely radical changes" (1968, 225).

Did Fanon, reflecting the revolutionary enthusiasm of the period, fail to fully comprehend how changes might not only be "reversed" but also channeled in other directions? Did Fanon realize too late, and perhaps not clearly enough, the importance of explicitly criticizing the revolution's direction and that preparing for the period after would be a philosophical as well as a practical project?

Thrown into the whirlpool of the revolution, the young ALN

recruits, fighters for liberation, went through an abrupt separation from prewar values and hierarchies. However, their political education was too quickly reduced to a military one and ideology reduced to mouthing slogans. Fanon tried to address this problem in a series of lectures to the ALN cadre and young fighters at Ghardimaou in 1961 that later became the "Pitfalls" chapter in *The Wretched of the Earth*. Earlier he spoke more generally of the crisis in African liberation, of its degeneration into military dictatorships, as an "absence of ideology." In Algeria, that problematic was overlaid by the contending and sometimes overlapping interests of the FLN militaires and Ulama clerics.

To the credo "Islam is our religion, Arabic our language, Algeria our fatherland," one needs to know specifically, what kind of Islam? Orthodox, reformist or fundamentalist, Sunni or Maraboutic? Would more than one school of Islam be allowed? Would secular Muslims be tolerated? What would be the relationship of Islam to politics and economics? How would Islam affect state formation and the rights of the people? What social relations, gender, class, and ethnicity would Islam justify? What groups would it seek to suppress?

On the question of language, for example, one needs to know what form of Arabic would be chosen, classical or modern? Since French colonialism had destroyed Algerian literacy, what other languages would be official? What about Berber languages? What about French? What about the hybrid "Algerian" (*faraber*)?[15]

On the question of the "fatherland," one needs to know, would a free Algeria be free for non-Arabs and non-Muslims, for the French and European Algerians or the Jews? Would Algeria be free for women?

These themes were touched on at the Soummam conference of 1956 and produced very different answers to the credo about the goal of the Algerian revolution. The platform announced that the revolution was not a "religious war." In contrast to the FLN's fairly contradictory first declaration of goals (November 1954) for the "restoration of an Algerian state," and for democracy, liberty, and individual rights within "Islamic principles," Soummam declared that its goal was not an Islamic state but a democratic, socialist, secular, multicultural, and "national struggle to destroy the anarchist regime of colonization." The national project was articulated as "a struggle for the birth of an Algerian nation," not for "a restoration of a monarchy or a dead theocracy."

The FLN leadership at Soummam, and particularly Abane, expressed the need to provide a political structure for the emerging mass movement, to establish the dominance of that social movement over military matters, as well as to organize the decentralized Wilayas (military districts) along national rather than local lines. However, after the "defeat" of the Battle of Algiers (1957) and a military solution to the "Abane problem," namely Abane's murder at the end of that year, the Soummam proposals began to be reversed. By 1958 "the control of the wilayas became blatantly militaristic" and the military commanders "lost track of political objectives" (Jackson 1977, 53). At the same time France came close to winning the war militarily though it could not translate its military successes into a political settlement. Similarly, the FLN preferred to address the deepening provincialism and disarray of the Wilayas by enforcing a stricter military model rather than by developing a far reaching political program. The party organization, which had reflected a vibrancy in its early years (1954–1956) never recovered from the internal disintegration after the Battle of Algiers. Abane's silencing reinforced the lack of internal discussion and, according to Henry Jackson, the FLN "ceased to function as a cohesive apparatus after 1958" (1977, 52). Fanon's involvement and experience of this period are important to an understanding of his political generalizations. The appropriation of Islam by FLN leaders after independence was a quick fix for national identity. It provided an ideological "screen" which ameliorated the developing social tensions and class cleavages.

Fanon's public entrance into the Algerian revolution came at its most radically articulated moment, that is, with the Soummam Platform. The moment continued to affect the theoretical issues explored in *A Dying Colonialism* and *The Wretched of the Earth*. With forty years' hindsight we can criticize Fanon's optimism, but was he wrong to think that revolution could strip away retrograde social relations? Grounded in a conception of culture and consciousness as changing and changeable, a revolution in values is certainly what he experienced.

Like Marx's concept of revolution, Fanon believed that the Algerian Revolution would also upset old ways of being. This process would be reflected in the contradictory development of a national consciousness and a national culture and forecasted the "reality of the nation" coming to be (Fanon's first title for *A Dying Colonialism*). Pierre Bourdieu expressed this sharply in 1958:

> No one is unaware of the fact that a deep gulf now separates Algerian society from its past and that an irreversible change has taken place. . . . The Revolutionary situation has upset the former social hierarchies, now associated with the system of outmoded values, and has substituted for them new men to whom authority was granted for reasons other than birth, wealth, or moral or religious ascendancy. (p. 184)

National culture is absolutely essential for a successful war of liberation, but such a culture is a dialectical development—"not a state but a becoming" (Irele 1983, 24). Neither imported into the struggle nor an unchanging element, "national culture" is formed and developed in the process of liberation. It would be mistaken to equate this movement with claims to religious orthodoxy. The Algerian war was a "total war" affecting everyone and fundamentally upsetting all social relations, including the sexual divisions of labor justified by religious authorities. In contrast to an "Islamic" nation, Fanon posited not simply secularism but a "new humanism." Though first declared in *Black Skin*, it would find its most concrete expression in the social movement's lived experiences.

What is of tremendous importance is understanding the development of Fanon's thought between *A Dying Colonialism* and *The Wretched*. Fanon is not uncritical of the revolution in *A Dying Colonialism* but the overriding movement is its inevitable success. In *The Wretched*, Fanon still celebrates the revolution's ability to change old ways of being and thinking but he also emphasizes that they are bare beginnings, the new subjectivities are already under threat. *The Wretched* represents a recollection of the high point of the revolution not as an end but as an expression of its serious contradictions. It is only by confronting these contradictions that the "future heaven" (Fanon 1967c, 30) can be realized.

Fanon's prescient critique of postindependence regimes is the subject of part four of *Rethinking Fanon*. The chapters, in quite different ways, consider the question of liberation and organization, and of spontaneity and theory. From my own (chapter 16) and Turner's (chapter 15) perspectives, Fanon emerges as a figure who is neither an uncritical supporter of the FLN nor a simple spontaneist. Turner brings Fanon to life as a political figure, unraveling the internal politics of the FLN and the influence of Ramdane Abane on Fanon's political outlook. Additionally, of singular importance in Turner's essay is his tracing Fanon's political praxis and theoretical generalizations derived from his Algerian experiences. Turner is insistent that rather than outside Algeria, as some critics contend, Fanon was in the thick of debates around the Battle of Algiers and the later factional struggles that led to the FLN's retreat from the Soummam perspective of a future democratic socialist secular state. The confusion about Fanon's whereabouts, the factional characterization of Fanon and Abane as "urban terrorists," often replayed in the literature, are connected to minimizing Fanon's role in the revolution.

In my essay I attempt to return to and articulate the vitality of dialectic in Fanon's thought. Fanon's critical engagement with Hegel does not entail an equation, as in some postcolonial theory, of dialectic with imperialism. His declaration at the end of *The Wretched of the Earth* to leave Europe, where the dialectic has changed into a "motionless movement," could be seen as a response to Hegel's attitude to Africa in *The Philosophy of History*. The tables are now turned, it is Europe, not Africa, that "lacks" dialectical development and it is Europe that must now take its impetus from Africa. Additionally, I attempt to explicate and get behind Fanon's conception of "radical mutation" that is central to *A Dying Colo-*

nialism and challenge the mistaken idea that he is a binary and Manichean thinker. Though an explicit philosophical grounding for Fanon's critique of ideology is not forthcoming, the relationship he envisions between intellectual and the common people, and the new humanism he trumpets at the end of *The Wretched of the Earth*, can be constructed in terms of an "untidy" dialectic. However, such untidiness is a bad traveler. Based on the privileging of action, Fanon's thought becomes problematic when one travels from an epoch of social revolution to an epoch dominated by the idea that there is no alternative to structural adjustment.

DOES FANON'S IDEA OF LIBERATION STILL TRAVEL?

> *Nationalism is not a political, nor a program doctrine.*
>
> Fanon

What happens, in a different period, when discussion about Africa's "future heaven" is reduced to electoral politics and the need to strengthen a "civil society" narrowly conceived as the capitalist market? Paradoxically, Fanon's declaration of the "impossibility of the bourgeoisie" has come under new scrutiny.[16] His analysis of kleptocracy (a regime of hucksters, as Fanon puts it) exists alongside the belief that a "true" (namely productive and noncorrupt) bourgeoisie can emerge and must emerge (and will emerge, given the enthusiastic figures of growth over the past couple of years) if Africa is to lift itself out of the cycle of debt and dependency. If this was simply the run off of over a decade of structural adjustments that would be one thing, but recently one of Fanon's most able critics has wondered whether Fanon is "open to the possibility of a redeeming role for members of the national bourgeoisie" (Sekyi-Otu 1996, 157). "Logically" Sekyi-Otu is not wrong to look for "enabling conditions" (p. 171) for the nationalist bourgeoisie in Fanon's writings. Fanon's text certainly opens up to such a possibility if one follows through the morality of their "betrayal" on one hand and the logic of capital on the other.

Indeed, that Fanon had explicitly based the proof of his analysis on action rather than logic (Fanon 1968, 175), indicates the constraining factor of history on his theory.

In this long "dry white season,"[17] a time when revolutionary action has seemingly come to a standstill, Fanon's predictive powers also seem raw. It is the "logic" of ambivalence within the boundaries of "colonial positionality" (Bhabha 1985, 94), of subversion not revolutionary action, that appears more promising. Colonial discourse analysis rightly understands and analyzes how "colonial power produces the colonized as a fixed reality which is at once an 'other' and yet entirely knowable and visible" (Bhabha 1983, 199), but by emphasizing ambivalence within colonial discourse it tends to reduce and forget the struggle to undermine it. At its worst, postcolonial theory avoids the constraints of historical specificity. Taken to an extreme, discourse theory goes even further than economic determinism, which proclaimed that colonialism was illogical from the standpoint of capital. Like capital logic theorists, discourse theory too often subsumes agency, avoiding its unpredictable variability.

Putting Fanon in context ("context" understood not passively but as movement, conflict, and tension) elucidates the richness of his thought and the audacity of the man. It elevates the conception of agency insofar as history, understood as history in the making, as the melding together of activity and intellect, is created by a man like Fanon. Here, at least for a passing moment, the historical possible and Fanon's social vision (itself a product of the drama of the revolutionary social movements) come together. The Algerian Revolution does not make Fanon a revolutionary but it does enable him to become a revolutionary practitioner. In other words, to fully understand Fanon's context one must situate him in the "epoch" of decolonization.

Black Skin, White Masks tells of his personal experiences of racism, but it is far from a personal account. It is a call for action to end of human alienation beginning by uprooting the causes of racism and Fanon engages in a critique of literature, film, philosophy, sociology, and psychoanalyses to do so. Fanon found all these modes of analysis problematic and, in short, struggled to transcend his context. In *Black Skin*, he articulated this in simple Marxian terms, not only to analyze the world but also to change it, to create a new humanism, a new understanding between human beings. He found an ability to realize this principle by participating in the Algerian Revolution, more exactly by throwing his life into it. Fanon was not a man of half measures; like Rosa Luxemburg, he believed that to remain human meant putting oneself on the scales of destiny. How do we understand such a man of suffering and passion?

Writing of Amilcar Cabral, Mustafah Dhada has spoken of the way in which a few people play key roles in politics:

> The few who do, do so because they are susceptible to that force—the force of the historical collective. They are listeners to a rhythm of a finer inner vision. They are willing instruments for a greater change. . . . They are players—men [and women] of action. But they are also prone to, although not totally consumed by, idealism. That is to say, they walk a fine line between ideals and reality. . . . That is not to say they are naive believers of the unreal. Rather they are realists, deeply rooted in the historical truth of the personal. . . . Their realism is a doer's realism. It is vibrant, potent realism. It is a realism fueled by an intellect on fire. (1993, xi–xii)

That's it. "A realism fueled by an intellect on fire," one can feel it in all of Fanon's books, but especially in *The Wretched*, written against his impending death, written with the rushing prose of an intellect on fire and with an absolute displeasure of those lazy intellectuals. Famously, he harangued Sartre for not staying up all night to discuss philosophy and politics, but it was the intellectuals of the newly independent nations who were the butt of his real anger.

The focus of this introduction has been to underline the richness of the context as well as its continuing legacy of Fanon's thought. The reader will find, throughout the volume, many criticisms of Fanon. Indeed, to some *The Wretched* is flawed because of its generalizations—its applicability of his experiences and analysis of the Algerian Revolution to the "Wretched of the Earth." To others Fanon's analysis of the Algerian Revolution itself, indeed his lack of analysis of "religion," is problematic. Nevertheless, to defend Fanon against such approaches does not put him beyond criticism. Certainly the reader will find many critical avenues to explore.

One inconsistency of Fanon's dialectic of national liberation and his profound critique of the nationalist leadership is apparent in his arguments about economic redistribution after colonialism. Instead of Fanon's "relentless dialectic" (cf. McCullogh 1983), he concludes in a subsection of chapter 1 of *The Wretched*, "Violence in the International Context," with appeals for reparations on one hand and for capital investment on the other. To avoid the capitalist crisis engendered by the decolonized countries' "collective autarky" and withdrawal from the world market, he argues, capitalist enterprises will find that their "true interest" lies in reinvesting and "in giving aid to the underdeveloped countries" (Fanon 1968, 105). But capitalism today, in other words, capitalism globalized more than ever before, is still not particularly interested in investing in Africa, a fact witnessed by the continuing net capital outflow from the continent. Rather capitalist enterprises are interested in the resources that can be shipped out of Africa and worked up elsewhere. Fanon knew this all too well, but stuck in the logic of underconsumptionism he is blinded by capitalism's need for markets rather than following out the new communications that could be established between the newly independent countries and mass struggles he believes will develop in Europe. In other words, rather than following through the dialectic of capital and the "new forces and new passions," as Marx put it, that will help overthrow it, Fanon returns us to the dead-end of capital investment in the newly independent countries. In doing he seems to have hemmed himself in and retreated from his most radical social vision. We are back to the problematic of the nationalist bourgeoisie.

Fanon is at his best when he is articulating the dialectic of the mass movements that seem to make everything possible. This is not to say that such movements are simply the result of sheer revolutionary will and led by a vanguard party. Unlike Nasser, who argued that the people had to be kept on a short leash, Fanon insisted that "people" did not need to be "driven" or "bossed" but kept involved in the political discussion (1968, 184). However, even if an assessment of the "radical mutations" that Fanon insists occur leads us back to the problem of having to situate in his thought in its historical context, we still should be able discern the philosophical ground that girds his tenacity. Thus rather than a preoccupation with simple intentionality we can begin to consider the question, What is living and what is dead in the thought of Frantz Fanon?

In *Black Skin, White Masks* Fanon has to keep reminding us and himself that the subject is not the "Negro" in general (who does not exist "in general"): "My observations and my conclusions," he writes, "are valid only for the Antilles," though he tells us that "In the beginning I wanted to confine myself to the Antilles. But, regardless of consequences, dialectic took the upper hand and I was compelled to see that the Antillean is first of all a Negro" (1967a, 16, 172). In addition he tells us that the subject is the educated Antillean who desires to turn white, and who Fanon then discusses in terms of gender. In the setting of postwar Paris the Antillean evolué find themselves walled in by color and viewed no differently than the "absolute other," the black Senegalese.

The impossibility of whiteness is the drama analyzed of *Black Skin, White Masks* and in contrast to the American black and the young Africans who "sought to maintain their alterity, [an a]lterity of rupture, of conflict, of battle" (1967a, 222), the Antillean, who has not struggled, was "doomed." Yet it was in Paris that the Antillean discovers a new route, discovers Africa, discovers his négritude roots. *Black Skin, White Masks*, Fanon hoped, would avoid "lumping all Negroes together" and "contribute to the dissolution of the affective complexes that oppose West Indians and Africans" (1967b, 18).

Some of the questions of *Black Skin, White Masks*, splendidly refashioned by Bhabha in the 1980s, of hybridity and ambiguity, of mis-fitting, were not only re-read in terms of the psychodrama of everyday life in colonial societies. In fact *Black Skin, White Masks* speaks of a period after colonialism as the "neurosis" of a subject people who had had "freedom" given them without a struggle: The Antillean who wants to "marry" whiteness in *Black Skin, White Masks* by sleeping with a white woman is reintroduced as the native who wants to take the place of the colonialist and sleep in his bed, with his wife in *The Wretched*. Both are doomed to *resentiment* (1967a, 222), to being enfranchised slaves. As I said earlier, despite Bhabha's insufficient interest in Fanon's politics and the historical context, his reading of *Black Skin, White Masks* was also related to the new configurations of blackness in Britain in the 1970s and 1980s (namely a second generation of Asians, Caribbeans, and Africans in Britain who considered themselves black British) where the black did not exactly fit the scheme the British wanted. Bhabha's Lacanian rereadings of *Black Skin, White Masks* were refreshing—even if Bhabha took little notice of Fanon's criticisms of Freud and Lacan—because they challenged the dominant reductive view of Fanon as simply an apostle of violence.

Today, I think, the overly psychoanalytic concerns of the rereading of these rereadings of *Black Skin, White Masks* take us further away from Fanon's texts and political problematics. There is a need to return to Fanon's whole corpus, including *The Wretched of the Earth* and *A Dying Colonialism*, to questions of political change and to Fanon's revolutionary praxis. This is not simply to place Fanon "irreducibly" in his own time but to find new avenues of enquiry that return us to Fanon.

For Fanon, revolutionary mass movements not only transgressed boundaries but also confronted the social system and thereby went beyond Manicheanism. Almost tautologically, though the point still needs to be made, as long as colonial power remained hegemonic its pronouncement that it was its own unceasing cause, having existed from the beginning of recorded time, appeared powerful. But as soon as it was radically challenged, its hegemony proved weak, and its ideology threadbare. Its illogical, irrational, and racist character becomes patently obvious to all. In many cases the colonialists' "rush" to decolonize reformulated its own racial ideology by adding an "educational" component. But it is the extent to which the ideology's racial frame was imbibed by nationalist leadership that became Fanon's concern.

Placing Fanon in his proper historical context helps illuminate contradictions but does not solve today's problems. At the same time, his analysis should not be confined to a critique of the forces of neocolonialism and global capitalism together with the internal corruption of the nationalist leaderships and indigenous elites. That would leave us stuck in the "logic" of hoping for a noncorrupt bourgeoisie. Fanon offers another legacy, one in which resistance can get *beyond* the debilitating mind-set of Manicheanism. A central element of this legacy is an exploration of the role intellectuals can play. Aware of the existential gulf between intellectuals and the people, he was critical of those intellectuals who reduced their role to being a "mouthpiece" of the everyday (Fanon 1968, 45). Instead, he proposes that one develops an organic, living relationship—a dialogue, and a critique (in the positive sense)—that requires ongoing theoretical labor. How to develop this constant relationship, during the "dry season" as well as during times of transformation?

Our times are marked by the failure to deepen the counter-hegemonic moments opened up by mass movements. Post-Apartheid South Africa is a case in point, showing the pitfall of a mass movement giving over political leadership to the nationalist organization. The rank and file of the social movements—the civic associations, youth groups, and trade unions that brought Apartheid to the negotiating tables—have been relegated to the background or as Fanon put it in *The Wretched of the Earth*, the appearance of the negotiation table signaled the silencing of the people. In a word, the movements are subsumed while a small elite helps repaint the juggernaut of capital. In a broader frame this shows how structural adjustment promotes (in its homegrown or World Bank sense) an authoritarian economism, a very narrow conception of "civil society" *qua* market, and a state as authoritarian enforcer against democratic challenges from below. Hussein Adam's "Fanon as Democratic Theorist" (chapter 4) inserts Fanon into the contemporary discussion. Adam argues that Fanon not only captures many of the demands made by current democratic opposition groups but goes beyond liberal democracy by including issues of radical decentralization and the democratization of local as well as central organs. Fanon's conception of political participation emphasizes the "ongoing and immediate activities in the everyday lives of the citizens." Popular participation, Adam contends, reemphasizing a point made earlier by Hansen, is grounded in Fanon's philosophic comprehension of social freedom and social praxis.

Fanon's *ongoing* critique of the "Pitfalls of National Consciousness"—both before and after the gaining of state power by the nationalist party—is still of relevance. What remains a philosophic project is how one begins to articulate the meaning of mass action, expand the new social consciousness derived from the cultures of resistance and solidarity into new creative directions. Too quickly rejected by our postmodern scholar today, Fanon's humanism still requires a serious critical engagement. Though that philosophic project remains the task of a future volume, the very fact that Fanon connects "new humanism" to the way people work and the types of labor they do—the kinds of questions that not only speak to "useful" employment—challenges the attitude that the masses work harder for the good of "the nation," "the people," "God," or other abstractions. Questions of what kind of labor human beings should do, which were not raised by a Left too concerned with immediacy, remain critical to envisioning a post-Apartheid South Africa "not in future heaven" (Fanon 1967c, 30). To repeat, Fanon does not provide the answers but he does provide a standpoint to consider the problems.

THE CONTINUING DIALOGUE

The explosion will not happen today. It is too soon . . . or too late.

Fanon

That Fanon is engrossing to critics on both sides of the postmodernist/modernist divide; that he is claimed by Afrocentrists and Marxists; that he is engaged by feminists and postcolonial literary critics; that he is the object of such varied appreciations as well as misconceptions is itself an accomplishment. But this book is neither a collection of appreciations nor another book on the genealogy of postcolonial theory. What is hoped is that it will stimulate other questions, engaging the creative tension between action and scholarship. In short, *Rethinking Fanon* seeks to build bridges and help generate discussion. Its interdisciplinary and intergenerational perspective will hopefully demonstrate continued critical relevance and bring Fanon's thought to life. Nearly forty years after his death, it will be wholly inadequate to apply his conclusions to current situations, but his thought can still provide a basis for alternatives and the challenge why "each generation must out of relative obscurity discover its mission, fulfill it, or betray it" (Fanon 1968, 206).

It goes without saying that our sense of Frantz Fanon, the man, has surely faded. Let me conclude with a vignette from Doctor Bertene Juminer who powerfully recalled Fanon's last years in an obituary for *Présence Africaine*.

In Fanon's presence a strange atmosphere was radiated, which cannot be described, but which was felt only by those who had the privilege of seeing him live, and of living in rhythm with him. Algeria was visibly insinuating itself into him, becoming his only raison d'etre. . . .

I know how imprudent it is to discourse about man, but how can I be silent when it was precisely in the intimacy of the family—either at his home or mine, in the presence of our wives and sons, or during our solitary colloquies—that Frantz revealed a humanity which bordered on humility! It is impossible not to recall that foggy autumn evening in 1959 when he related to me the details of his accident on the Algerian-Moroccan frontier (his jeep ran over a mine and he emerged with twelve fractured vertebrae, complicated by paraplegia and sphincteral disorders); or his transfer to Rome when the car in which he was to ride had been wired with explosives by the Red Hand,[18] but which exploded prematurely and killed two Italian children playing in the street nearby; or that sudden intuition he had, which led him to change rooms after reading a notice in the press to the effect that Dr. Omar, an Algerian leader, was in Room X at Clinic Y, and thereby escaped the obstinate killers who machine-gunned an empty bed during the night. This morbid prudence was henceforth demonstrated to the extent that he never entered the building in which he lived without first scrupulously examining the surrounding area. I had listened to him and observed him, and I could not help thinking that he had deliberately divested himself of all social style to which he had devoted the better part of his time to attain in the schools, on the battlefield and in Western universities. We were facing each other. One of his elbows was on the table and his face was resting in the palm of his hand. As he was accustomed to doing, he vigorously rubbed his face, breathed heavily through his nose, and passed his hand from his forehead to the nape of his neck : "I don't give a damn about Europe, its culture and diplomas, or the social institutions it tolerates which are just so many instruments of domination. We should chuck out all that garbage and tell ourselves we have nothing to lose by so doing. Otherwise, no liberation is possible!"

... Shortly after the 2nd Congress of the All-African Peoples' Conference held in Tunis in January 1960, he told me of his intended departure for Accra where he was going to represent the G.P.R.A. [Algerian Provisional Government]. I, in turn, had to return to Paris for a few months, so it was not until the summer of 1961, in the midst of the war in Bizerte, that we saw each other again. I had learned of his illness and avoided speaking to him of it. He put me at ease by telling me how it begun. "I lost about 28 lbs shortly after arriving there." He then described the embarrassment of a colleague who diagnosed his leukemia, but who did not dare tell him the result of the analysis. "I understood then that I didn't have more than three or four years to live. It then became necessary for me to hurry up to say and accomplish the maximum . . . but my Algerian brothers are asking me to be sparing of my efforts. The colonialists, are they sparing of theirs where we are concerned? . . ." "You see," he continued, "I have just completed *The Wretched of the Earth*. I should have liked to have written something more."

... At the table, after eating the water-melon which was the delight of the children, Frantz stretched out and for several hours attempted to amuse us with stories about psychiatry, and his Moscow discoveries of Russian humor. He had, however, spent his entire time in Russia in a hospital, and now found himself, although a doctor, on the other side of the stethoscope. What is more, he KNEW; he knew everything, from the diagnostic to the prognostic. He was in the habit of laughing when with us. We used to try to force ourselves to smile, and he would laugh even more to stimulate us to do so. But how could we dare when we were so afflicted by the imminence of his disappearance?

Once Olivier came into the room:

"Papa, a gentleman downstairs is asking for you."

"What is his name?"

"He said his name is Mr. X."

"Ah! Mr. X. Good. Go and tell him I left with Mr. Y."

And he laughed again.

Several days later he came to my house. He was visibly in bad shape. We had prepared a West Indian meal for him. He did not make much of it. Leaning towards my wife, he told her:

"Next time Michele, no West Indian dinner please."

"We'll make you some couscous next time."

"Good," he replied.

The next time! I stole a glance at his wife. She appeared to be calm, but I knew that this courageous Josy, like everyone who loved Frantz, was suffering, and she knew that I knew it.

One October morning he entered my laboratory. He was accompanied by a colonel of the A.L.N. "Analyze my blood, I feel fatigued," I pierced his finger and a drop of blood immediately formed.

"You don't seem to lack any" I told him.

He didn't seem concerned.

"When can you give me the results?"

"Tomorrow."

I did not know that this tomorrow would have been a day of hope for me, but for Frantz, a day of despair. In fact, everything was normal. And I was naively hoping that the previous diagnoses were erroneous. Maybe he was only overworked or parasitic. He dashed my hopes to the ground. "The result does not surprise me, I am under treatment. It's the Russian medicine, which has diminished the rate of the white globules. My illness nevertheless is going on. I'm going to leave for America." (1962, 139–42)*

*From Bertene Juminer, "Homage to Frantz Fanon," *Présence Africine* 12, no. 40 (1962). Reprinted with permission.

This volume was conceived during a journey to the 1991 African Studies Association conference in St. Louis where I organized a panel (with Lou Turner and Tsenay Serequeberhan) commemorating the thirtieth anniversary of Fanon's death.[19] Without Lou Turner's continual support and interest it probably would not have seen the light of day. My own interest in Fanon, sparked by Turner and Alan's essay (reprinted here), led to my first attempt to "work out" Fanon in another context: A commemoration of the twentieth year of his death in the context of the H-Block Hunger Strike in Northern Ireland (1981). Earlier that year Dave Black and I had started a dialogue with exiles of the Black Consciousness Movement on the basis of Fanon's relevance to South Africa's Steve Biko. But in terms of the British scene a turning point was reached that summer when black and white inner city youth rebelled against police harassment in Britain's major cities. The "triangular trade of ideas," among the United States, the Caribbean, and Africa, central to Turner and Alan's work, had found a "fourth port of entry." Alongside the well traveled routes, theory ranges across paths and scenarios not anticipated.

While the intervening seventeen years has seen the rise of new studies of Fanon, they have not, in the main, transgressed disciplinary boundaries but moved from the social sciences to the humanities. This should be lamented. Cross-disciplinarity, breaking disciplinary boundaries, should not result in shallow scholarship. Dabbling across boundaries is often provocative and suggestive. But, in fact, the oft-thought originality of "new" approaches is frequently mistaken. One finds that scholars in other fields have been asking similar questions in different ways. This is one reason why the scope of *Rethinking Fanon* is exciting and suggests a further investigation into the politics of Fanon studies as well as the ways in which Fanon has been subjected to the disciplines.

There is another interlocutor that operates at a different register in this articulation, namely Fanon's social vision. In the 1990s many radical scholars have felt the need to dissociate themselves from radical prescriptions. This is particularly striking when discussing a thinker like Fanon who passionately calls for social action. Like a kind of left Afro-pessimism, the iconization of Fanon mirrors the process of self-limitation. Certainly, if the specific context of Fanon's praxis is not to be reduced to mere academic interest neither should it become a paean to political will. To "rethink" Fanon should also engender new dialectical approaches to consciousness, knowledge and praxis. At least, I feel this is a tension underlining this volume of essays on Fanon.

Fanon's thought continues to be reconsidered, not alone because it cannot be fully claimed by one disciplinary framework and is open to reinterpretation and reconstruction but also because it remains vital. *Rethinking Fanon*, a collection that includes some of the most classic and enduring essays on Fanon, illustrates his vitality. It is hoped, therefore, that the volume will not only challenge the preconceptions and insularities of the academic disciplines but also offer other perspectives and challenges.

This volume has not only been a long time coming, it almost traveled the cul-de-sac experienced by other aborted volumes on Fanon (for example, Hansen and Jinadu's volume). Fortunately Prometheus Books saw the importance of bringing this Fanon collection into print when its initial publisher filed for bankruptcy. It is, however, an ongoing project. My own rethinking of Fanon continues. New questions, new problematics, introduced by friends, colleagues, or students, attract me back to Fanon's texts.

Many people have offered encouragement and shared their thoughts over its long period of gestation: Patrick Deer, Jonathan Dollimore, Lewis Gordon, Lolo, Richard Onwuanibe, Ato Sekyi-Otu, Andrew Rubin, Eloise Segal, and Lou Turner are just a few who deserve a special note. I would also like to thank George C. Bond at the Institute of African Studies at Columbia for our continued dialogues; my son Aidan for hooking me up into another world; and Kate Josephson who all too well knows this project's Blakean character and who continues to share my hopes and disappointments. Lastly to my friends at Sunday soccer for keeping my mind on the art of the game. The thought brings me back to a picture of Fanon and his brothers, "the forward line of the St. Pierre (Martinique) soccer team, 1946–47" (Geismar 1971, 134a).

Institute of African Studies
Columbia University, New York
November 1998

NOTES

1. I should mention the four-day International Memorial for Fanon (March 31–April 3, 1982), held in Fort de France with participants from all over the world including France, Algeria, French-speaking Africa, and the Caribbean. Speakers included Edouard Glissant, René Menil, Aimé Césaire, Marcel Manville, as well as Hussein Bulhan and James Forman from the United States.

2. For an overview of these debates, Immanuel Wallerstein's "Fanon and the Revolutionary Class" should be consulted.

3. Updating Bhabha's research one would still find it hard to uncover an article written by a British Leftist in a major British Left journal.

4. I am reminded of Fanon's reference to the native intellectual who will "try to make European culture his own. He will not be content to get to know Rabelais and Diderot, Shakespeare and Edgar Allen Poe; he will bind them to his intelligence as closely as possible" (1968, 218–19). The literature professors have paradoxically been part of making Fanon a "native intellectual."

5. *History and Class Consciousness* expresses Lukács's affiliation to Rosa Luxemburg's view against nationalism. For an interesting comparison see the essay by Joan Cocks, "On Nationalism: Frantz Fanon, Rosa Luxemburg and Hannah Arendt," in Bonnie Honig (ed.), *Feminist Interpretations of Hannah Arendt* (University Park, Penn.: Pennsylvania State University Press, 1995).

6. In my forthcoming *Frantz Fanon: Key Critical Thinker* (Polity Press) I consider this problem further.

7. I use the hyphenated "post-colonial" to designate a political regime. The nonhyphenated "postcolonial" refers to a school of thought or a particular thinker associated with that school.

8. And in fact are beginning to be. See for example, Robert Malley's

The Call from Algeria: Third Worldism, Revolution, and the Turn to Islam and Ricardo Laremont's "Islam and the Politics of Resistance in Algeria, 1983–1992."

9. Generally considered the "master-mind" of the Soummam and the instigator of the "Battle of Algiers," Abane is identified as advocating "indiscriminate urban terrorism" (Behr repeats this phrase three times in eleven pages [103, 111, 114], adding that he "could have stepped out of a Malraux novel"). The lack of scholarship when considering Abane is palpable. Horne states, without reference, that Abane's favorite dictum was "one corpse in a jacket is always worth more than twenty in uniform." John Ruedy simply repeats Horne.

In contrast, Quandt (writing in the late 1960s) argues that "according to many who knew him, [Ramdane Abane] was decisive without being authoritarian and was able to command the respect of those around him. Although a Kabyle, Abane is held in high regard by Arabs as well as Kabyles, and several elite members claim that he might have been the one Algerian who could have held the elite together after independence" (p. 100). The latter statement is more problematic since it was the elite who conspired to remove him in the first place.

A serious critique of the figure Lacoste, the "liberal" French governor-general of Algeria, called the movement's "best brain" is still to be written in English. As yet, Khalfa Mameri's biography of Abane has not been translated from the French.

10. Messali Hadj, the leader of the proletarian North Star party from which many of the FLN leadership had been members before the war, had been schooled by Sufi brethren. One wonders whether the Ulama's anti-Sufism and the FLN's anti-Messalism found a common enemy. Perhaps more importantly, the MTLD centralists who distanced themselves from Messali in the early 1950s, and from which a number of FLN militants received their political training, was the most secular of the nationalist organizations (see Gillespie 1961, 78–83).

To this day, despite forty years of attacks by the state and the fundamentalist clerics, the mass of rural Algerians still practice Sufi teachings.

11. Whereas the word "Marabout" can mean preacher or Muslim cleric, in Kabylia "Marabout" also refers to someone who belongs to the noble caste. In many Berber areas, such as Kabylia, regional traditions (animist religions) and the word of local sages take precedence over religious doctrine. It was these decentralized local authorities that Ulama sought to stamp out.

12. No doubt Fanon's name, Frantz, is related to his Alsatian ancestry. Richard Onwuanibe notes that his mother, "an illegitimate daughter of mixed parents, had Alsatian blood in her ancestry" (1983, vii–viii).

13. Kabylia saw a large amount of emigration. Like other nationalist movements, it was in France where the first militant nationalist organization, Messali's North Star (first connected to and supported by the Communist party) was organized.

14. On the surface Fanon might seem to be agreeing with dominant themes in modernization theory which spoke in Manichean terms of *Gemeinschaft* (community) and *Gesellschaft* (society). However, for Fanon there was no such thing as a pristine culture; peoples were always coming into contact, this was at the heart of "culture." The devastation brought about by French colonialism, in contrast, was wholly another type of meeting.

15. The written culture of Algeria has always been the language of the colonizer; St. Augustine wrote in the language of the Roman colonizers, Latin. Ibn Khaldun wrote in the language of the Arab colonizer, Arabic, and many modern authors write in French.

16. For example, Olufemi Taiwo suggests that we replace the word "Nigeria" every time we come across "nation" or "country" in Fanon's "Pitfalls" chapter (see his essay, "On the Misadventures of National Consciousness: A Retrospect on Frantz Fanon's Gift of Prophecy," in Gordon et al. 1996, 266).

17. Commenting on his work *A Dry White Season*, a title taken from a Wally Serote poem, André Brink has argued that it was "Biko's death which swung the novel in a different direction altogether." In other words, the "colonizer who refuses" the ambiguity and paradoxes of the black/white relations in South Africa and the very moral development of Brink's Ben Du Toit were related to social movements challenging Apartheid rule and had less to do with the internal logic of colonial ambivalence.

18. The Red Hand (La Main Rouge) is the name of a French Fascist gang, which specialized in assassination.

19. Versions of those papers appear in Lou Turner (1991), Nigel Gibson (1994), and Tsenay Serequeberhan (1994).

I
POLITICS AND REVOLUTION

1.

Frantz Fanon:
Portrait of a Revolutionary

Emmanuel Hansen

When Frantz Fanon died in December 1961, he was relatively unknown except among his fighting Algerian comrades, a small group of French Leftists who had been attracted to his writings, and a handful of radical Africans. Today in the United States and to a lesser extent in Western Europe, his name is a household word. . . .

Ironically, in Africa, where he spent a large portion of his adult life dedicating himself fanatically to the fight for African liberation, he is relatively unknown except in Algeria. In Ghana, where he lived as an Ambassador of the Algerian Provisional Government, today his name hardly draws a ripple.

There are a number of reasons why we in Africa should be concerned with Fanon. His was the most intriguing personality; he was a man full of apparent contradictions: One of the most assimilated of France's sons and yet perhaps its most passionate critic; a dedicated fighter of racial oppression, he was to die in Washington, the

Emmanuel Hansen, "Frantz Fanon: Portrait of a Revolutionary," *Transitions* 46 (1974), pp. 25–36. Copyright W. E. B. Dubois Institute and Duke University Press. Reprinted with permission.

heart of racist America; a man to whom violence was personally abhorrent, he was one of the most strident advocates of violence. Second, Fanon's life and work provide us with a model of what the African intellectual ought to be: a man who reflects and yet does not allow reflection to inhibit him from social action, and a man whose social action is guided by thought. To him the role of the intellectual and that of the political activist were not mutually exclusive. Like Marx he believed that what mattered was not to interpret the world but to change it, and he used his knowledge as a weapon in the battle for freedom. For him it was not enough to analyze a social situation and expose its undesirable nature. One must also include a program of action to change the undesirable situation and actually embark on activities which lead to change. In short, he was a man who lived his ideas. Third, Fanon's message is of extreme importance to Africa and the Third World. And if today Fanon is not read in Africa it is not because he is less relevant to Africa. It is because the national bourgeoisie which holds the reigns of power in Africa is committed to maintaining the colonial-bureaucratic state and is not prepared to propagate ideas which would change the status quo which benefits it so handsomely. Who was this extraordinary person whose life and ideas raised a controversy which has by no means been settled? What kind of life did he live? What were his ideas and what was his message to Africa and the Third World? What were his hopes, desires, and aspirations, and what do we learn from his experience? These are some of the questions we hope to touch on in this chapter.

Frantz Fanon's life history falls into five main parts: his birth, bourgeois upbringing and early education on the island of Martinique; his service in the French Army; his higher education in France and his exposure to the French intellectual Left; his work in North Africa as a psychiatrist committed to the cause of the Algerian revolution; his life and work as a professional revolutionary, both in North Africa and in sub-Saharan Africa. It is useful to look at Martinique in 1925 to understand the social environment in which Fanon grew up and the forces which molded his early life.

MARTINIQUE: SOCIAL STRUCTURE

The island of Martinique, where Fanon was born, was one of the Overseas Departments of France. Together with Guadeloupe it forms what is known as the French Antilles. As in other French Overseas territories, Martinican society consisted of a rigid class structure (for a detailed description of the life, politics, and social structure of Martinique see Geismar 1971, Murch 1971, and de Kadt 1972). Society was pyramidal. On top of the pyramid was a small group of whites, called creoles or *békès*. The whites formed a status group, and they consisted of native whites and whites from metropolitan France. Small in number, they formed a closely knit endogamous community. In the eyes of most blacks, the whites consisted of a single homogeneous and monolithic group. However, small as they were, some gradations could be discerned among them. Edith Kovatz has identified three main subgroups: *gros békè*, the *békè moyens*, and the *petits blancs* (Kovatz 1964, 49ff.).

Below the white group was a small but fairly prosperous middle class of blacks and at the bottom were the bulk of the black population. As happens in all cases of rigid class structure, those at the top of the pyramid tried to stress their social distance from those below them, and those at the bottom tried to stress their social nearness to those above them. In the nonwhite group also, there were some subgroups: the mulattoes and the blacks proper. The former were a socially well-to-do bourgeoisie, mostly city dwellers. They were mostly in the public service, business, and in the liberal professions, like law and medicine. Though economically some of them were better off than some of the whites, as a group they were considered socially inferior to the whites. Status coincided, though not absolutely, with color. The small white group formed a reference group for the mulatto and the black bourgeoisie, who tried to emulate it in every imaginable way. They tried to speak impeccable French, since it was the language of both the white upper class and the metropolitan power. In Martinique, as indeed in all colonial countries, the colonizer's language is associated with social class. In Martinique, the more impeccable one's

French, the higher was one's status. And one was considered human to the extent to which one mastered the language of the master and approximated his manners and ways of doing things. One writer has commented on the magic power of the white man's language on the island:

> Disembarking at Fort-de-France, the capital of Martinique, a person having good French or English is whisked through customs, while Creole-speaking blacks are searched for contraband goods. (Geismar 1971, 20)

Victor Wolfenstein, writing about Gandhi, remarks about a similar case:

> *Gandhi had tried to be like the English in order to be a man*: he was unable to master the task and he reverted to his mother's Hinduism, thereby arriving at a workable identity with himself. (Wolfenstein 1971, 208, emphasis added).

This is perhaps the most pernicious aspect of colonial rule. To be human one has to be white. The whites, though less than 1 percent of the population, owned the large firms, the construction companies, the newspapers, and most of the port facilities. They controlled the social, economic, and political life of the island. They were an ingrown, clannish group and, like their counterparts in other parts of the colonial world, namely preindependent Algeria or Kenya, or today's Rhodesia, they were hostile even to the whites of the metropolis. The lower class blacks who constituted the majority of the population did mostly manual work. Many worked in the fields as cane cutters, or on the banana and pineapple plantations. Some also worked in the sugar refineries or as dock workers, truck drivers, or domestic servants. Unlike the situation in other colonial areas, the nonwhite bourgeoisie of Martinique chose the path of assimilation instead of national independence.

BIRTH, FAMILY BACKGROUND, AND EARLY EDUCATION

Into one of these bourgeois families of small property owners Frantz Fanon was born on July 20, 1925. Of the father we hardly know anything except that he was a customs inspector and that he died in 1947, having been born in 1891 (Zahar 1970, 5). His mother was described as a mild-mannered and heavy-set woman, who considered herself just another French citizen (Geismar 1971, 8). The family was described as "conventional." They were integrated into the Martinican society in spite of the fact that in conversations, the brothers tended to agree with Frantz's analysis of European racism on the island (Geismar 1971, 11). Fanon's elder brother worked with a French separatist organization and for this reason he was exiled from the island. Fanon's father was described as a "free thinker" and a "freemason." In Catholic Martinique this provided the atmosphere in which independent thought could be developed, at least in matters of religion.

Of Fanon's preschool life we know very little. He was the youngest of the four sons, and as a child was quite restless and prone to getting into trouble. He was also the darkest of the eight children. Those who are attracted to psycho-history attach a great deal of importance to this (Gendzier 1973, 10). Among the speculations is that Fanon's preoccupation with recognition may have originated from maternal rejection which he might have interpreted in racial terms. The significance of color on the island is invoked to give weight to this. Preoccupation with recognition, however, is not a peculiar trait with Fanon. It is found in varying degrees among all colonial intellectuals. The tendency to interpret the drama of Fanon's life as an attempt to solve a personal psychosis is to say the least shallow, and I find totally unsatisfactory theories which class all innovators as psychopaths (Feuer 1969, 51).

Fanon's early education followed strictly along the lines laid down by French assimilationist policy. The only books available were the official school textbooks concentrating on the glories of the metropolitan power and the French Empire. As in other French colonies, the official policy was assimilation, by which the blacks or a chosen few of them were promoted to the status of French citizens, enjoying in theory all the privileges of the white man's existence.

Assimilation and French education were intertwined. Martinican children read the same books and took the same examinations as white students in metropolitan France. Their classrooms were decorated with pictures of the wine harvest in Bordeaux and winter sports in Grenoble (Geismar 1971, 15). They were taught the history of France as if it were their own history (Geismar 1971, 15). Fanon and his brothers learned French patriotic songs. French culture was exalted to the skies; French language, French literature, French history, French mannerisms were accepted with uncritical adulation as the only legitimate way of life. The effect of this was clear. It made the children develop a deep sense of personal identification with French culture and the French way of life. Corresponding to the exaltation of the French way of life was a deprecation of the African way of life. Training at home was no different. Fanon recounts that whenever he misbehaved he was told to "stop acting like a nigger" (Fanon 1967a, 191). The Martinicans, like some members of the older generation of black Americans, accepted the racist stereotypes about Africans. They did not regard themselves as Africans. They were Martinicans. The Africans lived in Africa. They spent evenings talking about the savage customs of the Africans in the same way as whites did. And of the Africans the Senegalese were held up as the worst of the black savages. They were the real Africans of whom the most incredible tales were told.

Looking back on these incidents of his personal life, Fanon writes:

> As a schoolboy, I had on many occasions to spend whole hours talking about the supposed customs of the savage Senegalese. In what was said there was a lack of awareness that was at the very least paradoxical. Because the Antillean does not think of himself as a black man; he thinks of himself as an Antillean. The Negro lives in Africa. *Subjectively, intellectually, the Antillean conducts himself like a white man.* (Fanon 1967a, 148, emphasis added)

We would here add that Fanon was not talking of the ordinary poor Martinican, but the educated bourgeoisie. He was thus subjected to colonial education in one of its most intensive forms. Thus, like most of the children of his age, his early training was to end in his alienation. His education led to identification with French culture and its values. It was not only identification with white French culture but also a deprecation of African culture. Several years later Fanon was to write: "I am a white man for unconsciously I distrust what is black in me, that is the whole of my being" (Fanon 1967a, 191). Little did he know that in France, no matter how much he approximated to the French European style of life, intellectual posture and achievements, he would still be regarded first and foremost as a black and different from the white Frenchman. He would be known not simply as a "doctor" but as a "black doctor," not simply a "student," but a "black student," etc. Europe would never forget his color.

VICHY TIMES

In 1940, after the fall of France to the Vichy Administration, the French fleet in the Caribbean declared its allegiance to the regime of Vichy. The United States immediately imposed a blockade on the island. In response, the French governor instituted a military dictatorship on the island with the support of the leading property owners (Zahar 1970, 5). Consequently, 5,000 French sailors descended on the island's city population of 45,000 for a prolonged holiday. Geismar gives a vivid description of the incident:

> The soldiers expropriated Fort-de-France's bars, restaurants, hotels, whorehouses, beaches, shops, sidewalks, taxis, and better apartments. . . . The military could afford to order the civilians around. The servicemen were rough too. . . . What money failed to do brute power accomplished. Cafes were immediately segregated: black waiters and women, white customers. In the stores sailors expected to be served before Martinicans. At first segregation came about for economic reasons: With the influx of military money prices went up and the islanders could no longer

afford to be customers. By 1941 . . . the color lines were firmly established. The servicemen weren't going to fraternize with black males. The women were another matter: The white visitors requisitioned them; they considered every young girl on the island a prostitute. Rape often replaced the remuneration of those unwilling to conform to the soldiers' expectations. The police, used to operating in a colonial environment where blacks were always in the wrong, dismissed rape victims as overpriced prostitutes. In the military courts, the navy's word always carried more weight than the Martinican's complaints. It was a totalitarian racism. (Geismar 1971, 22–23)

This was the condition of the island at the time of the Vichy regime. Overnight the island came to look like an occupied territory. The regime came to represent "rape, racism, and rioting" (Geismar 1971, 24). What effect did these incidents have on the young and sensitive mind of Fanon? Did Fanon begin to hate France and all that it stood for at this moment? Fanon was at this time beginning to develop what one might call "political consciousness." Like many other blacks on the island, he resented the "totalitarian racism" of the Vichy Administration. But at this time he did not link this to a questioning of the whole French presence, nor did he link racism with the colonial relationship. It was a resentment and hatred directed against the administration and the soldiers, and not the French as such. He identified them more with the Germans than with the French.

It was in such circumstances that Fanon left the island in 1943, halfway through his baccalaureate, in company of two of his close friends, to respond to the call of General de Gaulle to save France. Their enthusiasm to fight for the French was underlined by the fact that they had to pay their own fares to the Dominican Republic where they underwent military training. By 1943, however, Admiral George Robert had capitulated to the pressure of the American blockade and Fanon once more returned to the island. However, he did not obtain a discharge after the ouster of the Vichy Administration, but enlisted in the French Army and left for North Africa to fight for the "Free French."

Fanon left the island in the company of two of his close friends,

Mosole and Manville. Mosole was described as a cynic and a well-informed person, who by 1943 knew all about racism and exploitation. Manville was the son of a Martinican socialist, who defended blacks in lower courts without any fee. Manville, whose close association with Fanon might have had some impact on him, attempted to follow in his father's footsteps, and while at the lycée he was always taking up the cases of the defense of other students before the higher authorities (Geismar 1971, 30). Fanon, then, grew up in the company of two important catalysts: Mosole with a knowledge of racism and exploitation, and Manville with his emphasis on the need for action on behalf of the helpless.

After a short stay in southern Morocco, they arrived in Algeria, which was to become Fanon's country of adoption later on in life. While in Algeria, Fanon and his two companions volunteered for service in Europe. The rampant racism in the army and the conditions of poverty were too much for them. He left the army with the rank of a corporal in 1946 and he was cited for bravery.

THE FRENCH ARMY

Fanon's experiences in the French army and the war were to have lasting effects on him. In the army he came face to face with blatant racism. Admittedly the island had experienced racism in some of its worst forms, particularly during the time of the Vichy administration. This was resented by Fanon and all blacks, but, as we have said earlier, in the minds of the Martinicans, the Vichy Administration was identified more with the Germans than with the French. The French were different. They held the values of fraternité, egalité, and liberté. All through school, Fanon had been taught to regard himself as a Frenchman and he was quite unprepared for the treatment which awaited him. He realized that France reserved a different place for its black Frenchmen. On the trip to North Africa the white French troops had attempted to "requisition the 'services' of a group of female volunteers from Martinique and Guadeloupe" (Geismar 1971, 31). Fanon was deeply upset by this incident, which raised further doubts in his own mind about the nature of the reality of the black-white relationship and the hypocrisy of the white world.

Fanon also observed that black troops were always sent to the worst areas of the war and were quartered in some of the most inhospitable areas. He did not fail to notice that white troops were treated differently and preferentially. The whites looked down on the Arabs who also looked down on the blacks. And blacks from the Caribbean also looked down upon blacks from Africa. The Martinicans, on account of their supposed cultural assimilation, were treated in minor ways as whites, but in things which mattered were treated like the rest of the nonwhites.

Manville reports how African troops were sent back and forth, to and from southern France. Their classification as Europeans or Africans depended on changes in climatic conditions. The classification and assignment of the soldiers to areas in France was apparently done on the basis of the level of fluency in French and the degree of acculturation. Thus, though Martinique was in the tropical zone, its troops were sent, not to southern France where the climate was warm, but to northern France where the climate was cold, because that corresponded to their assimilated status. The white man, being civilized, lives in cold climates, so as the black man approximates the status of the white man through the process of assimilation, he is supposed to develop the same resistance to cold and be able to respond to the physical environment of the white world in the same way as the white man! Correspondingly, the Africans, who were supposed to be less culturally assimilated, were sent to southern France where the climate was warm, since that approximated to the level of their culturally assimilated status. One is supposed to be civilized to the extent to which one finds the hot weather unbearable. Fanon comments on the sudden inability of the Martinican to withstand the tropical heat after a visit to Europe:

> They need a minute to two in order to make their diagnosis. If the voyager tell his acquaintances, "I am so happy to be back with you. Good Lord, it is hot in the country, I shall certainly not be

able to endure it very long," they know: A European has got off
the ship. (Fanon 1967a, 37)[1]

Fanon was deeply angered by the record of German destruction of North Africa. He was also touched by the poverty, famine,
and destitution in Algeria. His concern about the conditions of
poverty and destitution among the Algerians is even more remarkable if we remember that he was aware that Arabs looked down
upon blacks as social inferiors: "Some ten years ago I was astonished to learn that North Africans despised men of color. It was
absolutely impossible for me to make any contact with the local
populace" (Fanon 1967a, 102).

His luck was to be better in the future. It is interesting to note that
Fanon did not react to Arab racism in the same way as he did to
European racism. In a way he tended to think that Arab racism was
part of the superstructure, a reflection of colonial racism occasioned
by the colonial experience. He viewed it in the same terms in which
he viewed Martinican expression of racist attitudes toward Africans.

In Europe too there were incidents which made him more bitter
against the French. In Toulon he had to watch white Frenchwomen
dancing with Italian prisoners of war after turning down requests
from black servicemen who, needless to say, had risked their lives to
save them (the French) from the Italians and the Germans.

By the end of the war, Fanon was becoming increasingly cynical about France and the French values he had been taught to
admire at school.

RETURN TO MARTINIQUE—
CÉSAIRE'S CAMPAIGN

A short period of political activity was to intervene between
Fanon's war years and his higher education. This was when he
went back to the island after the war to campaign for Aimé
Césaire, who was running on the Communist ticket as a parlia-
mentary delegate from Martinique to the first National Assembly
of the Fourth Republic. There is no evidence that Fanon was at this

time sympathetic to the Communist cause. He was more interested in the cultural nationalism of Césaire and his négritude philosophy at this time. His participation in the campaign activities of Aimé Césaire was very instructive. His brother Joby alerted him to the problems of political and social mobilization in a place like Martinique and pointed out to him the flaws in Césaire's campaign in that he never succeeded in reaching the peasants and the countryside (Geismar 1971, 40). It is significant to note that his brother Joby felt that it was important to involve the peasants in the politics of the island (see Fanon 1968). Fanon was not only to come to the same conclusion several years later but to make the peasantry the cardinal point of his revolutionary decolonization.

With the campaign over, Fanon went back to the lycée to complete his education. This was in 1946. The picture we have of Fanon at this time was that of an introspective, withdrawn, and serious student. It is possible to surmise that he was brooding and turning over in his mind his experiences in the French army. He turned his attention to the study of literature and philosophy and he studied the works of Nietzsche, Karl Jaspers, Kierkegaard, and Hegel. He was particularly interested in the works of Césaire and Jean-Paul Sartre, and for a while he thought of a career in drama.

HIGHER EDUCATION IN FRANCE

In 1947, after the death of his father, Fanon went to France for higher studies. He first enrolled in dentistry in Paris, but after three weeks' introductory courses he abruptly left Paris for Lyon to study medicine, complaining that there were too many "niggers" in Paris. Geismar gives as Fanon's reason that there were too many fools in dental school. He is also said to have claimed that he could live more cheaply in Lyon. These reasons, however, are hardly satisfactory, especially when we know that Fanon has always had the tendency to withdraw from an intolerable psychological situation. We have already noticed this "withdrawal syndrome" when he was in the army.[2]

If the statement "There are just too many niggers in Paris" is a reference to the revulsion which Fanon felt at the disgusting behavior of the black bourgeoisie in Paris which tried to be more French than the French, and which tried to imitate and assimilate French culture in every imaginable way, then one can say that, even at this early stage, he was keenly aware of the problems of cultural and intellectual alienation which afflict the black man in a white-dominated world, a theme he was to deal with so well in *Black Skin, White Masks*. If this interpretation is accepted, then how do we account for the fact that with such a knowledge he did try to assimilate French culture? The plain fact was that he had no choice; either he had to leave France or to stay in France and be assimilated. It could be argued that he sought full assimilation like anyone else, and to support this contention we may quote the following exclamation:

> What is all this talk of a black people, of a Negro nationality? I am a Frenchman. I am interested in French culture, French civilization, the French people. . . . I am personally interested in the future of France, in French values, in the French nation. What have I to do with a black empire? (Fanon 1967a, 203)

It is quite conceivable that Fanon was plagued all the time by an internal conflict between the demands of assimilation and the need for autonomy—the need to be oneself—and that sometimes he repressed one or the other. His abrupt flight from Paris could therefore be attributed to the constant reminder which the presence of the black bourgeoisie in Paris brought to him of his internal conflict, something which he was trying desperately to suppress. He thought Lyon would provide the conditions for psychic harmony. He was sadly mistaken in this.

After a year's preparatory work in chemistry, physics, and biology, Fanon entered medical school. At school he worked hard to earn the respect of his professors as a bright student.

While at the university, Fanon continued his interest in philosophy and literature. He read the existential philosophers: Husserl, Heidegger, and Sartre. He also read Marx and Hegel, and he attended the course of lectures of Jean Lacroix and Maurice Merleau-Ponty. He was greatly influenced by Sartre, especially his *Anti-Semite and Jew* and later by the *Critique de la Raison Dialectique*. According to Simone de Beauvoir, what impressed Fanon most about the *Critique de la Raison Dialectique* was Sartre's analysis of terror and brotherhood.

Fanon was also influenced by Aimé Césaire, an influence which is particularly noticeable in *Black Skin, White Masks*, with its numerous quotations from Césaire. While a medical student, he also immersed himself in playwriting and he completed three works: *Les Mains Paralleles, L'Oeil Se Noie*, and *La Conspiration*. These were written between 1949 and 1950. They still remain unpublished and according to Fanon's widow, it was his wish that they remain so. Dr Marie Perimbam, who has read them, says they reveal Fanon's attempt to solve human problems within the existential framework. They give the impression that Fanon was thinking of the world as a stage, life as an existential drama, and people as the actors. This was a period of intense reflection, introspection, and self-analysis. Some have called this the existentialist phase of Fanon's life. It should also be remembered that this was the time when he began to compose the essays which later were to appear collectively as *Black Skin, White Masks*, which deals with the problem of colonial alienation, the relations of superordination and subordination, the norm which guides all relations between the colonizer and the colonized, and the creation of a dependency complex. In short it is an examination of the ontological existence of the black man in a white-dominated world and covers the subject matter of the psychology of colonial rule, a topic notoriously neglected in college and university courses on colonialism.

Fanon was a restless student and side by side with his medical studies he was active in politics. While at the medical school, he helped to organize the Union of Students from Overseas France in Lyon, and put out the short-lived newspaper *Tam-Tam*. He was always involved in debates or going to left-wing meetings and touring occupied factories.

In November 1951, Fanon defended his medical thesis and left for Martinique. Much has been made of the fact that the thesis starts with a quotation from Nietzsche: "I dedicate myself to human beings, not to introspective mental process." But if a medical doctor does not dedicate himself to human beings to what else is he to dedicate himself? While in Martinique Fanon presented a copy of his thesis to his brother with this inscription:

> To my brother, Felix,
> I offer this work—
> The greatness of a man is to be found not in his acts but in his style. Existence does not resemble a steadily rising curve, but a slow, and sometimes sad, series of ups and downs.
> I have a horror of weaknesses—I understand them, but I do not like them.
> I do not agree with those who think it possible to live life at an easy pace. I don't want this. I don't think you do either . . .
> (Geismar 1971, 11)

These remarkable lines bring out forcibly some aspects of Fanon's personality: his restlessness, his impatience, his hatred of weakness, and the apparent contradictions of his personal life. For it is puzzling that a man who showed a deep sense of commitment to praxis should here place style above acts.

In the same year he went back to France to do his residency under Professor François Tosquelles, who was carrying out innovative experiments in the field of sociotherapy.* He was to make a deep impression on Fanon, who worked with Tosquelles for two years during which time they jointly published a number of research papers. His pioneering work in psychiatric medicine in Algeria and Tunisia bore strongly the impact of this association with Professor Tosquelles.

In 1952, he married Josie Dublé, a Frenchwoman whom he had met while at the lycée in Lyon.[3] Certain black radicals who have adopted Fanon have been uneasy about the fact of his marriage to a white woman. They claim it was not right and goes against Fanon's position. This is a complete misunderstanding of Fanon's position. Fanon never preached separation or segregation. His writings about the Manichean world are descriptive and not pre-

---

*Please refer to chapter 5 for a detailed discussion of sociotherapy. —Ed.

scriptive. It is precisely this idea of the black man being sealed in his blackness and the white man being encased in his whiteness which he wanted to avoid. Specifically on the question of marriage he says: ". . . I do not feel that I should be abandoning my personality by marrying an European, whoever she might be" (Geismar 1971, 202). Admittedly, Fanon has castigated the black bourgeoisie for deciding to marry white. It should, however, be remembered that his objection was not to marriage across color lines per se, but to marriage into the white society in order to escape one's blackness. In this case it is an indication of shame and hatred of one's color. Geismar comes near to suggesting that Fanon married a white woman because of the paucity of black women in Lyon or as a consequence of his yearning for "lactification."

> . . . it seems that Fanon fell in love only with white women. Maybe this was because there were few blacks living in the city, but Fanon himself gave a more interesting possible explanation in his first book, *Black Skin, White Masks.* He describes there the neurotic behavior pattern of a black man attempting to become white through love of a white woman. (Geismar 1969, 24)

Such a suggestion rests on a misunderstanding of Fanon. Fanon was not a man to marry a woman because she is black or white. This is precisely the Manichean world he denounced in the most strident terms. In Fanon's view, color or nationality should be entirely extraneous to the choice of a marital partner. His commitment was neither to a black nor to a white world. It was to a non-racial society. If Fanon avoided black women it was less on account of the color question. It was the same reason which occasioned his abrupt departure from Paris. Fanon has told us in *Black Skin, White Masks* of the kind of black women he encountered in France:

> I know a great number of girls from Martinique, students in France, who admitted to me with complete candor—completely white candor—that they would find it impossible to marry black men. (Get out of that and then deliberately go back to it? Thank you, no.) (Fanon 1967, 48).

Again, "I knew another black girl who kept a list of Parisian dance-halls 'where-there-was-no-chance-of-running-into-niggers'" (Fanon 1967a, 50). If these were the sort of black women in France at the time no psychological explanation is needed to account for Fanon's action. Any black man with his head on his shoulders would avoid such women.

Although Geismar does not cite anything from the text to support his claim of Fanon's marriage arising out of lactification, his contention perhaps rests on this passage:

> I marry white culture, white beauty, white whiteness. When my restless hands caress those white breasts, they grasp white civilization and dignity and make them mine. (Fanon 1967a, 33)

Although *Black Skin, White Masks* is autobiographical in tone, incidents related in the book do not always refer to incidents in Fanon's personal life. Sometimes it is only the style, not the incidents which are autobiographical. The work is an attempt to understand the world and the black man's place in it through introspection. The danger of using statements in *Black Skin, White Masks* undiscriminatingly as incidents in Fanon's personal life is evident from Geismar's work. Fanon, in *Black Skin, White Masks*, writes:

> A prostitute once told me that in her early days the mere thought of going to bed with a Negro brought on an orgasm. She went in search of Negroes and never asked them for money. But, she added, "going to bed with them was no more remarkable than going to bed with white men." (Fanon 1967a, 158-59)

Although there is nothing in the text to indicate so, Geismar turns this into an incident in Fanon's personal life.

> Not even the city's prostitutes wanted black clients. Except for one Fanon found, who confided she wanted him *because* he was black. She later admitted that she had had an orgasm the first time before he had begun sexual intercourse. (Geismar 1971, 47)

Fanon has discussed in detail in *Black Skin, White Masks*, buttressing his arguments with copious quotations from Mayotte Capecia's *Je suis Martiniquaise*, Abdoulaye Sadji's *Nini*, and René Maran's *Un homme pareil aux autres*, the phenomenon of "lactification" by marriage to the white woman, or vice versa. It is unlikely that a man so keenly aware of these problems which he analyzes would himself become a victim. Also, we know that *Black Skin, White Masks* was completed in 1951 and published in 1952. His marriage to Josie Dublé did not take place till 1952. Geismar's suggestions are therefore extremely unlikely.

In France, Fanon was exposed to the writings and the company of the French intellectual Left. He moved in the circles of Sartre and Simone de Beauvoir. He was particularly friendly with Dr. Colin, a leftist intellectual who edited a clandestine newspaper during the resistance. Fanon arrived in France when négritude was still fashionable among a number of black intellectuals in Paris. He was initially attracted to it and he reacted strongly against Sartre's criticisms of négritude. Sartre, though regarding négritude as revolutionary, nevertheless described it as "anti-racist racism" and pointed out its limitations, indicating that it is only a movement in the dialectic. Fanon's reaction to Sartre was swift and angry.

> When I read that page, I felt that I had been robbed of my last chance. I said to my friends, "The generation of younger black poets have just suffered a blow that can never be forgiven. Help had been sought from a friend of the colored peoples, and that friend had found no better response than to point out the relativity of what they were doing." (Fanon 1967a, 133)

He was later to recognize and acknowledge the same limitations.

While in France, he also experienced and reacted against white racism and the hypocrisy of the French with regard to their claims to be committed to universal ethical values. In Martinique it was easy to rationalize and interpret such behavior as the aberration of particular Europeans, and in the army one could always argue that soldiers everywhere are coarse and rough and do not typify the most decent and gentle of the nation. But when Fanon experienced the same things in France, and even from the leftist intellectuals, his reaction was no longer a matter of doubting French values, but it was a rejection of France and all that it stood for. Relating some of his experiences, Fanon writes: "When people like me, they tell me it is in spite of my color, when they dislike me, they point out that it is not because of my color. Either way, I am locked into the infernal circle" (Fanon 1967a, 116). Frenchmen could never forget that he was black and different from themselves. Color always played a central role in everything. Again Fanon writes:

> Not so long ago, one of those good Frenchmen said in a train where I was sitting: "Just let the real French virtues keep going and the race is safe. Now more than ever national union must be made a reality. Let's have an end of internal strife. Let's face up to the foreigners (here he turned toward my corner) no matter who they are." (Fanon 1967a, 121)

The blacks were never to be part of the French nation, no matter what their assimilated status was. They were the foreigners who had to be faced up to. He was treated primarily as a black man, not just as a human being. Fanon writes: "A man was expected to behave like a man. I was expected to behave like a black man or at least like a nigger" (Fanon 1967a, 114). Even in intellectual circles Fanon was not safe from this humiliation:

> . . . more than a year ago in Lyon, I remember in a lecture I had drawn a parallel between Negro and European poetry and a French acquaintance told me enthusiastically, "At bottom you are a white man." The fact that I had been able to investigate so interesting a problem through the white man's language gave honorary citizenship. (Fanon 1967a, 38)

Fanon was suspicious, and to his way of thinking the remark amounted to saying that for a black man his intellect was amazing. Incidents of this nature aroused his indignation, anger, and resentment and he hated France and all that it stood for.

Fanon was deeply affected by the hypocrisy of the French, even the Communist Left. He was also disgusted by the self-demeaning attitude of the black bourgeoisie who tried in every way to look as French as possible. He was angered by the oppression of man by man, by the dehumanization of man, and by the fact that France was a living negation of the values it claimed. As he was to say afterward: "When I search for Man in the technique and the style of Europe, I see only a succession of negations of man, and an avalanche of murders" (Fanon 1968, 312).

Fanon was entirely disillusioned with Europe and France, and if he had one consuming desire at the time it was to get away from it. No wonder that he was to write later:

> Let us waste no time in sterile litanies and nauseating mimicry. Leave this Europe where they are never done of talking about Man, yet murder men everywhere they find them, at the corner of every one of their own streets, in all corners of the globe. (Fanon 1968, 311).

It was no longer a question of appealing to Europe to live up to its proclaimed values. That was useless. He wanted to get to a place where he could search for his own identity and think of a way where he could contribute to the saving of humanity. The burden now was to be on the oppressed to do what Europe had been unable to do. Fanon writes: "Let us try to create the whole man, whom Europe has been incapable of bringing to triumphant birth" (Fanon 1968, 312). He wanted a place where he could feel solidarity with those who were contributing to the "victory of the dignity of the spirit," where man was saying "no" to "the attempt to subjugate his fellows." Algeria was godsent.

ALGERIA

In 1953, Frantz Fanon passed the all-important *Medicat des Hopitaux Psychiatriques* and was offered the directorship of a Martinican hospital. However, he turned it down and took up a position as *chef de service* in Algeria, after a short stay at Pontorson, a small quiet town on the Atlantic coast of France. Geismar contends that his choice was motivated by a consideration for his career, since Martinique lacked facilities for psychiatric care or research. He uses this to back up his claim that it was the Algerian situation which made Fanon a revolutionary, and that it was not for political reasons that he went there. Renate Zahar, however, maintains that Fanon had decided at the time of his marriage to Josie to work for a few years in Africa and then return to Martinique (Zahar 1970, 7). If we accept Zahar's account, then Geismar's position is somewhat weakened. If Fanon turned down the Martinican position because of his considerations for his career, i.e., lack of adequate equipment for the hospital, then how can we explain his plan to go back after a few years? There is no likelihood that in a few years the position at the hospital would have changed considerably. One would think that if Fanon was all that concerned with his career, Africa would be the least attractive place, if equipment for his work was very important to him. Zahar's claim is supported by the fact that Geismar himself admits that Fanon sought a position in Senegal, writing to Leopold Senghor, later to become president of Senegal, but his letter was not answered. He had known Senghor as one of the people connected with Society of African Culture and *Présence Africaine*. He wanted to leave France and go to Africa, which at that time was in a state of nationalist ferment. Ghana was making rapid advances toward self-government and Nigeria was following rapidly behind. In Central and East Africa there was political agitation. In Uganda, there was political agitation; in Kenya, politics was beginning to take a militant turn; Mau Mau had just begun.

Fanon wanted to be in the center of things. He wanted to be where the action was. We must not forget his commitment to praxis. We must also not forget that Fanon as a schoolboy had heard a lot about the Senegalese, and it is quite conceivable that Senegal still fascinated him and he wanted to go there himself. Reacting on his boyhood, Fanon had this to say about the Senegalese:

All I knew about them was what I had heard from the veterans of the First World War: "They attack with the bayonet and when that doesn't work, they just punch their way through the machine-gun fire with their fists." (Fanon 1967a, 162n)

If the above argument is accepted, then it means that Fanon had a political motive for wanting to go to Africa and his departure for Algeria should be seen in the same light. In sub-Saharan Africa, due to language difficulty, he could only go to French-speaking Africa; his attempt to go there was unsuccessful, so he went to North Africa. Here he would not have a language problem. Fanon had already shown some interest in North Africans in France by his essay "The North African Syndrome" (Fanon 1967b) in which he discusses the racially discriminatory practices against the Arab minority even among doctors in France. Besides, in Algeria, politics was beginning to take a militant turn. Geismar's position is further weakened by his own admission that Blida, where Fanon worked, did not have facilities for work therapy (Geismar 1971, 64). Why then should he want to go there? His argument that Fanon overcame his political phase toward the end of his studies and set himself up to be a successful professional is unpersuasive. This interpretation tends to regard Fanon's political interests and his commitment to praxis as the restless actions of an adolescent. He seems to think that Fanon was converted to revolutionary violence due to the existential situation in Algeria. It is quite plausible that toward the end of his medical training Fanon tried to concentrate more on his studies, but that he was committed to revolutionary violence before his trip to Algeria is evidenced in *Black Skin, White Masks*, where he writes:

> I do not carry innocence to the point of believing that appeals to reason or to respect for human dignity can alter reality. For the Negro who works on a sugar plantation in Le Robert, there is only one solution: to fight. (Fanon 1967a, 234)

This he wrote long before the trip to Algeria. Furthermore, Fanon quotes Hegel with relish to substantiate his contention for the necessity of revolutionary violence in the pursuit of freedom.

It is solely by risking life that freedom is obtained; only thus it is tried and proved that the essential nature of self-consciousness is not *bare existence*, is not the merely immediate form in which it at first makes its appearance, is not its mere absorption in the expanse of life. (Fanon 1967a, 218)

Fanon continues in his own words: "Human reality in-itself-for-itself can be achieved only through conflict and through the risk that conflict implies." Again he quotes from Hegel: "The individual who has not staked his life, may no doubt be recognized as a person, but he has not attained the truth of this recognition as an independent self-consciousness" (Fanon 1967a, 219).

In *Black Skin, White Masks*, Fanon advocates fundamental change in society. Echoing Marx, he writes:

But when one has taken cognizance of this situation, when one has understood it, one considers the job completed. How can one then be deaf to that voice rolling down the stage of history: "What matters is not to know the world but to change it"? (Fanon 1967a, 17)

In another passage he writes:

In no way should my color be regarded as a flaw. From the moment the Negro accepts the separation imposed by the European he has no further respite, and "is it not understandable that henceforth he will try to elevate himself to the white man's level? To elevate himself in the range of colors to which he attributes a kind of hierarchy?" We shall see that another solution is possible. It implies a restructuring of the world. (Fanon 1967a, 81–82).

"Restructuring of the world" is the change of social structure and value systems. In another passage Fanon is even more explicit:

What emerges then is the need for combined action on the individual and on the group. As a psychoanalyst, I should help my patient to become *conscious* of his unconscious and abandon his attempts at a hallucinatory whitening, but also to act in the direction of a change in the social structure. (Fanon 1967a, 100)

It is clear from the above that at the time of the composition of *Black Skin, White Masks*, Fanon was already convinced of the need for a change in social structure. When this commitment to fundamental change of social structure is viewed in conjunction with Fanon's argument for the necessity of violence to achieve freedom, it is difficult to avoid the conclusion that he was committed to revolutionary violence for the purpose of achieving freedom before he went to Algeria. His experiences in Algeria confirmed a thesis he had already arrived at intellectually. We can say that before he went to Algeria, Fanon was intellectually committed to revolutionary violence, but due to his experiences in Algeria, his commitment took a personal and practical form.

Fanon arrived in Algiers in November 1953. By then the revolution which was to engulf both France and Algeria was beginning. There were isolated incidents of terrorism which caused the French to isolate the casbah from the European quarter and to institute check points everywhere.

Initially, Fanon collaborated with the *Front de Libération Nationale* (FLN). During the day he treated the French torturers and by night he treated the Algerian tortured. By 1956 this double life was becoming impossible. There was terror all around him; his nurses were beginning to disappear, and he began to feel that he was becoming less effective. In these circumstances he resigned.

Fanon had also come to the view that in a colonial territory like Algeria, characterized by economic oppression, political violence, racism, torture, murder, and inhuman degradation, the psychiatric disorders from which the people suffered were the direct result of the social situation; it was, therefore, futile to treat a patient and send him back to the same environment. What had to be changed was not the people but the social and political conditions prevailing in Algeria.

In Algeria, Fanon saw a confirmation of the thesis he had developed earlier as a result of his observations in Martinique, namely that for the colonized the most serious problem standing in the way of self-realization and freedom was alienation. This alienation could only be cured by the destruction of the colonial system. In his letter of resignation he states:

If psychiatry is the medical technique that aims to enable man no longer to be a stranger to his environment, I owe it to myself to affirm that the Arab, permanently an alien in his own country, lives in a state of absolute depersonalization. . . . The function of social structure is to set up institutions to serve man's needs. A society that drives its members to desperate solutions is a nonviable society, a society to be replaced. (Fanon 1967b, 53)

And to underline his own commitment for praxis, he adds: "there comes a time when silence becomes dishonesty."

After participating in a strike of doctors sympathetic to the FLN, Fanon was expelled from Algeria in January 1957. Thus ended his short stay in Algeria.

FANON IN TUNISIA

After Fanon's expulsion, he stayed in Lyon for a short time with Josie's family and then left for Tunisia to work for the FLN. He was now a "professional revolutionary." He now belonged entirely to the organization. The Algerian Revolution was his life. He assumed whatever role the organization called upon him to perform. Whatever academic and intellectual interests he had were now only relevant to the extent to which they furthered the cause of the revolution.

While in Tunisia he worked as a member of the editorial staff of *El Moudjahid*, the FLN mouthpiece. Fanon turned it into a radical paper commenting on the social, economic, and political aspects of the revolution. He also published a number of articles on black Africa and on African unity.

In spite of his new status as a professional revolutionary, he also taught at the university of Tunis and practiced medicine at a government psychiatric hospital at Manouba, where he worked under the assumed name of Dr. Fares.

Here Fanon did not get along very well with some of his colleagues. The doctors resented his innovations and regarded him as overbearing. He, on the other hand, was a perfectionist, and tried to impose on others the same dedication which he applied to his work. The resentment against him from the doctors was such that they began to refer to him as "the nigger." Things got to such a pass that the head of the unit, Dr. Soltan, tried to fire Fanon on the ground that he was a spy for Israel, because he had earlier taken a stand against anti-Semitism.

> Anti-Semitism hits me head-on: I am enraged, I am bled white by an appalling battle, I am deprived of the possibility of being a man. I cannot disassociate myself from the future that is proposed for my brother. (Fanon 1967a, 55)

Fanon's singleness of purpose, his sincerity and dedication to the cause of freedom and justice, stand out clearly when it is noticed that not even incidents of this nature shook for a moment his total dedication to the cause of Algerian freedom.

It was while he was in Tunis that he published *The 5th Year of the Algerian Revolution* [*A Dying Colonialism*]. In some ways it bears a close resemblance to Marx's *The Eighteenth Brumaire of Louis Bonaparte*. It is a sociological study of the effects of the revolutionary war on Algerian society. It documents the changes which take place in social structure, social and political institutions, and in consciousness as a result of the war of liberation. In a way it should be seen as a sequel to Fanon's more illustrious work, *The Wretched of the Earth*, since it indicates the changes which would occur in the colonized society if the recommendations contained in *The Wretched of the Earth* were put into effect. The importance of the book for the liberation effort is evidenced by the fact that six months after its publication the French government ordered all copies seized and banned further publication.

In Tunis Fanon seemed to have achieved a total fusion of the role of the intellectual and that of the political activist. His life showed total dedication to the cause of Algerian liberation. In his writings, the reflective "I" which had characterized *Black Skin, White Masks* gave way to the committed "we," the Algerians.

Another role which Fanon played in the FLN was that of a diplomatic representative. In December 1958, he attended the All-

African People's Conference in Accra, where he met Kwame Nkrumah, and other nationalist leaders, including Patrice Lumumba, Felix Moumie, head of Union Populaire de Cameroun (UPC); Tom Mboya; and Holden Roberto. At the conference he argued for the necessity of violence for decolonization. In a report on the conference which he later wrote for *El Moudjahid*, he stated:

> The end of the colonial regime affected by peaceful means and made possible by the colonialist's understanding might under certain circumstances lead to a renewed collaboration of the two nations. History, however, shows that a colonialist nation is willing to withdraw without having exhausted all its possibilities of maintaining itself. Raising the problem of a non-violent decolonization is less the postulation of a sudden humanity on the part of the colonialist than believing in the sufficient pressure of the new ratio of forces on an international scale. (Fanon 1967b, 154–55).

In March 1959, he attended the Second Congress of Black Writers in Rome, and there he spoke as a member of the Antilles delegation. Fanon's internationalism was beginning to appear. Though completely dedicated to the Algerian cause, this did not inhibit him from participation in the Antillean delegation. In January 1960, he also participated in the Second Conference of African Peoples in Tunis as a member of the Algerian delegation. He was seen as the man who could bridge the gap between the predominantly Arab North Africa and the predominantly black sub-Sahara Africa.

Fanon's singular contribution to the cause of Algerian liberation at this time was to internationalize the Algerian struggle. In his writings and presentations at conferences he tried to project the Algerian struggle not only as an Arab nationalist movement, but as part of the whole world movement for the liberation of Africa and the Third World.

ACCRA

In March 1960, Fanon was appointed ambassador for the Algerian Provisional Government in Accra. In various other conferences which he attended—the International Conference for Peace and Security in Africa, the Afro-Asian Solidarity Conference of Independent African States at Addis-Ababa in June 1960—he went as the official representative of Algeria. As an ambassador in Accra he concentrated his attention on three main aspects of the African liberation struggle: the establishment of a southern flank in Mali through which recruits could be channeled to fight in Algeria; the attempt to recruit volunteers to fight in Algeria; the armed struggle in Angola and the events in the Congo.

He spent much time traveling to present the case for Algerian liberation and to propagandize for the formation of an African Legion for the fight for African liberation. Fanon's work in Accra was quite trying. His English was not fluent enough for him to be much involved in the social life of the country. Even if he had spoken very well, it is not likely that he could have got on well with the Ghanaian national bourgeoisie which was steeped in corruption, conspicuous consumption, authoritarianism, and a shameless display of affluence in the midst of poverty, the very issues which Fanon was to denounce most vehemently in *The Wretched of the Earth*. In Accra, he did not do any medical or psychiatric work. His official position as an ambassador would not allow him to do that.

In 1961 Fanon unsuccessfully sought posting to Cuba. There have been a number of speculations about this. One opinion has it that he was seeking to return to Martinique and wanted to go to Cuba to study it as a model (Geismar 1971, 173). It is also claimed that he wanted to go to Cuba as an ambassador to compensate for an earlier wounded pride in maternal rejection (Gendzier 1973, 16). Such an interpretation invests Fanon with a vanity out of keeping with the delineation of his character and personality. The more likely reason was that Fanon was becoming intellectually and politically bored with Accra. True enough Accra remained the headquarters of African liberation south of the Sahara, but behind the thin veil of political rhetoric there existed among the Ghanaian political leadership residual conservatism, ideological bankruptcy, political insensitivity, parochialism, incredible ignorance, or tolerance of international capitalist machinations which any serious revolutionary like Fanon would find most distressing. Looking around for a place to escape from such a revolutionary graveyard, Cuba appeared most attractive.

ASSASSINATION ATTEMPTS

Fanon's importance to the Algerian movement and to the whole of the liberation forces in Africa is underlined by the numerous attempts to assassinate him. In 1959 while he was traveling to a camp on the Algerian-Moroccan border his jeep was blown up. There are a number of speculations about the incident. Some claim that it was an accident, some that his car hit a land mine planted either by the French or someone within the ranks movement of the FLN who wanted to do away with Fanon. A third opinion is that there was a bomb planted in the car in which he was traveling. The true story is shrouded in mystery. Fanon was flown from Tunis to Rome for specialized treatment. In Rome there were two more assassination attempts: one when the car of the FLN representative who was to pick him from the airport was blown up and the second when the ward in which he was supposed to be occupying was machine-gunned. Fanon had had a premonition and had secretly requested a change of rooms the same night. The fact that there was strong evidence linking these attacks with the French Red Hand gives cause to think that it was the same group involved in the Algerian-Morocco border incident.

In 1960, there was another attempt to capture him. While an ambassador in Accra, he traveled frequently to various countries in West Africa, trying to open the southern flank where arms and men could be channeled to Algeria to aid the war effort. On one occasion he was returning to Conakry from Monrovia when there was an attempt to capture him. Geismar reports:

Fanon was informed that his scheduled flight to Conakry Guinea was filled. He would have to wait until the next day to get an Air France flight to the same city. His overnight expenses would be paid by the airline. That evening when a charming French airline hostess stopped at the hotel to tell him that the plane would be two hours late the next day, Fanon was suspicious. It was the kind of personal attention he had come to dread—especially after the 1959 incident in the Rome hospital. Revising plans, he and an FLN colleague left the Liberian capital by jeep and entered Guinea through the dark forest surrounding the border town of N'zerekore.

Air France still had Fanon, under the pseudonym of "Doctor Omar," on its passenger list for the next day. French intelligence had arranged for the plane to change courses from Guinea to the city of Abidjan, in the Ivory Coast. . . . Despite the fact that the final list didn't include "Omar" the aircraft was searched thoroughly at Abidjan before it was allowed to return to its normal flight plan. (Geismar 1971, 163)

It is something of a mystery that in spite of all this, Fanon eluded his enemies.

ILLNESS AND DEATH

Late in 1960, it was found that Fanon was suffering from leukemia. He went to the Soviet Union for medical treatment. The Russians advised him to go to the United States where the best center for the cure of leukemia was the National Institute of Health in Bethesda, Maryland, but he could not bring himself to go to the "nation of lynchers." He refused to allow the fact of his illness to dampen his activity. The treatment he had in the Soviet Union gave him relief for some time. He returned to Accra and threw himself furiously into his work. He began to plan projects as if nothing unusual existed.

By May 1961, Fanon was working on the last chapter of *The Wretched of the Earth*. As Geismar describes it, it was "a ten-week eruption of intellectual energies." After completing the drafts, he went to France to see Sartre, who had agreed to write the introduction.

Back in Tunis, Fanon had a relapse and his friends arranged for him to go to the United States for treatment. Joseph Alsop, a syndicated columnist for the *Washington Post*, claimed that it was the CIA which arranged for the transportation to Washington, and that the CIA had an interest in Frantz Fanon. He went on to mention the name of Ollie Iselin, a member of the U.S. diplomatic service, who was involved in the whole case. The story that the CIA managed to get information from the dying Fanon has been vigorously denied by both his wife, Josie, and his brother Joby.

There were some suspicious circumstances, however. Fanon was kept in Washington's Dupont Plaza for eight days before he was taken to the hospital, in spite of the fact that there were vacant beds at the hospital at this time. This raises the question of why he was not taken immediately to the hospital, considering the sad condition in which he was when he arrived in the country.

Fanon refused to recognize his illness and while on his deathbed he was still planning book projects. One was to deal with the extent and functioning of the FLN organization within metropolitan France; another, a psychological analysis of the death process itself, which was to be called *Le Leucemique et son double*. While he was in the hospital he received a number of visitors including Holden Roberto, and Alioune Diop, editor of *Présence Africaine*. Fanon had another relapse and died on December 6, 1961, after reading the proofs of *The Wretched of the Earth*, the work on which his reputation rests. In it he diagnoses the ills of Africa and the Third World. He argues that there has been no effective decolonization in Africa because the colonial structures have not been destroyed. What happened at independence was the Africanization of colonialism. There can be no effective decolonization and consequently no freedom so long as the colonial structures remain. And to destroy colonialism effectively, violence is indispensable. Violence destroys not only the formal structures of colonial rule, but also the alienated consciousness which colonial rule has planted in the mind of the native. Unlike the so-called dispassionate native intellectuals, he is not content with a mere description of the structure of politics or a catalogue of colonial injustices. He propounds a theory of social action and makes a passionate plea for revolutionary decolonization and the creation of a free society in which man would acquire authentic existence. His vision of the ideal society was that of a socialist populist democracy, a combination of Marx and Rousseau, in which man would be free to maintain and express his nature. We may criticize his vision or the means of its attainment, but we neglect the issues he raises only at our peril.

After his death a collection of some of the editorials he wrote for *El Moudjahid* and some of his presentations at international conferences were published collectively as *Toward the African Revolution*.

The portrait which emerges from this is that Frantz Fanon was a man of considerable courage, sincerity, and will power. He was a very sensitive person who dedicated his life to bringing about the end of oppression. His whole life was devoted to the cause of human freedom. He was a man of keen intellect and revolutionary zeal. Simone de Beauvoir described his intellect as "razor sharp." He was one for whom the role of the intellectual and that of the political activist posed no contradictions.

Peter Worsley, in a vivid description of his encounter with Fanon, gives us an insight into his qualities and personality:

In 1960, I attended the All African People's Congress in Accra, Ghana. The proceedings consisted mainly of speeches by leaders of African nationalism from all over the continent, few of whom said anything notable. When, therefore, the representative of the Algerian Revolutionary Provisional Government, their Ambassador in Ghana stood up to speak I prepared myself for an address by a diplomat—not usually an experience to set the pulses racing. I found myself electrified by a contribution that was remarkable not only for its analytical power, but delivered, too, with a passion and brilliance that is all too rare. I discovered that the Ambassador was a man named Frantz Fanon. At one point during his talk he appeared almost to break down. I asked him afterward what had happened. He replied that he had suddenly felt emotionally overcome at the thought that he had to stand there, before the assembled representatives of African nationalist movements, to try and persuade them that the Algerian cause was important, at a time when men were dying and being tortured in his country for a cause whose justice ought to command automatic support from rational and progressive human beings. (Worsley 1969, 30–31)

Like all revolutionaries, Fanon was sometimes impatient, brusque, and arrogant toward people whose commitment never went beyond the talking stage. He also tried to impose on others the same discipline which he imposed on himself, people who perhaps by temperament and constitution were not fit for the arduous tasks to which he subjected himself.

Aimé Césaire, in a tribute to Fanon, goes further than anyone in delineating his character, qualities, and personality. He writes:

> If the word "commitment" has any meaning, it was with Fanon that it acquired significance. A violent one, they said. And it is true he instituted himself as a theorist of violence, the only arm of the colonized that can be used against colonialist barbarity. . . .
>
> But his violence, and this is not paradoxical, was that of the non-violent. By this I mean the violence of justice, of purity and intransigence. This must be understood about him: his revolt was ethical, and his endeavor generous. He did not simply adhere to a cause. He gave himself to it. Completely, without reserve. Wholeheartedly. In him resided the absoluteness of passion. . . .
>
> A theorist of violence, perhaps, but even more of action. By hatred of talkativeness. By hatred of compromise. By hatred of cowardliness. No one was more respectful of thought than he, and more responsible in face of his own thought, nor more exacting toward life, which he could not imagine in terms other than of thought transformed into action. (Césaire 1962, 131–32).

It is clear from the portrait above that simplistic interpretations of Fanon as "apostle of violence," "glorifier of violence," "apologist for violence," "prisoner of hate" should be rejected. Fanon was a great humanist. It was in the name of man that he rose up against oppression; it was in the name of man that he fought against degradation, and it was in the name of man that he affirmed the dignity of man. If Fanon was a prisoner, he was a prisoner of a cause, the cause of the people, the cause of freedom. In a letter he wrote to Roger Tayed, one of his friends, just before he died, he said, "We are nothing on earth if we are not, first of all, slaves of a cause of the people, the cause of justice, the cause liberty" (quoted in Geismar 1971, 185). Che Guevara once said: "Let me say at the risk of seeming ridiculous that the true revolutionary is guided by great feelings of love." This we can say of Frantz Fanon.

NOTES

1. Incidents of this nature may appear improbable to the unacquainted with colonial alienation. However in Ghana, where it is claimed that on account of the indirect rule, the natives did not suffer such cultural emasculation which gives rise to such manifestations of alienation, it was not uncommon, especially in the 1950s and early 1960s for recent returnees from the white man's country to complain bitterly about the heat. Press them closely and you will find they were away for only a couple of months and in most cases in the summer.

2. This tendency to withdraw from an intolerable social situation seems to have characterized Fanon all his life. When Martinique fell to the Vichy forces he "withdrew" from the island by enlisting in the French army; while in North Africa, he "withdrew" by volunteering for service in Europe; in Paris he "withdrew" to Lyon; in France he "withdrew" to Algeria; in Accra, he wanted to "withdraw" by asking for a diplomatic post in Cuba. This shows his restlessness. For a man committed to praxis this is rather difficult to explain.

3. There have been some inconsistencies in the records about the date of Fanon's marriage. Irene Gendzier writes; "According to David Caute, *Fanon* (p. 99), it occurred in 1953; Tosquelles in our interview recalled, but with some hesitation, that it was in 1953; Geismar, on the other hand (p. 52), states that it occurred in 1952; Zahar in *L'oeuvre de Frantz Fanon* (p. 7), gives October 1952 as the date" (272). To make the issue more complicated, Phillip Lucas, *Sociologie de Frantz Fanon* (1971) gives 1950 as the date of the marriage. It is hoped further research will throw more light on this.

2.

Rescuing Fanon from the Critics

Tony Martin

"The Philosophers have only *interpreted* the world in various ways," said Marx. "The point, however, is to *change* it."[1] Fanon set out to change it. And the signs are already clear that, in spite of a thousand quibblings over minutiae by a thousand scholars betraying varying degrees of hostility, he will probably succeed.

The key to an appreciation lies in his personality. Fanon was no Draconian monster, as some have tried to paint him (see Isaacs 1965). On the contrary, he was an extremely sensitive individual whose outstanding personality trait was probably his ability to empathize with the abject suffering which he observed being meted out to his black brothers around the world. Nor did his abhorrence of suffering stop with the plight of black people. His humanism, on which his ideas were founded, reached out—to embrace all mankind, as I shall endeavor to show later in this chapter. This aspect of Fanon's character is eloquently summed up in a line he quoted from Aimé Césaire's *Et les Chiens se Taisent*: "In

Originally published in *African Studies Review* (December 1970): 381–99. Reprinted with permission.

the whole world no poor devil is lynched, no wretch is tortured, in whom I too am not degraded and murdered."

It would, of course, be surprising if this ability to empathize with the wretched in distant corners of the world were not to be matched by an equal earnestness to probe, to explain, and to prescribe a cure for the suffering which he himself had to endure at the hands of the inhabitants of the metropolis and that which he observed at close quarters.

"The attitudes that I propose to describe are real," Fanon announced in his first book. "I have encountered them many times" (Fanon 1967a, 12). And I can testify to the perceptiveness of his observations and the universality of their application, since there is nothing in the experiences described by this francophone West Indian who lived in France that I can identify as alien to my own experience and observation in the anglophone West Indies, or during my lengthy sojourns and peregrinations in the Anglo-Saxon metropolis. Indeed, the similarities are so striking as to extend even to trivia. Thus, for example, the episodes he mentions of young Martinicans returning home with French accents and supercilious airs have their exact counterparts on the Trinidad scene, where they are a favorite subject for largely apocryphal jokes and calypsoes.

Fanon's sensitivity to human suffering crops up in the most unexpected places. Despite the tendency of some critics to see him as a Sorel type advocate of violence, allegedly for its own sake,[2] Fanon abhors violence even while recognizing it as a necessary evil in some circumstances. Simone de Beauvoir in her autobiography recalls the pain which he experiences at the contemplation of the results of violence, whether inflicted by the enemy or his own side (1965; quoted in Seigel 1968). For he is too closely attuned to the desire of humanity for justice to view violence in strictly macro-political terms. He cannot ignore the suffering of *individuals*. For Fanon, the individual is never lost in a mass of statistics. Who can deny the heart-rending sincerity of these words:

No man's death is indispensable for the triumph of freedom. It happens that one must accept the risk of death in order to bring

freedom to birth, but it is not lightly that one witnesses so many
massacres and so many acts of ignominy. (Fanon 1967b, 95)

Indeed, perhaps the most eloquent testimony to the depravity
of French colonialism is provided by the fact that it could have
driven a man as desirous of justice and a true humanism as Fanon
was to the inescapable conclusion that violence was the only
answer. Fanon the humanist, the revolutionary who didn't want to
be a professional revolutionary (de Beauvoir 1965), who was
willing to sacrifice the future he worked for so many years to
secure to help his suffering brothers in Algeria, who in the midst
of an entry in his diary concerning a hazardous mission in enemy
territory (Fanon 1967b, 185) could write, "This part of the Sahara is
not monotonous. Even the sky up there is constantly changing.
Some days ago we saw a sunset that turned the robe of heaven a
bright violet"—yes, this was Fanon. . . .

FANON AND MARX

Fanon's writings reveal the influence of several people—Hegel,
Marx, Sartre, and Césaire, to name but a few. But most commenta-
tors have evaluated his philosophy around the concept of
Marxism. He has been described as a "Marxist ideologist," "not
Marxist . . . (but) populist," "(not) a dogmatic Marxist," "a
Marxist," and one whose "borrowings (were) heaviest from Mao"
(Brace 1965, Denis 1967, Geismar 1969, Grohs 1968, Isaacs 1965).
   Certainly, there are indications of his affinity to Marx which are
evident even without a close look at his philosophy—the fact, for
example, that two of his three books bore titles directly suggestive
of a conscious identification with Marx: *Les Damnes de la Terre*,
which is taken from the first line of the "Internationale," and *L'An
Cinq de la Revolution Algerienne* which bears an obvious similarity
to Marx's *The Eighteenth Brumaire of Louis Bonaparte*. These connections suffered with their translation into English. The translation of
L'An Cinq into Studies in a Dying Colonialism was particularly unfortunate, however picturesque the English rendering. Translators

will have to learn that sometimes a literal rendering is best, whatever they might have been taught at school!

The Eighteenth Brumaire seems to have had a special attraction for Fanon, for it provided him with the leitmotif of his philosophy. Toward the end of his first book he includes a lengthy and famous quotation from it beginning, "The social revolution . . . cannot draw its poetry from the past; but only from the future" (Fanon 1967a, 223). This theme recurs throughout Fanon's works and forms the basis for his controversial rejection of the Senghorian version of négritude.

There is another quotation from *The Eighteenth Brumaire* which does not appear in Fanon but which also sheds considerable light on his ideas, particularly his idea of history. It is this: "Men make their own history, but they do not make it just as they please; they do not make it under circumstances chosen by themselves, but under circumstances directly encountered, given and transmitted from the past." In this quotation, Marx effects a synthesis of the dialectical necessity inherent in historical development on the one hand, and human initiative on the other. And here Fanon follows him very closely. For though he nowhere specifically discusses his theory of history, his works are scattered with numerous references to a deterministic conception of history which nevertheless requires human involvement to realize the goals to which historical necessity is pointing. "Each generation," he says, "must, out of relative obscurity, discover its mission, fulfill it, or betray it" (Fanon 1968, 206). In other words, the mission is there, preordained by history, but it is up to individual initiative to discover and fulfill history. Again,

> The colonialist . . . reaches the point of no longer being able to imagine a time occurring without him. His eruption into the history of the colonized people is deified, transformed into absolute necessity. Now a "historic look at history" requires, on the contrary, that the French colonialist retire, for it has become historically necessary for the national time in Algeria to exist. (Fanon 1967c, 159; see 1967b, 70, 173)

There is another similarity between *L'An Cinq* and *The Eighteenth Brumaire*, and undoubtedly the main factor which led Fanon to base his title on Marx's work. This is the fact that both books are conceptually similar. Both are analyses of a given stage in a revolutionary situation (see Grohs 1968).

It follows from the foregoing that it is wrong to argue, as one commentator does, that Fanon's position in *Black Skin, White Masks* was nonexistent because he declared that he was not a prisoner of history (Seigel 1968). This conclusion is based on a faulty appraisal of Marx and a superior understanding of Fanon's theory of history.

Fanon can be considered a Marxist. This is not to say that he adhered rigidly to every word that has come down to us from Marx's pen. He didn't. But he was Marxist in the sense that Lenin or Castro or Mao are Marxist. That is, he accepted Marx's basic analysis of society as given and proceeded from there to elaborate on that analysis and modify it where necessary to suit his own historical and geographical context.

Furthermore, while on a political level he speaks very often of neutrality and the necessity to stand aloof from the Cold War, at the level of social organization he is quite clear as to what type of society he wants:

> The concrete problem we find ourselves up against is not that of a choice, cost what it may, between socialism and capitalism as they have been defined by men of other continents and of other ages. Of course we know that the capitalist regime . . . cannot leave us free to perform our work at home, nor our duty in the world. Capitalist exploitation and cartels and monopolies are the enemies of underdeveloped countries. On the other hand the choice of a socialist regime, a regime which is completely oriented toward the people as a whole and based on the principle that man is the most precious of all possessions, will allow us to go forward more quickly and more harmoniously, and thus make impossible that caricature of society where all economic and political power is held in the hands of a few who regard the nation as a whole with scorn and contempt. (1968, 99)

Thus by 1960, with four years of high-level contacts with African leaders behind him, he could lament in his diary the fact that, based on these contacts, it seemed to him that the greatest danger threatening Africa was not colonialism and its derivatives but the absence of ideology (1967b, 186).

Like the good Marxist that he is, Fanon sees the economic base of most things. This includes racism and colonialism. In his discussions of the economic basis of colonialism he is, in addition, very close to the Leninist stance, which he seems to have largely adopted.

His utterances on these matters reveal a Fanon torn in two directions. On the one hand, he is struggling to be true to the orthodox Marxist position of a community of interest between the metropolitan workers and the whole populations of the proletarianized Third World. On the other hand, he is faced with the clear evidence of French chauvinism which has transcended class lines. In two successive weeks in *El Moudjahid* he appears to make conflicting statements concerning the relationship of these two groups.

About one year later, however, he is able to make a dialectical reconciliation between these two conflicting positions by utilizing a Leninist Hobsonian analysis (Fanon 1967b, 76, 82, 144; 1967c, 55). According to his argument, it is both true that the solidarity between metropolitan workers and colonized peoples is a theoretical verity, and also true that experience has revealed many examples of the nonviability of this thesis. The apparent contradiction is explained by the fact that the retreat of imperialism in the face of national wars of liberation is accompanied by a deterioration in the economic position of workers in the metropolis. He continues in classic Leninist vein, "The 'metropolitan' capitalists allow social advantages and wage increases to be wrung from them by their workers to the exact extent to which the colonialist state allows them to exploit . . . the occupied territories." The struggle against this problem must therefore be intensified. So it is not entirely correct to say, as one critic does, that Fanon is contemptuous of international class solidarity (Worsley 1969).

His position vis-à-vis metropolitan intellectuals is not dissimilar. For while he recognizes the theoretical bonds linking progressive elements in the metropolis to the colonized masses, and appeals for the strengthening of these bonds, he has no time for those French left-wingers, who, when the chips are down, reveal themselves in all their "egocentric, sociocentric thinking which has become the characteristic of the French" (Fanon 1967b, 71), and their paternalism which "feeds on the ambivalent sources of kindness to the oppressed, or a thirst to *do* something, to be useful, etc." (Fanon 1967b, 100).

Fanon's elaborations on Marx begin to show themselves clearly in his discussions of the relative positions and constitutions of the main classes in society—bourgeoisie, proletariat, peasants, and lumpenproletariat.

Fanon's argument here begins with the observation that the African proletariat is both numerically minuscule and relatively pampered. This is an argument which, strangely, is repeated by Senghor, on whom Fanon frequently vents his antireactionary spleen. But whereas Senghor, in his *On African Socialism,* comes to the conclusion that workers' wages must be kept down, Fanon concludes that the peasant masses are the most revolutionary in the colonial situation and must be mobilized.

This does not mean, as one commentator has grotesquely suggested, that Fanon is in favor of a peasant-led Mau-Mau type jacquerie (Dieng 1967). Though he castigates the Kenyan nationalist leaders for not supporting the Mau-Mau uprising, he seems to favor a peasant revolution led by revolutionary intellectuals and urban militants who have rediscovered the masses. And it goes without saying that any mass uprising in Africa is likely to be a peasant uprising, since wage laborers constitute as little as 4 percent of the population in many countries (Davies 1966, 24).

Fanon is aware that the role of the peasantry has proved a thorny theoretical question for Marxists for a number of years. Marx himself, in his *Critique of the Gotha Program,* published posthumously by Engels, showed some awareness of the problem. There he suggested that peasant discontent could be channeled into support for proletarian-led parties. Fanon has taken this much further—"the peasants alone are revolutionary, for they have nothing to lose and everything to gain" (Fanon 1968, 61).

Indeed, if the word "peasantry" could be substituted for "proletariat," then Fanon's position here is, surprisingly, identical to Marx's early position as articulated in the *Communist Manifesto*. "All previous historical movements were movements of minorities, or in the interests of minorities. The proletarian movement is the self-conscious, independent movement of the immense majority, in the interests of the immense majority" (Marx 1978, 482).

Fanon's position is logically (if not theoretically) very near to this. For all he is saying is that the peasants in the colonies are the ones who comprise the vast underprivileged majority that the proletarians presented in mid–nineteenth-century England. This argument, however, probably will not appeal to too many Marxists. At least one has attacked Fanon for this position (Ghe 1963). This critic argues that the Vietnamese revolution, though overwhelmingly peasant in composition, has been proletarian-led.

On the other hand, an Algerian communist who has attacked Fanon in more than one journal admits in one place that the big mistake that caused the Algerian Communist party to remain aloof from the war of independence for most of the duration of the struggle "sprang from a persistent tendency to underestimate the national factor and the peasantry and to overestimate the role of the European workers" (Ali 1965; see Dieng 1967, Gordon 1966). This critic mentions in the same article that Algeria was 80 percent peasant on the eve of the revolution. His statistics further include about one million rural unemployed, 500,000 urban unemployed, a "middle bourgeoisie" of 11,000 families, a small, weak national bourgeoisie, and about 300,000 permanent and seasonal workers of whom the majority "had one foot in the village." He does not break down the figures into settlers and others, or give the total population, but even with these crude figures, if they are correct, it can be seen that among the proletarian minority, the majority were in fact only partly proletarianized. Indeed, the migrant and semipeasant nature of much of the African labor force has been noticed elsewhere (Davies 1966). Still, though these considerations highlight the problem of the narrowness of the proletarian base, they do not solve the problem of which class is the repository of the true revolutionary potential.

Yet, to return to Fanon, it is significant that even where he appears to make his greatest apparent deviation from classical Marxism, he characteristically grounds his theory in a solid base of the orthodox Marx. For as pointed out supra, he accepts Marx's analysis of the peasantry for the time and place that Marx was describing. His elaboration here, he emphasizes, is based on his analysis of the colonial situation, which has revealed a peasantry of a fundamentally different character from the nineteenth-century European peasants that Marx described. The main difference, for Fanon, is the fact that the individualistic behavior Marx ascribed to the peasants has now become the hallmark of the colonized proletariat.

Furthermore, and this is essential for an understanding of Fanon on the peasantry, he appears to consider the lumpenproletariat as merely an extension of the peasantry, its urban arm, so to speak. He refers, for example, to "the landless peasants, who make up the lumpenproletariat." The significant role which he assigns to the lumpenproletariat is partly masked by the Marx-like rhetoric in which he appears to denounce this classless element. Compare Marx, in *The Communist Manifesto*,

> The "dangerous class," the social scum, that passively rotting mass thrown off by the lowest layers of old society, may, here and there, be swept into the movement by a proletarian revolution. Its conditions of life, however, prepare it far more for the part of a bribed tool of reactionary intrigue. (1978, 482)

with Fanon,

> For the lumpenproletariat, that horde of starving men, uprooted from their tribe and from their clan, constitutes one of the most spontaneous and the most radically revolutionary forces of a colonized people. (Fanon 1968, 129)

The rhetoric is similar but the difference is clear. For Fanon, the revolutionary possibilities inherent in the lumpenproletariat have become revolutionary potential of the greatest significance, *and the lumpenproletariat is but an urban extension of the peasantry.*[3] And it is for them, more than any other element, that the revolutionary violence will prove a magnificent rehabilitation: "The prostitutes too, and the maids who are paid two pounds a month, all the hopeless dregs of humanity, all who turn in circles between suicide and madness will recover their balance . . . and march proudly in the great procession of the awakened nation" (Fanon 1968, 129). However, the difference with Marx must not be overstressed, for Fanon recognizes that, if not mobilized, the lumpenproletariat will be used against the revolution.

In his analysis of the colonized bourgeoisie and the process of decolonization, Fanon is at his most brilliant. He ruthlessly exposed the essential difference between a true bourgeoisie of the classical Marxist variety and the caricature that masqueraded under that name in the colonies. For the colonized so-called bourgeoisie were, and still are, insignificant as accumulators of capital and are devoid of the capitalistic ethic which, in metropolitan countries, drives the bourgeoisie relentlessly forward in a ceaseless quest for invention and expansion—"the psychology of the national bourgeoisie is that of the businessman, not that of a captain of industry," and there must be scarcely an economic journal in the Third World which will not reveal copious lamentations over this fact. Indeed, even the bourgeois-nationalist type of reactionary leader that Fanon describes can sometimes be heard to cry out in exasperation at the effeteness of his bourgeois-parasitic cronies (see, e.g., Trinidad 1964–1968, 4). Whereas for a true bourgeoisie the capitalist system "exercises a psychological compulsion to boundless extension" (Sombart), for Fanon, the colonized bourgeoisie is, quite literally, good for nothing.

This bourgeoisie has a central role in Fanon's model of decolonization, a model, moreover, whose predictive aspects can be successfully demonstrated by reference to almost any random sample of countries which have become independent in the last decade or so. The model runs, in outline, as follows. Independence is achieved to the accompaniment of a wave of sterile nationalism. The national bourgeoisie soon finds its role as intermediaries for the exploitation of the economy by foreign capitalists and attempts to reinforce its position as looters of the public purse by calling for nationalization of some industries. The economy, nevertheless, continues to be characterized by the neocolonial assembly-plant type of base. Meanwhile, the country is rapidly transformed into a rest house and brothel for the foreign bourgeoisie. This process is known as tourism. The national bourgeoisie excels itself in ostentatious living. The workers and other less-privileged elements get carried away by the nationalistic fervor. At their level, however, the only persons for them to turn against are foreign African traders and people like the Lebanese small-traders. Nationalism, therefore, is transformed into ultranationalism, from thence to chauvinism, and finally into tribalism. Meanwhile, protestations of African unity fly thick and fast. Nor is the colonialist rearguard slow to exacerbate these differences. The Church takes its rightful place among the neocolonialist agents inciting division. The bourgeoisie seeks solace in a single party and takes cover behind a nationalist leader, who expects the people to live forever on the charisma he generated during the preindependence period. The leader exposes himself as "the general president of that company of profiteers." Slowly and painfully realization dawns on the people. National flags and radio appearances by the leader can't feed empty bellies. The militants are excommunicated. Party organization disintegrates. The army and police loom as oppressive factors. A few honest intellectuals are disconcerted. They must be mobilized. The bourgeois phase in the Third World must be resolutely opposed and where possible prevented from appearing. To effect this, the middleman sector of the economy must be nationalized and given over to cooperatives of the people. "True liberation is not that pseudo-independence in which ministers having a limited responsibility hobnob with an economy dominated by the colonial pact" (Fanon 1967b, 105).

On the political level, a true neutralism must be achieved, aloof from the Cold War, and most of all from "the United States (who has) plunged in everywhere, dollars in the vanguard, with [Louis] Armstrong as herald and American Negro diplomats, scholarships, the emissaries of the Voice of America" (Fanon 1967b, 178).

There is one interesting theater of the struggle against neocolonialism which Fanon identifies in several places but which seems to have escaped the attention of all the commentators. This is the more surprising since this subject has already emerged as the cause of much strident debate. This is the question of the role of Africanist scholars from the metropolis. In *A Dying Colonialism*, for example, he points out that "it is on the basis of the analyses of sociologists and ethnologists that the specialists in so-called native affairs and the heads of the Arab Bureaus co-ordinated their work" of systematically attacking Algerian cultural resistance. Psychologists and sociologists seem to be the Africanists he singles out for most abuse. His vehemence on this subject gives a clear indication that he harbors no illusions about the potency of academic weapons if enlisted in the struggle against the Third World (Fanon 1967c, 37).

It is inevitable that a model of decolonization as fiercely uncompromising as this should attract at least an occasional backlash. This "historic mission," as Fanon might have called it, was duly performed by the French author of a Christian Socialist review, who came to the defense of colonialism by affirming, in between strident denunciations of Fanon and Sartre, that colonialism, contrary to Fanon, had preserved native culture and made decolonization possible by refraining from exterminating the natives! Nor was there any trace of humor in this article, which was severely condemned in a later issue of the same magazine by, of all persons, an unnamed "French cleric working in black Africa" (Domenach 1962, 454–63, 634–45; "A Propos..." 1962, 349).

TOWARD A TRUE DECOLONIZATION

Just as the process of decolonization outlined above shows the course that will be taken by those who accept the constitutionalist version of independence based on compromise with the colonial overlord, Fanon also explicitly maps out the course that will need to be taken by those who desire true decolonization. There is only one way for this to be achieved—through violence. Colonialism itself is the incarnation of violence. It is imposed and sustained by fire and sword, and Fanon can't bring himself to believe that such a situation can be changed fundamentally by inviting the Queen to preside over a flag-raising ceremony. The only road to real freedom is by making a clean break with colonialism. And a clean break necessitates violence.

Several of Fanon's interpreters suggest that he became aware of the necessity for violence as a result of his Algerian experience. This does not seem to be the case. For as early as his first book, written in 1950 but published in 1952, Fanon had unmistakably arrived at this conclusion by way of Hegel. In a section of that book devoted to "The Negro and Hegel," Fanon used the plight of the Negro to elaborate a theory of the conditions under which the Negro could liberate himself. Quoting Hegel's *The Phenomenology of Mind*, Fanon established that freedom of the human spirit can only be established by a dialectical progression in which the subjected individual imposes himself on the other in a violent demand for acceptance. In his own words, which at this point assume a Hegelian ponderosity,

> When it encounters resistance from the other, self-consciousness undergoes the experience of desire—the first milestone on the road that leads to the dignity of the spirit. Self-consciousness accepts the risk of its life, and consequently it threatens the other in his physical being. "It is solely by risking life that freedom is obtained; only thus is it tried and proved that the essential nature of self-consciousness is not *bare existence*." (Fanon 1967a, 218)

Furthermore, the peculiar influence of *The Eighteenth Brumaire* on Fanon has already been mentioned, and here the message is the same, "unheroic as bourgeois society is, it nevertheless took heroism, sacrifice, terror, civil war, and battles of peoples to bring it into being." And Fanon's endearment to this work dates, as has been mentioned, from his first book.

As usual, here as elsewhere, Fanon is on the lookout for ways in which the peculiarities of the colonial situation must call for a modification of the traditional line. This time it is Engels with whom he collides. He explains as against Engels's view that the poorly armed cannot defeat the mighty, that the new features of the Cold War, support from socialist countries, and competition for spheres of influence among capitalist countries, not to mention the new techniques of peoples' war and guerrilla warfare, all militate in favor of the weak and poorly armed in their struggle against the powerful. Further, he is fully aware of the deleterious influence of protracted struggle on the economic and political situation within the metropolitan countries themselves. And he can hardly be wrong when he says that no power can indefinitely occupy a subject country which has gone over to a peoples' war. But perhaps most important of all for him is the example of Korea, Indochina, Cuba, and his own Algerian struggle. He constantly reminds his African brothers that now is the time to strike—now, while France is already weakened to the point of exhaustion by the Algerian conflagration. He points out that the proferring of the *loi-cadre** as a palliative to Africa is evidence of France's weakness and fear. His arguments here are at one with Che Guevara's "many Vietnams" thesis. He even goes so far as to spearhead the formation, at the Accra Conference of 1958, of an African Legion to liberate the continent (Fanon 1967b, 130, 145, 156).[4]

But Fanon can never forget the price that the damned must pay for their freedom. The 45,000 innocent victims of French bombing at Setif in 1945, the 90,000 slaughtered in Madagascar in 1947, the fact that no Frenchman has ever been disciplined for the torture of Algerians, the perpetration of frighteningly unethical practices on Algerians by French doctors—all these are considerations which return to trouble him again and again.

Yet the fight must go on. Without a violent break, only suf-

Loi-cadre, or draft law, aimed at a political solution for Algeria that looked like a mixture of federalism and partition. LaCoste considered it his "masterpiece." It was adopted by the French legislature January 31, 1958 (see Horne 156). —Ed.

fering and neocolonialism lie ahead. The brotherhood of revolutionary violence cleanses, purifies, unifies, as Sartre claimed to have realized when viewing the new man produced by the Cuban revolution (de Beauvoir 1968, p. 619).

Here, as elsewhere, Fanon's critics have not been at a loss for wildly ridiculous arguments to oppose to his thesis. One critic, who should know better, concludes that "He has not freed himself from the White Mask and still believes that the blacks are less than men. Terrorism and murder are necessary because unless European institutions are totally destroyed they will prevail and corrupt the new world" (Zolberg 1966, 62).

This quotation contains almost as many misconceptions as words. It ignores the history of French brutality in Algeria and presents the violence of the damned as an action rather than a reaction. It fails to take cognizance of (or disbelieves) Fanon's own words:

> Having to react in rapid succession to the massacre of Algerian civilians in the mountains and in the cities, the revolutionary leadership found that if it wanted to prevent the people from being gripped by terror it had no choice but to adopt forms of terror which until then it had rejected. This phenomenon has not been sufficiently analyzed. (Fanon 1967c, 54)

It presents the violence of the damned as a confirmation of the White Mask whereas for the Hegelian basis of Fanon's thinking, revolutionary violence constitutes the very rending of the mask, the decisive action by which, to use Hegel's terminology, self-consciousness wrings acceptance from the other. It uses the term "European institutions," which can mean anything—the Church, Westminster-type government, racism, European-owned factories. It skillfully opposes the words "terrorism and murder" to "European institutions, " thereby making a thinly veiled allegation that Fanon was possessed of a blind undiscriminating hatred of Europe per se. This was not the case, as I shall endeavor to show.

Though Fanon's violence is usually to be taken quite literally, there seems to be at least one situation in which a violent break may be made with the colonial past without any blood being shed. This conclusion is being deduced here by inference from his often-expressed admiration for Sekou Touré. It would appear that Sekou Touré, by mobilizing a revolutionary intellectual elite in communion with the masses, and by taking a step against French colonialism which at least exposed him to the very real *risk* of a violent retort, may have fulfilled the requirements for a violent break. Fanon seems to be saying here that if, once you have showed your determination for a fight, colonialism withdraws without a violent confrontation, then there is no necessity to pursue the retreating enemy and pick a fight simply for the sake of shedding blood.

NÉGRITUDE, PAN-AFRICANISM, AND RACE

Fanon's thought has often been presented in the form of an evolutionary process culminating in *The Wretched of the Earth*. While there is nothing inherently wrong in this approach, it occasionally leads to misconceptions. It has already been shown that Fanon's theory of violence was stated clearly as early as his first book. The same is true concerning his position on négritude, contrary to the view, sometimes expressed, that he started with an acceptance of the concept of négritude and ended by rejecting it in his final work.

From the mass of material, especially in his first and last book on this subject, the following picture emerges. Fanon appreciates the necessity to rehabilitate the past—"this tearing away (from European cultural domination) painful and difficult though it may be, is, however, necessary." He nevertheless moves on to an apparently contradictory position against négritude. This is because he perceives the adherents of négritude overreaching themselves and going to the other extreme of completely whitewashing the past, so that what emerges tends uncomfortably toward a blind mystification of the past and a "banal exoticism." Furthermore, the négritude school is in danger of living in the past, which violates Fanon's *Eighteenth Brumaire* philosophy. For important as knowledge of the past is, progress for the present generation must be made in terms of contemporary realities. Culture should thus be subordinated to this goal. On a cultural level, the heterogeneity of black cultures should be recognized. This does not rule out the possibility—in fact, the necessity—for cooperation on a political level. And as long as exponents of negroism like Senghor and Rabemananjara can vote with France against the Algerian revolution, then something must clearly be wrong somewhere.

Thus unraveled (and the mass of scattered detail makes unraveling difficult), his apparently contradictory acceptance-rejection of négritude is resolved. That Fanon's arguments were often expounded in a dialectical fashion (he uses the world itself continuously) often masks his meaning to the superficial reader.

His rejection of négritude is influenced, further, by the fact that the generic term "negro" is the creation of the white man. It is a term, nevertheless, which was created to designate the white man's conception of the "quintessence of evil" and bestiality. Therefore, he cannot see why black people should revel in the fallacy of an undifferentiated negroness created for them by their oppressors.

This analysis he backed up, characteristically, in action. Through the pages of *El Moudjahid* there poured a steady stream of exhortations to African unity. And he frequently expressed pain at the obscurantism and chauvinism of people like Senghor, and, most of all, the traitor Houphouët-Boigny,* who was "objectively the most conscious curb on the evolution and liberation of Africa."

He was at pains to point out, in this regard, that his advocacy of national culture was not the same as nationalism. It was, on the contrary, the only real basis for a solid universalism which would include all humanity. "The Negro is not. Any more than the white man. Both must turn their backs on the inhuman voices which were those of their respective ancestors in order that authentic communication be possible" (Fanon 1967a, 231).

This quotation is a succinct statement of the ideal to which all of Fanon's work pointed—the ideal of a new humanity.

---

*Houphouët-Boigny, francophone president of the Ivory Coast, supported Charles de Gaulle. —Ed.

This statement also throws considerable light on Fanon's attitudes toward race relations. His sensitivity, his inability to separate an overview of social relationships from relationships at the level of the individual, his dialectical approach to most problems—all of this made it logically necessary that his unrelenting hatred of racism, and his uncompromising struggle to lift the black man out of the quagmire of psychological complexes into which racism had induced him, should be strictly divorced from a hatred of white people per se. For Fanon, there was no logical connection between the struggle against white racism and neocolonialism and the undiscriminating hatred of white people. Any white person who proved his sincere desire for a true humanism was a friend for Fanon, just as a traitorous black reactionary like Houphouët-Boigny would remain an implacable object of detestation. This is why Fanon's books are replete with expressions of concern for the Frenchmen working undercover for the revolution, for the French soldiers who deserted to the Algerian side, for an end of the egocentric paternalism of the French Left (see Fanon 1967a, 12; 1967c, 149). This is why, as Simone de Beauvior (1965) tells us, he could jokingly say that he would pay 20,000 francs a day to converse with Sartre for a fortnight (619).

This is why, too, he sets out with such honesty in *Black Skin, White Masks* to analyze the pathetic complexes which exposure to white racism has induced in the black people who come under his keen observation. All this is admirably borne out in the much misunderstood chapter "The Man of Color and the White Woman." Here, because he starts the chapter in the first person, superficial critics have been eager to associate him with the condition he describes.

The chapter revolves around the character Jean Veneuse, in René Maran's novel *Un Homme Pareil aux Autres*, whose love affair with a white woman displays all the negative qualities that Fanon would like to eradicate. His conclusions concerning Jean Veneuse leave the careful reader in no doubt as to where Fanon's own position lies:

there would be a . . . lack of objectivity . . . in trying to extend the attitude of Veneuse to the man of color as such . . . . (1967a, 81)

This sexual myth—the quest for white flesh—perpetuated by alienated psyches, must no longer be allowed to impede active understanding. (1967a, 81)

It is clear to me that Jean Veneuse, alias René Maran, is neither more nor less than a black abandonment-neurotic . . . who needs to be emancipated from his infantile fantasies . . . but let us remember that our purpose is to make possible a healthy encounter between black and white. (1967a, 79–80)

And the way to this healthy encounter, in characteristic Fanon fashion, is through "a restructuring of the world."

We are now in a position, therefore, to demolish perhaps the most slanderous piece of inaccurate superficiality that has emerged on Fanon's personal life. This particular opinion is all the more unfortunate because its author seems to have interviewed Fanon's wife (Geismar 1969, 24),[5] and his facile misconception can hardly be calculated to induce the lady to view with equanimity the inquiries of future, perhaps more genuinely motivated, researchers. For this gentleman, in one undocumented sweep of the pen in what is otherwise a reasonable article, assures us that Fanon's marriage to a white woman, though possibly occasioned by the absence of black people in Lyon where Fanon lived and studied, is more probably due to a desire on Fanon's part "to become white through love of a white woman" (Geismar 1969, 24). It can only be hoped that this bit of defamation is indeed based on superficial scholarship rather than malice. Certainly there is a discernible tendency in some critiques to subtly denigrate the man while grudgingly acknowledging the greatness of his ideas.

The impact of Fanon's ideas on Algeria (where, nevertheless, some critics suggest he may have been disappointed with the results of the revolution), on the student Left in Europe, and on black liberation struggle in the United States has been documented in several places (Gordon 1966, Worsley 1969). But the greatest battles over the applicability of Fanon's ideas are still to be fought. They will be fought in Africa and the Caribbean, the areas in which

Fanon was most interested and where disenchantment with the results of the black versions of bourgeois nationalism is already plain to see.

NOTES

1. Karl Marx, *Theses on Feuerbach*. Fanon himself quotes part of this line approvingly, though he does not give its source.

2. See Domenach 1962, pp. 634–45. Domenach also links Fanon, through Sorel, to Mussolini. For a similar view see Barnard 1968, p. 12.

3. This point has been overlooked by some critics, e.g., Cherif 1966. But for an interesting discussion of this point, see Worsley 1969, p. 40ff.

4. For a sterile and inaccurate attack on Fanon for his position vis-à-vis Engels, see Dieng 1967.

5. It is not entirely clear from the article whether he had yet spoken to Mrs. Fanon, though the fact that he had already interviewed Fanon's French acquaintances and is working on a Fanon biography means that she must have been on his list for interview; see also Armah 1969.

3.

Frantz Fanon, World Revolutionary

Lou Turner and John Alan

It is not accidental that Fanon's thoughts are relevant to the liberation struggles in South Africa, as manifested in the Black Consciousness movement. It was Fanon who had, in his *Black Skin,
White Masks,* both deepened the Hegelian concept of self-consciousness and in his sharp critique of "reciprocity," denied that
there is any reciprocity when the relationship of Master and Slave
has the additive of color. Quite the contrary. He made that the
foundation of revolutionary action. In the dialectical relationship
between the oppressed and the oppressor, the oppressed gains the
idea of his or her own being—one's own self-consciousness—and
the desire of being for self, and not for "other."

Fanon's philosophy of revolution has assumed the quality of actuality in the brutal life-and-death struggle between the black masses of
South Africa and the arrogant white ruling class that would, if it could,
reduce black humanity to a thing—an object among other objects.

From *Frantz Fanon, Soweto, and American Black Thought,* by Lou Turner and John
Alan. Reprinted with permission of *News and Letters,* Columbia University, New
York, New York.

It is not alone that banned copies of *The Wretched of the Earth* circulate among the South African youth of Soweto, nor that American intellectuals have chosen for their own reasons to present a truncated version of his thought, that makes us return to Frantz Fanon. Rather, it has been a resurgence of the African revolutionary spirit since the defeat of both Portuguese and U.S. imperialism in Angola—a spirit evident in the new wave of guerrilla wars of liberation in Zimbabwe and in Namibia—as well as the mass revolt in South Africa itself, that demands a new look at that world revolutionary figure, Frantz Fanon. A "new" understanding of Fanon becomes an imperative at this time, not as past history, but as living activity.

The Black Consciousness movement in South Africa which Steve Biko headed was powerful because it had re-established self-consciousness as a force of revolution. The idea that the black masses have the power to shake South Africa to its foundations has become the reality of South Africa.

In this early work, *Black Skin, White Masks*, Fanon had grasped that colonial domination of Third World peoples meant not only economic domination, but also the destruction of the spirit and the personality of the oppressed people. In the chapter on "The Negro and Hegel" in *Black Skin, White Masks*, Fanon is at his exciting best. What appears at first glance as a summation of the "Lordship and Bondage" section of Hegel's *Phenomenology*, is a brilliant exposition of the dialectical interrelationship of the independence and dependence of self-consciousness to the black situation in a racist society.

Here Fanon stresses the phenomenon that the self-consciousness of blacks has been sublated by oppression and that the other, white oppressors, do not regard black self-consciousness as real, but see in black only their own self-consciousness. As long as black self-consciousness is not recognized by the other, "the other will remain the theme of his [black] actions" (Fanon 1967, 222). If there is no reciprocity between the real self-consciousness of blacks and the other, the circuit is closed and ultimately blacks are deprived of being for themselves.

The recognition that blacks are saddled with a false consciousness of self—or rather two consciousnesses of self —is not new. In

1903, W. E. B. Du Bois wrote in *The Souls of Black Folk* that the American world "yields him [blacks] no true self-consciousness, but lets him see himself through the revelation of the other world."

Black people, in negating their living for the other, do not simply substitute white self-consciousness with their own—that is, simply take the place of the master—but move from one way of life to another, instead of one life to another. This was crucial for Fanon, because the role of the black and colonial revolutions is not a perpetuation of the old in "blackface," but says, "*No* to the exploitation of man. *No* to the butchery of what is most human in man: *freedom*" (Fanon 1967, 222).

The perils of domination are two-fold, striking with equal ferocity at both the body and the mind of the persecuted and the oppressed. The fact that Fanon understood this, both subjectively as a black colonial from Martinique, and philosophically through his mastery of Hegel's *Phenomenology of Mind*—especially the section on "Lordship and Bondage"—was to lay the foundation for a theory of revolution.

Because Fanon did not state, in so many words, "I reject bourgeois society," and because the language is existentialist, *Black Skin, White Masks* was treated as if Fanon were a "pupil" of Sartre. This was so, not only at the time of its publication, 1952, but even as late as his last work of genius, *The Wretched of the Earth*, 1961. In truth, a sharp critique of Sartre was included right in *Black Skin, White Masks*, in the section on "Orphée Noir," the very preface Sartre had written to introduce the writings of the négritude school, *Anthologie de la nouvelle poésie nègre et malgache*.

In quoting Sartre's analysis of class as the "universal and abstract" and race as the "concrete and particular," which led Sartre to the conclusion that "*négritude* appears as the minor term of a dialectical progression," Fanon writes: "*Orphée noir* is a date in the intellectualization of the *experience* of being black. And Sartre's mistake was not only to seek the source of the source but in a certain sense to block that source. . . . He was reminding me that my blackness was only a minor term. In all truth, in all truth I tell you, my shoulders slipped out of the framework of the world, my feet could no longer feel the touch of the ground" (Fanon 1967a, 134, 138).

Nor did Fanon, in that work which was a turning point in his revolutionary self-development, disregard the class struggle and the works of Marx. He chose as the frontispiece to "By Way of Conclusion," the very last chapter of *Black Skin, White Masks*, a quote from Karl Marx's *The Eighteenth Brumaire*:

> The social revolution . . . cannot draw its poetry from the past but only from the future. It cannot begin with itself before it has stripped itself of all its superstitions concerning the past. Earlier revolutions relied on memories out of world history in order to drug themselves against their own content. In order to find their own content, the revolutions of the nineteenth century have to let the dead bury the dead. Before the expression exceeded the content: now the content exceeds the expression. (1967a, 222)

The revolutionary humanist spirit that pervades the whole of the book is seen in Marx's sentence that had the greatest impact on Fanon: "In order to find their own content, the revolutions of the nineteenth century have to let the dead bury the dead." The expression "let the dead bury the dead" was Hegel's articulation of the passing of one epoch and the coming into existence of another. For Fanon and for us today, that new world was the wretched of the earth—the Third World. The transition to Fanon's work by the same name (which, after all, is the very first sentence of *The International*) took another nine years and signaled Fanon's giving up his French citizenship and his professional post at the Blida-Joinville Hospital for Algerian citizenship and revolutionary action.[1]

The Wretched of the Earth was to re-create the dialectics of liberation for the colonial world as it emerged out of the actual struggle of the African masses for freedom. Fanon saw the double rhythm of the colonial revolutions reflected in both the destruction of the old and the building of a totally new society. This was a break with all previous ideas about the African revolutions—especially the idea that the African revolutions had to first undergo a national bourgeois revolution before they could go on to a socialist, humanist society.

It is with this crucial situation facing the revolutionary masses of South Africa and Zimbabwe that Fanon's philosophy and understanding of the colonial revolutions assumes a greater concreteness for today than it may have had seventeen years ago. Fanon's commitment to the African masses, as the only real force and reason that could bring about a true revolutionary change in Africa, was total—and his analysis of African society, carried out in the very practice of revolution, was a concrete revelation that the African masses were the decisive element in African nationalism that could both achieve the goals of nationalism and move beyond them to international freedom. This concept was grounded in the specific historical existence of the African masses, who, out of necessity, demanded the creation of a dialectic of liberation.

Some have tried to reduce Fanon's creation of a dialectic of liberation to his writings on violence. But Fanon's conception of violence within the context of decolonization centered around what in the subject's objectivity was more than an expression of alienation, and was as well a pathway to freedom.

When the Algerians dared to hit out against the barbarism of colonial rule, the concept of the superiority of French culture showed itself to be a dimension of racism by attributing the violence to the "innate criminality" of the North African mind. Fanon showed the concepts of black alienation, of violence, and of emancipation to be historically determined phenomena.

Not only that, violence was not just having arms. Fanon took issue with what he thought Engels was saying on the theory of violence in *Anti-Duhring*, when Engels stressed that everything "depends on production." To Fanon, this sounded like "the leaders of reform . . . saying . . . 'With what are you going to fight the settlers? With your knives?'" (Fanon 1968, 64).

Fanon's contention was that at no time can violence be separated from ideology and that, in fact, revolutionary ideology is the greatest power. He then put the relationship of ideology to violence in its true historic context:

It so happens that the liberation of colonial countries throws new light on the subject. For example, we have seen that during the Spanish campaign which was a very genuine colonial war

Napoleon in spite of an army which reached in the offensives of the Spring of 1810 the huge figure of 400,000 men, was forced to retreat. Yet the French army made the whole of Europe tremble by its weapons of war. . . . Face to face with the enormous potentials of the Napoleonic troops, the Spaniards inspired by an unshakable national ardor, rediscovered the famous methods of guerrilla warfare, which, 25 years before, the American militia had tried out on the English forces. (Fanon 1968, 64)

Clearly, the violence that has a "cathartic effect"—which the American New Left took to mean violence, in and for itself—meant, to Fanon, the liberation struggle that is permeated with a philosophy of liberation.

The South African resistance movement, too, had to deal with the charge of violence, especially the leaders of a new organization, Umkonto We Sizwe (The Spear of the Nation), a new manifestation of black nationalism which appeared in 1961. Here is how one leader, Nelson Mandela, responded at the Rivonia Trial, April 20, 1964:

I admit, immediately, that I was one of the persons who helped to form Umkonto We Sizwe, and that I played a prominent role in its affairs until I was arrested in August 1962. . . . But the violence which we chose to adopt was not terrorism. . . . I was the Secretary of the Conference and undertook to be responsible for organizing the national stay-at-home which was subsequently called to coincide with the declaration of the Republic. . . . The African nationalism for which the ANC stands is the concept of freedom and fulfillment for the African people in their own land. (Benson 1976)

In every case, it was a question of the relationship of masses in revolt against armed oppressors, and not the simplistic question of "violence" versus "non-violence." History, to Fanon, was not just past events but history-in-the-making by live men and women, peasant masses most of all. This activist thinker was, however, not just an Algerian revolutionary, but involved in all of black Africa. Here, too, he was not uncritical. At one and the same time, he enthusiastically greeted each African revolution as it won independence from imperialism, and criticized the separation of leaders from masses after independence was won. Thus, he was to write:

> History teaches us clearly that the battle against colonialism does not run straight away along the lines of nationalism. . . . It so happens that the unpreparedness of the educated classes, the lack of practical links between them and the mass of the people, their laziness, and let it be said, their cowardice at the decisive moment of the struggle, will give rise to tragic mishaps. (Fanon 1968, 148)

Nothing, however, was to stem his overriding concern—a global concern—for fighting imperialism. This is what permeated his work as an editor of the newspaper *El Moudjahid*, and his whole life in the years 1956 to 1961, when leukemia struck him down at the age of thirty-six. Because he did have a global vision, he placed the African revolutions in the context of his view of world revolution and the urgent need to create a totally new kind of society. And yet what was to become a view of world revolution as well as the manifesto of the Third World was so concrete as to manifest worries of new fragmentations. Who today doesn't recognize the pertinence of Fanon's warning that "what must be avoided is the Ghana-Senegal tension, the Somalia-Ethiopia, the Morocco-Mauritania, the Congo-Congo tensions." Here is how Fanon continued:

> In reality the colonized states that have reached independence by the political path seem to have no other concern than to find themselves a real battlefield with wounds and destruction. It is clear, however, that this psychological explanation, which appeals to a hypothetical need for release of pent-up aggressiveness, does not satisfy us. We must once again come back to the Marxist formula. The triumphant middle classes are the most impetuous, the most enterprising, the most annexationist in the world. Not for nothing did the French bourgeoisie of 1789 put Europe to fire and sword. (1967b, 187)

Fanon's final decision—and only in part was it due to his terminal illness—was not to write the book he had planned on the

Algerian revolution, nor even to extend it only to African revolutions, but to develop a worldview of masses in motion, uprooting the old order as they created totally new human relations. He called it *The Wretched of the Earth*.

The main focus of *The Wretched of the Earth* is in three chapters dealing with "Spontaneity," "National Consciousness," and "National Culture." In these chapters Fanon is not speaking as a psychiatrist, nor as an angry prophet demanding retribution in blood for wrongs done, but as an activist-thinker acutely aware that in the historical process of revolution there exists simultaneously *both* revolution and counterrevolution.

The chapter titled "Spontaneity: Its Strength and Weakness" analyzes the conflict that exists between the self-activity of the colonial masses, who would destroy colonialism root and branch, and the symbiotic relationship between the national bourgeoisie and the colonial power. This is a great contribution to revolutionary theory, and it also represents what is profoundly new in Fanon's ideas that separates him from all the other theorists of the African revolutions. The recognition of this conflict between the leadership of the peasant masses of Africa is not presented as an abstraction, but is directly related to black leadership to revolutionary national leadership, to black culture.

Fanon points out that there exists a time lag, a difference of rhythm, between the national party and the masses of people. The rank and file demand a total improvement of their lot, while the leadership seeks to limit and to restrain. This is why the rank and file feel so cheated after a prolonged struggle which has been declared victorious by the leaders.

There is a built-in conservatism both within the elitist native intellectual class and the organizational forms that this class builds within the colony to mobilize and bring pressures on the colonial administration. The elitist intellectual leadership class, in spite of its conflicts with the white colonial administration, is a privileged section within colonialism.

The organizations that the elite build to combat colonialism—the national party, the trade union, etc.—are copies of European institutions which are unrelated to the struggle for freedom in the African colonies. Yet, "the elite will attach a fundamental importance to organization, so much so that the fetish of organization will often take precedence over a reasoned study of colonial society. The notion of the party is a notion imported from the mother country" (Fanon 1968, 108).

The importation and the mechanical application of the European vanguard type of political party to a colonial political situation, for Fanon, was a serious challenge to the success of the colonial revolution. To him, it meant that the elite national leadership was completely unaware of the indigenous organizational forms that the colonial masses had developed in the course of the long struggle against their colonial masters. Not only were the leaders not aware of these indigenous organizations, they were even too lazy and indifferent to find out about them. They simply brought in the European political party and proceeded to focus their organizing work solely around the skilled workers and civil servants in the cities—a tiny portion of the colonial population. This type of organizational attitude on the part of the national leadership was politically retrogressive and Fanon opposed it vigorously for obvious and concrete reasons.

The reality of the colonial world is that the overwhelming element in the population is poor peasants who are brutally exploited, miserably treated, and starved by colonialism, which at the same time robs them of their homeland. And, of all the classes in the colonial world, it is the poor peasants who stand in direct confrontation to the government and the white ruling class. Each day, every member of the poor peasantry has to struggle to survive and fight in order to retain a scrap of humanity. Too, on numerous occasions the peasants have rebelled against their colonial masters and suffered grievously for failure at the hands of the colonial police and the military.

To Fanon, a disregard for the black peasant masses, the only class in the colonies which kept the national consciousness alive by direct opposition to colonial exploitation, was tantamount to turning one's back on the revolution.

If the national party did pay attention to the colonial masses, they saw them as "blind inert tactical force: brute force, as it were" (Fanon 1968, 123), around which the national parties tried to erect an a priori program. This attitude of the national party, the elite leadership, to the peasant masses, Fanon reasoned, is due to the dual nature of *both* the party form *and* the leadership, where "the will to break colonialism is linked to another quite different will; that of coming to a friendly agreement with it" (Fanon 1968, 124).

The new national bourgeoisie does not end its connection with colonialism once independence is gained. The national middle class does not repudiate its own nature, insofar as it is bourgeois, that is, insofar as it is a tool of capitalism, nor does it make itself the willing tool of that revolutionary capital which is the people. The bourgeoisie of the ex-colony is weak and dependent upon world capitalism and because it has no link with the masses, it cannot throw off its colonial past, and, to hide its weakness, it commits all sorts of chauvinistic acts and futile militant gestures. When it nationalizes, or "Africanizes," institutions, Fanon says, it does so in the interest of its own privileges and not in the interest of the masses. Fanon criticizes this type of nationalization because it ends in rigid state control of consumer goods by the civil servants. There is praise for the leaders everywhere, but there is also widespread discontent among the masses: "The party, instead of welcoming . . . the free flow of ideas from the people up to the government, forms a screen, and forbids such ideas" (Fanon 1968, 183). Never could what Fanon was talking about be better understood than now. Here is how one West African describes the situation in Nigeria today:

> One thing that has been lacking in all the literature on Africa is the sense of a class consciousness. One talks of "Africans." Nobody talks of Chiang Kai-shek and Mao Tse-tung in the same breath, but somehow that sort of distinction is always missing in an analysis of Africa. Nigeria deserves emphasis on account of its sheer size: one out of every four Africans is a Nigerian and so, in that respect, what goes on in Nigeria is of tremendous importance to what happens in other parts of Africa.

The Nigerian press just says there has been a demonstration in South Africa and so many people were killed. There is never any mention of what they are protesting about. The Nigerian government does not want any aspect of a movement of a people against a ruling class brought up because it couldn't stand much scrutiny.

Someone wrote a letter to a Nigerian newspaper and said, "What is all this about South Africa? I live in a slum and I work in the reserve area. I work, and then I go back to the slum. So I don't want to hear any more about South Africa." At first sight that might look like a very reactionary view, but it does reflect why the government is reluctant to have people report in depth on what is going on in South Africa. They would prefer people to think it is Blacks wanting to get rid of whites. And in Nigeria, we don't have that problem, do we? Because we have a Black ruling class; so—problem solved.

At the very height of the Black struggles in Southern Africa, Nigeria hosted a Festival of Arts and Culture (FESTAC). It was supposedly a get-together of Africans to assert their identity. Millions were spent to let Westerners know we have a culture. A front page editorial in the government-owned *Daily Times* exclaimed "What a brilliant spectacle it turned out to be!" But a woman writer, Bisi Adebiyi, presented a much different view on the inside pages. In her column "Woman's Angle," she wrote:

"Just how liberated is the African woman? This was the crucial question before the celebrated FESTAC colloquium last week. But nobody cared to answer it. Perhaps because it has haunted the African man like the ghost of Ian Smith or John Vorster haunts all of us. . . . The point raised before the conference of eminent scholars was a recommendation that read: 'Emphasis must be given to women's education by according them equal opportunity in schools and colleges as a process of liberating them and enabling them to play equal roles as their male counterparts.' One after the other, the gentlemen of the colloquium raised hell over their bug-bear. 'The word "liberating" must be deleted from the recommendation,' they roared. 'The question of liberating the African woman simply does not arise because there's nothing to liberate her from.'

There were very few women delegates . . . If we can find large contingents of women on the stage of the National Arts Theatre wriggling their feminine buttocks to feed the lustful eyes of men, what more do we want, to claim full participation in FESTAC?

Barely two months before FESTAC, some of us were shouting ourselves hoarse for women in the northern states of Nigeria to have something as basic as the right to vote. They've now got it. Millions of women remain tucked away in the repressive culture of purdah. . . . And in the southern states, which claim to be better advanced, women in the rural areas continue to languish in a culture which survives on the economic contributions of women—their agricultural roles—but makes the more sophisticated agricultural tools available only to the men.

For the rural woman, the prospects are still the slow death from disease and unabated pregnancies. Watch her as she trudges home from the farm—a heavy sack on her head, a baby on her back and a 'bundle of joy' in her stomach, and you'll see how much the African woman can be liberated from."

There are classes in Africa. And events in Africa will continue to confuse, to befuddle, unless we face the fact that there are people in whose interest it is that things remain just as they are. . . . At the moment there is a new Constitution being debated in Nigeria. And right there in the Constitution it says Nigeria is made up of so many tribes! There is a class in Africa in whose interest it is that there should be tribes. What the masses of Nigerians are talking about has absolutely nothing whatever to do with tribes. They are talking about bread and butter issues. They are talking about inflation, which in Nigeria is running at about 40 percent. And there is an enormous gap in wages. So you really can't fool the people who are being oppressed about whether you have a new society. It is the intellectuals who get fooled. . .

What we have happening in Africa now is that there are changes coming from below. It's been a long time since imperialism was overthrown. Very soon it will be 20 years since Nigeria got independence, so the argument that we are being held back by the foreigners will soon start to make no impression on the people. I think we are entering the period where what will happen in Africa next will be mass- and class-oriented. Maybe what the revolution people have been talking about will actually begin to happen.

Fanon's development as a revolutionary thinker was part of a triangular relationship of Africa, the Caribbean, and France, which presented him with such deep contradictions at every level of human relations that he confronted the limitations of a merely psychological interpretation of subjectivity. He thus began his search for a philosophy of human liberation that could match the total transformation of society occurring in the Third World.

In the chapter titled the "Pitfalls of National Consciousness" in *The Wretched of the Earth*, Fanon states: "The party leaders behave like common sergeant-majors, frequently reminding the people of the need for 'silence in the ranks.' This party that used to call itself the servant of . . . the people's will, as soon as the colonial power puts the country into its control, hastens to send the people back to their caves" (Fanon 1968, 183). Fanon hastens to say that this "treason" is social, rather than individual.

Although Fanon paints a picture of the decrepit national bourgeois party in ex-colonial countries, he was not pessimistic about the future of the African revolutions. There must be a theory of revolution wedded to the mass struggles for freedom and above all, the black masses must not be considered muscle only, but human beings with ideas.

Fanon's analysis of the "Nationalist Consciousness" was a concrete breakthrough on the retrogressive role of so-called vanguard leadership in our age, a scathing critique not only of African, but also of European elitism.

He first reminded the Europeans that "not long ago Nazism transformed the whole of Europe into a veritable colony" (Fanon 1968, 101). He then showed that the two greatest events in 1956–57 were "Budapest and Suez"; in the case of the first, it was a Humanist liberation struggle against totalitarian Communism, and in the second, the Third World opposition to Western imperialism.

Fanon made clear the necessity not to mimic Europe: "Today we are present at the stasis of Europe. Comrades, let us flee from this motionless movement where gradually dialectic is changing into the logic of equilibrium. Let us reconsider the question of mankind" (Fanon 1968, 314).

By relating his analysis to the first wave of revolutions in Africa Fanon has shown that any leadership that does not spring out of, and retain dependence upon, the self-activity and the self-development of mass activities for freedom will ultimately find dependency upon neocolonialism.

When Fanon asked his African comrades to turn their backs on Europe, he did not have alone the subject of racism in his mind. He wanted them to flee from the "motionless movement of Europe where gradually dialectic is changing into the logic of equilibrium" where the static forms of party, unions, laws, and culture, conceal the true condition of men and women and attempt to stultify the self-development of humanity. "This new humanity cannot do otherwise than define a new humanism both for itself and for others. . . . National consciousness which is not nationalism, is the only thing that will give us an international dimension. . . . For Europe, for ourselves, and for humanity, comrades . . . we must work out new concepts, and try to set afoot a new man" (Fanon 1968, 246–47, 316).

Fanon's internationalism is not just rhetoric or an attempt to avoid the question of racism. We must realize that Western imperialism has taken all from Africa and given back nothing. African nations are still producers of raw material for the world market.

The third crucial chapter in *The Wretched of the Earth* is titled "National Culture." Why was Fanon so concerned with "National Culture"? After all, culture is a natural thing; people live within a culture and they build a culture out of various means and under different conditions. We recognize this universal aspect of culture but it was not so universally recognized that under colonialism the cultures of the colonial peoples are suppressed cultures, like the colonized people themselves. And, a foreign culture has been imposed in the place of their former indigenous culture. It is in the relationship between these two cultures that Fanon was seeking revolutionary development.

African intellectuals, particularly those of Senegal, developed the theory of "négritude" as an answer to the European contention that the black world had no culture. They did a great deal of intellectual work in rediscovering Africa's rich cultural heritage. They also organized societies and set out with great creative energy to educate European intellectuals about African art, African music, African dance, and above all the African's humanity.

However, in the harsh reality of the colonial world, not only is this not enough, but the leaders of what was once revolutionary négritude, like Senghor, are actually carrying out the Francophile imperialist policy. So thoroughly disgusted was Fanon with the leaders in power who had been creators of the négritude theory that he turned in utter indignation against the very closest comrade, the greatest poet, the one from whom he learned both revolutionary négritude and national struggle, Aimé Césaire, when he became mayor and welcomed the Gaullist, Malraux, to Martinique in 1958. To Fanon, culture without revolution lacks substance. He maintained that culture must not be mere "folklore" of an "abstract populism," but something that had to validate itself through the struggle for freedom.

Bringing to life the culture of an oppressed people is not just a question of harking back to history, but lies in grasping the reality of where that culture is today. If people are oppressed and impoverished, their culture suffers inhibition and lack of creativity. Only through the struggle for freedom will that cultural resurgence take on meaningful substance.

Ezekiel Mphahlele is quite eloquent on this point, and, in praise of the American blacks, he reminds us that it is not our "négritude" that will be brought to account during our struggles, but our "mastery of the techniques for bringing down the white power structure that will count. And, I insist, that this very struggle defines a culture. . . . Culture and political struggles define each other, and feed on each other, all the way" (Mphahlele 1971, introduction).

The question of culture, when it is the culture of revolution, is multidimensional; and sometimes what appears the least important becomes the most important. This became especially true during the Soweto revolt, when, seemingly out of nowhere, it became known that not only were copies of Fanon's *The Wretched of the Earth* circulating among the youth, but so were works by Martin Luther King Jr. and Malcolm X.

Sikose Mji, a twenty-one-year-old South African woman who was a member of the Black Consciousness Movement and participated in the Soweto demonstrations, put it this way: "We no longer feel isolated. As students we read a lot, even books which are banned. I don't know how students get these books, but we certainly have a lot, which we pass on to each other. As a result, we are more and more aware that other people are struggling too, and that other people are with us, and we with them."[2]

In a word, it is not that there would have been no Soweto if they had not read Fanon, King, and Malcolm X. It is that their not feeling isolated meant that the very ideas and revolts that they were engaged in were evidently revolts and ideas that others were part of. We have seen that to be true in every country of the world, whether it be U.S.A., Russia, China[3] or elsewhere.

It is a two-way road. The internationalism of the struggle in the U.S. certainly deepened with the struggles in South Africa and the Caribbean, and with the thought of Frantz Fanon.

NOTES

1. See Fanon's moving letter of resignation from the Blida-Joinville Hospital, "Letter to the Resident Minister," reprinted in the posthumous collection of his political essays, letters, and notes on colonialism published by the editor under the title *Toward the African Revolution*: "There comes a time when silence becomes dishonesty. . . . The decision I have reached is that I cannot continue to bear a responsibility at no matter what cost, on the false pretext that there is nothing else to be done."

2. From an interview published in *Southern Africa*, December 1976.

3. See Dunayevskaya (1977, 1996) especially the interview with the Chinese refugee in Hong Kong, who speaks of the frustration and anger of the Chinese students of Peking University when university officials blocked their attempts to socialize with the African students and learn from them about the African revolutions.

4.

Fanon as a Democratic Theorist

Hussein M. Adam

Current debates and reforms around the issue of democratization in Africa will, hopefully, encourage the development of indigenous political theories favoring democratization in the long run. This chapter is intended to emphasize that need by stimulating discussions around the ideas of one of the founding fathers of the African liberation movement, Frantz Fanon. . . .

Even though Fanon did not shed much light on certain detailed aspects of democratic politics—electoral mechanisms, for example—the corpus of his political writings is both compatible with and supportive of an understanding of democracy as a process in which individuals cooperate as free and equal participants in the demanding task of development and self-rule. Today we confront reordered global relationships. First, the Cold War has ended. Over thirty years ago, Fanon said, "The Cold War must be ended, for it leads nowhere" (1968, 105). The end of the Cold War removes any excuse by national and international forces to com-

Originally published in *African Affairs* 92, no. 369 (October 1993): 449–518. Reprinted with permission of the Royal African Society.

119

promise principles because of the fear of disturbing East-West loyalties. Second, popular revolts in Africa and elsewhere have shown that military power has become problematic as a tool of foreign policy and internal repression. Third, the nature, scope, power, and even conception of the nation state is being altered. These trends have facilitated a global democratization movement. The dramatic spectacle of former Communist states plunging toward democracy and market economies has overshadowed the striking events taking place within Africa. Obviously, a democratic South Africa would be a great boost to African democracy.

I could not find a concise definition for the concept of "democracy" that would adequately cover the issues and trends discussed here. However, the descriptions and elaborations should clarify the subject. For a brief working definition I prefer the commonsensical "Government of the people, for the people and by the people," which is still the foundation of democratic beliefs. However, because particular conceptions of democracy provide the frame of reference for all that is to follow, it is vital to cite the recent definition provided in the authoritative four-volume study titled *Democracy in Developing Countries*. The editors cite three conditions necessary to define democratic governance:

> meaningful and extensive *competition* among individuals and organized groups (especially political parties) for all effective positions of government power, at regular intervals and excluding the use of force; a highly inclusive level of *political participation* in the selection of leaders and policies, at least through regular and fair elections, such that no major (adult) social group is excluded; and a level of *civil and political liberties*—freedom of expression, freedom of the press, freedom to form and join organizations—sufficient to ensure the integrity of political competition and participation. (Diamond et al. 1988, xvi)

This liberal democratic definition captures many of the demands made by the current African opposition groups, parties, and movements. It contains notions that are employed directly or indirectly by Frantz Fanon in his trenchant critique of Africa's unmitigated slide into single-party autocracies, personal-rule authoritarianisms, and military dictatorships. While offering defensive reasons on behalf of liberal democracy in opposition to African dictatorial rule, Fanon goes beyond the definition to include radical decentralization, democratization of local, regional, and central state organs, as well as a preoccupation with issues of equity and gender. On political participation, Fanon emphasizes those that are more continuous or relevant to ongoing and immediately important activities in the everyday lives of citizens.

FANON AND SELF-DETERMINATION

Frantz Fanon and the other leaders of liberation movements in Africa and Asia share a certain vision of democracy that has been succinctly analyzed by C. B. Macpherson (1966). Fanon, however, does not stop here, he goes on to transcend this notion by emphasizing a vibrant participatory democracy. Macpherson asks:

> What does this vision of democracy amount to? . . . It is neither our Western liberal-democracy nor the democracy formulated by Marx and Lenin: It is newer than either of these, yet in a sense it is older than both. . . . The notion of democracy as rule by and for the oppressed people. (1966, 23–4)

Macpherson goes on to argue that this version of democracy puts emphasis on ends, not means. The classic formulator of this democratic doctrine was Rousseau, who argued

> Dignity, freedom, and humanity are to be achieved by re-establishing the equality that had been forcibly or fraudulently taken from them. This requires a revolution at once political and moral, an assertion of the will of an undifferentiated People as the only legitimate source of political power. (MacPherson 1966, 29)

Several critics have analyzed Fanon's ideas as regards the

Rousseau tradition (see Bondy 1966). Obviously Fanon shares this aspect of the notion of democracy. In normal anticolonial situations, national liberation stands for the democratic right of the colonized nation as a whole to independence from colonial rule and national self-determination. He is an advocate of the right of peoples to self-determination. He willingly and enthusiastically joined the Algerian freedom struggle against external French control, and he sacrificed his life for the freedom of Algeria (see Caute 1970). Nevertheless, he was quick to differentiate between authentic self-determination and false decolonization. Formal political independence he satirically calls "a fancy-dress parade and the blare of the trumpets. There's nothing save a minimum of readaptation, a few reforms at the top, a flag-waving: and down there at the bottom an undivided mass, still living in the Middle Ages, endlessly marking time" (Fanon 1968, 147).

Fanon transcends the issue of collective self-determination or state freedom and dialectically links it to the notion of individual freedom. He outlines a theory of democratized development through an emphasis on decentralization and participation. Before turning to Fanon's broadened conception of democracy, I will examine his contributions as a bitter critic of anti-democratic trends. In 1961, he predicted what became the most common pattern wherein a state moved to a single-party dictatorship, which was in turn replaced by a military regime. His uniqueness and originality in this endeavor are underlined by the fact that most African states achieved independence in 1960 only one year before he wrote his main book, *The Wretched of the Earth*. An analysis of the Latin-American experience helped him gain such prophetic insights.

FANON'S CRITICISMS OF ANTIDEMOCRATIC TRENDS

Like Marx, Fanon felt that "liberal democracy" is linked to an authentic national bourgeoisie and flourishing national market:

The national middle class which takes over power at the end of
the colonial regime is an under-developed middle class. It has
practically no economic power. . . . It is not engaged in production, nor in invention, nor building, nor labor; it is completely
canalized into activities of the intermediary type. . . . Under the
colonial system, a middle class which accumulates capital is an
impossible phenomenon. (Fanon 1968, 149–50)

Several consequences flow from this lack of an authentic national
bourgeoisie. The inability to sustain multiparty politics and therefore opt for one-party dictatorships is one consequence. Some of
the ruling elites resort to Rousseau-type concepts and argue for the
single-party as the dictatorship of an undifferentiated people (a
majoritarian mass). The single party is seen as representing an
undifferentiated General Will. The African pseudobourgeoisie or
neobourgeoisie

does not yet have the quiet conscience and the calm that economic power and the control of the state machine alone can give.
It does not create a state that reassures the ordinary citizen, but
rather one that rouses his anxiety. The state, which by its strength
and discretion ought to inspire confidence and disarm and lull
everybody to sleep, on the contrary seeks to impose itself in spectacular fashion. It makes a display, it jostles people and bullies
them thus intimating to the citizen that he is in continual danger.
The single party is the modern form of the dictatorship of the
bourgeoisie, unmasked, unpainted, unscrupulous, and cynical.
(Fanon 1968, 164–65)

At the level of theoretical argument and political practice, Fanon
demonstrates that the one-party dictatorship is neither necessary
nor inevitable. Incidentally, Martin Kilson makes a similar observation in his study of politics in Sierra Leone: "The party, having
usurped the field of political action, becomes the guarantor against
the precipitous and unwarranted populist demands; it constitutes
in effect, a veritable dictatorship of the black bourgeoisie" (Kilson
1966, 191).

Fanon differs with a number of social scientists such as Samuel Huntington and others, who have argued that developing nations need to emphasize stability and development and sacrifice democratic participation, at least for the short run. He also argues that the neobourgeois elite is incapable of providing stability, let alone facilitating socioeconomic development. In most cases, Africans will pay the price, in terms of rights and liberties, without gaining any benefits in return.

Fanon's position is also radically different from those in the modernization school (David Apter, for example), who distorted the Weberian concept of charisma to justify the "cult of the leader" in African one-party dictatorships. Historically, such a "populist" leader will come to be seen as"the fierce defender of these interests . . . of the national bourgeoisie and the ex-colonial companies. This honesty, which is his soul's true bent, crumbles away little by little" (Fanon 1968, 166).

Fanon's description recalls the late Kwame Nkrumah, who was president of Ghana while Fanon served as Algerian Provisional Government ambassador in Accra. He calls for a democratic concept of leadership: the need to empower citizens and to create a plurality of leaders in all spheres of political, economic, social, and cultural life. He sums up his critique of anti-democratic trends in African politics thus:

> That famous dictatorship, whose supporters believe that it is called for by the historical process and consider it an indispensable prelude to the dawn of independence, in fact symbolizes the decision of the bourgeois caste to govern the underdeveloped country first with the help of the people, but soon against them. The progressive transformation of the party into an information service is the indication that the government holds itself more and more on the defensive. The incoherent mass of the people is seen as a blind force that must be continually held in check either by mystification or by police force. The party acts as a barometer and as an information service. The militant is turned into an informer. He is entrusted with punitive expeditions against the villages. The embryo opposition parties are liquidated by beat-

ings and stonings. The opposition candidates see their houses set on fire. The police increase their provocations. In these conditions, you may be sure, the party is unchallenged and 99.99% of the votes are cast for the government candidate. (1968, 182)

In 1961 Fanon predicted that most of the civilian neobourgeois regimes will sooner or later be overthrown by military dictators. Within the neocolonial context, the army, trained and equipped by foreign technicians and finances, becomes not only the instrument used by the neobourgeoisie to control the people, but the instrument used by the metropole to enforce its policy of indirect government: "We may thus conclude that the ranks of decked-out profiteers . . . will sooner or later be men of straw in the hands of the army, cleverly handled by foreign experts" (1968, 174). Fanon criticizes the standing army as a destructive inheritance from colonial rule. Even in cases where guerrilla liberation armies have come to power, Fanon advocates a small, mobile, limited standing army surrounded by a peoples' militia. He sees armed citizens as the best guarantors of democratic rights and envisions militia training and participation as an informal school for civic and patriotic consciousness, literacy education, as well as technical and organizational know-how. Fanon joins those classical theorists of democracy who strongly emphasized the educative effect produced in the citizenry by participation. This is a key aspect of his participatory approach, intended to limit the power of narrow professional "castes." No discussion of democratization in Africa can be complete unless it raises the issue of the role, the size, and the objectives of Africa's standing armies and the international arms race. The declining Cold War and the destruction of sizable standing armies in Uganda, Liberia, and Somalia, as well as Ethiopia, give urgency and added significance to this crucial issue. Even powerful countries like the United States are obliged to rely on volunteer National Guards to meet emergency needs.

Over thirty years since Fanon's death, the military organization continues to pose the greatest threat to democracy in Africa. His citizen militias and related ideas were intended to prevent and/or facilitate the process of military withdrawal from power. Although there are cases such as Nigeria, Ghana, and the Sudan where the military has gone back to the barracks, the military continues to pose serious problems for democratic consolidation because of their propensity to reintervene under any pretext.

Fanon's criticisms of single-party dictatorships, personal rule, military rule, and standing armies constitute important aspects of his pro-democracy approach. In this section, Fanon provides negative reasons for democracy. He seems to be saying that if you are not convinced of the desirability for democracy, consider the alternatives. He changes the focus from obvious failures and political disasters to probable success to demonstrate that democracy has greater relevance to Africa's future. His existential background allowed him to reject historical and other forms of determinism. Even though the lack of an authentic bourgeoisie made the attainment of democracy extremely difficult, it has not made it impossible. Social and economic preconditions for democracy are helpful but not absolutely necessary. During this period, the majority of Western scholars and observers bent over backward to rationalize for African dictators and dictatorships. John Wiseman recalls: "To avoid the charge of ethnocentrism many scholars adopted a bogus Afrocentrism. . . . Although the same people would have been justifiably horrified if their own governments had decided to ban all opposition, they were quite willing to accept it in Africa" (1990, 5).

A number of African fiction writers have depicted Fanon-type criticisms of the African neobourgeoisie in their literary works. At least three such writers have acknowledged being directly influenced by Frantz Fanon: Ngugi Wa Thiong'o,[1] Ayi Kwei Armah, and Sembene Ousmane. Ngugi's satirical novel, written in prison in his native language, Gikuyu, *Devil on the Cross*, depicts a scene in which the budding "African capitalists" (read "thieves and robbers") give testimony before their foreign Western and Japanese masters in order to win the crown of modern theft and robbery. One such participant, Mwireri Wa Mukiraai, implores his fellow thieves to break the cycle of Western comprador domination in order to become a proper national bourgeoisie: "National robbers, national thieves, I have shown you the way." Mwireri's testimony causes a riot in the den of the thieves and robbers. The Master of Ceremonies profusely and humbly apologizes to the foreign capitalists present. Ngugi implies here that the Kenyan neobourgeoisie prefers its comprador, intermediary status. To rub in this bitter irony, Ngugi has Mwireri thrown out of the ceremonies and later killed for his heretical thoughts. Sembene's novel and film, *Xala*, depicts Senegal's mercantile class. El Hadji Beye is shown to be a capitalist of the intermediary export-import type. In this case, however, Sembene seems to see a spark of hope for this neobourgeoisie as the word *Xala* literally means "temporary impotence"! Africa's Nobel laureate writer Wole Soyinka has also expended a great deal of literary and political energy combating African dictatorships.

FANON'S PARTICIPATORY DEMOCRACY

So far we have analyzed Fanon's negative contribution: his criticisms of single-party dictatorships, cult of leaders, personal rule, and military authoritarianism. He considers freedom as man's defining characteristic and supreme goal. In a book he published as a young man and under the influence of Jean-Paul Sartre's existentialist philosophy, *Black Skin, White Masks*, Fanon wrote: "No attempt must be made to encase man, for it is his destiny to be free" (1967a, 230). The Algerian revolution allows Fanon to deepen his earlier notions of existentialist freedom to include social praxis and social freedom: organization, consciousness of freedom, self-expression, and respect for the freedom of others. In theorizing about democracy from a participatory perspective, he wishes to emphasize that democracy transcends the right to vote in a political system. It must include a whole set of rights and responsibilities for citizens if a decolonization is to be judged authentic and the new government is to be open, accountable, and participatory. His notion of development based on free choices and popular participation is best captured by the following quotation:

> If the building of a bridge does not enrich the awareness of those who work on it, then that bridge ought not to be built and the citizens can go swimming across the river or go by boat. The bridge should not be "parachuted down" from above; it should not be imposed by a *deus ex machina* upon the social scene; on the contrary, it should come from the muscles and the brains of the citizens. (Fanon 1968, 200–201)

Development is too important to be left to a few technicians or even to an authoritarian bourgeoisie of some sort. Development must involve the democratic participation of the people. Fanon understands perfectly well that democratic consultative mechanisms take time and might slow down developmental activities considerably. "In an under-developed country, experience proves that the important thing is not that three hundred people form a plan and decide upon carrying it out, but that the whole people plan and decide even if it takes them twice or three times as long" (Fanon 1968, 193).

Fanon's process orientation toward democratic development is in contrast to the product-oriented, top-down approach advocated by Kwame Nkrumah and a number of Africa's leaders. The statements cited above could be read as a refutation of Nkrumah's observation: "What other countries have taken three hundred years or more to achieve, a once-dependent territory must try to accomplish in a generation if it is to survive. Unless it is, as it were, 'jet-propelled,' it will lag behind and thus risk everything for which it fought" (Nkrumah 1957, x). Fanon's vision is one of voluntary self-propulsion, not coerced "jet propulsion."

Transcending existential freedom, Fanon seeks to establish social freedom, whereby man is liberated by liberating society, thus linking freedom, equality, and development. His democratic notions are strengthened by his stress on the necessity of extreme decentralization. He felt that this would not only take pressure off capital-city politics, but would also facilitate meaningful participation while contributing toward transparency, accountability, and predictability.[2] . . .

He conceived of the parliament as the apex of a pyramid of solid and active vertical, representative, and participatory institutions. These institutions were at the local village, district, and regional levels. Horizontal participatory institutions were the trade unions, youth and women's organizations, peasant cooperative associations, and a multiplicity of voluntary organizations. This was in keeping with Fanon's voluntarist, free-choice conception of democracy.

Even though he did not advocate multiple parties in the abstract, Fanon defended the need to have opposition parties, thus:

> The embryo opposition parties are liquidated by beatings and stonings. The opposition candidates see their houses set on fire. The police increase their provocations. . . . All the opposition parties, which moreover are usually progressive and would therefore tend to work for the greater influence of the masses in the conduct of public matters and who desire that the proud, money-making bourgeoisie should be brought to heel, have been by dint of baton charges and prisons condemned first to silence and then to a clandestine existence. (Fanon 1968, 182)

The late Emmanuel Hansen argued, "Fanon assumes that in his ideal society there will be a single-party system" (1977, 184). I believe this is not a correct reading of Fanon. Irene Gendzier correctly pointed out that in Fanon's view "whether there ought to be a single-party or a multi-party system was a secondary question" (1973, 221). In connection with the ruling party, Fanon wrote: "The living party, which ought to make possible the free exchange of ideas which have been elaborated according to the real needs of the masses of the people, has been transformed into a trade union of individual interests" (1968, 170). To enhance accountability Fanon advocated separating the party from the government:

> The party is not a tool in the hands of the government. Quite on the contrary, the party is a tool in the hands of the people; it is they who decide on the policy that the government carries out. The party is not, and ought never to be, the only political bureau

where all the members of the government and the chief digni-
taries of the regime may freely meet together. (Fanon 1968, 185)

In contradiction to his elaborate criticisms of the single-party
regime, is Fanon advocating a single-party system? I believe Adele
Jinadu is correct when he points out that Fanon is really "referring
to what *any* party ideally should be. What matters most to him is
the development of the social and political consciousness of the
African masses. Whatever the form of the party organization, its
task must be to facilitate the progressive attainment of this collective emancipation" (Jinadu 1986, 172). As explained above, Fanon
is aware of the nature of African de facto one-party states. What he
is definitely against is parties that cling to power by declaring
other parties illegal, by rigging elections, by cynical political
opportunism and/or the use of intimidation and force. A genuinely revolutionary party should seek to lead by exercising leadership as a result of prestige or hegemony, rather than naked
power. Its revolutionary catalysts should help educate the people
and provide organizational direction for a party that seeks to influence by setting itself up as a positive role model. It should operate,
like the state organs, on a highly decentralized model and its
leaders and cadres should live and work in rural areas among the
majority of the people. . . .

THE INTERNATIONAL DIMENSION

In their search for relative *autonomy* in an increasingly interdepen-
dent world, Fanon warned African and Third World leaders against
opting for autarchy: "An autarkic regime is set up and each state,
with the miserable resources it has in hand, tries to find an answer
to the nation's great hunger and poverty" (Fanon 1968, 98). This
attempt to create autarchy within excessive problems of scarcity
(perhaps best approached by Albania until recently) would only
pour fuel on the fires of Third World developmental dictatorships
that Fanon rejected. At one point he quipped that to exhort the

poverty-stricken masses to tighten their belts even further ignores the fact that they do not even have belts to tighten in the first place! Which is the way out of such dilemmas, autonomy or autarchy? "What counts today, the question which is looming on the horizon, is the need for a redistribution of wealth. Humanity must reply to this question, or be shaken to pieces by it" (Fanon 1968, 98). He calls for a form of humanistic and creative socialism (not the imitative top-down Stalinistic version) that is to be implemented through democratic consultations, persuasion, and education—and not through force and coercion.

> The choice of a socialist regime, a regime which is completely oriented toward the people as a whole and based on the principle that man is the most precious of all possessions, will allow us to go forward more quickly and more harmoniously, and thus make impossible that caricature of society where all economic and political power is held in the hands of a few who regard the nation as a whole with scorn and contempt. (Fanon 1968, 98)

For the most part, Fanon's reflections on democratizing development do not presuppose detailed government policies. At this point, however, he manifests a normative bias toward equalizing resources in society. With regard to participatory democracy, this will permit the less well-off to increase their relative weight in popular participation. Meaningful democracy requires the equalization of resources that facilitate the empowerment of the majority. This issue relates not so much to the form of "democracy" but rather to its substantive content.

Fanon calls on African countries to seek economies of scale by relying on Pan-African and Third World forms of solidarity. The New International Economic Order (NIEO) proposals put forward by Algeria at the 1974 Special Session of the United Nations General Assembly would be in line with Fanon's perspective: "We are strong in our own right, and in the justice of our point of view.... The Cold War must be ended, for it leads nowhere" (Fanon 1969, 105). Turning to the peoples of Western countries, Fanon urges them to transform foreign aid into genuine forms of international solidarity and partnerships:

> What [the Third World] expects from those who for centuries have kept it in slavery is that they will help it rehabilitate mankind, and make man victorious everywhere, once and for all. But it is clear that we are not so naive as to think that this will come about with the cooperation and good will of the European governments. This huge task which consists of reintroducing mankind into the world, the whole of mankind, will be carried out with the indispensable help of the European peoples, who themselves must realize that in the past they have often joined the ranks of our common masters where colonial questions were concerned. (1968, 106)

Fanon's democratic aspirations have a global, international dimension that could be best summed up by readapting the famous slogan of the international voluntary development movement: "Think globally, act locally" as well as its reverse,"Think locally, act globally."

IMPACT AND LINKS

To assess Fanon's impact fully would require considerably more research and a much longer chapter. To a large extent he has had an amorphous informal impact that is hard to measure. The links between Fanon and those who came after him arise out of similarity of roles (for example Amilcar Cabral) and partly out of conscious ideological emulation (as frankly admitted by writer Ngugi Wa Thiong'o). In a number of cases both are present and it is not easy to separate coincidence from conscious emulation.

As noted above, Fanon has had a direct impact on radical African writers such as Ngugi Wa Thiong'o, Ayi Kwei Armah, and Sembene Ousmane. My general impression is that his influence goes beyond these to include other Third World writers but I have not investigated enough to cite specific examples. In the social sciences, African studies in particular, his major impact consisted in unleashing the great debates around class versus ethnicity as research methods and approaches. Fanon felt that the bureaucratic African bourgeoisie faced domestic and external constraints that prevented it from developing into a productive national bourgeoisie. He wanted it controlled and substituted by institutions facilitating mass participatory democracy.

Partly by coincidence and partly by indirect influence through French agronomist Rene Dumont (1966), Julius Nyerere grasped the argument and tried to enact policies that would "freeze" Tanzanian class formation. The 1967 Leadership Code and similar measures were intended to prevent bureaucratic bourgeois expansion into the private sectors, thereby limiting conflicts of interest. Tanzania attained modest success in the beginning but on the whole the experiment seems to have failed. Robert Bates, in *Markets and States in Tropical Africa* (1981), echoes Fanon (by coincidence) in his criticism of urban elite–domination and resulting corruption. He is joined by others including the World Bank, in a perspective that differs from Fanon's, in believing that by rolling back state sector expansion, and by pursuing privatization and private sector policies, an African capitalism and a national bourgeoisie will be able to emerge. The historical jury is not yet in on the question of a productive African bourgeoisie.

Through activist writers such as Paulo Freire, Fanon has had an indirect influence on the liberation theology movement. His participatory vision of democracy is, to a varying extent, manifested in the statements and activities of a number of the indigenous and international voluntary development organizations; if there are any sectors of society where one could find echoes of Fanon's ideas they would be the universities, naturally, and the voluntary development sector. Drawing from diverse intellectual sources including Frantz Fanon and Paulo Freire, an alternative NGO position has emerged that defines development in terms of empowerment or training for transformation. Empowerment is not a simple project or projects; it is a process (Elliot 1987, 57–77; see also Clark 1991).

Recently, certain African radical democrats have followed Fanon in stressing the primacy of "development" and economic performance in their advocacy of democratization. Anyang' Nyong'o argues that nondemocratic African states are unable to tax the people, thus lack of democracy is a major obstacle to African development: "At the center of the failure of African states to chart viable paths for development (or industrialization) is the issue of lack of accountability, hence of democracy as well" (cited in Beckman 1989, 89). In rejecting Huntington and others, he parallels Fanon in arguing that it is the lack of democracy that breeds instability and coups d'etat.

Richard Jeffries's recent article (1992) on Jerry Rawlings's Ghana allows us to reflect on linkages between Fanon and later experimentation. Several of Rawlings's close advisors have been influenced by Fanon, and Rawlings is said to have read and to have been impressed by Paulo Freire's *Pedagogy of the Oppressed* which in turn was much influenced by Frantz Fanon. There is an indirect link, therefore, between Rawlings's and Fanon's ideas. There is also a good deal of coincidence.

A striking link between Fanon and Rawlings concerns the importance both attach to decentralization. Jeffries sums up Rawlings's decentralization measures thus:

> The aim of the local government reforms, then, was to decentralize the operation of the various government ministries to the district level so as to increase the range of governmental activities over which elected District Assemblies enjoyed jurisdiction. . . . Elected assembly members were to be required to report back regularly to their ward constituents. In this way, it was hoped . . . to enhance the political accountability of government activities. . . . With a larger proportion of the finance for development projects within each district having to be raised from local taxes, it was also hoped that this system would serve to educate the electorate . . . The electorate were to learn, as it were, that there are no free lunches. (Jeffries 1992, 10)

Ali Mazrui's TV series, *The Africans*, has an interesting portrayal of Jerry Rawlings. In "Part 6: Africa In Search of Stability,"

Mazrui shows Rawlings teaching a group of male and female Ghanaians how to use a gun. He says he wishes to see every citizen learning to use a gun to protect them from the domination of those who have a monopoly of guns. Like Fanon, Rawlings is advocating a popular militia and a diminished role for the professional army. He has unleashed a critical debate but it does not seem that he has had much success in implementing this policy. Africa has to carry out such experiments even though they are fraught with dangers: on the one hand they could trigger a militarist coup, on the other hand they could lead to armed anarchy as in Liberia and Somalia.

According to Jeffries, Rawlings "has remained, quite genuinely, a believer in what he terms 'participatory democracy' as the eventual goal of his revolution" (1992, 4). However, a number of his key associates tended to lean toward Jacobinism. As discussed by C. B. Macpherson above, they stress "democracy in unity" in order to achieve national development goals. Rawlings leaned toward a one-party state but after hesitation, he followed popular demands and conducted multiparty elections. His party won the elections though there are opposition charges of unfairness and fraud. He has been given a mandate to continue his reforms in favor of decentralization, popular militias and "participatory democracy."

CONCLUSION

Certain ambiguities and contradictions in Fanon cannot be explained by shortcomings in his poetic style. He offers a vision of democracy grounded on a historical process; however, he overlooks some of the details necessary to guarantee and sustain a participatory democratic process, for example: a democratic constitution, bill of rights, the rule of law, multiple parties, fair elections held at regular intervals, an independent judiciary, a free press, and voluntary associations. Fanon does refer to some of these elements but in connection with his critique of African authoritarianism rather than in his depiction of a desirable democratic society.

It could be suggested that he wanted to avoid offering a rigid blueprint. He wanted the participating masses to fill in their own details. This explanation receives paradoxical support in the younger Fanon of *Black Skin, White Masks*: "In no fashion should I undertake to prepare the world that will come later. I belong irreducibly to my time" (1967a, 13). However, the younger, existentialist Fanon has evolved into the mature historically engaged author of *The Wretched of the Earth* and *Toward the African Revolution*. Fanon risked his life and died in the struggle to bring about a better future for colonized Algeria in particular and the African continent in general. If we still admit he continued to retain an aspect of his earlier existentialist position, then he is subject to a criticism similar to that levelled at Marx and Rousseau, for example: by providing simply an outline of his vision he has facilitated the distortion of his ideas by others. Fascists and communists (Stalinists) have shown that mass participation can be manipulated. Obviously, Fanon is against top-down participation; he is advocating bottom-up grass-roots democratic participation. Unfortunately, he does not discuss the mechanisms that would ensure accountability of the leadership to the grass roots; that would rotate leaders and guarantee as well as sustain such democratic processes. The specific type of electoral system adopted may affect the prospects for the stability of any regime.

Fanon uses a modified social-class approach to understanding African politics. As mentioned, the opening salvoes in the great Africanist debate—class versus ethnicity—can be traced back to Frantz Fanon. This has led certain critics to accuse him of an incomprehension of the ethnic factors in African politics. He understood the role of primordial cleavages in African societies: ethnic groups (tribes, clans) and religious communities. The following quotation shows Fanon criticizing Africa's educated elite for ignoring important ethnic, traditional, and historical factors:

The traditional chiefs are ignored, sometimes even persecuted. The makers of the future nation's history trample unconcernedly over small local disputes, that is to say, the only existing national events, whereas, they ought to make of village history—the history of traditional conflicts between clans and tribes—a harmonious whole, at one with the decisive action to which they call on the people to contribute. The old men, surrounded by respect in all traditional societies, and usually invested with unquestionable moral authority, are publicly held up to ridicule. (Fanon 1968, 113)

Similar insights on ethnicity and traditions are to be found in various parts of *The Wretched of the Earth* and *A Dying Colonialism*. In promoting radical decentralization, Fanon is partially providing a method to handle primordial cleavages. Besides decentralization, he does not indicate other means to minimize ethnic conflicts and channel energies toward socially meaningful democratic participation . . . .

If, for the sake of simplicity, we were to categorize democratic theories, we would list liberal and consociational as pragmatic theories concerned with abstract principles as well as concrete issues, electoral systems and laws, for example. Fanon belongs to a third trend that, for convenience, we shall refer to as radical social democracy, which differs from moderate social democracy. The moderate social democratic parties in power and in opposition in Western Europe have more or less accepted the liberal or neoliberal framework of their societies. The gaps and omissions in Fanon's theory lead one to pose the question of practice: Is Fanon's participatory democratic vision feasible? We cannot point to any existing society as reflecting the ideal model Fanon proposed. The emerging political model is anti–Third World dictatorships, it is decidedly not Stalinist, and yet it is not fully liberal democratic.

Like other radical social democrats before him, Fanon had an excessively optimistic belief in human nature. This is one more reason why he spent little time suggesting rules, procedures, and mechanisms necessary to check the selfish aspects in all human beings. He placed great faith in sound leadership, in a strata of "revolutionary intellectuals" who would resolve contractions inherent in class/ethnic factors while facilitating participatory democracy. Fanon expects these revolutionary intellectuals to avoid the capital city and live among the rural masses.

Fanon is correct in arguing that in all societies there are corrupt as well as honest individuals. He gave various reasons for the presence of "honest intellectuals," for instance, solid religious and moral upbringing being one such explanation. However, he does not explain in a satisfactory manner how such honest intellectuals are able to gain power and to transfer it to the people. In relying on the spontaneous virtues of revolutionary intellectuals, Fanon neglected to focus on the systematic checks and balances of power. Though he clearly describes the natural tension between patriotic principles and the desire of neocolonial politicians to secure and maintain political power, with regard to revolutionary intellectuals he does not seem to see that clashes between democratic principles and self-interest are unavoidable. Somewhat naively he assumes a great deal of "voluntarism" on the part of his "revolutionary leaders." In reality, in radical countries such as Tanzania and Zimbabwe, which have adopted a leadership code, only a few leaders adhered to the precepts of the code.

Again, like other radical social democrats, Fanon's vision has a messianic touch. Paradoxically, this makes it both desirable and inapplicable. In attempting to implement Fanon's ideas, one would have to incorporate the practical and concrete mechanisms developed within the context of the other two trends in democratic theory. Even though human beings are political animals (Aristotle) they are not exclusively political. While Fanon assumes extremely high rates of interest in political participation among the citizens of his democratic polity, political interests vary. He wished to see democracy practiced in daily life, not just every four years or so: in factories, administrative offices, cooperative farms, schools and universities, as well as within the small army and large militia forces. Radical social democracy aims at transcending voting rights and related democratic mechanisms in favor of day-to-day decentralized participatory decision making. He believed that workplace and community participation offer greater potential for a democratized political culture than do sporadic campaigning and voting.

Perhaps the single most important element that glues Fanon's political thought together is his profound faith in the ability of the ordinary people for self-emancipation and self-rule. A number of his otherwise contradictory statements can be reconciled in light of this progressive optimism on his part. This not only explains much of his thinking, it is also the basis of his strategy for authentic decolonization and democratic development. He repeatedly argued against the view that the mass of the population in Africa does not understand or value democracy as patronizing, wrong, and ultimately dangerous.

Beginning with an existentialist interest in individual freedom and free choice, a process-oriented reading of Fanon shows that he continues to stress the voluntary relationship of individuals in the process of social choice as a necessary focus of democratic theory and practice. Praxis taught Fanon that only in specific communities marked by conditions of equality, autonomy, and relative self-reliance can individuals obtain concrete freedoms through their joint labor and association.

Fanon's stress on the peasantry was partly intended to ensure that Third World social movements be genuine movements of and for the majority of the people. Fanon's democratic thinking does have a majoritarian dimension. This "logic of the majority" includes the belief in the evaluation of all decisions in terms of what will be most beneficial to the poor majority of the population. This is a fundamentally democratic aspiration.

The process- and product-oriented aspects of democracy are not necessarily totally opposed to one another. For example, one can read Fanon and infer that democracy (a means) would facilitate development (the desired end). This would be a partial reading of Fanon. He does regard freedom as man's overriding goal, accordingly "democracy" for him is both a means and an end. Fanon wished to provide less political and social controls over outcomes, but a solid guarantee of the free expression of the needs and interests of all members of society, especially the majority who were women and peasants.

Fanon advocated an organic, self-centered movement toward democratization. He urged the development of indigenous political theories favoring democratization and participatory social development. He wished to see popular participation in various levels of decision making and administration and policies favoring distributive equity among the people. For him, this presupposed an understanding of democracy as a decision process constituting popular rule. The struggle for social development is, therefore, a struggle for equal, autonomous, and voluntary participation in the activity of decentralized popular rule.

NOTES

1. Both Ngugi Wa Thiong'o and Ousmane Sembene mentioned this during our 1991 discussions. During a 1990 public lecture at Holy Cross College, Ngugi pointed to Fanon's influences on Ayi Kwei Armah. See Ngugi (1987, 171); and Sembene Ousmane (1976), *Xala* (Lawrence Hill Books, Chicago, 1976); see, for example, Ayi Kwei Armah (1988); see also Neil Lazarus (1990). Lazarus argues that not only Ngugi, Sembene, and Armah but also Wole Soyinka and Chinua Achebe among others, tended to view the post-colonial situation in the light of the theories of the Third World analyst and revolutionary Frantz Fanon.

2. Chinua Achebe captures this issue of decentralization to facilitate local accountability best when, in his novel, *A Man of the People*, he states: "My father's words struck me because they were the very same words the villagers of Anata had spoken of Josiah, abominable trader. Only in their case the words had meaning. The owner was the village, and the village had a mind; it could say no to sacrilege. But in the affairs of the nation, there was no owner, the laws of the village became powerless.

5.

Revolutionary Psychiatry of Fanon

Hussein A. Bulhan

*I, the man of color, want only this: That the tool never possess the man.
That the enslavement of man by man cease forever.*

Fanon, *Black Skin, White Masks*

It is never enough only to expose a human problem or even to offer
conceptual paradigms exploring its structure and dynamics. The
exposition and paradigms, to be authentic and valid, require *action*
that puts the hypothetical against the actual and, above all, transforms what is to what *ought to be.* To commit oneself to the practice of
healing and rehabilitating tormented psyches is no doubt a form of
action—one that is always pregnant with heuristic and social import.
Yet as we have suggested, the action on behalf of the patient often
turns out to be against the interest and well-being of the patient.

Questions that often present themselves to therapists working
in situations of oppression can be posed thus: Is therapy really *for*
this patient? If so, what should the therapist do with respect to the

Originally published in Hussein A. Bulhan, *Frantz Fanon and the Psychology of Oppression* (New York: Plenum Publishing, 1985), chap 11. Reprinted with permission.

social forces that clearly undermine the well-being of his or her patient? And if one considers mental disorders also as a "pathology of liberty," is it possible to restore the well-being of the patient without at the same time endeavoring to restore his liberty?

This chapter looks at the contributions of Fanon toward a psychiatry of social and psychological liberation. It sketches the evolution of his clinical theory and practice to underscore the fact that a genuine endeavor to restore the health of the oppressed assumes a commitment to restore their liberty. This chapter highlights Fanon's attempt to delve into the experience of an oppressed people with a culture different from the one he had known. His own experience of oppression proved a critical bridge for comprehending "the truth" of others. Fanon's venture into ethnopsychiatry gradually led to an active challenge not only of establishment psychiatry, but also of the established social order. The chapter therefore shows Fanon's endeavor that the tool—in this case, psychiatry—never possess the man and that, with a bold application of it, enslavement cease wherever he found it.

EXPLORATION INTO ETHNOPSYCHIATRY

The Algiers School of Psychiatry represented one early predecessor of the subspecialty now called "ethnopsychiatry" or, more generally, "cross-cultural psychology." The views that the Algiers School propagated, and the historic function they served, were remarkably similar to those of behavioral scientists in other African colonies. Each colonial power, though relying primarily on military might, also had its own behavioral scientists whose task it was to explain and interpret the psyches and social behaviors of the colonized. All too frequently, however, the explanations and interpretations offered were substantively unoriginal, since these foreign scholars had simply given scientific trappings to the prevailing bigotry of Europeans.

Dr. Porto was thus the French counterpart of Dr. Carothers who, after fifteen years of service to the British Empire, authoritatively asserted that the African was a "lobotomized Western European." Certainly, significant changes in psychological conceptions of the African have occurred since the 1960s—a fact illustrated by the changing conception of depression among Africans (Prince 1967). A careful review of the literature in fact shows that changes in psychological conceptions correlate with changes in the sociopolitical domain. Hence the undisguised racism of the colonial era gave way to the subtle ethnocentrism of the neocolonial present (Bulhan 1981a).

Fanon was of the generation that effectively called colonialism into question and effected its demise in Africa. Yet to have been one of the few black psychiatrists at the time—and a sociopolitically committed one at that—was no doubt a major challenge itself. There were countless misconceptions to be corrected, an undisguised racism to be combated, and alternatives to be thought out. Fanon traversed this route pretty much alone as a black psychiatrist, even though he worked in collaboration with Europeans who shared his outlook if not his commitment.

Writing and professional symposia offered a medium in which Fanon challenged distorted conceptions and presented some alternative formulations. Fanon wrote on topics ranging from the strictly biomedical to the sociopolitical. In addition to the work he collaborated on with Azoulay, four of his untranslated articles can be clearly grouped under ethnopsychiatry. Two of them, which we will discuss, illustrate his ethnopsychiatric thinking between 1954, when the historic experiment* was reported, and 1956, when Fanon resigned from his job as *chef de service* at Blida Hospital to join the Algerian freedom fighters.

---

*The historic experiment, explained in chapter 10 of Bulhan's book (see especially pp. 215–17), was the attempt by Fanon to introduce a number of reforms at Bilda hospital. Bulhan writes: "The Tosquellean influence was unmistakable, at least at the beginning. Fanon introduced occupational, group therapy and collective gatherings in the attempt to create a therapeutic community" (1985, 216). Fanon organized a soccer team, and arranged weekly outings to the beach, the serving of traditional dishes, and a weekly publication, *Notre Journal*, for patients and staff. More controversially, Fanon desegregated the service.

Not all the reforms were successful, and it was the lack of success that proved

In September 1955, a year after the famous experiment in therapy, Fanon and Dr. Lacaton presented to a congress of psychiatrists and neurologists their "Confession in North Africa." The presentation, though brief, is crucial for at least three reasons. First, we glean from it Fanon's evolving interest in ethnopsychiatry. Second, we again find his critique of establishment psychiatry, particularly the Algiers School. Third, it intimates a critique of domination and of the prevailing social order. Themes subtly suggested here later become elaborated clearly and passionately.

On the surface, the article cross-culturally explores the psychological and social meaning of confession for criminal acts. At a more fundamental level, it exposes some of the human problematics that arise when a situation of oppression is imposed on a community. For a situation of oppression pits one group against another and constantly tests the allegiance of each member to his group. It leads to failure of communication, mutual incomprehension, and ontological insularity between members belonging to the two coexisting but opposing cultures. The dominant group imposes its ethico-legal precepts as it negates the validity and integrity of all that the oppressed uphold.

The oppressed on their part adopt a position of passive resistance, an autoprotective shield, which renders impossible any comprehension of their experience from the cultural perspective of the oppressor. The ontological insularity and mutual incomprehension come to play in court proceedings in which a member of the oppressed has allegedly committed a crime that must be

---

a crucial turning point for Fanon. Two separate groups, European women and Algerian men, were followed in the experiment. Whereas the Europeans readily participated in meetings and activities, the Muslim men failed to respond. The failure resulted in a fundamental reassessment by Fanon of the attempt to apply practices that had worked in Europe to a Muslim society. Fanon's remarkable "leap," as Bulhan puts it, involved a critique of the cultural biases of prevailing psychiatric thought as well as toward colonial claims of integration. "A revolutionary attitude was indispensable," Fanon declared in an article summing up his experiment. That attitude, notes Bulhan, involved becoming "timid" and "attentive" to the native culture.

judged. Fanon and Lacaton examined the problems that arose when a psychiatrist was requested to serve as an expert witness for court proceedings in North Africa.

Ordinarily, the authors argued, confession for wrongdoing has both existential and social dimensions, a private as well as a public import. Existentially, confession implies a willingness to assume personal responsibility and, in so assuming, to affirm the meaning of one's being revealed through the act. Not to assume such responsibility for one's action or to falsely deny it is to experience a fundamental alienation of one's being, at least at that moment. Socially, confession indicates that an "auto-condemnation" has been provoked in the conscience, that the values and ethical precepts of the community, if not already internalized, are now reinstalled in the actor.

Thus the intent if not the consequence of the confession becomes for the actor "the ransom for his re-insertion into the group." Having confessed, the actor is reinstated as a member either then and there or after some sanction has been imposed and subjectively accepted. A realignment of existential and social imperatives thereby occurs and the collective once again opens the way for his membership in the group, with the rights and responsibilities this implies. But all of this of course assumes a "reciprocal recognition of the group by the individual and of the individual by the group."

Under these circumstances, the task of the psychiatrist requested to evaluate the mental condition under which the criminal act was committed is relatively straightforward. He examines the ideas, values, and motivations that prompted and attended the criminal act. His obligation is to delve deeply into the psychology of the actor, "find the truth of the act which will be the foundation of the truth of the actor," and to offer a meaningful interpretation to the court as well as to the community it represents. Since the judge, the actor, and the psychiatrist share the same ethico-legal and cultural universe, the judicial proceeding, the psychiatrist's interpretation, the rendering of justice, the subjective acceptance of the sanction by the guilty one, and the potential reinsertion of the norm-violator into the group is relatively comprehensible. But this is not so in a situation of oppression in which a member of the oppressed is being tried and evaluated in a colonial court.

Fanon and Lacaton underscored the complexity of confession in North Africa and the problem of rendering justice in colonial courts. A "native" who allegedly committed a grave crime like murder is brought to court along with an "eloquent dossier" prepared by the police. The dossier indicates that the accused has already confessed, having in addition revealed where the arms were hidden. It may also show that several witnesses swore that they have seen him perform the act. The confession and the witnesses having confirmed the guilt of the person, the judge subsequently requests a psychiatric evaluation to determine if such a grave crime had been committed when the accused was psychotic. The psychiatrist who takes his obligations seriously then proceeds to examine the "truth of the act," its motivation and meaning, in order to arrive at the "truth of the actor," his existential and social being. He relies on the diagnostic value of the confession and conducts a psychiatric interview, hoping to be able to offer appropriate explanation and measures to the court. Unfortunately, however, he finds this to be extremely difficult in cases involving North Africans.

To begin with, it often happens that the accused absolutely denies that he committed the act or that he ever confessed. If indeed he confessed to the police, he asserts that this was done under torture. Not infrequently, even the witnesses retract their declarations. What is more, the medico-legal expert finds that the accused, vehemently asserting his innocence, is actually a lucid and coherent person. The psychiatrist thus loses not only the diagnostic value of the confession, now reduced to a police frame-up, but finds himself in the presence of one without signs of pathology. All that is left for him are the eloquent dossier and the criminal act without an actor. Further rendering "criminological comprehension" impossible in the North African is the fact that the accused states his innocence but does little to prove his innocence actively. The accused takes an attitude of resignation, saying he accepts any judgment of the court in the name of Allah.

Typically, the European psychiatrist faced with this type of situation fell back to such common stereotypes of the North African as a lazy, no-good liar. Indeed, the Algiers School of Psychiatry had provided him ample "scientific proofs" that the North African is degenerate, untrustworthy, and phylogenetically defective. But Fanon and Lacaton assert that such a simplification only obstructs comprehension, detracts from a search of the "truth," and makes any rendering of justice defective. What is more,

> To affirm that the race is suffering from a propensity to lie or to voluntarily dissimulate the truth, or that the population is incapable of discerning the truth from the false, or even that it does not integrate certain givens of experience, particularly by virtue of phylogenetic defect, this is to explain away the problem without really resolving it. (Fanon & Lacaton 1955, 659)

To grasp the "truth" of the native and therefore to comprehend his ontological system requires a fundamental shift in perspective. One must search for the condition under which confession is imbued with both existential and social validity, sanctions subjectively acceptable to the accused are imposed, and reinsertion into the group is possible. But how can confession have meaning when we have it only in a police dossier and the accused denies that he confessed to or committed the crime?

Even if confession is obtained without torture, does it have any value in the absence of reciprocal recognition of the group by the individual and of the individual by the group? Can the verdict be just and rehabilitative if all we have is an act without an actor, an accused who is unwilling to appropriate the act and unwilling to accept the condemnation? And how could reinsertion of the individual into the group be possible when there was no insertion in the first place?

Obviously, these questions suggest much that is amiss in the system of justice and human communication in a situation of oppression. Fanon and Lacaton trace the problem to the coexistence of two opposed and mutually exclusive groups—one dominant, the other dominated. Each group binds its members with its own social contract and ethical universe. Each inculcates a distinct ontological system in its members and instills allegiance only to its own ethical precepts. The North African before a judge thus finds that his social contract with, and allegiance to, his group are challenged, that he is being tried not only for an *act*, but also for his very *being*. Little wonder then that he resists, so unshakably if passively, and subverts the European judicial process—confessing then denying, bearing witness then retracting, declaring his innocence then failing to prove it.

In effect, an accused who confesses his crime to the judge is at once disapproving his act and legitimizing the "eruption of the public into the private." By failing to appropriate the act, by denying and retracting, the North African is essentially refusing an eruption of an alien public into his private world. He may perforce submit to such sanctions as a jail term but this should not be confused with his being won over to believe in the legitimacy of the judge, his judgment, and the underlying alien social contract.

The article is actually less direct in its argument than our interpretation of it. Why Fanon and Lacaton chose to be less direct is indeed intriguing. Was it because a clear expression of their views entailed political risks at the time? Was it because of an academic and professional ambience that tended to dampen discussion of highly controversial and seemingly esoteric topics? Or was it because a clear political stand and an unambiguous commitment to the cause of justice had not yet crystallized in the authors? Our guess is that the choice of a subtle and less direct approach was tactical in view of the fact that at the time a clear exposition would entail political and professional risks. In fact, both Fanon and Lacaton were by then considered the most radical psychiatrists at Blida-Joinville Hospital. Both had been alienated from their European colleagues at Blida for their ideas and practice, Fanon more than Lacaton. Both also ran a constant risk of police reprisal in the increasingly charged and dangerous atmosphere that then prevailed in Algeria. We will see later that Lacaton fell victim to police torture and humiliating physical abuse for his reformist outlook and that Fanon constantly ran the risk of a similar reprisal.

In 1956, Fanon, in collaboration with Dr. Sanchez, a resident at

Blida, wrote on the attitude of North African Muslims toward madness. The discussion here was less political and therefore less perilous than the one on confession. It nonetheless dealt with some misconceptions and aimed to restore respect to the North African approach to madness—an approach Europeans commonly considered primitive and senseless. In particular, Fanon and Sanchez refuted the view that North Africans look upon madness with absolute veneration and meaningless worship. Seeking to shed some light from the "inside" as psychiatrists in Blida, they first pointed out that establishments for treating the mad had been developed in the Muslim world before the Middle Ages, long before such institutions were introduced in Europe. This fact itself should suggest that a hasty condemnation of the North African attitude to madness is unwarranted and that perhaps something can be gained by a study of this attitude.

Fanon and Sanchez compared the attitude of Europeans toward madness to that of North Africans. They found differences in the human environment in which the mad find themselves in the two cultures, the marked difference of social stigma attached to madness, and the consequences these differences have to the psychology of the self in the afflicted. Implicit in the comparison was not only the desire to correct European misconceptions, but also the desire to find an appropriate psychiatric outlook relevant to the cultural and historical realities of the North African. We will see that this desire to be psychiatrically relevant, retaining the useful aspects in the indigenous society and introducing innovations found practical elsewhere, is a theme that remained with Fanon in subsequent years.

In comparing the two attitudes toward madness, Fanon and Sanchez pointed out that Westerners believe that madness is a *disease* that alienates the victim from others and from himself. Yet Westerners tend to forget this in their interactions with the patient. They hold him responsible for his illness and actions. They feel a moral obligation to provide for his needs, but they also resent their "servitude." Viewing him as a "social parasite" who readily exploits his illness, Westerners counter his aggression with a veiled and sometimes open retaliation. His actions offend them as if he willfully intended malice and harm. Even the medical personnel and the relatives of the patient take offense and retaliate. Thus, for instance,

> an attendant feeling himself wounded by the arrogance of a megalomaniac might remain angry from it until the occasion arises wherein he could deprive the patient a snack or a walk. Then there is the mother who feels she was poorly welcomed by her son whom she has come to see in the hospital to visit and consequently leaves very bitter. (Fanon and Sanchez 1956, 25)

All this is in striking contrast to the attitude of the North African toward persons afflicted with madness. Here the person is not held responsible for his illness. He is treated as an innocent victim of spirits (*genies*) over which he has no control. Since the affliction is an accidental occurrence, it could happen to anyone. If the afflicted acts aggressively, responsibility is imputed to spiritual forces that must collectively be appeased and confronted. But punishment, distrust, or exclusion of the afflicted rarely occurs. There is also no social stigma attached to madness and to those afflicted with it. The victim and relatives talk about the affliction openly and without embarrassment. One feels no need to conceal a condition for which he is not responsible and, moreover, spirits are not passed on genetically in any case. This social acceptance of the afflicted, the explanation of madness in terms of external causation, and the collective efforts to seek resolution—all these enhance the possibility of the patient's recovery and his reintegration into the society.

In particular, the *affliction* is not confused with the *person*, since madness is considered to affect "only the appearance never penetrating the underlying self." The authors do not endorse all the indigenous approaches to madness. They view therapeutic techniques as rudimentary, but they strongly recommend the humanistic and holistic attitude of the North African to madness:

Resting solidly on cultural bases, the system is of great human value which does not confine itself only to the efficacy of the North African therapy. This natural method of assistance is imprinted with a profoundly holistic thought which keeps intact the image of the normal man, in spite of the existence of afflic- tion. . . . [The North African] attitude is guided by a care of and respect to the person. It is not madness that creates the respect, the patience, the indulgence; it is rather the man affected by mad- ness, attacked by spirits; it is man as such. (Fanon and Sanchez 1956, 26)

The attempt to place madness in its sociohistorical and cultural perspective and to restore integrity to the indigenous conception was to Fanon analogous to the larger project of instituting political and social justice. The colonialism of Europe did not confine itself to economics or politics; it also permeated psychiatric concepts and practices. Fanon therefore endeavored to pioneer a psychiatry of liberation, at least within Blida-Joinville Hospital and among his professional colleagues. His writings on ethnopsychiatry con- tinued not only to inform Westerners, but also to search for a psy- chiatry appropriate to the needs and realities of his North African patients.

Fanon did not of course pioneer ethnopsychiatry. Others before him, including Emile Kraepelin, had long written on cross-cultural psychopathology. Writings on the topic accumulated over the years and cross-cultural psychology is today a popular and respected subject. But what differentiates Fanon's approach is this: His was a *radical* ethnopsychiatry that reached for the *roots* of the subject.

Most of those who write on ethnopsychiatry tend to study remote and non-Western societies with the aim of informing West- erners or of settling academic debates in their societies. They gather endless data, exploit the cooperation of their "subjects" abroad, and take a hasty retreat with stories of their exploits to their societies. Nothing comes back to the subjects and societies they studied—not even a report of their findings. In contrast, Fanon's ethnopsychiatry was rooted in the very people he studied. Not only did he endeavor to understand their world and serve their clinical needs, he also fully identified with those he wrote about—learning their language, respecting their person as well as their culture, and risking his life to help restore their human dignity.

PSYCHIATRY FOR SOCIAL LIBERATION

The year 1954 was not only a turning point for the direction Fanon's psychiatric work was to take, it was also a historic watershed in Algerian history. In that year, the Algerian struggle for liberty took a decisive turn as the various Algerian movements, previously divided and in disarray, forged the foundation for a united and frontal attack against colonialism. The ensuing war of liberation was to last nearly eight long and bloody years until 1962, when Algeria became an independent nation. The hemorrhage and psychic dislocation caused by the war was to be so massive that an ordinary psychiatric practice on isolated private problems became untenable if not dishonest.

Fanon's critical inquiry into psychiatric theory and practice was at first confined to an institutional context and professional circles. Reforms at Blida-Joinville Hospital and presentations at psychiatric conferences remained the foci of his endeavors. But as social unrest heightened among the Algerian populace and colonial administrators reacted with brutal repression, Blida-Joinville Hospital became less and less sheltered from the turmoil and reprisals that increasingly came to characterize life in Algeria. The psychiatric work at Blida and the critique of establishment psychiatry gradually led Fanon to conclusions similar to those others had arrived at by different means. In time, Fanon's critical inquiry into psychiatry merged with the highest and most practical critique of domination—namely, the popular struggle for liberation. The merger was gradual and perilous, but momentous when it was complete.

The Algerian struggle against colonialism did not of course begin in 1954. As exemplified by the early and popular uprising of Abdel Kader, resistance to colonial domination started in the 1830s when the French colonized Algeria. Abdel Kader's rebellion and the Kabyle insurrection of 1871 were defeated with superior arms, a better military organization, and the defections of tribal chiefs. The so-called pacification of natives subsequently opened the way for installing *colons,* European settlers, into Algerian soil.

The quest for political and social rights was thereafter met with brutal repression on the one hand, and promises of reforms on the other. This stick-and-carrot policy remained effective so long as a significant portion of the Algerian elite, led by the vacillating Ferhat Abbas, was convinced that assimilation into French society and the rights this implied were attainable. The vast majority of the Algerian population nonetheless clung to their Islamic tradition and Afro-Arab culture. The riots and rebellions that occurred before 1954 were sporadic and without lasting consequence. For decades, the Algerian populace tended to mark time and offered a passive but impermeable resistance with an underlying psychology that escaped European authorities.

The obstinacy of French colonialism in Algeria cannot be adequately realized without appreciating the special status Algeria held in the French imperial system. Algeria was a prized French colony not only for economic and strategic reasons, but also because there was a large and powerful settler community in that colony. Of all the colonies, Algeria in particular was considered an integral part of France. The expropriation of land and labor in Algeria, among the most intense of all the French colonies, began soon after conquest. Thus in 1840, Marshal Bugeaud, the conqueror of Algeria, advised the Chamber of Deputies: "Wherever good water and fertile land are found, settlers must be installed without questioning whose land it may be" (Davidson 1978, 119).

Marshall Bugeaud's advice was taken and countless Algerians were displaced from their land or forced into temporary tenancy. By 1890, about 4 million acres of the best land fell into European ownership. European settlements gradually intensified and, by 1940, no less than 6 million acres, about one-third of the profitably cultivatable land, came to be owned by about 2 percent of the whole population, mainly European settlers. The settlers were not all of French stock; an overwhelming majority of them were southern Europeans of different nationalities. Algeria became a new frontier where land was grabbed without question and native labor exploited with impunity.

Much of the land expropriated was used for vineyards to make Algeria an "export enclave" of wine within the French imperial system. The irony was that most Algerians, professing the Muslim faith, did not drink wine and that the huge vineyards used land sorely needed for food production. It is estimated that, for instance, by the middle 1950s "cereal production stood at the same level as in the 1880s, although the population had tripled" (Davidson 1978, 119). Thus hunger and disease increased among Algerians as the wealth and well-being of settlers soared. A Manichean psychology founded in this economics of inequity also became well entrenched. The system of governance too was devised to give European settlers absolute power. Establishment psychiatry generally and the Algiers School of Psychiatry particularly gave scientific trappings to the bigotry of settlers and justified the status quo of oppression.

The Algerian elite was for decades manipulated and kept under control with promises of reform and a policy of assimilation. Successive administrations in the colony espoused the policy of assimilation with the effect of dividing and hence ruling Algerians. But French administrators may not have been adverse to the assimilation of a small Algerian elite in theory, although such a notion itself was deeply abhorrent to European settlers. These settlers were violently opposed to any and all political concessions even to the moderate native elite, the so-called évolués, who actually saw their destiny in assimilation into French culture. This deracinated and alienated petit bourgeoisie gradually realized that their colonial status was never temporary and that their hope for reform through peaceful means was futile. Any remaining illusions were dashed by such savage assaults as the Setif massacre of 1945, when riots, reprisals, and counterreprisals left thousands dead and many more wounded.

In 1954 various Algerian movements, which previously had

differed in ideology, tactics, and organization, began to unite around the *Comité Révolutionnaire pour l'Unité et l'Action* (CRUA). The CRUA grew out of and replaced the paramilitary and clandestine *Organisation Spéciale* (OS) formed two years after the Setif massacre. The name was soon changed to the *Front de Libération Nationale* (FLN). Gradually those who for decades sought assimilation into French society and the traditional nationalists joined forces in the FLN.

The Algerian war of independence was dramatically inaugurated at dawn of All Saints Day, November 1, 1954, when the FLN staged a well-coordinated assault against French military installations, police headquarters, communication facilities, and public utilities throughout Algeria. The FLN and military wing subsequently initiated guerrilla warfare in rural as well as urban areas, focusing on key government facilities, settler farms, and collaborators with the colonial regime. Following each engagement, the guerrillas mixed with the population.

The colonial authorities and settlers responded with ruthless and increasingly indiscriminate retaliation. They held collectively responsible all villages and neighborhoods suspected of harboring FLN guerrillas. The settler vigilante groups in particular carried out wanton, widespread killings of Muslim Algerians in what they called "rat-hunts." Villages were bombed; many of their residents were resettled in poor and crowded areas where they could be easily monitored. Electrified barbed-wire fences were installed along parts of the border and in some urban areas to stem the mobility and growing strength of the FLN.

The repressed and festering violence of colonial Algeria suddenly erupted. By 1956, France had deployed well over 400,000 soldiers to Algeria, along with sophisticated air and naval forces. One interesting irony here is that the French general, Raoul Salan, who had personally decorated Fanon for heroic action during World War II, was assigned to command French forces in Algeria at a time when Fanon was already an active FLN member.

Nearly eight years of war brought an immense loss of lives. Estimates are that over 1 million Algerians and about 20,000 Europeans were killed. The ruthless way the war was conducted, the violence and counterviolence, and this immense human loss no doubt influenced Fanon's theory of violence. In reading about the struggle against colonialism in Algeria, one cannot help but be impressed by the stubborn refusal of the oppressors to acknowledge the humanity of the other, thereby engendering untold violence.

Vested interests and formed habits, always difficult to change, are even more difficult to modify in a situation of oppression. The last to make changes and amends are oppressors. They tend to learn little from history unless shocked into a rude awakening. It was in fact in 1954 that French colonialism suffered a humiliating defeat at Dien Bien Phu in Indochina. Yet it took nearly eight more years in Algeria and thousands of casualties before France came to acknowledge the Algerian people's right to self-determination. In any case, on July 3, 1962, after 132 years of French colonial rule, Algeria was declared an independent country.

Fanon's open support of the Algerian war of independence began in 1956 when he resigned his job as *chef de service* at Blida-Joinville Hospital. The decision to resign was both clinically and politically influenced. The reevaluation of Eurocentric psychiatry outlined in the 1954 article written in collaboration with Azoulay was followed by other works that, in retrospect, suggest that some form of confrontation with the colonial social order was in the making well before the resignation. For one thing, these works showed a growing interest in radical ethnopsychiatry—an interest itself of significant clinical and political import.

At the same time, the growing social ferment in Algeria and the brutal reprisals taken by the colonial administrators increasingly intruded into Fanon's clinical practice within Blida-Joinville Hospital. The social unrest and ruthless reprisals also underscored the fact that clinical and political problems could no longer be isolated and that a clinician's professional duties also entailed social responsibility. Indeed, periods of relative peace and stability tend to obscure this intimate relation between clinical and political concerns as between professional and social responsibility. But the

Algeria of the 1950s made the connection starkly clear, particularly to a person like Fanon who asked himself if, by acting or failing to act, he contributed to the improvement or impoverishment of the human reality.

Fanon's radical outlook and his empathy toward Algerians preceded his arrival as *chef de service* in Algeria. But the practice at Blida and life in Algeria further radicalized his outlook and transformed his empathy into an unambiguous identification with the Algerians. How Fanon first made contact with the FLN and what services he provided it are documented by Geismar (1971). Fanon's initial work with the FLN involved a clandestine medical service for Algerian freedom fighters. Some of the captured freedom fighters were brought to Blida-Joinville Hospital after devastating torture by French authorities, as shown in the chapter, "Colonial Wars and Mental Disorders," in *The Wretched of the Earth*. Others suffered war neuroses and came for treatment. But Fanon and the Algerian male nurses kept secret the political affiliations of these patients and the causes of their disorders.

Fanon's formal contact with the FLN was arranged by Pierre Chaulet, the son of a European settler who was an active collaborator with the FLN. The two men met in 1955 at Blida. Chaulet, himself a physician, was on a mission to establish a local unit of a supposedly charitable organization that was actually raising funds for FLN fighters and their families. Chaulet confided in Fanon his role in the work of the FLN and soon found in him a committed comrade. Fanon secretly committed himself to the struggle for national liberation while still the *chef de service* at Blida.

His life and work during this period reveal remarkable courage and personal stamina. He provided clandestine service to wounded FLN fighters at his home while regularly performing his "normal" duties at Blida, here also treating other freedom fighters, broken in torture or yet unapprehended. Some of the Algerian male nurses who worked with Fanon were themselves FLN members or sympathizers. It is said that Si Saddik, a top FLN administrator, was secretly treated by Fanon and hidden in his home until he recovered from severe nervous exhaustion. Simone de Beauvoir who, along with Sartre, had developed a personal friendship with Fanon reported some of his clandestine work with the freedom fighters for a year while still a *chef de service* at Blida. According to de Beauvoir , not only did he harbor guerrillas in his home or hospital, provide them sorely needed medicine, and teach them how to treat their wounded, but also:

> Eight assassination attempts out of ten were failing because the "terrorists," completely terrorized, were either getting discovered straight off or else bungling the actual attack. "This just can't go on." They would have to train the Fidayines. With the consent of the leaders, he took the job on; he taught them to control their reactions when they were setting a bomb or throwing a grenade; and also what psychological and physical attitudes would enable them to resist torture. He would then leave these lessons to attend to a French police commissioner suffering from nervous exhaustion brought on by too many "interrogations." (1965, 593)

As the intensity of the war increased, the rat-hunt for collaborators and sympathizers intruded into the hospital. A number of the staff at Blida were arrested, and some of them were tortured while others disappeared forever. For instance, Dr. Lacaton, who worked for reform in the hospital and wrote with Fanon the article on confession, was arrested on suspicion of collaborating with the liberation movement. The "standard interrogation" of him led nowhere and therefore pushes and punches followed. These too failed to produce a self-incriminating confession or revelation of who else collaborated with the FLN, and the security police then subjected Dr. Lacaton to such "standard torture" as submersion in a bathtub, enemas of soapy water, and electrical shock to the genitals.

The authorities later decided that Dr. Lacaton was neither directly involved with the national liberation movement as suspected nor actively opposed to it as expected of a patriotic Frenchman. He was released, but in a most humiliating manner reserved for "ambiguous personalities." Half-conscious, Dr. Lacaton was taken to the farm of a European settler and dumped in a pigsty.

This placed him in danger of being attacked by pigs and trampled on, itself a most obscene form of torture and execution. Fortunately, the doctor regained consciousness and escaped before the pigs could harm him. After a convalescence, Dr. Lacaton packed up and departed for France (Geismar 1971, 77).

Fanon too constantly ran similar risks or worse. Yet he escaped arrest primarily because he was a "foreigner," neither an Algerian nor a European, and the authorities did not want to have word of their brutal torture leaked to the international community. This leniency was however only relative and quite circumscribed. Still, Fanon's commitment to the welfare of his patients superceded all other considerations. The length to which Fanon took his commitment is shown not only by his clandestine activities while at Blida but also by his bold complaints to authorities. For instance,

> There was an air force base close to the hospital. . . . Sometimes, throughout the night, jet bombers would come in and out of the base making a deafening roar over the wards. Fanon, along with the other doctors, knew that the planes were disturbing the patients' sleep and retarding their recovery; but only Fanon dared to complain . . . to the Chief of Staff of the air force in Algeria then to the Resident Minister's office. (Geismar 1971, 79)

Fanon's request to change the pattern of air flights was complied with for nearly a year. He also complained about the frequent and unexpected intrusion of authorities on the hospital grounds, arresting patients and staff alike. "In 1955, because of Fanon, police were no longer permitted to carry loaded guns when they entered the hospital grounds. If possible they were to complete their business in the guardhouse at the gate of the institution" (Geismar 1971, 80).

These small but significant changes could not of course forestall the tragic and devastating ravages of the war. There continued the brutal violence, the psychiatric casualties of both the freedom fighters and their torturers, both of whom Fanon treated, and the engulfing madness of a society at war. The moment fast approached for a decisive and unambiguous stand. Thus in 1956, Fanon resigned from his post as *chef de service* in Blida-Joinville Hospital. His letter of resignation, showing the integrity and courage of the man, was both a political act and a personal reaffirmation. In response, the Resident Minister ordered Fanon's departure from Algeria in forty-eight hours, or he would face imprisonment.

Following a short stay in France, Fanon moved to the FLN headquarters in Tunis. He served there as an editor and commentator for its most crucial periodical, *El Moudjahid*, and soon established himself as a key spokesman of the Algerian Revolution. He also served as an ambassador of the FLN, enlisting political and material support from sub-Sahara Africa. Still, claims to the contrary notwithstanding, Fanon did not abandon psychiatry for politics. His clinical practice continued in Tunis, initially in the Psychiatric Hospital at Manouba and later in the Charles Nicolle Hospital. So did his work with FLN health centers and his professional writing on psychiatry.

At Manouba, Fanon attempted to introduce the reforms he brought to Blida. But conditions were quite different from those at Blida. For one thing, he ran into conflict with the Tunisian director who was said to have been very touchy about bureaucratic hierarchy and formalities, neither of which was to Fanon's liking. Fanon's attempts to introduce reforms were resisted by the director, first on the grounds of limited budget. The conflict between the two men intensified as Fanon persisted in his reforms. When Fanon won the endorsement of the Tunisian Minister of Health, the director accused Fanon of being a Zionist and a spy of Israel, using as evidence his earlier writings against anti-Semitism and his association with Jewish doctors. The accusations however failed to discredit Fanon even in the charged climate of war and suspicion.

In fact, Fanon's revolutionary and professional credentials were by then well established within the FLN and increasingly recognized both in Tunis and abroad. Local and foreign interns sought to work with him. Once again, his closest professional allies were interns and indigenous nurses. In spite of the resistance to his reforms, Fanon was able to remove from his pavilion locked doors, straitjackets, and closed wards. He also introduced some aspects of milieu therapy. As in Blida, he fully committed himself to patient care and expected the same from his colleagues. Failure to meet these expectations brought harsh rebuke. His use of his own rare commitment and stamina as benchmarks for evaluating others often caused gnawing resentment. His belligerence and his readiness to take offense also made him a difficult person to work with, particularly when competence or commitment was in question. And once again doctors at Manouba, disagreeing with Fanon's views or joining the director's camp, called him "The Nigger" behind his back (Geismar 1971, 138).

Fanon's active commitment to social liberation also entailed a commitment to psychological liberation. In spite of claims to the contrary, he never abandoned psychiatry for politics, nor did he neglect the relations between individual travails and the prevailing social order. It was indeed his ability to connect psychiatry to politics or private troubles to social problems and, having made the connection conceptually, to boldly act that made him a pioneer of radical psychiatry. It was certainly an important step to place the psychiatric institution at Blida and its demoralized patients within the larger colonial milieu. But more decisive was the conclusion that, if therapy aims at restoring integrity of mind and body, then the colonial order undermined that integrity in the first place and did not permit its restoration in the second place.

As he joined in the struggle for a social revolution that it was hoped would give birth to the "new man" and "new society," there still remained the immediate and serious predicament of those incarcerated within the walls of psychiatric institutions and by social exclusion. His work in the psychiatric hospital at Manouba and in the FLN Health Centers—where the anguish of dislocated Algerian refugees was particularly grave—further emphasized the fact that the project for psychological liberation had hardly begun. More and more, the centrality and urgency of liberty for psychiatric patients had become as obvious as it was for the colonized.

And if madness is a pathology of liberty, as it was later defined, then the therapeutic task was primarily one of restoring liberty. Now how did Fanon endeavor to restore liberty for psychiatric patients? And what theoretical formulations guided this endeavor? After his resignation from Blida-Joinville Hospital in 1956 to his death in 1961, Fanon wrote five psychiatric articles in addition to numerous sociopolitical works, most notably *A Dying Colonialism* and *The Wretched of the Earth.* The psychiatric articles, written alone or in collaboration with others, remain untranslated and relatively inaccessible. The neglect of these articles is unfortunate because some of them reveal a further and important evolution of Fanon's psychiatry. These works reveal his fundamental disillusionment with psychiatric hospitalization, his significant departure from Tosquellean approaches, his clear reformulation of madness as the pathology of liberty, and his firm conviction that therapy should, above all, restore freedom to patients. After several years of intensive application of the institutional therapy inspired by Tosquelles, Fanon concluded that therapy is most meaningful and effective within the dialectic of concrete, living society.[1]

The article on agitation was written while Fanon was in Blida, although it was published on the very month he received the letter of expulsion and was forced to leave Algeria (Fanon and Asselah 1957). This article is significant not only because it was written at a critical point in Fanon's psychiatric and political career, but also because, for the first time, we find in it an open critique of Tosquelles and of psychiatric hospitalization. Both critiques were elaborated in the subsequent articles on day hospitalization.

The article on agitation began with a distinction Tosquelles made between agitation of the "expressive type" and agitation of the "percepto-reactive type." Such a distinction implies generally the old *nature* versus *nurture* duality common in psychological conceptions and specifically the *instinct* versus *environment* opposition found in psychoanalytic thought. Fanon in any case argued that Tosquelles's distinction, although heuristically interesting, contained serious doctrinaire problems. In essence, he argued that the distinction was too simplistic, mechanistic, and clinically, not helpful.

In Fanon's view, the notion that one type of agitation is reactive and another nonreactive neglects the fact that agitation, like most other forms of psychopathology, emerges out of reciprocal relations, that it is provoked and maintained in human interaction, and that the sadomasochistic character of institutionalization exacerbates rather than ameliorates agitation. Fanon argued that, except in patients with severe organic defect, agitation is expressive *and* reactive. Since it emerges in reciprocal relations, agitation cannot be understood and effectively treated apart from the human context that initiates, maintains, and exploits it.

Instead of accepting Tosquelles's distinctions, Fanon argued that it is clinically more useful to distinguish agitation that is predominantly motor from predominantly verbal and verbo-motor agitations. In its pure state, according to Fanon, the motor type is most commonly observed among the severely retarded and the senile. Agitation that is predominantly verbal seems to be less neurologically based and more comprehensible, except in the stereotypic, archaic, and incoherent soliloquy of the organically defective. The verbo-motor type, best exemplified by mania, is the most studied because "precisely it restores the base melody of existing man." Thus in his view, agitation reveals a deeper existential and social meaning inasmuch as the human organism becomes comprehensible only by *saying* and *doing* in a temporo-spatial structure. Hence, "agitation is not only an enlargement, a 'psychemotor' cancer. It is also and especially a modality of existence, a type of actualization, an expressive style" (Fanon and Asselah 1957, 24).

Fanon's critique of his former teacher and his proposed alternative typology are interesting. But more substantive however is the dialectic of agitation he expounded from an interpersonal and institutional perspective. This dialectic, he argued, is most blatant in the psychiatric milieu that is supposedly a therapeutic instrument, but is in reality a repressive "second internment" with sadomasochistic aspects. The aggressivity and meanness observed in hospitalized patients are often provoked by this brutal internment. What is more, the internment provokes avoidable agitation and hallucinations.

Already rejected by society, the patient comes or is brought to the institution as a final refuge where at last he could be understood. In reality, according to Fanon, the institution "amputates and punishes" the patient. It rejects, excludes, and isolates him. In so doing, it confirms and legitimizes society's attitudes toward the patient. The rejection, exclusion, and isolation also provoke more psychopathology and a vicious cycle in which the patient remains entrapped is begun. Isolated from real, living relations, the patient is forced into the unreal world of fantasy and hallucination. Rejection of his *symptoms*—provoked in or out of the institution—leads him to infer that what is rejected is his very *being*.

It was Fanon's view that agitation in particular and psychopathology in general test the degree of institutional resistance—its solidity and flexibility. A therapeutic milieu worthy of the name is, on the one hand, *solid* in structure to provide a base for psychologically uprooted patients and, on the other, *flexible* to permit the expression of human problems others could not tolerate. This dual character of solidity and flexibility thus forces us to comprehend and help the patient. Even when not induced by hospitalization, agitation tests the degree of institutional resistance, its solidity and flexibility. To reject the patient, to exclude and isolate him, is to compromise the therapeutic aim and to miss an opportunity for compassionate service.

Society has already rejected the patient, having earlier imposed requirements that are intolerably formal and somewhat monolithic. Yet the psychiatric institution has no organizational plan but to be repressive and punitive: "The lines of force which participate in the erection of the phenomenal field [in the institution] are of a disastrous poverty." The biological and emotional rhythm of the patient is disturbed, arrested, and forced into a second internment. The psychiatric personnel whose responsibility it is to understand and to heal become alarmed with signs of agitation and react in ways that further disrupt the fragile equilibrium of the patient.

Indeed one finds among the psychiatric staff a sadistic tendency as they hasten to subdue, threaten, and retaliate, producing a chain reaction. An attendant comes to the doctor and asserts: "Doctor, this patient has broken everything"; "Doctor, this patient has wounded three personnel"; "Therefore, Doctor, we have to restrain this patient." The straitjacket, the exclusion, and medication are quickly justified by the claim that all is to the interest of the patient. The patient thereby finds himself confronting a punitive doctor and his collaborators: "In effect, it is the service itself which is sadistic, repressive, rigid, non-socialized, with a catastrophic manifestation" (Fanon and Asselah 1957, 22).

The patient already rejected by society finds his or her rejection further confirmed in the institutional milieu. Rejection by the real world and subsequent rejection by the psychiatric personnel foster the need for and the emergence of a pseudoworld with its novel relations and significations. For to isolate the patient is not only to confirm his rejection, but also to produce the metabolic and emotional conditions required for hallucination. In this sense, hallucination and agitation are fundamentally reactions, provoked conditions, and an experience integral to a disturbed social existence. Disillusioned with the repressive and custodial character of psychiatric institutions, Fanon sought an alternative in day hospitalization. This mode of psychiatric management has three basic aims: (a) to reduce the incarcerative character of full hospitalization, (b) to provide psychiatric treatment with greater efficiency, and (c) to keep the patient in close contact with his own community. Historically, the first day hospital started in Moscow in 1932 out of such practical exigencies as a shortage of facilities rather than on theoretical or ideological grounds (Dzhagarov 1944). Within the first four years of its service, this day hospital in Russia cared for 1,225 patients, most of whom were psychotic—a remarkable accomplishment given the dismal failure of traditional hospitalization. Almost independently, other countries subsequently introduced day hospitalization as an alternative to twenty-four-hour, full hospitalization. Such hospitals for severely disturbed patients were established by the 1940s in England, Canada, and the United States.

Day hospitalization is today so common a component of psychiatric care in industrialized countries that it becomes difficult to sufficiently appreciate the significance of adopting it in Tunis during the 1950s. Africa was at the time undergoing a marked sociopolitical upheaval and the colonial powers that had stunted its development were under attack. In countries like Tunisia, in which independence was granted, the colonial powers, having developed a minimum infrastructure, left with the limited technology and expertise they brought, and in some cases vindictively destroyed what few facilities they had established. Tunisia had recently become independent and the national government was in dire economic and political need. It is, in fact, remarkable that its leaders had the will and courage to allow the experiment of day hospitalization—something most African countries have yet to attempt twenty years later.

When in 1958 the first day hospital was introduced in Tunis, partial hospitalization and the "open-door" policy in psychiatric care were largely confined to highly industrialized countries. Day hospitalization burgeoned mostly in the "Anglo-Saxon" countries of Western Europe and North America. A theoretical and methodological question, unanswered at the time, was if in fact day hospitalization could be introduced to treat severely disturbed patients, both chronic and acute, in a less developed country like Tunis. That Fanon and his colleagues provided an affirmative and empirical answer to this question was indeed significant. But more important in our view is the theoretical and moral justification Fanon presented for day hospitalization. Day hospitalization was first introduced elsewhere for varying reasons and exigencies, whereas day hospitalization was inaugurated in Tunis through a distinctly Fanonian perspective. This perspective had far-reaching implications for the conception and treatment of madness. It is unfortunate that Fanon did not live to refine and extend this perspective beyond the notion of day hospitalization.

There are two articles in which the work on day hospitalization in Tunis is discussed (Fanon and Geronimi 1959, 713–32). The first article was by Fanon alone and the second was written in collaboration with Dr. Geronimi, a former intern at Blida and a committed colleague in Tunis. The first article is primarily empirical, showing the impressive results achieved through day hospitalization in an underdeveloped country. The second is mainly theoretical, discussing the values and limits of day hospitalization. The first article is also a telling illustration of how rigorously empirical Fanon pursued problems when time and resources permitted. This point is important because his works that were translated in English do not reflect it and some, like Woddis (1972), have thereby concluded that Fanon was unempirical and a man given to wild speculation. In the first article, Fanon reviewed the history and principles of the "open door" policy for psychiatric care. Traditional hospitalization removed the patient from his social milieu and hence his conflictual and necessary milieu. The institution promised to offer a "protective shield" to the patient from society, to the society from the patient, and to the patient from himself. But this proved to be a false protection in all three respects. Hospitalization became, in effect, a brutal internment characterized by repression, lethargy, and depersonalization. Day hospitalization was started in Tunis with the goals, first, of early diagnosis as well as early treatment and, second, of keeping the patient in maximal contact with his exterior social milieu. Fanon pointed out that at the time they started day hospitalization in Tunis, there existed "at most twenty day hospitals in the world," all in highly industrialized countries, and "never an experience of day hospital was attempted in an underdeveloped country" (Fanon and Geronimi, 1959, 690). In reality, the total number of day hospitals then is subject to debate, but it is clear that Fanon was unaware of the interesting and pioneering work of Dr. Lambo in Nigeria.[2] Nonetheless, the questions Fanon posed were pertinent. From a methodological standpoint, can day hospitalization be viable and effective in an underdeveloped country like Tunis? From a doctrinal standpoint, can this type of service meet *all* the psychiatric demands of such a country? Day hospital service in Tunis was started as a component of Charles Nicolle Hospital, a general hospital that had had a neuropsychiatric unit for more than forty years. It had a different policy for admission than traditional asylums, but it relied on the same rigid, repressive, and punitive measures. Like asylums of the worst type, it used straitjackets, cells, bars, closed doors, and the other ugly tools of large establishments. The Tunisian government wanted to expand its psychiatric facilities, but the futility of building the same old structures became obvious. A plan for a day hospital was therefore considered and eventually implemented within the Charles Nicolle Hospital. It was agreed that the new day hospital remain of small capacity so that its "therapeutic efficacy could be rationally studied and augmented." How the plan was implemented and the role given to patients are themselves noteworthy. The Ministry of Health having boldly endorsed the plan, a team of patients was put to work to demolish the prison-like cells. The bars, the straitjackets, the handcuffs, and all the instruments of incarceration and repression were removed. The building was renovated and refurbished. The new center was limited to eighty beds: forty men and forty women. Six small beds were, in addition, reserved for children in the women's section. The old staff who, accustomed to the sadomasochistic relations of the old institution, looked at the patient not as "the most important part of the service" but rather as the veritable "enemies of the personnel's tranquility," was transferred. A new, better educated staff was employed and rigorously trained, with high premium placed on competence and a "welcoming attitude" toward patients. Each member was in charge of no more than six to eight patients with whom he or she worked every day and throughout the period of their hospitalization. The quality and efficiency of communication between patients and personnel, between relatives and personnel, and between staff and doctors in charge were particularly emphasized. There was regular psychological and medical surveillance. Patients' dreams, anxieties, relations with family members, sleeping habits, and behavior in the center were carefully recorded. New crises or relapses were immediately attended to and monitored.

Alone or accompanied by relatives, patients arrived at the Neuropsychiatric Day Center at 7:00 A.M. and stayed there until 5:30 P.M.

The center closed its doors by 6:00, when all the patients left for home. Except on Sundays, the center provided daily services. On arrival in the center, each patient was received by the assigned staff member who, after breakfast was served, reviewed the patient's medical and psychological regimen. Therapeutic activities were carefully planned for maximal effect and tailored to the needs of each patient. These included psychotherapy, sleep and relaxation therapy, insulin therapy, electroshock therapy, and chemotherapy. Some of these techniques are today considered archaic and even brutal. That Fanon used them shows how much he was rooted in his own time, even as he endeavored to question and transcend it.

Of particular interest is the form of psychotherapy Fanon employed. His approach to psychotherapeutic technique was what today may be called "eclectic." He employed psychoanalytic psychotherapy, behavioral therapy, and existentialist-oriented psychotherapy. In particular, Fanon adopted Sandro Ferenczi's psychoanalytic techniques in which the therapist takes an *active* and *involved* role in therapy.[3] The behavioral techniques he utilized were based on the Pavlovian theory òf Second Signal System.[4] Along with individual and group therapy, he used sociodrama for which the content, significantly, was *biographical* rather than *fictional*. Patients were encouraged to recount their personal experiences to the group who, in turn, gave their opinion, criticism, support, and the opportunity for feedback as in "identification through mirror." Each patient was encouraged to confront himself and others through verbalization, explication, and taking a stand. But attacking a patient's *conscience* or *being* was at all times avoided. Patients did not pay the doctor—a fact that was carefully taken into account because it modified the quality of transference and countertransference. A major portion of Fanon's article empirically describes the demographic and diagnostic characteristics of the patients seen during the first eighteen months of the center's existence. Data for 1958 and 1959 are compared and contrasted, and some changes and remarkable accomplishments are shown for that period. During the last seven months of 1958, 345 patients were admitted to the center. The volume of admissions almost doubled in the next eleven months, to a total of 670 patients. Thus, during the eighteen months considered, over 1,000 patients were admitted of whom fewer than 0.88 percent required full hospitalization. In twenty months, more than 1,200 were admitted and treated with the average duration of stay shortened to twenty-five days. No suicide, homicide, or violence of medico-legal import occurred during this period. This level of efficiency and efficacy is particularly remarkable when one considers that during the first year there was only one *chef de service·* who, in the absence of interns, "assumed all therapeutic" needs of the eighty patients. We are not informed who that clinical director was, although one suspects it may have been Fanon himself. In a footnote to the second article on day hospitalization, written in collaboration with Dr. Geronimi, another intriguing point is made, that one of the two doctors had started the first day hospital in Algeria. If in fact it was Fanon who started the first day hospital in Algeria, more research is needed on his work at Blida.

The impressive results of the first article are actually exceeded by the poignant theoretical and humanistic articulations of the second article. The latter focuses on considerations of doctrine and the values and limits of day hospitalization. Fanon and Geronimi pointed out that two characteristics distinguish their neuropsychiatric day center from other psychiatric establishments in Tunis: First was its attachment to a general hospital and second its "formula of hospitalization." Given the social stigma and isolation of traditional asylums, the authors emphasized the need for integrating psychiatric care in the professional and material infrastructure of a general hospital. Such an integration makes possible effective utilization of the services of internists, radiologists, surgeons, and others who can immensely contribute to patient care. It can also rehabilitate the psychiatrist in the eyes of his colleagues, since his isolation in closed asylums confers on him a "mysterious and, taken together, disquieting" character. But most of all, in the eyes of the patient, the psychiatrist becomes a doctor among other doctors and the mental patient comes to be viewed only as a "sick person" like other sick persons.

More fundamental than their endorsement of the medical model is the theoretical and moral justification they offer for day hospitalization. They argue that day hospitalization breaks away from the brutal practice of coercion as well as confinement and most of all that it aims to restore the *freedom* of the patient. The liberty day hospitalization confers is, they regretfully admit, never real and complete. For it is indeed relative and limited. What is more, there is often the temptation of doctors to oppose the exit of an obviously very ill patient who would rather have his freedom than be hospitalized. The doctors in the center sometimes succumbed to this temptation, but very rarely.

The authors nonetheless emphasized that their experience amply demonstrates that partial hospitalization that permits patients to go to their homes and immerse themselves in their world of relations is more acceptable to them and therapeutically more effective. Day hospitalization, they pointed out, minimizes the dialectic of the *master-slave* or *prisoner-jailer* relationship that characterizes traditional approaches. The sadomasochistic relations engendered by confinement and isolation are also attenuated. The doctor-patient relationship regains a "sense of normalcy." Their encounter becomes more and more the meeting of "two free people [which] is necessary in all therapy, and more so in psychiatry " (Fanon and Geronimi 1959, 717). The patient comes without coercion, he also leaves without feeling an unrealistic gratitude to a doctor who allowed it. Confinement disarms the patient, forces him to give himself up completely; it is a battle between unequals, a submission to the doctor's every whim. "Day hospitalization, on the other hand, offers a passive support, a momentary freedom, a reinforcement of the personality, like a prolonged and therapeutic visit" (Fanon and Geronimi 1959, 715).

Basic to the doctrine enunciated is a particular conception of psychopathology, a firm commitment to the being of the patient, and a therapeutic approach aiming to restore freedom in the very society in which it was lost. Madness comes to be defined as a pathology of liberty. The patient's liberty is constantly undermined psychologically—by anxieties, obsessions, inhibitions, contradictions—and socially—by victimization, rejection, coercion, and confinement. Denied his right of liberty by forces within and without, the patient is condemned to exercise his liberty in the unreal world of phantoms.

Traditional psychiatry simply reinforces and legitimizes this brutal reality even as it ostensibly claims to have the interest of the patient at heart. It is from this perspective that one can appreciate "the attitude of revolt" against hospitalization found among patients who are least disorganized—those who still retain a measure of an *active self* and have not yet renounced their *world of relations*. Although day hospitalization is accepted by such patients, those who have an inactive self and have renounced life in the real world prefer complete hospitalization. These are the ones who have totally succumbed to the pathology of liberty. The therapist must understand and reinforce this attitude of revolt as he combats this tendency to surrender liberty.

Fanon and Geronimi emphasized that the real context for sociotherapy is the dynamic and living society itself. No genuine healing or restoration of liberty can be effected apart from it. In fact, their disillusionment with the institutional therapy that Tosquelles pioneered is clear, although they concede its advantages in large and dehumanizing asylums. They pointed out that in such establishments the "neo-society" of institutional therapy was an important advance because it counteracted the regressive tendencies of patients as it offered them a modicum of social contact and tasks in the closed asylum. It also helped the therapists to understand what could have "happened outside," while fruitfully studying mechanisms like identification, projection, and instinctual inhibition. But then comes their incisive critique.

It must always be remembered that with institutional therapy we create frozen institutions, strict and rigid rules, schemes which rapidly become stereotypical. In the neo-society, there is no invention, no creative dynamism, no newness. There seem to be no veritable dislocation, no crises. The institution remains that "cadaveric foundation" of which Mauss speaks. . . . [Moreover]

the inert character of the pseudo-society, its strict spatial limitation, the restricted number of movements and, why hide it, the
actual experience of confinement-imprisonment, considerably
limit the curative and rehabilitative value of its sociotherapy.
(Fanon and Geronimi 1959, 719–21)

That is why we believe today that the true milieu for sociotherapy
is concrete society itself.

Day hospitalization keeps the patient in the social and familial
milieu out of which his problems arose and in which he must take
his rightful place. The therapist every day confronts a living
person having active relations with the living world: This patient
has not "cut antenna," so to speak. At night and whenever the
patient chooses, he returns to his family and friends. On his way to
and from the center, he rides the bus or train with others whom he
knows in his neighborhood and place of work. One took special
care to avoid disengagement of others from the patient and of the
patient from others. At all times, his world of relations retains its
reality and density. The therapist therefore faced, on the one hand,
a personality in crisis at the very heart of its environment and, on
the other, a real, dynamic, and active society in the very heart of
the patient. It is from this perspective that one clearly observes the
rupture in the "synthetic unity" of the person to his milieu and
seeks to restore that unity. Symptoms and troubled affectivity are
no longer abstracted or isolated from their source. They are offered
dialectically and the therapist thinks and acts dialectically. One is
forced to abandon the symbolic and imaginary games of institutional therapy and becomes immersed in society itself, not its caricature. This orientation to a dynamic and living reality forces a
rethinking of conceptions and techniques. The reification of
descriptive semiology and nosology gives way to an existential
approach that takes into account the activities, assaults, and vulnerabilities of the self in a dynamic social milieu. It is in this psy-
chosocial dialectic that the therapist decides the time, place, and
type of his intervention. At the center, the patient is provided his
own space, his privacy is respected, and no demand is made upon

his liberty or immediate appearance. He wears and brings what he wants. What is questioned is not "the form of his being," but rather "the form of his existence."

Fanon and Geronimi concluded that day hospitalization is inappropriate in cases in which "the organic participation in the illness" is massive and dominant, therefore requiring constant medical surveillance. However, they added that even for such cases, thanks to chemotherapy, the period of complete hospitalization could be reduced, and early transfer to day hospitalization becomes possible. The other categories they thought inappropriate for day hospitalization are patients who present clear danger to others or to themselves and of course those in police custody. They further emphasized that each center be small and "avoid at all cost the creation of those monsters which are classical psychiatric hospitals." Significantly, they urged stronger legislation for patients' rights and appropriate consideration to those who live in distant or rural areas. Their last sentence is most noteworthy: "In summary, a very strict legislation should be established, guaranteeing to the maximum the liberty of the patient in getting rid of every incarcerative and coercive aspect of internment" (Fanon,1967b, 53–55).

This was Fanon's psychiatry until his death at the age of thirty-six. The noble project of restoring liberty to captives of colonialism and of the psychiatric establishment had only begun when he died. There have been some advances made here and there, but that project still awaits realization. Liberty continues to elude the majority—whether colonized or neocolonized, incarcerated or overdrugged. A small elite, sham and corrupt, has usurped what many have fought, bled, and dreamed for in those colonies that Europe underdeveloped to develop itself. The mental health profession too has betrayed its declared goals of prevention and healing once it joined in the rampage for profit, power, and control. It caters willingly to those who can afford it, at the same time neglecting or abusing those victims for whom hope of liberty remains frustrated.

Fanon presents an alternative for those who desire that the tool never possess the man and that enslavement cease, if not forever, at least in their own personal and professional life. The letter of resignation he wrote while in Blida is a moving and principled document rare in psychological literature. It summarizes the revolutionary and humanistic thrust of his psychiatry.

> If psychiatry is the medical technique that aims to enable man no longer to be a stranger to his environment, I owe it to myself to affirm that the [colonized and, we may add, the patient], permanently an alien in his own country, lives in a state of absolute depersonalization. . . . The function of a social structure is to set up institutions to serve man's needs. A society that drives its members to desperate solutions is a non-viable society, a society to be replaced.
>
> It is the duty of the citizen to say this. No professional morality, no class solidarity, no desire to wash the family linen in private, can have a prior claim. No pseudo-national mystification can prevail against the requirement of reason. (Fanon 1967c, 53–54)

NOTES

1. Earlier writers, including Gendzier (1973), have strangely ignored Fanon's critique of Tosquelles. This article and others show that, contrary to Gendzier, in particular, Fanon departed significantly from Tosquellean theory and practice.

2. T. A. Lambo (1956) started an innovative day hospital at Aro Hospital in Nigeria.

3. Sandor Ferenczi, a Hungarian psychoanalyst and a close disciple of Freud, is best known for his innovations in therapeutic technique. He emphasized the need for shortening therapy through greater *activity* and *involvement* on the part of other analysts of his time, including Freud, but that was later gradually assimilated in psychoanalysis. For details, see Paul Roazen (1974, pp. 363–71).

4. Ivan Pavlov had used mainly dogs, later monkeys and gorillas, for his pioneering work on conditioning. But as his interest shifted to human neurophysiology, he postulated the Theory of Second Signal System to take into account the human capacity for language and complex associations as in speech and writing.

II. Cultural Criticism

6.

Remembering Fanon: Self, Psyche, and the Colonial Condition*

Homi Bhabha

O my body, make of me always a man who questions!

Fanon

In the popular memory of English socialism the mention of Frantz Fanon stirs a dim, deceiving echo. *Black Skin, White Masks, The Wretched of the Earth, Toward the African Revolution*—these memorable titles reverberate in the self-righteous rhetoric of "resistance" whenever the English Left gathers, in its narrow church or its Trotskyist camps, to deplore the immiseration of the colonized world. Repeatedly used as the idioms of simple moral outrage, Fanon's titles emptily echo a political spirit that is far from his own; they sound the troubled conscience of a socialist vision that extends, in the main,

*Thanks to Stephen Feuchtwang for shepherding these ideas; Stuart Hall for discussing them; A. Sivanandan and Hazel Walters for their archival assistance at the Institute of Race Relations; Pete Ayrton for his patience; and Jackie Bhabha for the engaged combat of comrades.

Originally published as the introduction to *Black Skin, White Masks* (London: Pluto Press, 1986). Reprinted with permission.

179

from an ethnocentric little Englandism to a large trade union internationalism. When that laborist line of vision is challenged by the
"autonomous" struggles of the politics of race and gender, or threatened by problems of human psychology or cultural representation, it
can only make an empty gesture of solidarity. Whenever questions of
race and sexuality make their own organizational and theoretical
demands on the primacy of "class," "state," and "party," the language of traditional socialism is quick to describe those urgent,
"other" questions as symptoms of petty bourgeois deviation, signs of
the bad faith of socialist intellectuals. The ritual respect accorded to
the name of Fanon, the currency of his titles in the common language
of liberation, are part of the ceremony of a polite, English refusal.

There has been no substantial work on Fanon in the history of
the *New Left Review*; one piece in the *New Statesman*; one essay in
Marxism Today; one article in *Socialist Register*; one short book by an
English author. Of late, the memory of Fanon has been kept alive
in the activist traditions of *Race and Class*, by A. Sivanandan's stir-
ring indictments of state racism. Edward Said, himself a scholar
engagé, has richly recalled the work of Fanon in his important T. S.
Eliot memorial lectures, *Culture and Imperialism*. And finally,
Stephan Feuchtwang's fine, far-reaching essay, "Fanon's Politics of
Culture" (*Economy and Society*) examines Fanon's concept of culture with its innovatory insights for a nondeterministic political
organization of the psyche. Apart from these exceptions, in Britain
today Fanon's ideas are effectively "out of print."

Memories of Fanon tend to the mythical. He is either revered
as the prophetic spirit of Third World liberation or reviled as an
exterminating angel, the inspiration to violence in the Black Power
movement. Despite his historic participation in the Algerian revolution and the influence of his ideas on the race politics of the
1960s and 1970s, Fanon's work will not be possessed by one political moment or movement, nor can it be easily placed in a seamless
narrative of liberationist history. Fanon refuses to be so completely
claimed by events or eventualities. It is the sustaining irony of his
work that his severe commitment to the political task in hand,
never restricted the restless, inquiring movement of his thought.

It is not for the finitude of philosophical thinking nor for the finality of a political direction that we turn to Fanon. Heir to the ingenuity and artistry of Toussaint and Senghor, as well as the iconoclasm of Nietzsche, Freud, and Sartre, Fanon is the purveyor of the transgressive and transitional truth. He may yearn for the total transformation of Man and Society, but he speaks most effectively from the uncertain interstices of historical change: from the area of ambivalence between race and sexuality; out of an unresolved contradiction between culture and class; from deep within the struggle of psychic representation and social reality.

To read Fanon is to experience the sense of division that prefigures—and fissures—the emergence of a truly radical thought that never dawns without casting an uncertain dark. His voice is most clearly heard in the subversive turn of a familiar term, in the silence of a sudden rupture: *"The Negro is not. Anymore than the white man."* The awkward division that breaks his line of thought keeps alive the dramatic and enigmatic sense of the process of change. That familiar alignment of colonial subjects— Black/White, Self/Other—is disturbed with one brief pause and the traditional grounds of racial identity are dispersed, whenever they are found to rest in the narcissistic myths of négritude or white cultural supremacy. It is this palpable pressure of division and displacement that pushes Fanon's writing to the edge of things: the cutting edge that reveals no ultimate radiance but, in his words, "exposes an utterly naked declivity where an authentic upheaval can be born" (1967a, 218).

The psychiatric hospital at Blida-Joinville is one such place where, in the divided world of French Algeria, Fanon discovered the impossibility of his mission as a colonial psychiatrist:

> If psychiatry is the medical technique that aims to enable man no longer to be a stranger to his environment, I owe it to myself to affirm that the Arab, permanently an alien in his own country, lives in a state of absolute depersonalization . . . The social structure existing in Algeria was hostile to any attempt to put the individual back where he belonged. (1967b, 63)

The extremity of this colonial alienation of the person—this end of the "idea" of the individual—produces a restless urgency in Fanon's search for a conceptual form appropriate to the social antagonism of the colonial relation. The body of his work splits between a Hegelian-Marxist dialectic, a phenomenological affirmation of Self and Other, and the psychoanalytic ambivalence of the Unconscious, its turning from love to hate, mastery to servitude. In his desperate, doomed search for a dialectic of deliverance Fanon explores the edge of these modes for thought: His Hegelianism restores hope to history; his existentialist evocation of the "I" restores the presence of the marginalized; and his psychoanalytic framework illuminates the "madness" of racism, the pleasure of pain, the agonistic fantasy of political power.

As Fanon attempts such audacious, often impossible, transformations of truth and value, the jagged testimony of colonial dislocation, its displacement of time and person, its defilement of culture and territory, refuses the ambition of any "total" theory of colonial oppression. The Antillean *evolué* cut to the quick by the glancing look of a frightened, confused, white child; the stereotype of the native fixed at the shifting boundaries between barbarism and civility; the insatiable fear and desire for the Negro: "Our women are at the mercy of Negroes. . . . God knows how they make love" (Fanon 1967a, 157–58); the deep cultural fear of the black figured in the psychic trembling of Western sexuality—it is these signs and symptoms of the colonial condition that drive Fanon from one conceptual scheme to another, while the colonial relation takes shape in the gaps between them, articulated in the intrepid engagements of his style. As Fanon's text unfolds, the "scientific" fact comes to be aggressed by the experience of the street; sociological observations are intercut with literary artifacts, and the poetry of liberation is brought up short against the leaden, deadening prose of the colonized world.

What is this distinctive force of Fanon's vision that has been forming even as I write about the division, the displacement, the cutting edge of his thought? It comes, I believe, from the tradition of the oppressed, as Walter Benjamin suggests; it is the language of a revolutionary awareness that "the state of emergency in which we live is not the exception but the rule. We must attain to a concept of history that is in keeping with this insight" (Benjamin 1968, 257). And the state of emergency is also always a state of *emergence*. The struggle against colonial oppression changes not only the direction of Western history, but challenges its historicist "idea" of time as a progressive, ordered whole. The analysis of colonial depersonalization alienates not only the Enlightenment idea of "man," but challenges the transparency of social reality, as a pre-given image of human knowledge. If the order of Western historicism is disturbed in the colonial state of emergency, even more deeply disturbed is the social and psychic representation of the human subject. For the very nature of humanity becomes estranged in the colonial condition and from that "naked declivity" it emerges, not as an assertion of will nor as an evocation of freedom, but as an enigmatic questioning. With a question that echoes Freud's *what does woman want?* Fanon turns to confront the colonized world. "What does a man want?" he asks, in the introduction to *Black Skin, White Masks,* "What does the black man want?"

To this loaded question where cultural alienation bears down on the ambivalence of psychic identification, Fanon responds with an agonizing performance of self-images:

> I had to meet the white man's eyes. An unfamiliar weight burdened me. In the white world the man of colour encounters difficulties in the development of his bodily scheme. . . . I was battered down by tom-toms, cannibalism, intellectual deficiency, fetishism, racial defects. . . . I took myself far off from my own presence. . . . What else could it be for me but an amputation, an excision, a hemorrhage that spattered my whole body with black blood? (1967a, 110–12)

From within the metaphor of vision complicit with a Western metaphysic of Man emerges the displacement of the colonial relation. The black presence ruins the representative narrative of

Western personhood: Its past tethered to treacherous stereotypes of primitivism and degeneracy will not produce a history of civil progress, a space for the Socius; its present, dismembered and dislocated, will not contain the image of identity that is questioned in the dialectic of mind/body and resolved in the epistemology of "appearance and reality." The white man's eyes break up the black man's body and in that act of epistemic violence its own frame of reference is transgressed, its field of vision disturbed.

"What does the black man *want*" Fanon insists and in privileging the psychic dimension he changes not only what we understand by a *political* demand but transforms the very means by which we recognize and identify its *human agency*. Fanon is not principally posing the question of political oppression as the violation of a human essence, although he lapses into such a lament in his more existential moment. He is not raising the question of colonial man in the universalist terms of the liberal-humanist ("How does colonialism deny the Rights of Man?"); nor is he posing an ontological question about Man's being ("*Who* is the alienated colonial man?"). Fanon's question is not addressed to such a unified notion of history nor such a unitary concept of Man. It is one of the original and disturbing qualities of *Black Skin, White Masks* that it rarely historicizes the colonial experience. There is no master narrative or realist perspective that provides a background of social and historical facts against which emerge the problems of the individual or collective psyche. Such a traditional sociological alignment of Self and Society or History and Psyche is rendered questionable in Fanon's identification of the colonial subject who is historicized as it comes to be heterogeneously inscribed in the texts of history, literature, science, myth. The colonial subject is always "overdetermined from without," Fanon writes. It is through image and fantasy—those orders that figure transgressively on the borders of history and the unconscious—that Fanon most profoundly evokes the colonial condition.

In articulating the problem of colonial cultural alienation in the psychoanalytic language of demand and desire, Fanon radically questions the formation of both individual and social authority as they come to be developed in the discourse of Social Sovereignty. The social virtues of historical rationality, cultural cohesion, and the autonomy of individual consciousness assume an immediate, utopian identity with the subjects upon whom they confer a civil status. The civil state is the ultimate expression of the innate ethical and rational bent of the human mind; the social instinct is the progressive destiny of human nature, the necessary transition from nature to culture. The direct access from individual interests to social authority is objectified in the representative structure of a General Will—law or culture—where psyche and society mirror each other, transparently translating their difference, without loss, into a historical totality. Forms of social and psychic alienation and aggression—madness, self-hate, treason, violence—can never be acknowledged as determinate and constitutive conditions of civil authority, or as the ambivalent effects of the social instinct itself. They are always explained away as alien presences, occlusions of historical progress, the ultimate misrecognition of Man.

For Fanon such a myth of Man and Society is fundamentally undermined in the colonial situation where everyday life exhibits a "constellation of delirium" that mediates the normal social relations of its subjects. "The Negro enslaved by his inferiority, the white man enslaved by his superiority alike behave in accordance with a neurotic orientation." Fanon's demand for a psychoanalytic explanation emerges from the perverse reflections of "civil virtue" in the alienating acts of colonial governance: the visibility of cultural mummification" in the colonizer's avowed ambition to civilize or modernize the native which results in "archaic inert institutions [that function] under the oppressor's supervision like a caricature of formerly fertile institutions"; or the validity of violence in the very definition of the colonial social space; or the viability of the febrile, phantasmatic images of racial hatred that come to be absorbed and acted out in the wisdom of the West. These interpositions, indeed collaborations of political and psychic violence *within* civic virtue, alienation within identity, drive Fanon to describe the splitting of the colonial space of consciousness and society as marked by a "Manichean delirium."

The representative figure of such a perversion, I want to suggest, is the image of post-Enlightenment man tethered to, *not* confronted by, his dark reflection, the shadow of colonized man, that splits his presence, distorts his outline, breaches his boundaries, repeats his action at a distance, disturbs and divides the very time of his being. This ambivalent identification of the racist world—moving on two planes without being in the least embarrassed by it, as Sartre says of the anti-Semitic consciousness—turns on the idea of Man as his alienated image, not Self and Other but the "Otherness" of the Self inscribed in the perverse palimpsest of colonial identity. And it is that bizarre figure of desire, which splits along the axis on which it turns, that compels Fanon to put the psychoanalytic question of the desire of the subject to the historic condition of colonial man.

"What is often called the black soul is a white man's artifact," (1967a, 10), Fanon writes. This transference, I've argued, speaks otherwise. It reveals the deep psychic uncertainty of the colonial relation itself; its split representations stage that division of "body" and "soul" which enacts the artifice of "identity"; a division which cuts across the fragile skin—black and white—of individual and social authority. What emerges from the figurative language I have used to make such an argument are three conditions that underlie an understanding of the *process of identification* in the analytic of desire.

First, to exist is to be called into being in relation to an Otherness, its look or locus. It is a demand that reaches outward to an external object and as J. Rose (1981) writes, "it is the relation of this demand to the place of the object it claims that becomes the basis for identification." This process is visible in that exchange of looks between native and settler that structures their psychic relation in the paranoid fantasy of boundless possession and its familiar language of reversal: "when their glances meet he [the settler] ascertains bitterly, always on the defensive, 'They want to take our place.' It is true for there is no native who does not dream at least once a day of setting himself up in the settler's place" (1968, 39). It is always in relation to the place of the Other that colonial desire is articulated: that is, in part, the phantasmatic space of possession that no one subject can singly occupy which permits the dream of the inversion of roles.

Second: the very place of identification, caught in the tension of demand and desire, is a space of splitting. The fantasy of the native is precisely to occupy the master's place while keeping his place in the slave's *avenging* anger. "Black skins, white masks" is not, for example, a neat division; it is a doubling, dissembling image of being in at least two places at once which makes it impossible for the devalued, insatiable evolué (an abandonment neurotic, Fanon claims) to accept the colonizer's invitation to identity: "You're a doctor, a writer, a student, you're *different*, you're one of *us*." It is precisely in that ambivalent use of "different"—to be different from those that are different makes you the same—that the Unconscious speaks of the form of Otherness, the tethered shadow of deferral and displacement. It is not the Colonialist Self or the Colonized Other, but the disturbing distance in between that constitutes the figure of colonial otherness—the white man's artifice inscribed on the black man's body. It is in relation to this impossible object that emerges the liminal problem of colonial identity and its vicissitudes.

Finally, as has already been disclosed by the rhetorical figures of my account of desire and Otherness, the question of identification is never the affirmation of a pre-given identity, never a self-fulfilling prophecy—it is always the production of an "image" of identity and the transformation of the subject in assuming that image. The demand of identification—that is, to be *for* an Other—entails the representation of the subject in the differentiating order of Otherness. Identification, as we inferred from the illustrations above, is always the return of an image of identity which bears the mark of splitting in that "Other" place from which it comes. For Fanon, like Lacan, the primary moments of such a repetition of the self lie in the desire of the look and the limits of language. The "atmosphere of certain uncertainty" that surrounds the body certifies its existence and threatens its dismemberment.

Look a Negro. . . . Mama, see the Negro! I'm frightened. . . . I could
no longer laugh, because I already know there were legends, stories, history and above all historicity. . . . Then assailed at various
points, the corporal schema crumbled its place taken by a racial
epidermal schema. . . . It was no longer a question of being aware
of my body in the third person but in a triple person. . . . I was
responsible for my body, for my race, for my ancestors. (1967a, 112)

In reading *Black Skin, White Masks* it is crucial to respect the difference between "personal identity" as an intimation of reality, or an
intuition of being, and the psychoanalytic problem of identification
that, in a sense, always begs the question of the subject—"What
does a man want?" The emergence of the human subject as socially
and psychically authenticated depends upon the negation of an
originary narrative of fulfillment or an imaginary coincidence
between individual interest or instinct and the General Will. Such
binary, two-part identities function in a kind of narcissistic reflection of the One in the Other which is confronted in the language of
desire by the psychoanalytic process of identification. For identification, identity is never an a priori, nor a finished product; it is only
ever the problematic process of access to an "image" of totality. The
discursive conditions of this psychic image of identification will be
clarified if we think of the perilous perspective of the concept of the
image itself. For the image—as point of identification—marks the
site of an ambivalence. Its representation is always spatially split—
it makes *present* something that is *absent*—and temporally
deferred—it is the representation of a time that is always elsewhere, a repetition. The image is only ever an *appurtenance* to
authority and identity; it must never be read mimetically as the
"appearance" of a "reality." The access to the image of identity is
only ever possible in the *negation* of any sense of originality or plen-
itude, through the principle of displacement—and differentiation
(absence/presence; representation/repetition) that always renders
it a liminal reality. The image is at once a metaphoric substitution,
an illusion of presence and by that same token a metonym, a sign
of its absence and loss. It is precisely from this edge of meaning and

being, from this shifting boundary of otherness within identity, that Fanon asks: "What does a *black* man want?"

> When it encounters resistance from the other, self-consciousness undergoes the experience of desire. . . . As soon as I desire I ask to be considered. I am not merely here and now, sealed into thingness. I am for somewhere else and for something else. I demand that notice be taken of my negating activity in so far as I pursue something other than life. . . . I occupied space. I moved toward the other . . . and the evanescent other, hostile but not opaque, transparent, not there, disappeared. Nausea. (1967a, 112)

From that overwhelming emptiness of nausea Fanon makes his answer: the black man wants the objectifying confrontation with otherness; in the colonial psyche there is an unconscious disavowal of the negating, splitting moment of desire. The place of the Other must not be imaged as Fanon sometimes suggests as a fixed phenomenological point, opposed to the self, that represents a culturally alien consciousness. The Other must be seen as the necessary negation of a primordial identity—cultural or psychic—that introduces the system of differentiation which enables the "cultural" to be signified as a linguistic, symbolic, historic reality. If, as I have suggested, the subject of desire is never simply a Myself, then the Other is never simply an *It-self*, a font of identity, truth, or misrecognition.

As a principle of identification, the Other bestows a degree of objectivity but its representation—be it the social process of the law or the psychic process of the Oedipus—is always ambivalent, disclosing a lack. For instance, the common, conversational distinction between "the letter and spirit" of the law displays the otherness of law itself; the ambiguous grey area between "justice" and judicial procedure is, quite literally, a conflict of judgment. In the language of psychoanalysis, the Law of the Father or the paternal metaphor, again, cannot be taken at its word. It is a process of substitution and exchange that inscribes a normative, normalizing place for the subject; but that metaphoric access to identity is exactly the place of prohibition and repression, precisely a conflict of authority. Identification, as it is spoken in the *desire of the Other*, is always a question of interpretation for it is the elusive assignation of myself with a one-self, the elision of person and place.

If the differentiating force of the Other is the process of the subject's signification in language and society's objectification in law, then how can the Other disappear? Can desire, the moving spirit of the subject ever, evanesce?

In his more analytic mode Fanon can impede the exploration of these ambivalent, uncertain questions of colonial desire. The state of emergency from which he writes demands more insurgent answers, more immediate identifications. At times Fanon attempts too close a correspondence between the *mise-en-scène* of unconscious fantasy and the phantoms of racist fear and hate that stalk the colonial scene; he turns too hastily from the ambivalences of identification to the antagonistic identities of political alienation and cultural discrimination; he is too quick to name the Other, to personalize its presence in the language of colonial racism—"the real Other for the white man is and will continue to be the black man. And conversely" (1967a, 161 n. 25). These attempts, in Fanon's words, to restore the dream to its proper political time and cultural space, at times, blunt the edge of Fanon's brilliant illustrations of the complexity of psychic projections in the pathological colonial relation. Jean Veneuse, the Antillean evolué, desires not merely to be in the place of the white man but compulsively seeks to look back and down on himself from that position. The white man does not merely deny what he fears and desires by projecting it on "them"; Fanon sometimes forgets that paranoia never preserves its position of power for the compulsive identification with a persecutory "they" is always an evacuation and emptying of the "I."

Fanon's sociodiagnostic psychiatry tends to explain away the ambivalent turns and returns of the subject of colonial desire, its masquerade of Western Man and the "long" historical perspective. It is as if Fanon is fearful of his most radical insights: that the space of the body and its identification is a representational reality; that the politics of race will not be entirely contained within the humanist myth of man or economic necessity or historical progress, for its psychic affects questions such forms of determinism; that social sovereignity and human subjectivity are only realizable in the order of Otherness. It is as if the question of desire that emerged from the traumatic tradition of the oppressed has to be denied, at the end of *Black Skin, White Masks*, to make way for an existentialist humanism that is as banal as it is beatific:

> Why not the quite simple attempt to touch the other to feel the other, to explain the other to myself? . . . At the conclusion of this study, I want the world to recognize, with me, the open door of every consciousness. (1967a, 231–32)

Such a deep hunger for humanism, despite Fanon's insight into the dark side of Man, must be an overcompensation for the closed consciousness or "dual narcissism" to which he attributes the depersonalization of colonial man: "There one lies body to body, with one's blackness or one's whiteness in full narcissistic cry, each sealed into his own particularity—with, it is true, now and then a flash or so." It is this flash of "recognition"—in its Hegelian sense with its transcendental, sublative spirit—that fails to ignite in the colonial relation where there is only narcissistic indifference: "And yet the Negro knows there is a difference. He wants it . . . The former slave needs a challenge to his humanity" (1967a, 231). In the absence of such a challenge, Fanon argues, the colonized can only imitate, never identify, a distinction nicely made by the psychoanalyst Annie Reich: "It is imitation when the child holds the newspaper like his father. It is identification when the child learns to read." In disavowing the culturally differentiated condition of the colonial world—in demanding *"Turn White or disappear"*—the colonizer is himself caught in the ambivalence of paranoiac identification, alternating between fantasies of megalomania and persecution.

However Fanon's Hegelian dream for a human reality *in itself-for itself* is ironized, even mocked, by his view of the Manichean structure of colonial consciousness and its nondialectical division. What he says in *The Wretched of the Earth* of the demography of the colonial city reflects his view of the psychic structure of the colonial relation. The native and settler zones, like the juxtaposition of black and white bodies, are opposed, but not in the service of "a higher unity." No conciliation is possible, he concludes, for of the two terms one is superfluous.

No, there can be no reconciliation, no Hegelian "recognition," no simple, sentimental promise of a humanistic "world of the You." Can there be life without transcendence? Politics without the dream of perfectibility? Unlike Fanon, I think the *nondialectical* moment of Manicheanism suggests an answer. By following the trajectory of colonial desire—in the company of that bizarre colonial figure, the tethered shadow—it becomes possible to cross, even to shift the Manichean boundaries. Where there is no human *nature* hope can hardly spring eternal; but it emerges surely and surreptitiously in the strategic return of that difference that informs and deforms the image of identity, in the margin of Otherness that displays identification. There may be no Hegelian negation but Fanon must sometimes be reminded that the disavowal of the Other always exacerbates the "edge" of identification, reveals that dangerous place where identity and aggressivity are twinned. For denial is always a retroactive process; a *half* acknowledgement of that Otherness which has left its traumatic mark. In that uncertainty lurks the white-masked black man; and from such ambivalent identification—black skin, white masks—it is possible, I believe, to redeem the pathos of cultural confusion into a strategy of political subversion. We cannot agree with Fanon that "since the racial drama is played out in the open the black man has no time to 'make it unconscious'" (1967a, 150), but that is a provocative thought. In occupying two places at once—or three in Fanon's case—the depersonalized, dislocated colonial subject can become an incalculable object, quite literally, difficult to place. The demand of authority cannot unify its message nor simply identify its subjects. For the strategy of colonial desire is to stage the drama of identity at the point at which the black mask *slips* to reveal the white skin. At that edge, in between the black body and the white body, there is a tension of meaning and being, or some would say demand and desire, which is the psychic counterpart to that "muscular tension" that inhabits the native body: "The symbols of social order—the police, the bugle calls in the barracks, military parades and the waving flags—are at one and the same time inhibitory and stimulating: for they do not convey the message 'Don't dare to budge'; rather, they cry out 'Get ready to attack'" (1968, 53). It is from that tension—both psychic and political—that a strategy of subversion emerges. It is a mode of negation that seeks not to unveil the fullness of Man but to manipulate his representation. It is a form of power that is exercised at the very limits of identity and authority, in the mocking spirit of mask and image; it is the lesson taught by the veiled Algerian woman in the course of the revolution as she crossed the Manichean lines to claim her liberty. In Fanon's essay "Algeria Unveiled" the colonizer's attempt to unveil the Algerian woman does not simply turn the veil into a symbol of resistance; it becomes a technique of camouflage, a means of struggle—the veil conceals bombs. The veil that once secured the boundary of the home—the limits of woman—now masks the woman in her revolutionary activity, linking the Arab city and the French quarter, transgressing the familial is liberated in the public and colonial boundary. As the "veil" is liberated in the public sphere, circulating between and beyond cultural and social norms and spaces, it becomes the object of paranoid surveillance and interrogation. Every veiled woman, writes Fanon, became suspect. And when the veil is shed in order to penetrate deeper into the European quarter, the colonial police see everything and nothing. An Algerian woman is only, after all, a woman. But the Algerian *fidai* is an arsenal and in her handbag she carries her hand-grenades.

Remembering Fanon is a process of intense discovery and disorientation. Remembering is never a quiet act of introspection or retrospection. It is a painful re-membering, a putting together of the dismembered past to make sense of the trauma of the present. It is such a memory of the history of race and racism, colonialism and the question of cultural identity, that Fanon reveals with greater profundity and poetry than any other writer. What he achieves, I believe, is something far greater: for in seeing the phobic image of the Negro, the native, the colonized, deeply woven into the psychic pattern of the West, he offers the master and slave a deeper reflection of their interpositions, as well as the hope of a difficult, even dangerous, freedom: "It is through the effort to recapture the self and to scrutinize the self, it is through the lasting tension of their freedom that men will be able to create the ideal conditions of existence for a human world" (1967a, 231). Nobody writes with more honesty and insight of this lasting tension of freedom in which the self—the peremptory self of the present—disavows an image of itself as an originary past or an ideal future and confronts the paradox of its own making.

For Fanon, in *Black Skin, White Masks*, there is the intricate irony of turning the European existentialist and psychoanalytic traditions to face the history of the Negro which they had never contemplated, to face the reality of Fanon himself. This leads to a meditation on the experience of dispossession and dislocation—psychic and social—which speaks to the condition of the marginalized, the alienated, those who have to live under the surveillance of a sign of identity and fantasy that denies their difference. In shifting the focus of cultural racism from the politics of nationalism to the politics of narcissism, Fanon opens up a margin of interrogation that causes a subversive slippage of identity and authority. Nowhere is this slippage more visible than in his work itself where a range of texts and traditions—from the classical repertoire to the quotidien, conversational culture of racism—vie to utter that last word which remains unspoken. Nowhere is this slippage more significantly experienced than in the impossibility of inferring from the texts of Fanon a pacific image of "society" or the "state" as a homogeneous philosophical or representational unity. The "social" is always an unresolved ensemble of antagonistic interlocutions between positions of power and poverty, knowledge and oppression, history and fantasy, surveillance and subversion. It is for this reason—above all else—in the twenty-fifth anniversary of his death, that we should turn to Fanon.

In Britain, today, as a range of culturally and racially marginalized groups readily assume the mask of the black not to deny their diversity but to audaciously announce the important artifice of cultural identity and its difference, the need for Fanon becomes urgent. As political groups from different directions gather under the banner of the black, not to homogenize their oppression but to make of it a common cause, a public image of the identity of otherness, the need for Fanon becomes urgent. Urgent, in order to remind us of that crucial engagement between mask and identity, image and identification, from which comes the lasting tension of our freedom and the lasting impression of ourselves as others.

> In the case of display . . . the play of combat in the form of intimidation, the being gives of himself, or receives from the other, something that is like a mask, a double, an envelope, a thrown-off skin, thrown off in order to cover the frame of a shield. It is through this separated form of himself that the being comes into play in his effects of life: and death. (Lacan 1981, 107)

The time has come to return to Fanon; as always, I believe, with a question: How can the human world live its difference? How can a human being live Other-wise?

NOTE

Fanon's use of the word "man" usually connotes a phenomenological quality of humanness, inclusive of man and woman and, for that very reason, ignores the question of gender difference. The problem stems from Fanon's desire to site the question of sexual difference within the problematic of cultural difference—to give them a shared origin—which is suggestive, but often simplifies the question of sexuality. His portrayals of white women often collude with their cultural stereotypes and reduce the "desire" of sexuality to the desire for sex, leaving unexplored the elusive function of the "object" of desire. In chapter 6 [of *Black Skin, White Masks*] he attempts a somewhat more complex reading of masochism but in making the Negro the "*predestined* depository of this aggression" (my emphasis) he again preempts a fuller psychoanalytic discussion of the production of psychic aggressivity in identification and its relation to cultural difference by citing the cultural stereotype as the predestined aim of the sexual drive. Of the woman of color he has very little to say. "I know nothing about her," he writes in *Black Skin, White Masks*. This crucial issue requires an order of psychoanalytic argument that goes well beyond the scope of my chapter. I have therefore chosen to note the importance of the problem rather than to elide it in a facile charge of "sexism."

7.

Travelling Theory Reconsidered

Edward W. Said

In an essay ("Travelling Theory") written several years ago, I discussed the ways in which theories sometimes "travel" to other times
and situations in the process of which they lose some of their original power and rebelliousness. The example I used was Georg
Lukács's theory of reification, which is fully explained in the famous
fourth chapter of his masterpiece, *History and Class Consciousness*.
Underlying my analysis was a common enough bias which, even
though I tried to guard against and mitigate its influence, remains in
the essay. This bias can be put simply as follows: The first time a
human experience is recorded and then given a theoretical formulation its force comes from being directly connected to and organically
provoked by real historical circumstances. Later versions of the
theory cannot replicate its original power; because the situation has
quieted down and changed, the theory is degraded and subdued,

Reprinted from *Critical Reconstructions: The Relationship of Fiction and Life*, edited
by Robert M. Polhemus and Roger B. Henkle with the permission of the publishers, Stanford University Press. ©1994 by the Board of Trustees of the Leland
Stanford Junior University.

made into a relatively tame academic substitute for the real thing whose purpose in the work I analyzed was political change.

As a revolutionary in early twentieth century Hungary, Lukács was a participant in the dramatic social upheavals that in his work he linked to the whole social deformation of alienation, the radical separation of object and subject, the atomization of human life under bourgeois capitalism. To resolve the crisis represented by these things, Lukács spoke about "the viewpoint of the proletariat," a dynamic theoretical reconciliation of subject with object that was enabled by getting beyond fragmentation and imagining a revolutionary vision of "totality." *History and Class Consciousness* is full of the agony of life in a brutally capitalist society: the way in which every human relationship and impulse is compelled into "alienated" labor, the bewildering rule of facts and figures with no bonds between people except those of the cash nexus, the loss of perspective, the fragmentation of every experience into saleable commodities, the absence of any image of community or wholeness. When he comes to the remedy for such diminishments and deprivations Lukács presses into service a Marxism that is principally the result of an alteration of consciousness. To be conscious of how widespread is reification—how everything is turned into a "thing"—is for the first time to be aware of the *general* problem of life under capitalism, and for the first time to be conscious of the class of individuals, the proletariat, who are capitalism's most numerous victims. Only in this way can subjectivity understand its objective situation, and this in turn makes possible an understanding of what kept subject and object apart, and how they can be rejoined.

The point I made about all this was that when they were picked up by late European students and readers of Lukács (Lucien Goldmann in Paris, Raymond Williams in Cambridge) the ideas of this theory had shed their insurrectionary force, had been tamed somewhat, and became considerably less dramatic in their application and gist. What seemed almost inevitable was that when theories travelled and were used elsewhere they ironically acquired the prestige and authority of age, perhaps even becoming a kind of dogmatic orthodoxy. In the setting provided by revolutionary Budapest,

Lukács's theory of the subject-object split and of reification was actually an inducement to insurrectionary action, with the hope that a proletarian perspective in his highly eccentric view of it would see "reality" as eminently changeable because it was largely a matter of perspective. His later readers regarded the theory as essentially an interpretive device, which is not to take away from their work some considerable and even very brilliant achievements.

What now seems to me incomplete and inadequate in such an account of Lukács's theory and its subsequent travels, is that I stressed the reconciliatory and resolvable aspects of his diagnosis. Those who borrowed from Lukács—and for that matter Lukács himself—saw in the reifications imposed epistemologically on the split between subject and object something that could be remedied. For such a view Lukács of course was indebted to Marx and Hegel before him, in whose theories the dialectic between opposed factors was routinely to result in synthesis, resolution, transcendence, or *Aufhebung*. Lukács's particular elaboration (some would say improvement) on the Hegelian and Marxian dialectic was to stress both the extraordinarily widespread infection of all of human life by reification—from the family, to professional pursuits, psychology, and moral concerns—as well as the almost aesthetic character of the reconciliation or healing process by which what was split asunder could be rejoined.

In this perhaps more comforting phase of the theory the work of several recent Lukács scholars, chief among them Michael Löwy (1979), is useful. They have shown the powerful influence on the young Lukács, the romantic anticapitalist, of Dostoevsky and Kierkegaard, whose explorations of modern angst found so devastatingly thorough and analytic a realization not only in *History and Class Consciousness* but also in his earlier treatises, *Soul and Form* and *Theory of the Novel*. But, it can be argued, so too can the Kierkegaardian and Dostoevskian influences be found in Lukács's specifically Marxist resolution, or even redemption. As contained in subject-object reconciliation within the largely unreal, projected or "putative" category of "totality," Lukács's leap from present misery to future healing recapitulates (if it does not actually repeat) the great nineteenth-century irrationalists' leaps of faith.

But what if some of Lukács's readers, totally influenced by his description of reification and the subject-object impasse, did not accept the reconciliatory denouement of his theory, and indeed deliberately, programmatically, intransigently refused it? Would this not be an alternative mode of travelling theory, one which actually developed away from its original formulation, but instead of becoming domesticated in the terms enabled by Lukács's desire for respite and resolution, flames out so to speak, restates and reaffirms its own inherent tensions by moving to another site? Is this different kind of dislocation so powerful as retrospectively to undermine Lukács's reconciliatory gesture when he settles the subject-object tensions into what he calls "the standpoint of the proletariat?" Might we then not call this surprising later development an instance of "transgressive theory," in the sense that it crosses over from and challenges the notion of a theory that begins with fierce contradiction and ends up promising a form of redemption?

Let us return briefly to the early Lukács. In the principally aesthetic works that anticipate *History and Class Consciousness* (1923) he brilliantly examines the relationship between different aesthetic forms on the one hand, and the concrete historical or existential experience from which they derive and to which they are a response. The most famous of these early works is *Theory of the Novel* (originally published in 1920), premised on the notion that in a world abandoned by God the novel embodies the trajectory of an epic whose hero is either demonic or mad, whose constitutive element is a temporality basically disappointing and demystifying, and whose representative status as the art-form of modernity is based on its tremendous constitutive ironies, the irony of "errant souls [adventuring] in an inessential, empty reality," or that of speaking "of past gods and gods . . . to come" but never of what is present, or "the irony [which] has to seek the only world that is adequate to it along the *via dolorosa* of interiority but is doomed never to find it there" (1971b, 92).

Before he becomes a Marxist, therefore, Lukács's overpowering sense of the disjunctions of modernity (which in his *Logos* essay of 1917 he abstracted into "the subject-object relationship") led him to regard the aesthetic as a site where their contradictions are manageable, and even pleasurable. For this view he is indebted to both Kant and Schiller, although his inflection of the thesis is largely original. Each art form, he says, is itself in a sense the incarnation of a particular phase in the subject-object relationship. The essay, for example, is about heralding a resolution but never giving it; the tragedy is the fatal clash between subjects, and so forth. That the novel has a special privilege in modernity is underscored by its scope, its hero and, although Lukács never actually says this, by the fact that theoretical discourse (such as his) can express and by its sheer complexity represent the form's quintessential ironies. The transformation in Lukács's politics that occurs after *Theory of the Novel* and in *History and Class Consciousness* is that Marxism, as borne and reflected in "the class consciousness of the proletariat," is explicitly revealed to be the theoretical discourse resolving the subject-object relationship.

Nevertheless, Lukács actually says that that resolution is almost by nature postponed and thus hasn't happened yet. There is an unwonted certainty in his accents which, it must be said immediately, supplies his later work with its gruffly dogmatic authority and assertiveness. Clearly, however, not every reader of Lukács went as far in *that* direction as the dogged stubbornness of Adorno quite plainly shows. Adorno, I believe, is virtually unthinkable without the majestic philosophical beacon provided by *History and Class Consciousness*, but he is also unthinkable without his own great resistance to its triumphalism and implied transcendence. If for Lukács the subject-object relationship, the fragmentation and lostness, the ironic perspectivism of modernity were supremely discerned, embodied, and consummated in narrative forms (the rewritten epics both of the novel and the proletariat's class consciousness), for Adorno that particular choice was, he said in a famous anti-Lukács essay, a kind of false reconciliation under duress. Much more typical, more in keeping with the irremediably "fallen" character of modernity was "new" music which, for Adorno, was Schoenberg, Berg, and Webern, *not* Stravinsky and Bartok.

II

Philosophie der neuen Musik (Philosophy of Modern Music, 1948) is a quite spectacular instance of travelling theory gone tougher, harder, more recalcitrant. In the first place its language is a good deal more difficult to decode even than Lukács's which, in the reification essay of *History and Class Consciousness*, had already had a programmatically unattractive density and philosophical obscurity to it. Lukács's choice of the history of classical philosophy— here too the *narrative* of increasing desperation and abstraction was an illustration of subject-object tension unrelieved by reconciliation—was meant to show how deeply alienation had penetrated and therefore where in its most abtruse version it could be analyzed as a pure symptom of the overall *anomie* of modern life. Adorno goes a step further. Modern music, he says, is so marginal, so rarified, so special an expression as to represent a total rejection of society and any of its palliatives. This is why Schoenberg is such a heroic figure to Adorno. No longer is the composer a figure like Beethoven, who stands for the newly triumphant bourgeoisie, or like Wagner, whose sorcerer-like art camouflages the irreconcilability between the aesthetic and the commercial. The twentieth century composer stands outside tonality itself, proclaiming an art of so totally, irrecusably rebarbative a mode as to reject listeners altogether. Why? Because according to Schoenberg as described by Adorno "the middle road . . . is the only one which does not lead to Rome" (1973, 40 and ff).

For indeed the subject-object compromise enacted by Lukács does resemble a middle-of-the-road synthesis; whereas Schoenberg's twelve-tone theory was based upon and, more definitively than any other language, reasserted the impossibility of synthesis. Its premise was dissonance, the subject-object impasse raised to the level of an uncompromisable principle, "forced into complete isolation during the final stage of industrialism" (Adorno 1973, 6). Standing apart from society with a uniquely brooding severity and a remorseless self-control, the new music's loneliness pitilessly showed how all other art had become kitsch, other music ruled by "the omni-present hit tune," "false interpretations and stereotyped audience reaction patterns." These, Adorno said, sternly needed to "be destroyed." Any illusions that the tonality rejected by Schoenberg was somehow natural are rejected: According to Adorno, tonality corresponds to "the closed and exclusive system [of] mercantile society," music submitting to the demands of trade, consumerism, administration. Not for nothing then in a later essay did Adorno attack Toscanini as the *maestro* of conventional music, with its limitless reproducibility, inauthentic perfection, and heartless rhythms contained in the conductor's iron-like dominance and precision.

For Lukács the atomized individual consciousness in surveying its alienation from the product of its own labor desired a kind of healing unity; this was afforded it by "class consciousness" made tenuous, it is true, because, in Lukács's rather circumspect description, consciousness was not empirical or actually and immediately experienceable but "imputable" (*zugerechtnetes*). Such a deferral of the clubby gregariousness normally associated with class feeling undercuts the "vulgar Marxism" that Lukács was so polemically energetic in trying to discredit. But it also allowed him to reharness the aesthetic powers of imagination and projection that had been central to his work before he became a Marxist. "Imputable consciousness" was a daring composite made up not only of what was later to be called Marxist humanism, but in addition it borrowed from Schiller's play instinct, Kant's aesthetic realm, and Bans Vaihinger's *als ob*. In all, then, a good deal of optimism and even enthusiasm for the promised reconnection of the subject with itself, other subjects, and objects.

None of this is permitted by Adorno in his stirringly bleak account of Schoenberg's emergence and rather repellent triumph. Instead of social relevance Schoenberg's aesthetic chooses irrelevance; instead of amiability the choice is intransigence; instead of antinomian problematics being overcome (a central notion in

Lukács's history of classical philosophy) they are vindicated; instead of class consciousness there is the monad; instead of positive thinking there is "definitive negation."

> In the process of pursuing its own inner logic, music is transformed more and more from something significant into something obscure—even to itself. No music today, for example, could possibly speak in the accents of "reward." Not only has the mere idea of humanity, or of a better world no longer any sway over mankind—though it is precisely this which lies at the heart of Beethoven's opera [*Fidelio*]. Rather the strictness of musical structure, wherein alone music can assert itself against the ubiquity of commercialism, has hardened music to the point that it is no longer affected by those external factors which caused absolute music to become what it is. . . . Advanced music has no recourse but to insist upon its own ossification without concession to that would-be humanitarianism which it sees through, in all its attractive and alluring guises, as the mask of inhumanity. (Adorno 1973, 19–20)

Music thus insistently becomes what Lukács's reconciled consciousness has given up—the very sign of alienation which, says Adorno, "preserves its social truth through the isolation resulting from its antithesis to society." Not that this isolation is something to be enjoyed as, say, an 1890s aesthete might have enjoyed the status of arty eccentric. No; in the awareness of an advanced composer that his work derives from such appalling "social roots" as this, there is consequently a recoil from them. So between that awareness and an attitude that "despises [the] . . . illusion of reconciliation" stands new music. Precisely because its constitutive principle is the disjunctive twelve-note series, its harmony a mass of dissonances, its inspiration the remorseless "control" of the composer who is bound by the system's unbreakable laws, music aspires to the condition of theoretical knowledge. Of what? The contradiction.

With this clearly stated, Adorno proceeds resolutely to an account of Schoenberg's career or "progress" (the word is fairly loaded down with irony) from the early expressionist works to the late dodecaphonic masterpieces. As if affectionately recalling and then angrily refuting Lukács, Adorno describes the twelve-tone method in terms taken almost verbatim from the subject-object drama, but each time there is an opportunity for synthesis Adorno has Schoenberg turn it down.

The further irony is that very far from liberating him, Schoenberg's mastery of the atonal technique he invented for escaping "the blind domination of tonal material" ends up by dominating him. The severity, objectivity, and regulatory power of a technique that supplies itself with an alternative harmony, inflection, tonal color, rhythm—in short a new logic for music, the object of the subject's compositional skill—become "a second blind nature," and this "virtually extinguishes the subject" (Adorno 1973, 68–69). In Adorno's descriptions here there is a breathtakingly regressive sequence, a sort of endgame procedure by which he threads his way back along the route taken by Lukács; all the laboriously constructed solutions devised by Lukács for pulling himself out of the slough of bourgeois despair—the various satisfactory totalities given by art, philosophy, Marxism—are just as laboriously dismantled and rendered useless. Fixated on music's absolute rejection of the commercial sphere, Adorno's words cut out the social ground from underneath art. For in fighting ornament, illusion, reconciliation, communication, humanism, and success, art becomes untenable:

> Everything having no function in the work of art—and therefore everything transcending the law of mere existence—is withdrawn. The function of the work of art lies precisely in its transcendence beyond mere existence. Thus the height of justice becomes the height of injustice: the consummately functional work of art becomes consummately functionless. Since the work, after all, cannot be reality, the elimination of all illusory features accentuates all the more glaringly the illusory character of its existence. This process is inescapable. (Adorno 1973, 70)

An even more drastic statement comes later, when Adorno avers as how the fate of new music in its illusionless self-denial and ossified self-sacrifice is to remain unheard: "music which has not been heard falls into empty time like an impotent bullet" (Adorno 1973, 133).

Thus the subject-object antithesis simply disappears because Adorno has Schoenberg rejecting even the ghost of achievement and experience. I say it this way to underscore Adorno's manipulation of Schoenberg, and also to contrast it with Mann's *Doctor Faustus* (based on Adorno's book), a tamer version of Adorno's Schoenberg. Mann's hero is an Adornian emanation, but the novel's technique, especially the presence of Serenus Zeitblom, the humanist narrator, recuperates and to a degree saves or domesticates Adrian by giving him the aura of a figure representative of modern Germany, now chastened and perhaps redeemed for postwar elegiac reflection.

III

But Lukács's theory has voyaged elsewhere too. Recall that between Lukács and Adorno there is first of all a common European culture and more particularly the affinity stemming from the Hegelian tradition to which they both belong. It is therefore quite startling to discover the subject-object dialectic deployed with devastating intellectual and political force in Frantz Fanon's last work, *The Wretched of the Earth*, written in 1961, the very year of its author's death. All of Fanon's books on colonialism show evidence of his indebtedness to Marx and Engels, as well of course as Freud and Hegel. Yet the striking power that differentiates his last work from, say, the largely Caribbean setting of *Black Skins, White Masks* (1952) is evident from the unflagging mobilizing energy with which in the Algerian setting Fanon analyzes and situates the antinomy of the settler versus the native. There is a philosophical logic to the tension that is scarcely visible in his previous work, in which psychology, impressions, astute observation, and an almost novelistic technique of insight and vignette give Fanon's writing its ingratiatingly eloquent inflections.

Two things seem to have happened between *L'An V de la révolution algérienne* (1959), his first collection of essays after he changed his focus from the Caribbean to North Africa, and *The Wretched of the Earth*. One of them, obviously, is that the progress of the Algerian revolution had deepened and widened the gulf between France and its colony. There was a greater drive toward separation between them, the war had become uglier and more extensive, sides were being taken both in Algeria and in the metropolis, with rifts, and internecine conflicts in both of the two great hostile encampments. Second—and here I speculate—Fanon seems to have read Lukács's book and taken from its reification chapter an understanding of how even in the most confusing and heterogenous of situations, a rigorous analysis of one central problematic could be relied on to yield the most extensive understanding of the whole. The evidence I have is, to repeat, not firm, but is worth noting: a French version of Lukács's central work, *Histoire et conscience de classe* appeared in 1961, in an excellent translation by Kostas Axelos and Jacqueline Bois, published by Editions de Minuit. Some of the chapters had already appeared in *Arguments* a few years earlier, but 1961 was the first time the entire book had made its appearance anywhere at all, ever since Lukács had recanted the book's most radical tenets a generation earlier. In his preface Axelos compared Lukács to Brecht's Galileo, associating him also with those other martyrs to truth, Socrates, Christ, and Giordano Bruno; according to Axelos, the main point for twentieth century thought, however, was that Lukács's great treatise was expunged both from history and class consciousness, with no visible effects on those working people the book was designed to assist.

How strongly the subject-object dialectic resonated *outside* Europe, and for an audience made up of colonial subjects, is immediately apparent from the opening pages of *The Wretched of the Earth*. The Manicheanism Fanon describes as separating the clean, well-lighted colonial city on the one hand, and on the other the vile, disease-ridden darkness of the *casbah* recalls the alienation of Lukács's reified world. And Fanon's whole project is first to illuminate and then to animate the separation between colonizer and colonized (subject and object) in order that what is false, brutalizing, and historically determined about the relationship might become clear, stimulate action, lead to the overthrow of colonialism itself. As Lukács put it in his supremely Hegelian 1922 preface to *History and Class Consciousness*: "It is of the essence of dialectical method that concepts which are false in their abstract one-sidedness are later transcended" (Lukács 1971a, xlvi). To this Fanon will answer that there is nothing abstract or conceptual about colonialism which, as Conrad once said, "mostly means the taking it [land] away from those who have a different complexion or slightly flatter noses than ourselves." Thus, according to Fanon,

> for a colonized people the most essential value, because the most concrete, is first and foremost the land: the land which will bring them bread and, above all, dignity. But this dignity has nothing to do with the dignity of the human individual: for that human individual has never heard tell of it. All that the native has seen in his country is that they can freely arrest him, beat him, starve him: and no professor of ethics, no priest has ever come to be beaten in his place, nor to share their bread with him. As far as the native is concerned: morality is very concrete; it is to silence the settler's defiance, to break his flaunting violence—in a word, to put him out of the picture. (1968, 44)

Lukács's dialectic is grounded in *The Wretched of the Earth*, actualized, given a kind of harsh presence nowhere to be found in his agonized rethinking of the classical philosophical antinomies. The issue for Lukács was the primacy of consciousness in history; for Fanon it is the primacy of geography in history, and then of history over consciousness and subjectivity. That there is subjectivity at all is because of colonialism—instituted by Europeans who like Odysseus came to the peripheries to exploit the land and its people, and thereafter to constitute a new aggressive selfhood—and once colonialism disappears the settler "has no longer any interest in remaining or in co-existing" (1968, 45). The subjective colonizer has turned the native into a dehumanized creature for whom zoological terms are the most apt; for the settler the terms used to falsify and palliate his repressive presence are borrowed from "Western culture," which whenever it is mentioned "produces in the native a sort of stiffening or muscular lockjaw" (1968, 43).

At the same time that Fanon uses the subject-object dialectic most energetically he is quite deliberate about its limitations. Thus, to return to the relationship between the colonial enclave and the native quarter: these "two zones are opposed," says Fanon, "but not in the service of a higher unity . . . They both follow the principle of reciprocal exclusivity. No conciliation is possible, for of the two terms one is superfluous" (1968, 38–39). At the same time that he uses what is a patently Marxist analysis Fanon realizes explicitly that such "analysis should always be slightly stretched" in the colonial situation. For neither the colonist nor the colonized behaves as if subject and object might someday be reconciled. The former plunders and pillages; the latter dreams of revenge. When the natives rise in violent insurrection, it "is not a rational confrontation of points of view. It is not a treatise on the universal, but the untidy affirmation of an original idea propounded as an absolute" (Fanon 1968, 41).

No one needs to be reminded that Fanon's recommended antidote for the cruelties of colonialism is violence: "the violence of the colonial regime and the counter-violence of the native balance each other and respond to each other in an extraordinary reciprocal homogeneity" (Fanon 1968, 88). The logic of colonialism is opposed by the native's equally strict and implacable counter-logic. What operates throughout the war of national liberation is therefore a combative subject-object dialectic whose central term is violence which at brief moments appears to play a reconciling, transfiguring role. True, Fanon says there is no liberation without violence and certainly he admits that there is no "truthful behavior" in a colonial setting: "good is quite simply that which is evil for 'them'" (Fanon 1968, 50). But does Fanon, like Lukács, suggest that the subject-object dialectic can be consummated, transcended, synthesized, and that violence in and of itself is that fulfillment, the dialectical tension resolved by violent upheaval into peace and harmony?

The by now conventional notion about Fanonist violence is exactly that, a received idea, and is a caricatural reduction more suited to the Cold War (Sidney Hook's attack on Fanon being a case in point) than to what Fanon actually says and to how he says it. In other words, Fanon can too easily be read as if what he was doing in *The Wretched of the Earth* was little more than a replication of Lukács, with the subject-object relationship replaced exactly by the colonizer-colonized relationship, the "new class-consciousness of the proletariat," Lukács's synthesizing term, replaced by revolutionary violence in Fanon's text. But that would be to miss Fanon's crucial reworking and critique of Lukács, in which the *national* element missing in *History and Class Consciousness*—the setting of that work, like Marx's, is entirely European—is given an absolute prominence by Fanon. For him, subject and object are European and non-European respectively; colonialism does not just oppose the terms and the people to each other. It obliterates and suppresses their presence, substituting instead the lifeless dehumanizing abstractions of two "masses" in absolute uncommunicating hostility with each other. Whereas Lukács saw the subject-object antinomy as integral to European culture, and as in fact its partial symbol, Fanon sees the antinomy as imported from Europe, a foreign intrusion that has completely distorted the native presence. "Thus the history which he [the colonist] writes is not the history of the country which he plunders but the history of his own nation in regard to all that she skims off, all that she violates and starves" (Fanon 1968, 51).

Fanon had made earlier use of the subject-object dialectic in an expressly Hegelian manner; this is most notably evident in *Black Skins*, where he uses the master-slave dialectic to show how the Negro had been turned by racism into an "existential deviation." Yet even there Fanon distinguished the dialectic as Hegel envisioned it for white Europe, and how it might be used by whites against Negroes: "here [in the colonial relationship between races] the master differs basically from the master described by Hegel. For Hegel there is reciprocity; here the master laughs at the consciousness of the slave. What he wants from the slave is not recognition but work" (1967a, 220). In *The Wretched of the Earth* existential racial relationships have been superseded in a sense: they are now located and resituated geographically in the colonial setting. And from this derives that "world divided into compartments, a motionless Manicheistic world, a world of statues" (1968, 51).

In short, the colonial antinomy can now be reinterpreted as an antagonism between nations, one dominating the other, and in the process actually preventing the other from coming into being. The new complication therefore is nationalism, which Fanon introduces as follows:

> The immobility to which the native is condemned can only be called in question if the native decides to put an end to the history of colonization—the history of pillage—and to bring into existence the history of the nation—the history of decolonization. (Fanon 1968, 51)

The unresolvable antinomy is the opposition between two nations which in the colonies cannot be brought to coexist. Fanon matches two sets of terms: pillage and colonization versus the nation and decolonization, and they emerge in the anticolonial struggle itself as absolutely opposed as they were before it began, before the liberation movement was born, before it started to fight, before it challenged the colonizer. The violence of decolonization is no more than an explicit fulfillment of the violence that lurks within colonialism, and instead of the natives being the object of colonial force, they wield it back *against* colonialism, as subjects reacting with pent-up violence to their own former passivity.

Were liberation therefore only to consist in the violence of nationalism, the process of decolonization might be seen as leading inevitably to it, one step along the way. But Fanon's essential point—and here he also rejects Lukács's own resolution—is that nationalism is a necessary but far from sufficient condition for liberation, perhaps even a sort of temporary illness which must be gone through. By the approximate terms of the subject-object antinomy, the natives who reject their reified status as negation and evil, take on violence as a way of providing themselves with "a royal pardon" (1968, 86): since they stand outside the European class system about which Lukács spoke, colonized natives need an extra measure of rebelliousness to afford them the dubious position of antagonists (their dreams, Fanon remarks, are full of jumping, swimming, running, climbing, as if trying to imagine what it would be like *not* to stay in place). Once antagonists of the colonizers, however, they are only the *opposite* of colonialism: this is why Fanon says that only at an initial stage can violence be used to organize a party. Colonial war is of the colonial dialectic, the replication of some of its mutually exclusive and antagonistic terms on a national level. The opposites reflect each other. For the Europeans this will lead to expulsion; for the native this will mean that national independence will be achieved. Yet both expulsion and independence belong essentially to the unforgiving dialectic of colonialism, enfolded within its unpromising script. Thereafter Fanon is at pains to show that the tensions between colonizer and colonized will not end, since in effect the new nation will produce a new set of policemen, bureaucrats, merchants to replace the departed Europeans. And indeed after his opening chapter on violence Fanon proceeds to show how nationalism is too heavily imprinted with the *unresolved* (and unresolvable) dialectic of colonialism for it to lead very far beyond it. The complexity of independence, which is so naturally desirable a goal for all colonized people, is that simultaneously it dramatized the discrepancy between colonizer and colonized so basic to colonialism, and also a discrepancy (*décalage*) between the people and their leaders, leaders who perforce are shaped by colonialism. Thus after the opening chapter on violence, Fanon proceeds to develop the new difficulties of nationalism as it continues the war against colonialism decreed by the subject-object antinomy, while at the same time an entirely new consciousness—that of liberation—is struggling to be born.

It is not until the chapter titled "The Pitfalls of National Consciousness" that Fanon makes clear what he has been intending all along: national consciousness is undoubtedly going to be captured by the colonial bourgeois elite, the nationalistic leaders, and far from guaranteeing real independence this will perpetuate colonialism in a new form, a "sterile formalism." Thus, he says, if nationalism "is not enriched and deepened by a very rapid transformation into a consciousness of social and political needs, in other words, into humanism, it leads up a blind ally" (1968, 204). Borrowing from Aimé Césaire, Fanon suggests that the necessity is to "invent souls," not to reproduce the solutions and formulas either of colonialism or the tribal past. "The living expression of the nation is the moving consciousness of the whole of the people; it is the coherent, enlightened action of men and women" (Fanon 1968, 204). A few sentences later he states that a national government (the only government ever known!) ought to cede its power back to the people, dissolve itself.

Fanon's radicalism, I think, is and has been since his death too strenuous for the new postcolonial states, Algeria included. The gist of his last work plainly indicts them for this insufficiently visionary response to the colonialist dialectic, from which they have never fully liberated themselves, satisfied as they have been with the imitations and simulacra of sovereignty that they simply have taken over from European masters. But even in this extraordinary turn Fanon relies to some degree on Lukács, although it is a Lukács which had been either rejected or toned down by Lukács himself. So that even for a colonial setting, as he criticized the subject-object reconciliation advocated by *History and Class Consciousness* as the "class consciousness of the proletariat," Fanon takes from Lukács the real dissatisfaction with that resolution that surfaces briefly near the end of the essay on "Class Consciousness," the short essay that precedes the reification chapter. "The proletariat," says Lukács, "only perfects itself by annihilating and transcending itself. . . . It is equally [therefore] the struggle of the proletariat against itself" (1971, 80).

There is concurrence here between Fanon and this more (and perhaps only momentarily) radical Lukács on the one hand, and between Lukács and Adorno on the other. The work of theory, criticism, demystification, deconsecration, and decentralization they imply is never finished. The point of theory therefore is to travel, always to move beyond its confinements, to emigrate, to remain in a sense in exile. Adorno and Fanon exemplify this profound restlessness in the way they refuse the emoluments offered by the Hegelian dialectic as stabilized into resolution by Lukács—or the

214 Said: Travelling Theory Reconsidered

Lukács who appeared to speak for class consciousness as something to be gained, possessed, held onto. There was of course the other Lukács which both his brilliant rereaders preferred, the theorist of permanent dissonance as understood by Adorno, the critic of reactive nationalism as partially adopted by Fanon in colonial Algeria.

IV

In all this we get a sense, I think, of the geographical dispersion of which the theoretical motor is capable. I mean that when Adorno uses Lukács to understand Schoenberg's place in the history of music, or when Fanon dramatized the colonial struggle in the language of the manifestly European subject-object dialectic, we don't think of them simply coming after Lukács, using him at a belated second-degree so to speak, but rather as pulling him from one sphere or region into another. This movement suggests the possibility of actively different locales, sites, situations for theory, without facile universalism or overgeneral totalizing. One would not, could not, want to assimilate Viennese twelve-tone music to the Algerian resistance to French colonialism: the disparities are too grotesque even to articulate. But in both situations, each so profoundly and concretely felt by Adorno and Fanon respectively, is the fascinating Lukácsian figure, present both as travelling theory and as intransigent practice. To speak here only of borrowing and adaptation is not adequate. There is in particular an intellectual, and perhaps moral, community of a remarkable kind, *affiliation* in the deepest and most interesting sense of the word. As a way of getting seriously past the weightlessness of one theory after another, the remorseless indignations of orthodoxy, and the expressions of tired advocacy to which we are often submitted, the exercise involved in figuring out where the theory went and how in getting there its fiery core was reignited is invigorating—and is also another voyage, one that is central to intellectual life in the late twentieth century.

8.

Resistance Theory/ Theorizing Resistance or Two Cheers for Nativism

Benita Parry

It is not the literal past, the "facts" of history, that shape us, but images of the past embodied in language. . . . We must never cease renewing those images, because once we do, we fossilise.

Brian Friel

That the colonized were never successfully pacified is well known to the postcolonial study of colonialism and the long and discontinuous process of decolonization.[1] But proposals on how resistance is to be theorized display fault-lines within the discussion that rehearse questions about subjectivity, identity, agency, and the status of the reverse-discourse as an oppositional practice, posing problems about the appropriate models for contemporary counter-hegemonic work. An agenda which disdains the objective of restoring the colonized as subject of its own history does so on the grounds that a simple inversion perpetuates the colonizer/colonized opposition within the terms defined by colonial discourse,

Reprinted from *Colonial Discourse/Postcolonial Theory*, edited by Francis Barker, Peter Hulme, and Margaret Iversen (Manchester, U.K.: Manchester University Press,) pp. 172–96. Reprinted with permission.

remaining complicit with its assumptions by retaining undifferentiated identity categories, and failing to contest the conventions of
that system of knowledge it supposedly challenges. Instead the
project of a postcolonial critique is designated as deconstructing
and displacing the Eurocentric premises of a discursive apparatus
which constructed the Third World not only for the West but also
for the cultures so represented.[2]

The performance of such procedures does display Richard Terdiman's contention that "no discourse is ever a monologue; nor
could it ever be analyzed intrinsically . . . Everything that constitutes it always presupposes a horizon of competing, contrary
utterances against which it asserts its own energies" (Terdiman
1985, 36). However, the statements of the theoretical paradigms,
where it can appear that the efficacy of colonialism's apparatus of
social control in effecting strategies of disempowerment is total-
ized, are liable to be (mis)read as producing the colonized as a
stable category fixed in a position of subjugation, hence foreclosing
on the possibility of theorizing resistance. Even if this is a crass
misrepresentation of the project, the colonized's refusals of their
assigned positions as subjected and disarticulated are not—and
within its terms cannot be—accorded center stage.

The premise to modes of criticism within the postcolonial critique which are attentive to those moments and processes when
the colonized clandestinely or overtly took up countervailing
stances is that no system of coercion or hegemony is ever able
wholly to determine the range of subject positions. For although
the colonial is a product of colonialism's ideological machinery, the
formation of its differentiated and incommensurable subjectivities
is the effect of many determinants, numerous interpellations, and
various social practices.[3] A postcolonial rewriting of past contestation, dependent as it is on a notion of a multiply (dis)located native
whose positions are provisional, and therefore capable of annul-
ment and transgression, does not restore the foundational, fixed,
and autonomous individual; what it does resort to is the discourse
of the subject inscribed in histories of insubordination produced
by anticolonial movements, deciphered from cryptic cultural

forms and redevised from vestiges perpetuated through constant transmutation in popular memory and oral traditions.

There is of course abundant evidence of native disaffection and dissent under colonial rule, of contestation and struggle against diverse forms of institutional and ideological domination. Inscriptions and signs of resistance are discernible in official archives and informal texts, and can be located in narrativized instances of insurrection and organized political opposition. Traces of popular disobedience can also be recouped from unwritten symbolic and symptomatic practices in which a rejection or violation of the subject positions assigned by colonialism is registered. Here the modes of refusal are not readily accommodated in the anticolonialist discourses written by the elites of the nationalist and liberation movements. Since they were not calculated to achieve predetermined political ends or to advance the cause of nation-building, the anarchic and nihilistic energies of defiance and identity-assertion, which were sometimes nurtured by dreams, omens, and divination, and could take the form of theater, violated notions of rational protest.[4]

If we look at the work of contemporary critics recounting figures of colonial resistance, not from the rhetorical strategies of the dominant discourses but by revisiting dispersed and connotative informal sources, these projects do not appear as preoccupied with victimage, or as enacting a regressive search for an aboriginal and intact condition/tradition from which a proper sense of historicity is occluded—charges which have been made against such undertakings. As an instance of a resistant mode available to the colonial Caribbean, Wilson Harris cites limbo dancing, a practice stemming from Africa and reinterpreted on the slave ships of the Middle Passage, and which although indebted to the past—as is voodoo—is not an imitation of that past but rather "a crucial inner re-creative response to the violations of slavery and indenture and conquest" (Harris 1974, 14).

> Such a strategy is not the total recall of an African past since that African past in terms of tribal sovereignty or sovereignties was

modified or traumatically eclipsed with the Middle Passage and
with generations of change that followed. Limbo was rather the
renascence of a new corpus of sensibility that could translate and
accommodate African and other legacies within a new architecture of cultures. (Harris 1974, 10)

Does revisiting the repositories of memory and cultural sur-
vivals in the cause of postcolonial refashioning have a fixed retrograde valency? Such censure is surely dependent on who is doing
the remembering and why: Certainly as Rashmi Bhatnagar suggests, in some situations the mythologizing of beginnings can be
suspect "in that it can unwittingly serve the reactionary forces of
revivalism. Nowhere is this danger greater than in the Indian context, where the search for the source of Hindu identity in Vedic
times has almost invariably led to a loss of commitment to our contemporary plural/secular identity" (1986, 5).[5] A very different
impulse toward recuperating a very different history marked by
discontinuities and erasures is attested by Edouard Glissant whose
repeated references to the Acoma tree intimates that the need to
renew or activate memories is distinct from the uncritical attempt
to conserve tradition: "One of the trees that has disappeared from
the Martinican forest. We should not get too attached to the tree,
we might then forget the forest. But we should remember it" (1981,
260). In his aphoristic and fragmentary critical writings Glissant
urges a postcolonial construction of the past that, far from being a
desire to discover a remote paternity, is an imaginative reworking
of the process of *metissage* or an infinite wandering across cultures
including those of Africa. Because the slave trade snatched
African-Caribbeans from their original matrix, erasing memory
and precluding the ability to map a sequence, Glissant contends
that it is the function of a contemporary counter-poetics to
engender that tormented chronology:

> For history is not only absence for us. It is vertigo. The time that
> was never ours we must now possess. We do not see it stretch
> into our past and calmly take us into tomorrow, but it explodes

in us as a compact mass, pushing through a dimension of emptiness where we must with difficulty and pain put it all back
together. (1989, 161–62)

Since these are definitions of a discursively produced resur-
gent subjectivity that is volatile, polyglot, and unconcerned with
discovering the persistence of an original state, it would seem that
critics who continue to valorize the identity struggle, and to
reclaim forms of situated agency asserted in the struggle over representation, do so without returning to the notion of an ahistorical
essential and unified self. In this vein Stuart Hall has braved the
reprobation directed against ethnic identitarianism, to make a
carefully modulated case for decoupling ethnicity from its equiva-
lence with nationalism, imperialism, racism, and the state as it
functions in the dominant discourse, and appropriating it for a different usage in the current post-colonial discussion: "The term
'ethnicity' acknowledges the place of history, language and culture
in the construction of subjectivity and identity, as well as the fact
that all discourse is placed, positioned, situated, and all knowledge is contextual" (1988c, 29). Now although Hall is wary of postmodernism's "absolutist discourse," since he considers that "the
politics of absolute dispersal is the politics of no action at all," he
defines subjectivity as "a narrative, a story, a history. Something
constructed, told, spoken, not simply found" (1987, 45), and identity as an invention "which is never complete, always in process,
and always constituted within . . . representation" (Hall 1990, 222).
    Hall is quite aware of the colonial subject as the product of
multiple constitutions, of the contradictions and overdetermina-
tions of postcolonial ideological positions—having written of these
as always negotiated and negotiable—and of ethnic and cultural
difference as sites of articulation. He has all the same directed
attention to the indispensable role played in all colonial struggles
by a conception of "'cultural identity' in terms of one shared culture, a sort of collective 'one true self' . . . which people with a
shared history and ancestry hold in common." This, he adds, "continues to be a very powerful and creative force in emergent forms

of representation amongst hitherto marginalized peoples. . . . We should not . . . underestimate or neglect . . . the importance of the act of imaginative rediscovery which this conception of a rediscovered essential identity entails" (Hall 1990, 223, 224). And before we pillory Hall for reviving the myth of an organic communality, we should note that he emphasizes the impossibility of its indivisible, homogeneous meaning, recognizing this to be an "imaginary reunification," imposing an "imaginary coherence" on the experience of dispersal and fragmentation, and acknowledging that its other side is rupture and discontinuity.

Because in another register Henry Louis Gates Jr. has reclaimed the *ethnos* from vilification as false consciousness (Gates 1990), it could appear that there is a move to restore affect to the fiction of identity, and rather than the toleration extended to its expedient use in political mobilization, we see it embraced as a pleasure, and one that is all the greater because identity is now perceived as multi-located and polysemic—a situation that characterizes postcoloniality and is at its most evident in the diasporic condition. An uninhibited statement of the gratification of inhabiting many cultures and identifying with all oppressions and persecutions, while electing to be affiliated to one's natal community, comes from the artist R. B. Kitaj, in whose paintings Rosa Luxemburg and Walter Benjamin are emblematic figures of that particular and permanent condition of diaspora in which he is at home:

> The compelling destiny of dispersion . . . describes and explains my parable pictures, their dissolutions, repressions, associations, referrals, their text obsessions, their play of difference . . . People are always saying that the meanings in my pictures refuse to be fixed, to be settled, to be stable: that's Diasporism. . . . Diasporist art is contradictory at its heart, being both internationalist and particularist. . . . The Diasporist's pursuit of a homeless logic of ethnie may be the radical core of a newer art than we can yet imagine. . . . the Jews do not own Diaspora, they are not the only Diasporists. . . . They are merely mine. (Kitaj 1989, 35, 37, 39, 21)

There are moreover critics who testify to the possibility that the identity struggle of one community can serve as a model for other resistant discourses, since the self-definition articulated by, say, the black or the Jew in defiance of received representations can be communicated to different situations of contest against the authority of the dominant by marginals, exiles, and subjugated populations (see Diawara 1991 and Grosz 1990).

II

When we consider the narratives of decolonization, we encounter rhetorics in which "nativism" in one form or another is evident. Instead of disciplining these, theoretical whip in hand, as a catalogue of epistemological error, of essentialist mystifications, as a masculinist appropriation of dissent, as no more than an antiracist racism, etc., I want to consider what is to be gained by an unsententious interrogation of such articulations which, if often driven by negative passion, cannot be reduced to a mere inveighing against iniquities or a repetition of the canonical terms of imperialism's conceptual framework. This of course means affirming the power of the reverse-discourse[6] by arguing that anticolonialist writings did challenge, subvert, and undermine the ruling ideologies, and nowhere more so than in overthrowing the hierarchy of colonizer/colonized, the speech and stance of the colonized refusing a position of subjugation and dispensing with the terms of the colonizer's definitions.

The weak and strong forms of oppositional discursive practices have been designated as counter-identification and disidentification (Pêcheux 1982), and re/citation and de/citation (Terdiman 1985). For Pêcheux a "discourse-against" is that in which the subject of enunciation takes up a position of separation "with respect to what 'the universal subject' gives him to think . . . (distantiation, doubt, interrogation, challenge, revolt) . . . a struggle against ideological evidentness on the terrain of that evidentness, an evidentness with a negative sign, reversed on its own terrain." Disidentification, however, "constitutes a working (transformation-displacement) of the *subject-form* and not just its abolition" (Pêcheux 1982, 157, 159). In Terdiman's terms, the technique of re/citation seeks "to surround the[ir] antagonist and neutralize or explode it"; whereas de/citation, a total withdrawal from the orbit of the dominant, strives "to exclude it totally, to expunge it" (Terdiman 1985, 68, 70). Neither writes off the force of the counter-discursive, and Terdiman, who concedes that reverse-discourses are always interlocked with and parasitic on the dominant they contest—working as opposition without effacing the antagonist, inhabiting and struggling with the dominant which inhabits them—maintains that they function to survey the limits and weaknesses of the dominant by mapping the internal incoherences: "From this dialectic of discursive struggle, truths about the social formation—its characteristic modes of reproduction and its previously hidden vulnerabilities—inevitably emerge" (Terdiman 1985, 66).

A recent discussion of nativism condenses many of the current censures of cultural nationalism for its complicity with the terms of colonialism's discourse, with its claims to ancestral purity and inscriptions of monolithic notions of identity cited as evidence of the failure to divest itself of the specific institutional determinations of the West. Although allowing the profound political significance of the decolonized writing themselves as subjects of a literature of their own, Anthony Appiah's critique, which is principally directed against its current forms, extends to older (all?) articulations. In exposing the operation of a "nativist topology"—inside/outside, indigene/alien, Western/traditional—it installs a topology of its own, where the colonizer is dynamic donor and the colonized is docile recipient, where the West initiates and the native imitates. Thus while the reciprocity of the colonial relationship is stressed, all power remains with Western discourse. For example: "the overdetermined course of cultural nationalism in Africa has been to make real the imaginary identities to which Europe has subjected us (Appiah 1988, 164); the rhetoric of "intact indigenous traditions" and the very conception of an African personality and an African past are European inventions; the Third World intellectual is Europhone, immersed in the language and lit-

erature of the colonial countries. These statements could be modulated without underplaying or obscuring a necessary registration
of Western discursive power: Europe's fabrications of "Africa"
were deflected and subverted by African, Caribbean, and African-
American literary discourses; "African identity" is the product of
refusing Europe's gaze and returning its own anticolonialist look;
Europhone colonials transgress their immersion in European languages and literatures, seizing and diverting vocabularies,
metaphors, and literary traditions.

The occasion for Appiah's case against nativism is *Toward the
Decolonization of African Literature*—whose authors, Chinweizu,
Jemie, and Madubuike, invite censure for taking an unqualified
position on cultural autonomy—but its object is a critique of cultural nationalism's entrapment in a reverse-discourse:

> Railing against the cultural hegemony of the West, the nativists
> are of its party without knowing it. Indeed the very arguments,
> the rhetoric of defiance, that our nationalists muster are . . .
> canonical, time tested. . . . In their ideological inscription, the cul-
> tural nationalists remain in a position of counteridentification . . .
> which is to continue to participate in an institutional configura-
> tion—to be subjected to cultural identities they ostensibly decry.
> . . . Time and time again, cultural nationalism has followed the
> route of alternate genealogizing. We end up always in the same
> place; the achievement is to have invented a different past for it.
> (Appiah 1988, 162, 170)

The effect of this argument is to homogenize the varieties of
nationalisms and to deny both originality and effectivity to its
reverse-discourses. Such a contention is disputed by Partha Chatterjee's study which, despite a subtitle (*A Derivative Discourse*)
encouraging selective citation in the interest of relegating nationalist thought as mimetic and while recognizing the inherent contradiction of its reasoning within a framework of knowledge
serving a structure of power it seeks to repudiate, is concerned to
establish its *difference*: "Its politics impel it to open up that frame-

work of knowledge that presumes to dominate it, to displace that framework, to subvert its authority, to challenge its morality" (Chatterjee 1986, 42).

Some of the implications of arguments according a totalizing power to colonialist discourses emerges in Rosalind O'Hanlon's discussion of current research concerned to emphasize the British "invention" of nineteenth-century caste as a challenge to "the notion of an ageless caste-bound social order," but which maximizes the effectivity of "colonial conjuring," and by occluding the "complex and contradictory engagements with colonialist categories . . . often produces a picture of Indian actors who are helpless to do anything but reproduce the structures of their own subordination" (O'Hanlon 1989, 98, 104, 100). In this connection Ranajit Guha's eloquent inventory establishing the presence of an "Indian idiom of politics" discernible in the many languages of the subcontinent, demonstrates that the modes of subaltern colonial resistance, far from being determined by forms and vocabularies borrowed from the dominant culture, were rearticulations of pre-colonial traditions of protest (Guha 1989).[7]

Mindful of Robert Young's caution that the search for a "nativist alternative" may simply represent "the narcissistic desire to find an other that will reflect Western assumptions of selfhood" (Young 1990, 165), I will argue that something quite different animates those modes of postcolonial critique concerned to reconstruct a story from tales, legends, and idioms which are themselves transcriptions and improvisations of dissent that was never formally narrativised, and to produce an uncensorious but critical interrogation of colonial resistances when they were. It will be evident that the interest of such readings is to retain in the discussion that realm of imaginary freedom which these histories prefigured or configured, as well as to register decolonizing struggles as an emancipatory project despite the egregious failures these brought in their wake. Although the assumption here is that the discourses or discursive retracings of past dissidence come to us already encoded with the elements of a counter-narrative (which diminishes the critics' claim to be performing the insurgent act), it is we who by appropriating it to our theoretical purposes alter the material, in the process making visible its erasures, suppressions, and marginalizations, evident for example in the foregrounding of male figures of praxis and authority.

Elleke Boehmer's discussion of narratives of nationalist recuperation, identity reconstruction, and nation formation shows how images of the female body were used to embody ideals of the wholeness of subjectivity, history, and the state. Thus, while reversing colonialist iconography figuring penetration, pillage, and dismemberment—"repression upon the objectified, enslaved, colonised body"—such invocations of the female body "rest[s] upon the assumption of predominantly masculine authority and historical agency," nationalism's core concepts nesting in the metaphor of the maternal body. Because, Boehmer argues, postcolonial discourses of self-determination "have a considerable investment in nationalist concepts of 'selving' and of retrieving history, the gender specifics of nationalist iconography are accepted, or borne with, or overlooked," the deconstructions of such configurations only now being effected in postcolonial literatures (Boehmer 1991). In a related register, Ella Shohat writes that "Anticolonial intellectuals, though not particularly preoccupied with gender issues, have . . . used gender tropes to discuss colonialism," Césaire and Fanon implicity subverting representations of rape by violent dark men and cultures, and fantasies of rescuing virginal white and at times dark women, "while at the same time using gendered discourse to articulate oppositional struggle" (Shohat 1991, 56, 57).[8]

Such modulated attention to the retention of patriarchal positions in anticolonialist discourses points up the inadvisability of using the sources to write an optimistic narrative of liberation struggles as "ideologically correct." But in order to do justice to their histories—to borrow a phrase from Jonathan Dollimore[9]—it is surely necessary to refrain from a sanctimonious reproof of modes of writing resistance which do not conform to contemporary theoretical rules about discursive radicalism. Instead I would argue that the task is to address the empowering effects of constructing a coherent identity or of cherishing and defending against calumniation altered and mutable indigenous forms, which is not the same as the hopeless attempt to locate and revive pristine pre-colonial cultures.[10] It is an unwillingness to abstract resistance from its moment of performance that informs my discussion of Césaire and Fanon as authors of liberation theories which today could stand accused of an essentialist politics. For, as I read them, both affirmed the invention of an insurgent, unified black self, acknowledged the revolutionary energies released by valorizing the cultures denigrated by colonialism and, rather than construing the colonialist relationship in terms of negotiations with the structures of imperialism, privileged coercion over hegemony to project it as a struggle between implacably opposed forces—an irony made all too obvious in enunciations inflected, indeed made possible, by these very negotiations.

III

These remarks are a prelude to my considering whether those articulations of cultural nationalism I examine can be disposed of as a reverse ethnocentrism which simply reproduces existing categories, performing an identical function and producing the same effects as the system it contests. My route will be to Fanon via négritude, an unsafe road since, despite its heterogeneous languages and its interrogations of Western thought, this body of writing is routinely disparaged as the most exorbitant manifestation of a mystified ethnic essentialism, as an undifferentiated and retrograde discourse installing notions of a foundational and fixed native self and demagogically asserting the recovery of an immutable past. Perhaps this would account for the current tendency to ignore Fanon's voyage into and then around négritude or to dismiss it as a detour not mapped onto his theories. However, as the path of his project passed through the thickets of uncertain affiliation and irresolute withholding before emerging as unequivocal denunciation, this suggests that the appointment of Fanon as exemplar of anticolonialist theory liberated from identitarian thinking should perhaps be qualified.

In his unsententious critique of decolonizing discourses Edward Said suggests a progression from nativist through nationalist to liberation theory. While acknowledging the transgressive energies of the former in deranging the discourses of domination ranged against the colonized, and recognizing the achievement of nationalist movements in winning statutory independence for the occupied territories, it is liberation writing which is credited with producing a politics of secular illumination, articulating a transformation of social consciousness beyond ethnicity and reconceiving the possibilities of human experience in nonimperialist terms (see, for example, Said 1988, 1993). Not only are the stages less disjunct than the periodization suggests—messianic movements and Pan-Africanism were utopian in their goals; Nkrumah's nationalism was not exclusively Africanist, acknowledging as it did the recombinant qualities of a culture which had developed through assimilating Arabic and Western features; and so on—but the liberation theory of Fanon and Césaire was more impure than is here indicated, nativism remaining audible despite the strenuous endorsements of a post-European, transnational humanism as the ultimate goal.

Négritude's moment of articulation and reception—before the nationalist movements in Africa and the Caribbean had gained momentum, but after Marxist critiques of colonialism had been developed within the Indian independence struggle—may testify to both its originality as a cultural-political position and its limitations as an ideology. Many of the contemporary objections to négritude came from those who had welcomed its inception, and were delivered from a Marxist standpoint. These can be arranged into the following categories: systemized mystification construing "black being" as irrational and "black culture" as genetically determined, unified, and transnational, thus fostering the universalizing myth of a unified black identity in the face of its multiplicity and diversity; political error in failing to represent the anticolonial struggle as the national liberation of all classes, or to acknowledge the specificities of each national culture in the colonized world and, in the case of the Caribbean, in driving a wedge between African and other oppressed communities; and theoretical error in distorting African worldviews and overlooking that the synthesizing of indigenous with foreign elements in the colonized world had issued in complex and particularized modes of *mestizaje* or creolization[11]—sometimes, though rarely, this fusing being differently represented as the reconciliation of the African with the Western, or even complete cultural acclimatization to the West.[12]

What is notable is that many critics of négritude were prepared either to concede its liberating effects in fostering new modes of consciousness[13] or to offer alternative means of constituting reconceived identities. To counter the mystifications of négritude, the Haitian writer Jacques Stéphen Alexis in the 1950s proposed "marvellous realism" as a literary practice appropriate to producing the fantastic reality of the Caribbean's broken histories, different temporalities, and creolized cultural identities (Dash 1973). In another register, René Depestre, who dissociated himself from négritude's indifference to the diverse material conditions of cultural constitution and national character, emphasized the "syncretic elaboration of cultural elements taken from Africa and Europe," offering an alternative and not dissimilar program of ideological "*cimarronaje*" as the means for Caribbeans to resist depersonalization: "This cultural escape is an original form of rebellion which has manifested itself in religion, in folklore, in art and singularly in Caribbean literatures," the people in search of their identity becoming aware "of the validity of their African heritage latent in our society" (Depestre 1976, 62, 63).[14]

The sustained attack on négritude as an irrational ideology which perpetuated Western stereotypes came during the 1960s from a new generation of African philosophers and intellectuals concerned to expose the errors in notions of Africanism and the African personality. Scholars such as Stanislas Adotevi, Marcien Towa, and Paulin Hountondji attacked notions of the African as an intuitive being, of a fixed black essence and a static African culture, and dismissed "ethnophilosophy" for failing to distinguish between cultural anthropology and philosophy's critical activity when attempting to demonstrate the existence of a distinctive African mode of philosophical thinking (Irele 1986, Mudimbe 1988). According to Irele, Hountondji refuses to concede "any positive significance to the effort to rehabilitate African culture," asserting that the relationship between négritude and the ideology it intends to combat revealed "a peculiar ambiguity, a pathetic correspondence between the terms of African affirmation and the opposite system of ideas or representations proposed by the colonial ideology in its image of Africa" (Irele 1986, 147). The revolutionary socialist Towa, however, despite his repudiation of a cultural nationalism that seeks to resuscitate a heritage of past values irrelevant to the modernizing preoccupations and goals of contemporary Africa and his hostility to the state négritude of Senegal and the Cameroons, acknowledges the inspiration of Césaire and has referred to him as the prophet of the revolution of black people: "he announced the freedom of the Black [Nègre], he prophesied with his great voice the 'Beautiful City,' a world in which the Black could be himself, master of his destiny" (cited in Arnold 1981, 172).[15]

The presence of absolutist denunciations of négritude makes it necessary to recall its historical juncture and to differentiate between the articulations subsumed under its rubric. As a structure of feeling and a seizure of the means of self-representation by a rebellious elite, négritude was anticipated by the Haitian literary movement of the nineteenth century and in the United States by the Back to Africa movements and later by Dubois's Pan-Negroism and Pan-Africanism.[16] The definitive articulations of négritude are however usually attributed to the activities of students, writers, and intellectuals from the French colonies, who were closely associated with African-American expatriates in Paris during the early 1930s, the prime movers being Senghor from Senegal, Césaire from Martinique, and Léon Damas from French Guiana. (The subsequent dissemination of the movement was promoted by Alioune Diop's Présence Africaine which began publication in 1947.) Irele (1970) has characterized négritude as the francophone equivalent

of Pan-Africanism and a distinct current in African national consciousness and cultural nationalism. All the same, the extent to
which négritude was embraced by the African-Caribbean diaspora
is significant both to the willed construction of Africa as a country
of the mind, rather than a representation of a geohistorical place,
to the notion of "Africa" as the homeland of dispersed populations
in search of solidarity, and to the construing of black identity as
creolized and dislocated. Here it could be noted that if there were
exponents prone to definitions of an intrinsic black nature and a
unified black culture centered on an eternal Africa, others
deployed "black" as a multi-inflected signifier of oppression and
resistance, energizing a discursive stance from which colonialism's
most eloquent creatures interrogated the essentializing definitions
foisted on peoples of African origins. In this mode, exemplified by
Césaire's poetry, négritude is not a recovery of a pre-existent state,
but a textually invented history, an identity effected through figurative operations, and a tropological construction of blackness as a
sign of the colonized condition and its refusal.

Commentators on négritude tend to distinguish between Senghor's biologically determined notion of blackness as a distinctive
mode of being and a collective identity in which emotion and intuition are located as the essential attributes of the race (though Senghor did insist on the actuality and desirability of cross-cultural
fertilization), and Césaire's historical/cultural concept. Arnold
(1981), however, suggests that at the outset their views approximated, both having been influenced by the obscurantist ethnological notions of the subsequently discredited Frobenius, and by
antirational philosophers such as Spengler and Bergson. But by the
1940s Césaire, at the time a member of the Communist party, with
which he broke in 1958,[17] was concerned, in his analysis of colonialism as economic exploitation and cultural aggression, to establish a theoretical rather than a metaphysical basis to négritude,
hence rejecting the attempt to essentialize an African worldview or
to define it as a closed system. The perspective in his *Discourse on
Colonialism* is resolutely transnational and, while honoring an ante-
European past, looks to a post-European future, the dossier on the

West's sham humanism anticipating Fanon's execration in *The Wretched of the Earth*:

> The Indians massacred, the Moslem world drained of itself, the Chinese world defiled and perverted for a good century; the Negro world disqualified; mighty voices stilled forever; all this wreckage, all this waste, humanity reduced to a monologue, and you think that all this does not have its price? The truth is that this policy *cannot but bring about the ruin of Europe itself*, and that Europe, if it is not careful, will perish from the void it has created around itself. . . . What else has bourgeois Europe done? It has undermined civilizations, destroyed countries, ruined nationalities, extirpated "the root of diversity." (Césaire 1972, 57, 59)

Where Césaire is sure to be faulted by those who deplore nativist nostalgia is in his lament for what colonialism has destroyed:

> The wonderful Indian civilizations—and neither Deterding nor Royal Dutch nor Standard Oil will ever console me for the Aztecs and the Incas . . . [for] extraordinary *possibilities* wiped out. . . . For my part I make a systematic defense of the non-European civilizations. . . . They were communal societies, never societies of the many for the few. They were societies that were not only ante-capitalist . . . but also anti-capitalist. . . . I systematically defend our old Negro civilizations; they were courteous civilizations. (Césaire 1972, 20, 22, 23, 31).

An explicit reconstruction of négritude's beginnings can be found in Césaire's 1967 interview with the Haitian writer and political activist René Depestre, where he speaks of the program as a collective creation of Africans, North Americans, Antilleans, Guianans, and Haitians who came together in Paris during the 1930s to give expression to their struggle against alienation and the politics of assimilation:

> We adopted the word *nègre* as a term of defiance. . . . We found a violent affirmation in the words *nègre* and *négritude*. . . . It is a concrete rather than an abstract coming to consciousness. . . . We

lived in an atmosphere of rejection, and we developed an inferiority complex. . . . I have always thought that the black man was
searching for his identity. And . . . if what we want is to establish
this identity, then we must have a concrete consciousness of what
we are—that is of the first fact of our lives: that we are black; that
we were black and have a history . . . [that] there have been beautiful and important black civilizations . . . that its values were
values that could still make an important contribution to the
world. (Césaire 1972, 74, 76)

This concrete coming to consciousness was realized by Césaire
as a poet; and because many of the writings of négritude are open
to some or all of the charges made against it as an ideological tendency, any argument that as a literary practice it performed a textual struggle for self-representation in which the indeterminacy of
language ruptured fixed configurations, invented a multivalent
blackness, and wrenched "Africa" out of its time-bound naming
and into new significations, is most readily made by referring to
his over-determined and polysemic poetry. Although made possible, as he concedes, by surrealism, this exceeded the influence of
European modes and violated its forms in what Arnold calls a
"sophisticated hybridization, corrosion and parody" of Western
traditions.[18]

In an essay on Césaire, James Clifford argues for uncoupling
his coinage of négritude from the "elaboration of a broad black
identity" and attaching it to "very specific affirmations and negations," citing the passage in *Notebook* beginning "my négritude is
not . . ." (see below). However Clifford's selective citation of "The
verb 'marronner'/for René Depestre, Haitian poet" suggests that
the trajectory of his case is directed at dissociating Césaire from
négritude. The poem, written in 1955 and subsequently published
in numerous revised versions, was Césaire's response to
Depestre's ready compliance with the Communist party's decree
against surrealism and for accessible and committed verse. Clifford's reading is appropriately concerned with how "Césaire
makes rebellion and the remaking of culture—the historical

maroon experience—into a . . . necessary new verb [that] names the New World poetics of continuous transgression and coopera- tive cultural activity" (Clifford 1988, 181). But what is occluded is, as Arnold argues, that the poem appeals to Depestre not to abandon his négritude—"Courageous tom-tom rider / is it true that you mistrust the native forest . . . is it possible / that the rains of exile / have slackened the drum ˙ skin of your voice?"— entreating him to "escape the shackles of European prosody" (Arnold) just as in the past slaves had escaped from bondage, to this end coining the neologism "marronner": "shall we escape like slaves Depestre, like slaves" (in an earlier version this read: "Let's escape them Depestre let's escape them / As in the past we escaped our whip-wielding masters") (Césaire 1983, 369–71).

It is possible to disregard Césaire's account of his intentions when he speaks of his poetry as a way to break the stranglehold of accepted French form in order to create a new language, "an Antillean French, a black French . . . one capable of communi- cating the African heritage" (Césaire 1972, 66, 67). However, we cannot overlook that poetry which adapted the structure of some African languages, and drew on African folklores and cosmolo- gies, does effect an identification with Africa—"from brooding too long on the Congo / I have become a Congo resounding with forests and rivers" (Césaire 1983, 51)—and does construct an imaginary Africa as signifier of the legacy shared by Africans of the continent and the diaspora. The "Guinea" of his "Ode to Guinea," written before the name was adopted by a postindepen- dence territory, is the mythic land of the Caribbean creole lan- guages—the "Africa" or "Guinea" that is the heaven of black peo- ples—and the "Ethiopia" of "Ethiopia . . . / for Alioune Diop" embodies what Eshleman and Smith call "the dignity lost to other African peoples," a location occupying a special place "in the per- sonal mythology of Négritude writers" (see Eshleman and Smith 1983, 11, and Arnold 1981, 218).

By rewriting the stories of Africa's long oppressions—see "All the way from Akkad, from Elam, from Sumer" and "Africa"— Césaire derives an ethos common to all blacks, out of which an anticolonial and ultimately an anticapitalist identity can be constituted, as in "A Salute to the Third World / for Léopold Sedar Senghor" where connections between the Caribbean dispersal and the African motherland are forged before gesturing toward a larger and more inclusive solidarity.

Arnold's attention to the shifting values produced by images of blackness in *Notebook of a Return to a Native Land* convinces that this is indeed "The epic of négritude" and a classic in the literature of decolonization. What Arnold traces is how through the creation of a new style, the transformation of black consciousness and the self-construction of an African-Caribbean identity is enacted, the neologism "négritude" occurring both to hail past glories in Haiti and to signify abjection before its "third and decisive statement of négritude" as reconciled to itself[19]: "my négritude is not a / stone, its deafness hurled against the clamour of the day . . . / my négritude is neither tower nor cathedral / it takes root in the red flesh of the soil / it takes root in the ardent flesh of the sky" (Césaire 1983, 67, 69). As an instance of what Ella Shohat calls the use of gendered discourse in articulating anticolonialist struggles, she cites Césaire's remark about adventurers violating Africa "to make the stripping of her easier" (Shohat 1991, 57). Yet although his poetry does invoke Africa as inscribed on the woman's body (see "Ode to Guinea,""Hail to Guinea,""Africa," "Ethiopia," and "A Salute to the Third World"), and while the authoritative voice is masculine, the figure of suffering and endurance is not invariably the woman, and in *Notebook* the trope of négritude is doubly gendered: "all our blood aroused by the male heart of the sun / those who know about the feminity of the moon's oily body / the reconciled exultation of antelope and star / those whose survival travels in the germination of grass! / Eia perfect circle of the world, enclosed concordance" (Césaire 1983, 69).

The multivalencies of Césaire's négritude preempts both closure and fixity, making it available to rearticulations covering other modes of oppression. It has since been reinvoked by national liberation movements and continues to be renewed in unforeseen ways within the postcolonial critique—as when James Snead, while acknowledging the necessity of preserving the specificity of historical experience, commends a "broad-based, even militant usage of the term black as a unifying metaphor," and an object of cultural identification and ideological bonding (Snead 1988, 48); or when Kobena Mercer looks back to the redefinition of black identity in Britain during the early 1980s as "an empowering signifier of Afro-Asian alliances" (Mercer 1990, 77). What was it then in négritude that caused Fanon to recognize it as liberating and resist it as mystifying before launching a concerted attack which was at pains to signal that its hold on his thinking had been relinquished?

IV

The somewhat schematic summary which Mudimbe (1988), in an otherwise modulated account of the movement, gives of Fanon's relationship to négritude—namely that an initial affiliation gave way to a position based on situating African ideologies of otherness as the antithesis to colonialist constitution, the synthesis to be realized in political liberation—tends to smooth over the persistent instabilities in Fanon's writings where proclamations of a future beyond ethnicity continue to be intercepted by affirmations of the immediate need to construct an insurgent black subjectivity. In another register, what Abiola Irele neglects when he claims that Césaire's poetry provided "the essential ground-plan for Fanon's phenomenological reflection on black existence" in Black Skin, White Masks (Irele 1986, 138) is that, despite its many salutations to Césaire's liberating influences and its moments of unstable identification, the study effects the problematization of négritude. Fanon may well have perceived his mode of thinking as dialectical; however, the language of his flamboyant writing (he wrote a number of plays which he chose not to publish) is witness to the conflicting predications remaining disjunct. Although such incommensurability is especially marked in Black Skin, White Masks, where Marxism coexists with existentialism and psychoanalysis, scholarly citation is juxtaposed to anecdote, and the torsions of self-analysis art precariously balanced against the poised interpretation of a historical condition, none of his writings—with the exception of the last section of *The Wretched of the Earth*—is without the discord of incompatible testimony. Hence I will argue that Fanon's writings function at a point of tension between cultural nationalism and transnationality, without resolving the contradiction and without yielding an attachment to the one or the aspiration to the other.

It is this "historical Fanon" who never quite abandoned "all fixity of identity," an ironic figure who resists recuperation as the paradigmatic figure of liberation theory that is recognized by Henry Louis Gates Jr. (see chapter 9 this volume). Thus when Fanon moved from the many different first-person-singular voices deployed in the psycho-autobiography of an assimilated and insulted Martinican tempted by négritude to the "we" of Algerians and unspecified African communities in polemical writings proclaiming a new international community, he continued to concede the importance of valorizing pre-colonial histories and cultures that had been systematically disfigured and devalued by colonialism:

> It was with the greatest delight that they discovered that there was nothing to be ashamed of in the past, but rather dignity, glory and solemnity. The claim to a national culture in the past does not only rehabilitate that nation and serve as a justification for the hope of a future national culture. In the sphere of psycho-affective equilibrium it is responsible for an important change in the native. (Fanon 1968, 170)

As I read it, both an intellectual apprehension of blackness as a construct ("what is often called the black soul is a white man's artifact" [1967a, 16]) and a visceral attachment to the powerful fiction of black identity are always evident in *Black Skin, White Masks*, the language of criticism repeatedly interrupted by articulations of empathy with the impulse. What I will try to trace is how the precise statements of intention as laid down in the introduction—i.e., a clinical study of the attitudes of the modern Antillean Negro and a psychopathological explanation of the state of being an Antillean

Negro—mutate into the multivocal enunciations of the essays that follow, and where the stated brief is exceeded when specified Negroes are displaced by "the Negro" in the white world. (All existing translations of Fanon use this term for the black person of African descent.) At the start, which appears to have been written first and does not attempt to elide the ensuing contradictions, Fanon outlines his project as the attempt to effect the disalienation of the depersonalized Negro by offering a psychological analysis of the massive psychoexistential complex produced through the juxtasposition of the white and black races. Although a passage from Césaire's *Discourse on Colonialism* serves as the epigraph, and the importance of social and economic realities is acknowledged, no further reference is made to colonialism as the specific situation of the pathological juxtaposition. What is given space in an address directed at white and black brothers is the perspective of transcending the present and an insistence that if the existing structure is to be eliminated and the Negro extricated from his universe, then unilateral liberation is insufficient.

So here we find the vision of a condition beyond ethnicity already in place—"I believe that the individual should tend to take on the universality inherent in the human condition"—while the attempt of blacks "to prove to white men, at all costs, the richness of their thought, the equal value of their intellect" (Césaire 1972, 12) is designated as a symptom of that vicious circle where whites are sealed in their whiteness and blacks in their blackness. To break out of this entrapment, fervor is eschewed, and digging into one's flesh to find meaning is scorned, the narrative voice in "The fact of blackness" distancing itself from its portrayal of the desperate struggle of the educated Negro, "slave of the spontaneous and cosmic Negro myth . . . driven to discover the meaning of black identity," who "with rage in his mouth and abandon in his heart . . . buries himself in the vast black abyss" (Césaire 1972, 16).

The incommensurable enunciations of *Black Skin, White Masks* produce a dissonance that is something other than ambivalence, for the adoption of heuristic procedures in order to establish négritude as a pathology involves the speaking subject voicing opposing stances with an equally passionate intensity—the process of discovering a black identity and history registering intimacy with that impulse simultaneously with recoil from the extravagance of its rhetoric and its recourse to the paralogical (see especially Fanon 1967a, 113, 115, 122, 123–27). The graph of this learning process—if this is what it is—continues when the speaker adopts the stance of one who turns to antiquity in order to establish black creativity and achievement. Up to and including this moment, and let us suppose always in forensic mode, the strategies of affirming blackness, embracing unreason, and reclaiming the past had been explored and found wanting, every move having been determined and countermanded by the white world's demands and reactions: "Every hand was a losing hand for me" (Fanon 1967a, 132). But how are we to read the protest against Sartre which is delivered in a register of unalloyed identification when the speaker takes up the position of that black person who had determined "on the level of ideas and intellectual activity to reclaim my négritude," only to find that "it was snatched away from me. . . . Proof was presented that my effort was only a term in the dialectic . . . I felt I had been robbed of my last chance" (Fanon 1967a, 132, 133).

This is a reference to Sartre's *Black Orpheus,* which appeared in 1948 as the preface to Senghor's anthology of new Negro and Malagasy poetry, and which Fanon designates as "a date in the intellectualization of the experience of being black" when challenging its mistake not only in seeking "the source of the source" but in blocking that source (Fanon 1967a, 134).[20] Sartre's essay applauded the act whereby the oppressed seized a word hurled at them as an insult and turned it into a means of vindication, while at the same time relegating the movement as "the weak stage of a dialectical progression." In his schema, the theory and practice of white supremacy is the thesis, and négritude the moment of negativity and thus dedicated to its own destruction: "it is passage and not objective, means and not ultimate goal" (Sartre 1963, 60), this being the passing into the objective, positive, exact notion of the proletariat. Despite which Sartre commended the fashioning of a black subjectivity and the invention of an "Africa beyond reach, *imaginary* continent" (Sartre 1963, 19), grasping as others since have not always done the revolutionary project carried out by poets of négritude who, in "degallicizing" the oppressor's language, shattered its customary associations.

Is Fanon wearing one of the many masks he dons for exegetical purposes when he accuses Sartre of attributing négritude to the forces of history? "And so it is not I who make a meaning for myself, but it is the meaning that was already there, preexisting, waiting for me" (Fanon 1967a, 134). This anger appears to be sustained when he censures the born Hegelian for forgetting that to attain consciousness of self, to grasp one own's being, "consciousness has to lose itself in the night of the absolute" (p. 133). In destroying black zeal, what Sartre had failed to understand was that "I needed to lose myself completely in Négritude . . . In terms of consciousness, black consciousness is immanent in its own eyes. I am not a potentiality of something, I am wholly what I am. I do not have to look for the universal . . . My Negro consciousness does not hold itself out as a lack. It is its own follower" (p. 135).[21]

If this could appear to be a vindication of négritude's project, then in the last chapters, specified in the introduction as an attempt at "a psychopathological and philosophical explanation of the state of *being* a Negro" (p. 15), Fanon again disavows not only the Antillean Negroes' attempt to be white but the effort to maintain their alterity—"Alterity of rupture, of conflict, of battle" (p. 222). By the time of the conclusion, the impulse to discover a black past is unequivocally repudiated: "In no way should I dedicate myself to the revival of an unjustly unrecognized Negro civilization" (p. 226), the denunciations moving toward a lofty detachment—"I do not have the right to allow myself to be mired in what the past has determined. I am not the slave of the Slavery that dehumanized my ancestors . . . The body of history does not determine a single one of my actions. I am my own foundation" (pp. 230–31)—before rising/collapsing into the utopianism of his ultimate desire: "That it may be possible for me to discover and to love man, wherever he may be. The Negro is not. Any more than the white man" (p. 231).

The "drama of consciousness" performed in *Black Skin, White Masks* can be read as Fanon directing a scenario in which the players are alienated Antillean blacks learning or being weaned from the errors of both assimilation and négritude, and hence as charting the move from the reactional, in which there is always resentment, to the actional (p. 222). But perhaps it traces the path of the author effecting his own cure within the space of its pages— négritude marking the transgressive moment of emergence from the colonized condition, and the transition from négritude to universal solidarity signalling disalienation and the transcendence of ethnicity. The problem here is that subsequent writings replay the dilemma of fashioning/disavowing black identity. Some years later in "West Indians and Africans" Fanon continued to affirm Césaire's positive influence in valorizing what West Indians had rejected, teaching them to look in the direction of Africa, and instead of identifying with and mimicking the white world, recognizing themselves as transplanted children of black slaves. But now, writing in the third person about the West Indian, Fanon detaches himself from what he had proclaimed in the first person as a transformation of consciousness, by denying the existence of a Negro people, deriding the Africa of the West Indian imagination—"Africa the hard and the beautiful, Africa exploding with anger, tumultuous bustle, splash, Africa land of truth" (1967b, 26)—and pronouncing that "It thus seems that the West Indian, after the great white error, is now living in the great black mirage" (p. 27).

The retreat from a wavering empathy with négritude becomes an ambiguous critique in Fanon's address to the First Congress of Negro Writers and Artists in Paris in 1956. In his disobliging account of the meeting, where he intimates that the agenda was incoherent and the platform much given to demagogy, James Baldwin (1961) observes that what Césaire left out of his eloquent speech reviling the colonial experience was precisely that it had produced men like himself. Since this is now something of a platitude, it is notable that Fanon did not dwell on his own colonialist formation, concentrating instead on colonialism as expropriation and spoliation matched by "the sacking of cultural patterns," the natives having been induced by the overwhelming power and authority of the oppressor to repudiate their original forms of existence (1967b, 33). Having earlier protested at Sartre's relegation of négritude to a minor term, Fanon now essentially follows his model, and while like Sartre he commends black affirmations in the face of white insult, the negative/positive evaluations of cultural revaluations interrupt each other in a double-voiced critique of the native intellectual's abrupt movement from ardent assimilation to the swooning before tradition:

> This culture, abandoned, sloughed off, neglected, despised, becomes for the inferiorized an object of passionate attachment. . . . The culture put into capsules, which has vegetated since the foreign domination, is revalorized. It is not reconceived, grasped anew, dynamized from within. . . . The past, becoming henceforth a constellation of values, becomes identified with the Truth. (1967b, 41, 43)

But at the moment when a reader could assume that this predicates a total rejection of négritude's project, the perspective again shifts when cultural affirmation is marked as a necessary moment in the realization of a combative position: "This rediscovery, this absolute valorization almost in defiance of reality, objectively indefensible, assumes an incomparable and subjective importance. . . . The plunge into the chasm of the past is the condition and source of freedom" (1967b, 43).

Fanon's argument characterizes native culture under colonialism as inert, stultified, lethargic, rigid, uncreative, with the natives reduced to despising their indigenous modes of existence—assertions for which much countervailing evidence can be adduced. However, for Fanon it was only when the movement for decolonization was set in motion that there occurred a qualitative leap from stagnation to modernity, from passivity to insurgency. It is this "zone of occult instability where the people dwell . . . that fluctuating movement which they are just giving a shape to" (1968,

182) that remains unknown to those native writers and artists who, lagging behind the people and going against the current of history by seeking to revive abandoned traditions, forget "that the forms of thought and what it feeds on, together with modern techniques of information, language and dress have dialectically reorganized the peoples' intelligences" (1968, 181). Hence his eloquent defense of the natives' discovery of the past as a means of rehabilitation is countermanded when, and as it were in the same breath, disdain is directed at the recovery of old legends that will be "interpreted in the light of a borrowed aestheticism and of a conception of the world which was discovered under other skies . . . the poetic tom-tom rhythms breaking through the poetry of revolt" (1968, 179–81). In Fanon's argument the condition of possibility for producing a literature of combat is that writers take up arms on the side of the people, since only such writings will mold the national consciousness "giving it form and contours and flinging open before it new and boundless horizons" (1968, 193). That he could be formulaic in his appreciation of the arts is apparent in his comments on the blues as the black slave's lament, "offered up for the admiration of the oppressor," and his prophecies that the "end of racism would sound the knell of great Negro music" (1967b, 37), or that as soon as the Negro comes to an understanding of himself, the jazz howl that whites perceived as an expression of nigger-hood will be replaced by "his trumpet sound[ing] more clearly and his voice less hoarsely" (1968, 195).[22]

Fanon's writings on national culture can be read as a response to Césaire's address to the First Congress in 1956 where, in countering Senghor's metaphysical version of négritude, he had argued that whereas a culture must be national, a civilization can be supranational, and that whereas specific African cultures had been decimated by enforced dispersal and colonial aggression, important elements of an African civilization had persisted ("Culture and Colonization," cited in Arnold 1981, 185–87). By this time Fanon's disenchantment with the official cultural nationalism of the newly independent African states had been exacerbated by the apostasy to the cause of the national liberation struggles of its most

eloquent exponents—Senghor had underwritten De Gaulle's proposed Franco-African community and withheld Senegal's support
for the Algerian liberation struggle; Césaire had backed the constitutional referendum on the Fifth Republic whereby Martinique
would become an overseas department of France, and Jacques
Rabemananjara of Malagasy had voted against the Algerian
people in the General Assembly of the United Nations (I will evade
any questions of whether a theorist's public acts can be held to
invalidate the theories he or she espouses). Fanon now took the
position that any notion of a continental African culture, of
"Negroism," was a blind alley, stressing instead the heterogeneity
of Negro and African-Negro cultures and the different concrete
problems confronting specific black populations, and insisting that
solidarity was forged not in declamations of a common culture but
in political struggle. In his statement to the Second Congress of
Black Artists and Writers in Rome in 1959 (1968), Fanon declared
that culture is necessarily the expression of the nation, just as the
nation is the condition of culture, once again pointing to the error
of the native intellectual's ways, whether assimilationist or
"Negroist." Distinguishing between national consciousness and
nationalism, Fanon maintained that the former was the most elaborate form of culture, and declared that the national period was
the necessary space for the growth of an international dimension
and of universalizing values.[23]

To the end there are signs of Fanon's links with the négritude
movement—the title of his last essays taken from *The Internationale*
had previously been adapted by Jacques Roumain in a poem
calling for a black revolt against the bourgeois white world, and he
remained in touch with the editors of *Présence Africaine*.[24] Yet his
repudiation of négritude in his 1959 address to the congress is
unqualified. Like Trotsky, who scorned the notion of a proletarian
culture since the proletariat would be abolished on the attainment
of classless society, so Fanon now rejected black culture as an
abstract populism: "To believe that it is possible to create a black
culture is to forget that niggers are disappearing, just as those
people who brought them into being are seeing the break-up of

their economic and cultural supremacy" (Fanon 1968, 188–89). This optimism of the intellect is what Albert Memmi addresses when he remarks that for Fanon "the day oppression ceases, the new man is supposed to appear before our eyes immediately" (Memmi 1968, 88), although it should be noted that Fanon predicated this leap into the future, this instant emancipation on the transformative powers of a principled decolonizing struggle: "After the conflict there is not only the disappearance of the colonized man. . . . This new humanity cannot do otherwise than define a new humanism for itself and others. It is prefigured in the objectives and methods of the conflict" (Fanon 1968, 197).

The verso of these epiphanies to a future transcending ethnicity and nationalism is a measured demystification of Europe's "spiritual adventure" undertaken at the expense of the rest of the world, and a call that the oppressed should slough off enslavement to its values by recognizing the failure of its claims: "Let us try to create the whole man, whom Europe has been incapable of bringing to triumphant birth" (Fanon 1968, 253). Here Fanon's writings appear as prematurely postcolonialist and are reminiscent of what Anthony Appiah, in discussing Ouologuem's "postrealist" novels, describes as writings of delegitimation that inscribe a postnativist politics and a transnational rather than a national solidarity: "they reject not only the Western imperium but also the nationalist project of the postcolonial national bourgeoisie . . . The basis for that project of delegitimation cannot be the postmodernist one: rather it is grounded in an appeal to an ethical universal" (Appiah 1991, 353). In turning away from Europe as a source and model of meanings and aspirations, Fanon's last writings look not to the fulfillment of the Enlightenment's ideals within the existing order but to decolonization as the agency of a transfigured social condition; hence holding in place that vision of the anticolonial struggle as a global emancipatory project and projecting the radical hope of an oppositional humanism. What is less certain is whether the time for transnational politics had come when Fanon was writing, whether it has now, and whether the prospect of his postnativist "whole man" is one that wholly delights.

NOTES

1. For Fanon, the colonized prior to modern movements for national independence were passive, stultified, unproductive. Presumably this characterization applied only to the Caribbean and sub-Saharan Africa, since Algeria is credited with sustained military and cultural resistance against the French occupiers (1967b, 65).

2. This position is elucidated and underwritten by Robert Young (1990).

3. These issues are addressed by amongst others Paul Smith (1988), Diana Fuss (1989), and, in a colonial context, Rosalind O'Hanlon (1988; see especially pp. 204–205). The framing of the agon of structure and agency has been questioned by Anthony Appiah (1991).

4. Instances are the upsurge during the late nineteenth century of messianic movements and Ethiopian or Zionist Churches in sub-Saharan Africa which Thomas Hodgkin (1957) has described as precipitating a clash between colonial and prophetic power; maroonage or the flight of slaves from the plantation and post-plantation systems of the Americas to an outlaw life in the mountains and forests or to other territories; the concealment of meaning from master and overseer in creole and carnival; the parodic inversions of the colonizer's images in song and dance; noncooperation with projects of "social improvement"; adherence to traditions the occupiers sought to reform; idleness and malingering to circumvent and undermine the demands of enforced and indentured labor regulations; and—if one is tempted to adapt the schema of silent majorities devised by Baudrillard (1983) to specify inertia as opposition to a contemporary condition saturated by information technology—silence as a weapon against political authority. The problem here is that silence can be read either as a sign of resignation to subjugation—being reduced to silence, as marking the refusal to speak or be heard within the oppressor's system of meanings—or as a form of nonspeaking subjectivity; it can also register an exclusion operated by the text—the hole in the narrative. Some of the modes listed above have been problematized by David Theo Goldberg, who maintains that "The discourses promoting resistance to racism must not prompt identification with and in terms of categories fundamental to the discourse of oppression." As examples of the failure to make this distinction, he cites the black separatist movement and the tactics of resistance used by plantation slaves: "slow work

and malingering undermined the plantation economy but reinforced the stereotype of laziness; self-mutilation increased labor costs but steeled the stereotype of barbarism" (1990, 313 and 318 n.58). The terms of this strong reservation impinge on the argument for the effectivity of a reverse discourse pursued in this essay.

5. Ranajit Guha however has maintained that "the appropriation of a past by conquest carried with it the risk of rebounding on its conquerors. It can end up by sacralizing the past for the subject people and encouraging it to use it in their effort to define and affirm their own identity" (1989, 212).

6. A case for the power of the reverse-discourse which uses the same categories and vocabulary as the texts of social control it contests is made by Jonathan Dollimore, citing Foucault's argument in *History of Sexuality*, vol. 1: "Deviancy returns from abjection by deploying just those terms which relegated it to that state in the first place—including 'nature' and 'essence.' . . . A complex and revealing dialectic between the dominant and the deviant emerges from histories of homosexual representation, especially from the homosexual (later gay) appropriations of nature and essence" (1991, 95–96).

7. See Guha: "peasant uprisings variously called *hool, dhing, bidrohal hangama, fituri,* etc.; . . . *hizrat* or desertion *en masse* of peasants or other laboring people . . . *dharma* or protest by sitting down in the offender's presence with the pledge not to move until the redress of grievance; . . . *hartal* or the general suspension of public activity; . . . *dharmaghat* or withdrawal of labor; . . . *jat mara,* or measures to destroy the offender's caste by refusal to render such specialist services as are required to insure him and his kin against pollution; . . . *danga* or sectarian, ethnic, caste and class violence involving large bodies of the subaltern population" (1989, 267).

8. Where Shohat seems to be overstating her case is in suggesting that stories of sexual violence against Third World women are "relatively privileged" over those of violence toward Third World men.

9. See Dollimore who argues for avoiding a "theoreticist" writing off of the histories of "essentialist politics" (1991, pp. 44–45).

10. But nor should the cost of the "hybridity" effected by colonialism's invasions be uncounted: glossing Edward Brathwaite's definition of creolization "as one's adaptation to a new environment through the loss of parts of oneself and the gain of parts of the Other," Manthia Diawara adds that "one must be aware of the fact that in fusing Whiteness with the seductiveness of hybridization, one is also sacrificing not

only a part of Blackness, but certain Black people" (Diawara 1990–91, 82). These "certain Black people," inhabiting extant although neither static or intact autochthonous cultures, emerge in Caroline Rooney's reading of a story by Ama Ata Aidoo where she draws attention to a narration which legitimates "a culture that predates and is not erased by colonial founding fathers, who are not then an originating point of reference," and criticizes the amnesia of those who, having embraced the metropolitan culture, renounce their natal communities (1991, 222).

11. In the late 1940s African writers and political activists close to the Communist party—Gabriel d'Arboussier, Albert Franklin and Abdoulaye Ly—attacked négritude for failing to give expression to the anti-imperialist revolution as a national liberation struggle fought by all classes, dismissing it as a mystification which placed the accent on the irrational aspects of African life and claimed the existence of a unique Negro culture—charges of which Césaire was exonerated (Hyams 1971). Compare Wole Soyinka (1976), who faults négritude for negative and contradictory definitions, distortions of the African worldview, and reinstalling blasphemies about the African as a nonanalytic being.

12. During the 1950s and 1960s black writers who were the stepchildren of an Anglophone oppression tended to emphasize their Western formation—see, for example, Baldwin (1961) and Mphahlele (in Hyams 1971)—or to stress the fusion of African strains with other lines in the making of African American identity (see Ellison 1967).

13. Mphahlele (Hyams 1971) allowed the historical fact of négritude as both a protest and a positive assertion of African cultural values, and Soyinka conceded that "it had provided a lifeline along which the dissociated individual could be pulled back to the source of his material essence and offered a prospect for the coming into being of new black social entities" (1976, 64).

14. Depestre was subsequently to put a greater distance between his stance and that of négritude, attributing its "original sin . . . and the adventures that destroyed its initial project" to "the spirit that made it possible: anthropology," a criticism which Mudimbe reads as referring to techniques of ideological manipulation (cited by Mudimbe 1988, 187).

15. Towa's article "Aimé Césaire, prophete de la révolution des peuples noirs" was published in *Abbia* (Cameroon) no. 21, 1969; see Bjornson on Abbia, founded in 1962 by William Eteki whose influential policies/politics attempted to reconcile négritude with scientific knowledge in constructing a new African philosophy (1991, 173–74).

16. There was apparently some continuity in Haiti where during the 1920s the journal *Revue indigène* was established, while in the 1930s a group of intellectuals and writers calling themselves *Les Griots* (a name borrowed from an African term for the profession of poet–historian–musician) coined the word *nigrité* to signal a rejection of assimilation and the reconstruction of an African identity. Similarly there were moves by literary coteries in Puerto Rico, Cuba, and Brazil to locate the black communities of the territories within an African continuum and effect a bond of solidarity with other products of the African dispersal—as there were in the Harlem Renaissance.

17. Césaire's *Letter to Maurice Thorez* (1956) criticized the Communist party's position on the Caribbean dependencies; questioned the applicability of orthodox Marxist analysis to Martinican conditions; rejected the thesis that the urban proletariat, which scarcely existed in Martinique, was necessarily the vanguard of revolution; and reiterated his adherence to négritude (cited by Arnold 1981, 172). Two years later Césaire, apparently at the behest of André Malraux, supported De Gaulle's constitutional referendum whereby Martinique became an overseas department of the Fifth Republic.

18. So novel are language, syntax, and trope that commentators have in glossing his poetry been moved to their own displays of stylistic pyrotechnics: "A poem of Césaire . . . bursts and turns on itself as a fuse, as bursting suns which turn and explode in new suns, in a perpetual surpassing. It is not a question of meeting in a calm unity of opposites but rather a forced coupling into a single sex, of black in its opposition to white" (Sartre 1976, 36).

19. Cf. Irele: "Césaire's poetry . . . becomes quite literally an affect; a drama of consciousness, a sloughing off of processes by which the complex of negative associations through which the black subject has been forced to perceive himself is overturned and transformed into a mode of mental liberation and ultimately of self-acceptance" (1986, 137). In their introduction to Césaire's poetry, Eshleman and Smith refer to French usages of words to designate things or persons belonging to the black race: the euphemistic "Noir," the derogatory "negro," and the more neutral; "nègre": "it is in this light that one must read Césaire's use of the word 'nègre' and its derivatives 'négritude,' 'négrillon' and 'négraille': He was making up a family of words based on what he considered the most insulting way to refer to blacks. The paradox, of course, was that this implicit reckoning with the blacks' ignominy, this process of self-

irony and self-denigration, was the necessary step on the path to a new self-image and spiritual rebirth" (Césaire 1983, 27).

20. For Mudimbe and Irele, Sartre's contribution was to have shifted négritude from an ethnic to an historical concept and a revolutionary project, Mudimbe crediting Sartre with transforming it into a major political event and a philosophical critique of colonialism, while at the same time subjugating "the militant's generosity of mind and heart to the fervor of a political philosophy" (1988, 84).

21. The movement of Fanon's argument resembles the tropological production of blackness's different registers in *Notebook of a Return to the Native Land*.

22. The cultural agenda proposed by Fanon, in which an "upward springing trend" is required in writing, dancing, and singing, iterates the desiderata heard before and since in the program for the arts drawn up by radical political movements, bringing to mind Césaire's ironic reprimand to Depestre for supporting the then party line on poetry: "Comrade Depestre / It is undoubtedly a very serious problem / the relation between poetry and Revolution / the content determines the form / and what about keeping in mind as well the dialectical / backlash by which the form taking its revenge / chokes the poem like an accursed fig tree" (1983, p. 371).

23. Writing on cultural resistance, Amilcar Cabral looked forward to the emergence of a "universal culture," while calling for "a spiritual reconversion of mentalities, a re-Africanization that will aim at the development of a people's culture and of all aboriginal positive cultural values" (1980, p. 153). In his Memorial Lecture for Eduardo Mondlane, "National liberation and culture," Cabral, who calls national liberation "an act of culture," steers a course between concessions to and rejections of négritude, advocating that a people freeing themselves from foreign rule must "recapture the commanding heights of its own culture" and reject "any kind of subjection to foreign culture," while repudiating the "rather byzantine discussion of which African cultural values are specific or non-specific to Africa" (1974, 15–16). All the same he writes of the armed war of liberation as an "expression of our culture and our African-ness. It must be expressed when it comes, in a ferment signifying above all the culture of the people which has freed itself" (p. 17). In the editorial, Cabral is cited as denouncing a notion, held even by the Left, "that imperialism made us enter history, at the moment when it began its adventures in our countries," substituting instead "We consider that when imperialism arrived in Guine, it made us leave history—our history."

24. Peter Worsley suggests that "It is more than possible that Roumain's poem rather than the Internationale, was the source of Fanon's title. It is a poem that saw the revolt of color and the revolt of class as overlapping. . . . Roumain, after a 'furious embittered rhapsody on the sufferings of the Negro,' stops himself short with a POURTANT in capital letters—'And yet! I only want to belong to your race / workers and peasants of all countries'" (1972, 197).

9.

Critical Fanonism

Henry Louis Gates Jr.

This book, it is hoped, will be a mirror.

Fanon

One of the signal developments in contemporary criticism over the past several years has been the ascendancy of the colonial paradigm. In conjunction with this new turn, Frantz Fanon has now been reinstated as a global theorist, and not simply by those engaged in Third World or subaltern studies. In a recent collection centered on British romanticism, Jerome McCann opens a discussion of William Blake and Ezra Pound with an extended invocation of Fanon. Donald Pease has used Fanon to open an attack on Stephen Greenblatt's reading of the Henriad and the interdisciplinary practices of the new historicism. And Fanon, and published interpretations of Fanon, have become regularly cited in the rereadings of the Renaissance that have emerged from places like Sussex, Essex, and Birmingham (see McGann 1989, 85–107 and Pease 1991).

Originally published in *Critical Inquiry* 17, no. 3 (1991): 457–70. Reprinted with permission of the University of Chicago Press.

251

My intent is not to offer a reading of Fanon to supplant these others, but to read, even if summarily, some of these readings of Fanon. By focusing on successive appropriations of this figure, as both totem and text, I think we can chart out an itinerary through contemporary colonial discourse theory. I want to stress, then, that my ambitions here are extremely limited: What follows may be a prelude to a reading of Fanon, but does not even begin that task itself.[1]

Fanon's current fascination for us has something to do with the convergence of the problematic of colonialism with that of subject-formation. As a psychoanalyst of culture, as a champion of the wretched of the earth, he is an almost irresistible figure for a criticism that sees itself as both oppositional and postmodern. And yet there's something Rashomon-like about his contemporary guises. It may be a matter of judgment whether his writings are rife with contradiction or richly dialectical, polyvocal, and multivalent; they are in any event highly porous, that is, wide open to interpretation, and the readings they elicit are, as a result, of unfailing symptomatic interest: Frantz Fanon, not to put too fine a point on it, is a Rorschach blot with legs.

We might begin with a recent essay by Edward Said, entitled "Representing the Colonized" (1989). To Jean-François Lyotard's vision of the decline of grand narrative, Said counterposes the counternarratives of emergent peoples, the counternarratives of liberation that Fanon (as he says) "forces on a Europe playing 'le jeu irresponsable de la belie au bois dormant.'" And Said goes on to argue:

> Despite its bitterness and violence, the whole point of Fanon's work is to force the European metropolis to think its history *together with* the history of colonies awakening from the cruel stupor and abused immobility of imperial dominion. . . . I do not think that the anti-imperialist challenge represented by Fanon and Césaire or others like them has by any means been met; neither have we taken them seriously as models or representations of human effort in the contemporary world. In fact Fanon and

Césaire—of course I speak of them as types—jab directly at the question of identity and of identitarian thought, that secret sharer of present anthropological reflection on "otherness" and "difference." What Fanon and Césaire required of their own partisans, even during the heat of struggle, was to abandon fixed ideas of settled identity and culturally authorized definition. (1989, 223)

I've given some space to these remarks because it is, preeminently, in passages such as this one that Fanon as global theorist has been produced.

And yet some have found cause for objection here. Reading the passage above, they say that given the grand narrative in which Fanon is himself inserted, it seems beside the point to ask about the extent to which the historical Fanon really did abandon all fixity of identity; beside the point to raise questions about his perhaps ambivalent relation to counternarratives of identity; beside the point to address his growing political and philosophical estrangement from Aimé Césaire. Fanon's individual specificity seems beside the point because what we have here is explicitly a composite figure, indeed, an ethnographic construct. It's made clear by the formulaic reference to Fanon, Césaire, and "others like them." It's made clear when he writes, "of course I speak of them as types": to which some readers will pose the question, why "of course"? And they will answer: because the ethnographer always speaks of his subjects as types. Or they find the answer in Albert Memmi, who explains that a usual "sign of the colonized's depersonalization is what one might call the mark of the plural. The colonized is never characterized in an individual manner; he is entitled only to drown in an anonymous collectivity" (Memmi 1965, 85).

Thus, while calling for a recognition of the *situatedness* of all discourses, the critic delivers a Fanon as a global theorist *in vacuo*; in the course of an appeal for the specificity of the Other, we discover that his global theorist of alterity is emptied of his own specificity; in the course of a critique of identitarian thought, Fanon is conflated with someone who proved, in important respects, an ideological antagonist. And so on. These moves are, I think, all too predictable: and, yes, even beside the point. Said has delivered a brief for a usable culture; it is not to be held against him that his interest is in mobilizing a usable Fanon. Indeed, this is his own counternarrative, in the terrain of postcolonial criticism. But Said's use of Fanon to allegorize the site of counterhegemonic agency must also be read as an implicit rejoinder to those who have charged him with ignoring the self-representations of the colonized. Homi Bhabha's objection that Said's vision of Orientalism suggests that "power and discourse is possessed entirely by the colonizer" is typical in this regard (Bhabha 1983a, 200). Certainly Bhabha's own readings of Fanon are the most elaborated that have been produced in the field of poststructuralism. And his readings are designed to breach the disjunction Said's essay may appear to preserve, that is, between the discourse of the colonized and that of the colonizer. For Bhabha, colonial ambivalence "makes the boundaries of colonial 'positionality'—the division of self/other— and the question of colonial power—the differentiation of colo- nizer/colonized—different from both the Hegelian master/slave dialectic or the phenomenological projection of Otherness" (Bhabha 1986b, 169). Accordingly, he has directed attention to (what he sees as) the disruptive articulations of the colonized as inscribed in colonial discourse, that is, the discourse of the colo- nized. Bhabha's reading requires a model of self-division, of "alienation within identity," and he has enlisted Lacanian psycho- analysis to this end:

> [Minority discourse] is not simply the attempt to invert the balance of power within an unchanged order of discourse, but to redefine the symbolic process through which the social Imaginary— Nation, Culture, or Community—become "subjects" of discourse and "objects" of psychic identification. (Bhabha 1983a, 200)

From Fanon, he educes the question, "'how can a human being live Other-wise?'" And he juxtaposes to his reflections on *Black Skin, White Masks* the following remarks of Jacques Lacan's:

In the case of display . . . the play of combat in the form of intimidation, the being gives of himself, or receives from the other,
something that is like a mask, a double, an envelope, a thrown-
off skin, thrown off in order to cover the frame of a shield. It is
through this separated form of himself that the being comes into
play in his effects of life and death. (Quoted by Bhabha; in this
volume p. 195)

Bhabha may be Fanon's closest reader, and it is an oddly touching
performance of a coaxing devotion: He regrets aloud those
moments in Fanon that cannot be reconciled to the poststructuralist
critique of identity because he wants Fanon to be even better than
he is. Benita Parry has described Bhabha as proffering Fanon as "a
premature poststructuralist," and I don't think Bhabha would dis-
agree (Parry 1987, 33). In this same vein, Bhabha redescribes
Fanon's "Manichean delirium" as a condition internalized within
colonial discourse, as a form of self-misrecognition. "In articulating
the problem of colonial cultural alienation in the psychoanalytic
language of demand and desire, Fanon radically questions the formation of both individual and social authority as they come to be
developed in the discourse of Social Sovereignty" (this volume pp.
184–85). Fanon's representation "turns on the idea of Man as his
alienated image, not Self and Other but the 'Otherness' of the Self
inscribed in the perverse palimpsest of colonial identity" (this
volume p. 186). It's interesting to note, however, that Bhabha's
mobilization of Lacan stands as an explicit correction of Fanon's
own citation of Lacan in *Black Skin, White Masks*. Here, then, is the
originary irruption of Lacan into colonial discourse theory. With
reference to the mirror stage, Fanon writes:

When one has grasped the mechanism described by Lacan, one
can have no further doubt that the real Other for the white man
is and will continue to be the black man. And conversely. Only
for the white man The Other is perceived on the level of the body
image, absolutely as the not-self—that is, the unidentifiable, the
unassimilable. For the black man, as we have shown, historical
and economic realities come into the picture. (1967a, 161 n.25)

(Hence for the delirious Antillean, Fanon tells us, "the mirror hallucination is always neutral. When Antilleans tell me that they have experienced it, I always ask the same question: 'What color were you?' Invariably they reply: 'I had no color'" [1967a, 162 n.25].)

Bhabha cautions, however, that

> The place of the Other must not be imaged as Fanon sometimes suggests as a fixed phenomenological point, opposed to the self, that represents a culturally alien consciousness. The Other must be seen as the necessary negation of a primordial identity—cultural or psychic—that introduces the system of differentiation which enables the "cultural" to be signified as a linguistic, symbolic, historic reality. (this volume p. 189)

In other words, he wants Fanon to mean Lacan rather than, say, Jean-Paul Sartre, but acknowledges that Fanon does tend to slip:

> At times Fanon . . . turns too hastily from the ambivalences of identification to the antagonistic identities of political alienation and cultural discrimination; he is too quick to name the Other, to personalize its presence in the language of colonial racism. . . . These attempts . . . can, at times, blunt the edge of Fanon's brilliant illustrations of the complexity of psychic projections in the pathological colonial relation. (this volume p. 190)

Bhabha is charmingly up front about the pulling and pushing involved in turning Fanon into *le Lacan noir*; he regrets the moments when Fanon turns to "an existentialist humanism that is as banal as it is beatific" (this volume p. 175). Indeed, Bhabha's rather passionate essay, entitled "Remembering Fanon," can as easily be read as an index to all that Bhabha wants us to forget.

For some oppositional critics, however, the hazards of Bhabha's approach may go beyond interpretive etiquette. Thus, in a prelude to his own Lacanian reading of colonial discourse, Abdul JanMohamed takes Bhabha to task for downplaying the negativity of the colonial encounter; and not surprisingly, his critique pivots on his own positioning of Fanon. JanMohamed writes: "Though he cites Frantz Fanon, Bhabha completely ignores Fanon's definition of the conqueror/native relation as a 'Manichean' struggle—a definition that is not a fanciful metaphoric caricature but an accurate representation of a profound conflict." "What does it mean, in practice, to imply as Bhabha does that the native, whose entire economy and culture are destroyed, is somehow in 'possession' of colonial power?" he asks. JanMohamed charges that Bhabha asserts "the unity of the 'colonial subject'" and so "represses the political history of colonialism" (1986, 11). The critical double bind these charges raise is clear enough. You can empower discursively the native, and open yourself to charges of downplaying the epistemic (and literal) violence of colonialism; or play up the absolute nature of colonial domination, and be open to charges of negating the subjectivity and agency of the colonized, thus textually replicating the repressive operations of colonialism. In agency, so it seems, begins responsibility.

But of course JanMohamed does not argue that colonialism completely destroyed the native's culture. Conversely, it can't be the case that Bhabha ignores Fanon's discussion of colonialism's self-representation as a Manichean world, since he explicitly reflects on what Fanon calls the "Manichean delirium." But certainly Bhabha's different account of colonialism makes it unlikely that he posits a unity of the colonial subject in the way JanMohamed construes it, for Bhabha's account denies the unity of either subject in the first place. Properly reframed, JanMohamed's argument might be seen as another version of a critique of Lacan advanced by (among others) Stephen Heath, who argues that "the importance of this idea of the Other [as the "locus" of the symbolic, which produces the subject as constitutively divided] and the symbolic is crucial to Lacan exactly because it allows him to abstract from problems of social-historical determinations" (1983, 77). As against Fredric Jameson's famous injunction, then, Lacan's motto would turn out to be: "Never historicize, never explain." But far from turning against the psychoanalytic model of colonial discourse, JanMohamed's concern is, of course, to advance an explicitly Lacanian account of these discourses. To be sure, the allure of Lacan for both Bhabha and JanMohamed is only tangentially related to its appearance in Fanon: As I've suggested, Lacan's discourse exemplarily maps a problematic of subject-formation onto a Self-Other model that seems to lend itself to the Colonial Encounter. On the other hand, it's unclear whether JanMohamed really wants to make space for all the distinctively Lacanian ramifications spelled out by Bhabha.

For his part, JanMohamed reinstates the notions of alterity that Bhabha rejected. "Faced with an incomprehensible and multifaceted alterity," he writes, "the European theoretically has the option of responding to the Other in terms of identity or difference" (1986, 83). Here, the Other exists as such prior to and independent of the encounter; but a little further we find the limits of the Lacanian register in JanMohamed's analysis: "Genuine and thorough comprehension of Otherness," he writes, requires "the virtually impossible task of negating one's very being" (1986, 84). This "virtually impossible" encounter is neither a provisional, negotiated difference nor the Lacanian Other in whose field the self must constitute itself. Rather, it is a close encounter of the third kind, involving the disputed notion of radical alterity."[2]

And the duality supports his division of colonialist literature into the two categories of the imaginary and the symbolic. In the imaginary text, the native functions as mirror—though in fact as a negative image. The symbolic text uses the native as mediator of European desires, introducing a realm of "intersubjectivity, heterogeneity, and particularity" (1986, 85) as opposed to the infantile specularity of Otherness that the imaginary text enacts.

While this use of Lacan to demarcate literary categories has uncertain value as a means of classifying colonial literature (it has been criticized as crudely empiricist), it has appeal in classifying postcolonial theorists. Here one might station JanMohamed's penchant for Manichean allegories in the imaginary register, Bhabha's negotiations in the symbolic. I suppose (to continue the conceit) we might cast Fanon as the Other that mediates between them and the historical Real.

Yet the most problematic feature of JanMohamed's theorizing is what critics describe as an overly mimetic conception of oppositional literature. Here we should turn to a recent overview of colonial discourse theory by the radical South African expatriate, Benita Parry. In the course of her explicitly Fanonian critique of JanMohamed's study, Parry finds him lacking "Fanon's grasp of the paradoxes and pitfalls of 'rediscovering tradition' and re-presenting it within a Western system of meanings. What for Fanon is a transitional process of liberating the consciousness of the oppressed into a new reality, JanMohamed treats as the arrival of the definitive oppositional discourse" (1987, 47). In fact, she is concerned even more with the critique of alteritism as pursued in the work of Bhabha and Gayatri Chakravorty Spivak. Parry asks: "What are the politics of projects which dissolve the binary opposition colonial self/colonized other, encoded in colonialist language as a dichotomy necessary to domination, but also differently inscribed in the discourse of liberation as a dialectic of conflict and a call to arms?" (1987, 29). Thus Parry says of Bhabha's reading that it "obscures Fanon's paradigm of the colonial condition as one of implacable enmity between native and invader, making armed opposition both a cathartic and a pragmatic necessity" (1987, 32). (To be sure, Fanon also spoke of the metaphysics of the dualism as "often quite fluid" [1967a, 10].)

Of both Spivak and Bhabha, Parry asserts: "because their theses admit of no point outside of discourse from which opposition can be engendered, their project is concerned to place incendiary devices within the dominant structures of representation and not to confront these with another knowledge" (1987, 43). Considering the subaltern voice to be irretrievable, they devalue the actual counternarratives of anticolonialist struggle as mere reverse discourse. But what Fanon shows us, according to Parry, and what "colonial discourse theory has not taken on board," is that "a cartography of imperialist ideology more extensive than its address in the colonialist space, as well as a conception of the native as historical subject and agent of an oppositional discourse is needed" (1987, 45).

To such positions in contemporary theory, Parry contrasts what she implies is a more properly Fanonian critical mode, one that

> also rejects totalizing abstracts of power as falsifying situations of domination and subordination, land in which the notion of hegemony is inseparable from that of a counter-hegemony. In this theory of power and contest, the process of procuring the consent of the oppressed and the marginalized to the existing structure of relationships through ideological inducements, necessarily generates dissent and resistance, since the subject is conceived as being constituted by means of incommensurable solicitations and heterogeneous social practices. The outcome of this agonistic exchange, in which those addressed challenge their interlocutors, is that the hegemonic discourse is ultimately abandoned as scorched earth when a different discourse, forged in the process of disobedience and combat, occupying new, never colonized and "utopian" territory, and prefiguring other relationships, values, and aspirations, is enunciated. (1987, 43–44)

Some people might describe this utopian moment as the externalization of the quest romance. But note the emergence here of the familiar historicist dialectic of subversion and containment: that power produces its own subversion is held to be a fact about the constitution of the subject itself. And some will be skeptical about the notion of a revolutionary literature that is implicit here: If Said made of Fanon an advocative of post-postmodern counternarratives of liberation; if JanMohamed made of Fanon a Manichean theorist of colonialism as absolute negation; and if Bhabha cloned, from Fanon's theoria, another Third World poststructuralist, Parry's Fanon (which I generally find persuasive) turns out to confirm her own rather optimistic vision of literature and social action.

"This book, it is hoped, will be a mirror," wrote a twenty-six-year-old Fanon, and in rereading these readings, it's hard to avoid a sort of tableau of narcissism, with Fanon himself as the Other that can only reflect and consolidate the critical self.

And perhaps we can hear a warning about the too uncritical appropriations of a Fanon in Spivak's recent rebuttal to the criticism concerning the recuperation or effacement of the native's voice. The course we've been plotting leads us, then, to what is, in part, Spivak's critique of Parry's critique of JanMohamed's critique of Bhabha's critique of Said's critique of colonial discourse.

Now, in Spivak's view, Parry "is, in effect, bringing back the 'native informant syndrome' and using it differently in a critique of neocolonialism." "'When Benita Parry takes us—and by this I mean Homi Bhabha, Abdul JanMohamed, Gayatri Spivak—to task for not being able to listen to the natives or to let the native speak, she forgets that we are natives, too. We talk like Defoe's Friday, only much better'" (cited in Koundoroura 1989, 91–92). Thus, in straining for a voice of indigenous resistance, we can succumb to another quest romance, this time for the

> transparent "real" voice of the native. This has so many of the properties of a somewhat displaced model in the 19th-century class-stratified management of the culture of imperialism, that I believe that it is my task now to be vigilant about this desire to hear the native. Also, let me tell you that the native is not a fool and within the fact of this extraordinary search for the "true" native which has been going on for decades, perhaps even a century or more, the native himself or herself is aware of this particular value. (Koundoura 1989, 92–93)

So we need to reject, says Spivak, that insidious image of the native as a parahuman creature "who is there to give us evidence that we must always trust (as we wouldn't trust the speech of people to whom we ascribe the complexity of being human)" (Koundoura 1989, 93).

I think this is an elegant reminder and safeguard against the sentimental romance of alterity. On the other hand, it still leaves space for some versions of Parry's critique. I suggest that we try to distinguish more sharply between the notions of cultural resistance, on the one hand, and of cultural alterity, on the other, even as we note the significance of their conflation. There may well be something familiar about Spivak's insistence on the totalizing embrace of colonial discourse, and Parry's unease with the insistence.

My claim is that what Jacques Derrida calls writing, Spivak, in a brilliant reversal, has renamed colonial discourse. So it is no accident that the two terms share precisely the same functionality. The Derridian mot, that there is nothing outside the text, is reprised as the argument that there is nothing outside (the discourse of) colonialism. And it leads, as well, to the argument that this very discourse must be read as heterogeneous to itself, as laced with the aporias and disjunctures that any deconstructive reading must elicit and engage. (It's in just these terms that Spivak joins in the critique of alteritism: "I am critical of the binary opposition Colonizer/Colonized. I try to examine the heterogeneity of 'Colonial Power', and to disclose the complicity of the two poles of that opposition as it constitutes the disciplinary enclave of the critique of imperialism" (Spivak 1985, 9). Indeed, I think Spivak's argument, put in its strongest form, entails the corollary that all discourse is colonial discourse.

But perhaps the psychoanalytic model of culture makes this a foregone conclusion. When Fanon asserted that "only a psychoanalytical interpretation of the black problem" could explain "the structure of the complex" (1967a, 12), he was perhaps only extending a line of Freud's, which Greenblatt has focused attention on: "'Civilization behaves toward sexuality as a people or a stratum of its population does which has subjected another one to its exploitation.'"[3] Freud's pessimistic vision of "analysis interminable" would then refer us to a process of decolonization interminable. I spoke of this double session of paradigms, in which the Freudian mechanisms of psychic repression are set in relation to those of colonial repression; but it's still unclear whether we are to speak of convergence or mere parallelism. Again, the Fanonian text casts the problem in sharpest relief. Stephan Feuchtwang has recently argued, in an essay entitled "Fanonian Spaces," that

> the use of psychoanalytic categories for descriptions of social situations has tremendous analogical virtues. One is their capacity to indicate a directionality of affect in the situations, of forces mobilized and immobilized rather than a mere disposition of

intelligible elements and their rationality. Another is their focus on the relational, truly the social facts. Fanon does not analyze the colonial situation as a contact of cultural subjects or as an interaction of interested subjects as if they were logically prior to the situation. Instead, the relations of the situation are analyzed to see how their organization forms cultural subjects. (1987, 127)

Feuchtwang speaks of "tremendous analogical virtues": but are they *merely* analogical! Further—accepting the force of the Freudian rereading—do we really want to elide the distance between political repression and individual neurosis: the *positional* distance between Steve Biko and, say, Woody Allen? On the other hand, Feuchtwang does point to the problematic relation between individual case studies and analyses of the collective state in *Black Skin, White Masks*. We've heard Fanon speak of the necessity for the "psychoanalytic interpretation"; yet he subsequently juxtaposes a notion of socioanalysis to Freud's psychoanalysis: "It will be seen that the black man's alienation is not an individual question. Beside [the Freudian contribution of] phylogeny and ontogeny stands sociogeny" (1967a, 13). Or as Memmi simplifies the question, in the preface to his classic *The Colonizer and the Colonized*: "Does psychoanalysis win out over Marxism? Does all depend on the individual or on society?" (Memmi 1965, xiii). And, of course, the tension—which we endlessly try to theorize away—persists in all political appropriations of the psychoanalytic.

Indeed, doesn't this tension plague our appropriation of Fanon as a collectivized individual, as alterity in revolt, as the Third World of Theory itself? I speak of course, of our Fanon, of whom Sartre wrote in the preface to *The Wretched of the Earth*: "the Third World finds *itself* and speaks to itself through his voice" (1968, 10). I speak of the black Benjamin who, as McGann writes, presents "the point of view of a Third World, where the dialectic of the first two worlds is completely reimagined," because he writes from "the perspective of an actual citizen of the actual Third World" (McGann 1989, 86, 87).

So I want to turn, finally, to yet another Fanon, the ironic figure analyzed by the Tunisian novelist and philosopher Albert Memmi. Memmi's Fanon is, emphatically, not the Fanon we have recuperated for global colonial discourse theory. He is, indeed, a far more harried subject, a central fact of whose life is his dislocation from the "actual Third World." Of course, we know from his biographers and from his own account that Fanon, whose mother was of Alsatian descent, grew up in Martinique thinking of himself as white and French: and that his painful reconstitution as a black West Indian occurred only when he arrived at the French capital. Yet at this point—again, in Memmi's narrative—Fanon loses himself as a black Martinican: *"Fanon's private drama is that, though henceforth hating France and the French, he will never return to négritude and to the West Indies,"* indeed, he "never again set foot in Martinique" (Memmi 1971, 5; emphasis added). Yet his attempts to identify himself as an Algerian proved equally doomed. As Fanon's biographers remind us, most Algerian revolutionaries scant [reduce] his role and remain irritated by the attention paid to him in the West as a figure in Algerian decolonization: to them— and how ironic this is to his Western admirers—he remained a European interloper.

Though he worked as a psychiatrist in Algeria and Tunisia, in neither country did he even understand the language: his psychiatric consultations were conducted through an interpreter (see Memmi 1971, 5). And the image here—of the psychoanalysis of culture being conducted, quite literally, through an interpreter— does speak eloquently of the ultimately mediated nature of the most anticolonialist analysis.*

Far from championing the particularities and counternarratives of the oppressed, Memmi's Fanon is an interloper without the patience or interest to acquaint himself with the local specificities of culture: "He grew impatient, and failed to hide his scorn of regional particularisms, the tenacity of traditions and customs that distinguish cultural and national aspirations, not to speak of contradictory interests" (1971, 5). And while Memmi's own insertion

*For a different view, see chapter 5, this volume. —Ed.

in colonial politics is certainly complex, his version is consistent with that of the revolutionary elite of postindependence Algeria.

Memmi's Fanon was devoted to a dream of a third world, a third world where he could look into a mirror and have no color: yet he lived in the Third World, which rebuffed his most ardent desires for identification. What remained for him, Memmi writes, "but to propose a completely novel man?" (1971, 5).

We've seen inscribed on the Fanonian text (as well as in contemporary colonial discourse theory more widely) the disruptive relation between narratives of subject-formation and narratives of liberation. Here, Memmi is quite blunt: Fanon does, on the one hand, claim an absolute disjunction between colonial representations of the colonized and the subject of representation. But doesn't colonialism inscribe itself on the colonized? "For that matter, is Fanon's own thinking on this point really coherent? I too could cite a great many contradictory passages of his, where he speaks of 'mutilation,' 'inferiorization,' 'criminal impulsion,'—results, obviously, of colonization." Actually, Memmi goes on to say, Fanon must have seen that the personality of the colonized was affected in these ways. But

> he found them embarrassing and repulsive. This is because, like many other defenders of the colonized, he harbored a certain amount of revolutionary romanticism . . . As for most social romantics, so for him the victim remained proud and intact throughout oppression; he suffered but did not let himself be broken. And the day oppression ceases, the new man is supposed to appear before our eyes immediately. (Memmi 1968, 88)

But, says Memmi, this is not the way it happens.

I believe that the Antillean mirror which reflects no color at all haunts Fanon. Memmi is surely right to locate the utopian moment in Fanon in his depiction of decolonization as engendering a "kind of *tabula rasa*," as "quite simply the replacing of a certain 'species' of men by another 'species' of men" (1968, 35); so that the fear that we will continue to be (as Fanon puts it) "overdetermined from

without" was never reconciled with his political vision of emancipation. This may be the clearest way of representing Fanon's own
self-divisions, that is, as an agon between psychology and a politics, between ontogeny and sociogeny, between—to return to
Memmi—Marx and Freud.

Fanon's vision of the New Man emerges as a central tableau in
identity politics, for us as for him. At the intersection of colonial
and psychoanalytic discourse, Fanon wonders how to create a new
identity. The problem remains, again for us as for him, that—as
Memmi remarked about Fanon's own project of personal transformation—"one doesn't leave one's own self behind as easily as all
that" (1971, 5).

Rehistoricizing Fanon, we can hear a lament concerning the limits
of liberation, concerning the very intelligibility of his dream of
decolonization. And while the colonial paradigm proved valuable
in foregrounding issues of power and position, it may be time to
question its ascendance in literary and cultural studies, especially
because the "disciplinary enclave" of anti-imperialist discourse
has proved a last bastion for the project, and dream, of global
theory. In the context of the colonial binarism, we've seldom
admitted fully how disruptive the psychoanalytic model can be,
elaborating a productive relation between oppressed and
oppressor—productive of each as speaking subjects. And yet we
can chart the torsional relation of the discourses in the exceptional
instability of Fanon's own rhetoric.

But this requires of us that we no longer allow Fanon to remain
a kind of icon or "screen memory," rehearsing dimly remembered
dreams of postcolonial emancipation. It means reading him, with
an acknowledgment of his own historical particularity, as an actor
whose own search for self-transcendence scarcely exempts him
from the heterogenous and conflictual structures that we have
taken to be characteristic of colonial discourse. It means not to elevate him above his localities of discourse as a transcultural, tran-
shistorical global theorist, nor simply to cast him into battle, but to

recognize him as a battlefield in himself. Fanon wrote, with un-canny and prescient insistence: "In no fashion should I undertake to prepare the world that will come later. I belong irreducibly to my time" (1967a, 15). This is one proviso we ignore at our own risk.

Do we still need global, imperial theory—in this case, a grand unified theory of oppression; or, indeed, even the whole universal-izing model of Theory that it presupposes, a model of total theory that quests for finality and an exclusive lien on the last word? It's no longer any scandal that our own theoretical reflections must be as provisional, reactive, and local as the texts we reflect upon. Of course, discarding the imperial agenda of global theory also means not having to choose *between* Spivak and Said, Greenblatt, Pease, or Jameson, Bhabha or JanMohamed or Parry, even Fanon or Memmi; or, rather, it means not representing the choice as simply one of epistemic hygiene. And it requires a recognition that we, too, just as much as Fanon, may be fated to rehearse the agonisms of a culture that may never earn the title of postcolonial.[4]

NOTES

1. A properly contextualized reading of Fanon's *Black Skin, White Masks*, the text to which I most frequently recur, should situate it in respect to such germinal works as Jean Paul Sartre's *Reflexions sur la question Juive* (Paris, 1946), Dominique O. Mannoni's *Psychologie de la colonization* (Paris, 1950), Germaine Guex's *La Nevrose d'abandon* (Paris, 1950), as well as many lesser known works. But this is only to begin to sketch out the challenge of rehistoricizing Fanon.

2. Gayatri Chakravorty Spivak may keep him company here: "No perspective critical of imperialism can turn the Other into a self, because the project of imperialism has always already historically refracted what might have been the absolutely Other into a domesticated Other that con-solidates the imperialist self" (Spivak, "Three Women's Texts and a Cri-tique of Imperialism," in *"Race," Writing, and Difference*, p. 272). The "absolutely other" here seems to be something we find (or fail to find), rather than make. I should stress that it's not the notion of otherness as such but of absolute otherness that I want to question.

3. Quoted in Stephen Greenblatt, *Renaissance Self-Fashioning: From*

More to Shakespeare (Chicago, 1980), p. 173. See Sigmund Freud, *Civilization and Its Discontents*, trans. James Strachey (New York, 1962); p. 51.

4. This paper was originally prepared for and delivered (in abridged form) at the 1989 Modern Language Association panel on "Race and Psychoanalysis," at the invitation of Jane Gallop, which partly explains why my references to Fanon are largely to his first and most overtly psychoanalytic book, *Black Skin, White Masks*. Since Fanon's oeuvre receives scant attention in my paper, I should remind readers unfamiliar with his works that early and late Fanon (say) cannot be simply conflated, and that many oppositional critics regard the later essays to be his most valuable contribution. See, for example, *Toward the African Revolution: Political Essays*. Finally, I'm grateful to Hazel Carby, Jonathan Culler, K. A. Appiah, Arnold I. Davidson, Benita Parry, and Henry Finder, who commented on an earlier draft, even though I have failed to respond to their criticisms as I would have wished.

III. Fanon, Gender, and National Consciousness

10.

Women, Nationalism, and Religion in the Algerian Liberation Struggle*

Marie-Aimée Helie-Lucas

The image that the outside world has formed of women in the Algerian liberation struggle is shaped by Frantz Fanon's books, a very widely distributed film called *The Battle of Algiers*, and the true story of a few national heroines. From these sources, the Algerian woman appears as a freedom fighter who carried arms against French colonialism and its army, a "terrorist" who planted bombs in the city during the Battle of Algiers, who was equal to men in the struggle and who shared decision-making both at the political and at the military levels.

These myths hardly match personal experience. They are now also challenged by Djamila Amrane, a freedom fighter from 1957 to 1962. Hers is the only serious study produced on women in the struggle since independence. As a registered veteran, she was allowed access to the Ministry of Veterans archives for her research (Amrane 1980).

*Presented to the international Symposium on Women and the Military System at Siunto Baths, Finland in 1987. Earlier versions of this paper were produced by the Peace Movement in Finland and Wheatsheaf Books of Brighton, England. The version reproduced here was originally published in *Opening the Gates: A Century of Arab Feminist Writing*, edited by Margot Badran and Miriam Cooke (Bloomington: Indiana University Press, 1990), pp. 104–14.

From her study one can question who was registered as a veteran by the Ministry. The request for registration had to be supported by a documented, stamped file of extensive testimonies. This cumbersome bureaucratic procedure made it difficult for poor and illiterate people to register. Amrane emphasizes the added difficulty for peasant women who were not only illiterate but also sometimes veiled and secluded. Registration procured advantages: jobs, promotion, retirement benefits, etc. Hence, it did not benefit women, since only 2.1 percent were employed. Few registered. Those who did represent only 3.25 percent of the total number of veterans. Official agencies did not encourage women to register and there was a universal desire immediately after independence to have women back in the home. Hence statistical data derived from the archives of the Ministry of Veterans are not indicative of the number of women who participated in the independence struggle.

From these statistics, one can also ask who is a fighter, a veteran? Most of the fighting took place in rural areas, little in the cities. The peasants helped the armed fighters in numerous ways: guiding, hiding, feeding, carrying messages, buying arms, observing the French army moves, taking over the arms of killed fighters. Whereas a line can be drawn between fighter and civilian in the city, it is not so easily done in the country. Yet gender distinctions persisted. If a man carried food to the armed fighters at great personal risk, he was called a "fighter." A woman doing the same was called a "helper." If a man risked his life to hide armed fighters or wanted political leaders, he was called a "fighter." A woman doing the same was simply performing the female task of "nurturing." Nor was she considered a fighter when she collected fuel or food for the fighters, or carried their guns, or guided them through the mountains. She was merely helping the men. Only the French army acknowledged her action by imprisoning and torturing her in concentration camps and killing her. This explains why even fewer women are registered as veterans in the country. The official data is therefore even more biased and not representative of the reality, in which, in these types of guerrilla liberation struggles, the whole population is involved, f not by will, by force. Hence we can consider that most peasant women were involved in the Algerian revolution.

Out of 10,949 registered women 9,194 were designated as "civilians" and 1,755 as "military." This means that 81 percent worked for the Civil Organization of the National Liberation Front (OCFLN) supporting guerrilla and urban terrorism: 19 percent were part of the army and worked in the bush, 78 percent of the women worked in the countryside, and 20 percent were in the cities. This corresponds to the male ratio. One out of five women were jailed, tortured, or killed. They were from all age groups, from under twenty to over fifty, though 41.7 percent were between thirty-one and fifty; all of the latter were married and mothers. In the civilian branch (OCFLN) 47.3 percent were between thirty-one and fifty. These figures show the overall participation of women, their heavy repression, and the involvement of mature women and mothers.

Amrane's study details women's civilian and military tasks. They were as follows:

1. Supervision of hiding places and food collection (63 percent in the civilian branch; 2.9 percent in the military, i.e., only six women performed such tasks in the military). Amrane remarks that several women worked together and that only one (the leader) was allowed to register as a veteran.
2. Liaison and guides (22.1 percent civilian, none in military out of a total of 677 women).
3. Collection of funds, medicine, and ammunition (9.3 percent in civilian, i.e., 286 women, none in military).
4. Nursing (1.8 percent in civilian, i.e., 56 women, 49.3 percent in military, i.e., 101 women).
5. Cooking and washing (none in civilian, 44.4 percent in military, i.e., 91 women).
6. Terrorists (2.1 percent in civilian, i.e., 65 women, none in military).
7. Tailoring (0.6 percent in civilian, i.e., 19 women, 1 in military).
8. Secretarial (0.7 percent in civilian, i.e., 5 women, 0.4 percent in military, i.e., 3 women).

9. Political commissaries (none in civilian, 1 percent in military, i.e., 2 women).
10. Armed fighters (none in civilian, 0.5 percent in military, i.e., 1 woman).

Although we know that many more women were in the struggle, these biased figures still give a fair idea of the fact that even in the hardest times of the struggle, women were oppressed, confined to tasks that would not disturb the social order in the future. Although these tasks were absolutely essential, they should not have absorbed all female energy. One woman bore arms, none was in a decision-making position! Sixty-five dealt with bombs in the urban sectors (probably carrying spare parts) and two political commissaries?

So much for Fanon's and others' myth of the Algerian woman liberated along with her country. These liberated women were in the kitchen, they were sewing clothes (or, flags!), carrying parcels, typing. Nevertheless, since there was "no humble task in the revolution" we did not dispute the roles we had. It would have been mean to question the priority of liberating the country, since independence would surely bring an end to discrimination against women. What makes me angrier in retrospect is not women's confinement but the brainwashing that did not allow us young women even to think of questioning. What makes me angrier still is to witness the replication of this situation in other struggles for independence. It angers me to see women covering the misbehavior of their fellow men and hiding, in the name of national solidarity and identity, crimes which will be perpetuated after independence.

This is the real harm which comes with liberation struggles. The overall task of women during liberation is seen as symbolic. Faced with colonization the people have to build a national identity based on their own values, traditions, religion, language, and culture. Women bear the heavy burden of safeguarding this threatened identity. And this burden exacts its price.

Probably most of the women present at this symposium [at which this paper was originally presented] take for granted that they belong to a country or a nation which does not have to prove its existence. For them, the concept of nation can be transcended and criticized. This is not true for Algeria nor for other decolonized or still colonized countries at war with imperialism. For us it is much more difficult to criticize the nation, and even the state which claims to represent the nation.

One of the earliest slogans of nationalism in Algeria was promoted by the *ulama*: "Arabic is our language. Islam is our religion. Algeria is our country." Women were supposed to raise sons in the faith and preserve traditional moral standards and to teach the language of the forefathers.[1]

Women should be bound by tradition, while men had some access to modernity. Yet, it is now commonplace that tradition serves the purposes of those in power. Tradition is seen as ahistorical and immutable, modernity draws from the wealthy West—whatever that means.

Let us now discuss two examples of traditions as symbols of national identity during the Algerian struggle. The first is the veil, the second tobacco and alcohol.

Although there is no doubt that veiling women is a measure for control and oppression, it became for a time a symbol of national resistance to the French. During the war, French officials had insisted that Algerian women should be freed from the oppression of the veil. French army trucks had transported village women to urban areas. There these women were forced to unveil publicly, thereby proving their renunciation of outworn traditions. Both Algerian men and women resented this symbolic public rape. In addition to its symbolic role, the veil was supposed to have a practical function. Fanon praised the revolutionary virtue of the veil—it allowed urban women freedom fighters to escape the control of the French army. They could hide their guns under their veils and travel incognito for underground purposes. How, therefore, could we take up the issue of the veil as oppressive to women without betraying both the *nation* and the *revolution*? Many young women, even those brought up in liberal families, chose to don the veil as a demonstration of their belonging to the oppressed Algerian people—in their lives and in their symbolic existence.

The FLN (the National Liberation Front) encouraged such an attitude that emphasized women's modesty and could also be labeled
"fighting for the Cause." More recently, we have seen another such
example in Iran.

It is important to view this sexist program as part of another
which denies the individual control over private matters. At the
time of the Battle of Algiers, the FLN engaged in a campaign
against tobacco and alcohol, which they branded antirevolu-
tionary. Use of either could lead to a death sentence, or at least to
the cutting off of the culprit's nose! The reasoning was that all
Algerians were supposed to be Muslims; Islam forbids the consumption of tobacco and alcohol: those who consume are not true
believers; and infidels are allies of colonialism. Similarly, the
Ramadan fast became symbolic for Algerian identity and it was
universally enforced. Slowly and surely, the entwining of concepts
as heterogeneous as nation, religion, and ethnicity began to shape
the future of independent Algeria.

I feel the need to remind us all that we women, we nonreli-
gious beings, we internationalists, did not raise our voices—it
would have been difficult and dangerous—or our consciousness.
We did not recognize the implications of such ideological confusion. We, too, were afraid to betray the people, the revolution, and
the nation. At no point did we see that a power structure, predicated on the control of private life and of women, was being built
on our mental confusion. Obedience, morality, and conformity
were necessary to the revolution. In a struggle where secrecy is the
basis for action, one cannot question the decisions of the comrades
in charge. This leads to blind obedience. In a struggle that demanded anonymity, militants had to conform, to wear traditional
clothes, even the veil. Soon the morality, particularly sexual, of the
militants was controlled. Women were the first to be affected.
During this crucial period, women were assigned a place in society
which could not be challenged without questioning both the past
(as tradition) and the future (as revolution).

Immediately after independence, Algerian leaders evolved a
discourse about Algeria which increasingly retreated from the

lived experiences of the Algerian people. We used to elaborate on the discourse, and the discourse on the discourse became our reality. We talked endlessly of Algerian socialism, even though there was no attempted socialism (see Helie 1967).[2] State capitalism was in transition to private capitalism because there was no private, indigenous capital to be invested at the time of independence (see Mrabet 1965 and 1967). We talked about Algerian models of self-management, while self-management in industry was being converted into state-owned industries less than one year after independence, and self-managed farms were being converted into state-owned farms soon thereafter. We talked about democratic institutions while the police state and its army were daily gaining in strength. We denied the political use of religion and the growth of Islamic groups later to become powerful fundamentalists, since the socialism that was proclaimed shielded us from such evils. And of course we congratulated ourselves on the freedom that women had gained during the struggle. We were inside the myth talking about the myth.

In fact, what started during the war of liberation continued to unfold. Under the Constitution, as long as it conformed with the *Sharia*, women were equal to men. Later we were to learn what this meant. Minimum marriage age for girls was fixed at eighteen years, but the law was not enforced. Forced marriages still took place, sometimes followed by suicide. Women were beaten and secluded by their male relatives and they had no recourse (Benhourya 1980). Education for girls was compulsory, but there were not enough schools nor will there ever be enough schools for girls. Women's employment was legal, but there were no jobs, nor will there ever be enough jobs for women. Women could legally walk in the streets, but the men and the police harassed them: What was an honest woman doing outside her home? When men started to beat women in the streets, no one came to their rescue for fear of being questioned by the police: "You sided with her. Do you know her? What were you doing there?" In the very summer of independence, the FLN army patrolled the streets of the capital, arresting men and women who were walking together in groups:

"Who is married to whom here? This one. Is she someone's sister or wife?" A valid marriage certificate had to be produced. People retreated into their homes in fear of the authorities and of denunciation by neighbors. More women veiled. We were free to be ourselves . . . but, beware of foreign ideologies. Ramadan was observed—police locked up those who did not fast. Hypocrisy grew as neighbors, colleagues, friends, and even family members became informants: "Mother must not know that I am not fasting." "Officially" people did not drink alcohol or smoke in the presence of their fathers. A law was passed—and intermittently enforced—forbidding Algerians from buying alcohol. Those who denounced this state of affairs were persecuted by the authorities as traitors. We developed a split personality.

It is important to stress the role of what was officially called "specific socialism" in the context of decreasing political liberties and growing religiosity that disadvantaged women in particular. Why specific? This differentiated it from "scientific socialism," which was atheism, and it included Islam. Another trick by those in power to delude those who had given so much for national independence.

We were already silenced by fears of accusations of betrayal and by the nationalist myth. But this socialist label was the most effective silencer. We could not oppose the politics of this socialist state without opposing socialism. Because the people were in power, we could not oppose the regime without being anti-people. This rhetoric successfully silenced the Left in most East European countries also.

It took years to dare to become a dissident. We knew that speaking out could be used by the right both in and outside Algeria to undermine socialist ideas that promised justice and equality. As long as we remained separate from the international Left, from other dissident socialists, we were riddled with guilt.

Nationalism, socialism, and religion were used as tools for the elaboration of antiwomen state policy. At independence, Algeria was still under that old nationalist French law of 1920 which forbade not only the use but also all knowledge of contraception. Like other laws this one could not be immediately replaced, so there

was "tacit prorogation." We women hoped that after independence we would have access to some means of contraception. But
many men died during the struggle and the state policy was to
replace them. Moreover, the concept of patriotic motherhood was
still in force. Fortunately, if I may say so, the United States was at
that time trying to enforce a brutal policy of birth control in the
Third World which culminated with their attempt to put pressure
on governments to adopt their world plan, the "fertility target," at
the World Conference on Population at Bucharest.

Algeria, as the champion of the liberation of Africa, as the
champion of socialism, could not accept such a policy. As we all
know population policies are not *the* way to develop. Could we
women disapprove of that? Could we socialists not support the
international policy of our government? No. We supported its
views and did not protest when the natalist law was not changed.
Although we managed to get statements from the highest Islamic
authorities stating that contraceptive practices were not forbidden
by religion, nothing was to change for a whole decade.

The anti-imperialist stand on birth policy suited the needs of
those in power. Women had to pay a high price. In about ten years,
the average number of children per woman was 7.9. The number of
pregnancies ranged from fourteen to around twenty-one. We do not
know about illegal abortions or maternal death. The population
growth reached 3.5 percent—one of the highest in the world. Within
ten years a socialist bureaucracy became a conventional capitalism
with the ruling classes nervous of the lumpen proletariat. Suddenly,
birth control was legalized, contraception clinics were opened, and
their numbers increased rapidly. Therapeutic abortion was legalized. Population growth came down to 3.2 percent within a few
years. In January 1981, the law of finances suddenly penalized large
families: the more the children, the higher the taxes. Women, however, had no say. Reproduction was in the hands of the state.

Although the Constitution guarantees equality, the Family Code
is closer to the *Sharia*. From 1963, three projects were drafted: one
under Ben Bella, the first president of Algeria, two under Boumedienne, the second president. Each project canonized women's inferi-

ority and subjection to the authority of a man who had legal tutelage over her. In 1981, under President Chadili, a new, secret project was drafted. Ministers and deputees were allowed to read, though not to keep, a copy of the project during a special session. We never heard that any of them protested. Some women succeeded in getting hold of a copy. They demonstrated in the streets for the first time since independence. They stopped a law, labeled Quranic, which would have forbidden women the right to choice in marriage, to divorce, to work without permission from a male guardian, to a rightful share in inheritance. However, in May 1984, without warning or discussion, a family code reproducing this fourth project with the exception of the right to work, was finally passed.

It is now a legal fact that women have lost many rights which were guaranteed by the Constitution on the grounds that these rights were anti-Islamic. Fundamentalist Muslims, known in Algeria as Muslim Brothers, are coming to the fore throughout the Arab world. In Algeria, the number of mosques has increased so that each housing block, each school, and each university has at least one huge prayer room. These improvised mosques collect large numbers of young men who rule their female relatives according to the prescriptions of their leaders. Also, ministers of justice in the Arab world and in South Asia meet in attempts to regularize family codes in a way that is even more restrictive to women. One of the most striking elements of fundamentalist philosophy is a rationalism expressed as a "going back to tradition," especially insofar as this relates to women, in the face of Western imperialism. Muslims who believe that Islam mandates equality see no contradiction in the inequalities that Islamic laws force on women. They also claim that Islam demands of each believer to be fair to his women, and yet polygamy and repudiation are now legal in socialist Algeria.

During wars of liberation women are not to protest about women's rights. Nor are they allowed to before and after. It is never the right moment. Defending women's rights "now"—this now being any historical moment—is always a betrayal of the people, the nation, the revolution, religion, national identity, cultural roots. Leftist

Algerian men are the first to accuse us of betrayal, of adhering to "imported ideologies," of Westernism. They use the same terminology that our government uses against the Left at large. We are caught between two legitimacies: belonging to our people or identifying with other oppressed women.

It is difficult to persist in total isolation in denouncing regression in terms of the woman question on the part of so many once-revolutionary countries. We are prevented from speaking for women, from thinking, from dreaming. We are not even aware of the differences between one Muslim country and another. Let Muslim women step out of their national ghettos. Let them see that the clitoridectomy practiced in Africa is unthinkable in Asia, that the veil worn in Arab countries is absent in sub-Saharan Africa, that none of these practices are based on religious precepts, but that religion everywhere backs such practices whenever they allow for greater control over women.

Let us dream of secular states. Let us dream of the separation of religion and state. Let us dream of the end of using nationalism to further oppress the already oppressed.

When I was in Pakistan recently, I heard comments about Iranian women in exile. Their detractors said details of their oppression should not be voiced in the West lest this be used as ammunition against the Iranian people, Muslim countries, and Islam. But who are the Iranians? Are they those in power? Or those who are oppressed? Were the Germans who denounced Hitler during the Second World War anti-German or anti-Nazi? Whom does silence benefit?

In Algeria, many, including myself, kept silent for a whole decade after independence. We gave those in power the time to strengthen and organize and to enforce discriminatory laws against women. Even now Algerian feminists are trying to analyze their oppression from within the Algerian context alone. They refuse to acknowledge the international aspect for fear of being accused of betrayal. And yet the same thing is happening throughout the Islamic world. In India, Muslim fundamentalists have persuaded Muslim women activists to stop their campaigns against the Muslim

Personal Law in the face of Hindu fundamentalist riots and massacres. They claim that these campaigns may be used "against the community." Women must, therefore, suffer discrimination both from dominant Hindus and from their own Muslim community.

We have everything to gain by being truly internationalist. We must exchange information and support one another. We must create such solidarity so that we will be able to retain control over our protest.

Recently we set up the Network of Women Living under Muslim Laws. Women and women's groups from seventeer countries or communities now communicate with each other through the network, ask for documentation, compare so-called Muslim laws in different countries, send appeals for solidarity, inform each other about their strategies in very practical terms, for example, how to write marriage contracts. Through the network we have learned of projects of unification of family codes, both in Arab countries and in South Asia. We are learning how young fundamentalists are trained. We have been informed about progressive interpretations of Islam from the times of the Prophet until today, and about what happened to the courageous pioneers, both men and women, who spoke of an egalitarian interpretation of religion. We have realized in concrete terms that most of our regimes leave no room for agnosticism or atheism and that religion is forced down our throats because of the constant ideological confusion among religion, culture, and nationality. We must work toward a clear-cut definition of these concepts. We are supporting each other from within and are decrying discriminatory situations throughout the Islamic world. We are leaving less and less ground for nationalist justifications for silence. Internationalism must prevail over nationalism.

NOTES

1. We will not discuss here the legitimacy of Arabic in a country where the dominant ethnics are Berber and speak Berber languages.

2. Socialism was simply a good recipe for the primitive accumulation of capital.

11.

Fanon and Gender Agency

Anne McClintock

As male theorists of nationalism go, Frantz Fanon is exemplary, not only for recognizing gender as a formative dimension of nationalism but also for recognizing—and immediately rejecting—the Western metaphor of the nation as a family. "There are close connections," he observes in *Black Skin, White Masks* "between the structure of the family and the structure of the nation" (1967a, 141). Refusing, however, to collude with the notion of the familial metaphor as natural and normative, Fanon instead understands it as a cultural projection ("the characteristics of the family are projected onto the social environment") that has very different consequences for families placed discrepantly within the colonial hierarchy (1967a, 142). "A normal Negro child, having grown up within a normal family, will become abnormal on the slightest contact with the white world" (1967a, 143).

The challenge of Fanon's insight is threefold. He throws radi-

Originally published in *Imperial Leather: Race, Gender, and Sexuality in the Colonial Conquest*, by Anne McClintock (New York: Routledge, 1995), pp. 360–68. Reprinted with permission.

cally into question the naturalness of nationalism as a domestic genealogy. At the same time, he reads familial normalty as a product of social power—indeed, of social violence. Fanon is remarkable for recognizing, in this early text, how military violence and the authority of a centralized state borrow on and enlarge the domestication of gender power within the family: "Militarization and the centralization of authority in a country automatically entail a resurgence of the authority of the father" (1967a, 141–42).

Perhaps one of Fanon's most provocative ideas is his challenge to any easy relation of identity between the psychodynamics of the unconscious and the psychodynamics of political life. The audacity of his insight is that it allows one to ask whether the psychodynamics of colonial power and of anticolonial subversion can be interpreted by deploying (without mediation) the same concepts and techniques used to interpret the psychodynamics of the unconscious. If the family is not "a miniature of the nation," are metaphoric projections from family life (the Lacanian "Law of the Father," say) adequate for an understanding of colonial or anticolonial power? Fanon himself seems to say no. Relations between the individual unconscious and political life are, I argue, neither separable from each other nor reducible to each other. Instead, they comprise criss-crossing and dynamic mediations, reciprocally and untidily transforming each other, rather than duplicating a relation of structural analogy.

Even in *Black Skin, White Masks*, the most psychological of Fanon's texts, he insists that racial alienation is a "double process" (1967a, 13). First, it "entails an immediate recognition of social and economic realities." Then, it entails the "internalization" of inferiority. Racial alienation, in other words, is not only an "individual question" but also involves what Fanon calls a "sociodiagnostic" (1967a, 13). Reducing Fanon to a purely formal psychoanalysis, or a purely structural Marxism, risks foreclosing precisely those suggestive tensions that animate, in my view, the most subversive elements of his work. These tensions are nowhere more marked than in his tentative exploration of the gendering of national agency.

Gender runs like a multiple fissure through Fanon's work, splitting and displacing the "Manichean delirium" to which he repeat-edly returns. For Fanon, the colonial agon appears, at first, to be fun-damentally Manichean. In *Black Skin, White Masks*, he sees colonial space as divided into "two camps: the white and the black" (1967a, 10). Nearly a decade later, writing from the crucible of the Algerian resistance in *The Wretched of the Earth*, Fanon once again sees anti-colonial nationalism as erupting from the violent Manicheanism of a colonial world "cut in two," its boundaries walled by barracks and police stations (1968, 29). Colonial space is split by a pathological geography of power, separating the bright, well-fed settler's town from the hungry, crouching Kasbah: "This world . . . cut in two is inhabited by two different species" (1968, 30). As Edward Said puts it: "From this Manichean and physically grounded statement Fanon's entire work follows, set in motion, so to speak, by the native's violence, a force intended to bridge the gap between white and non-white" (Said 1993, 326). Yet the fateful chiaroscuro of race is at almost every turn disrupted by the criss-crossings of gender.

Fanon's Manichean agon appears at first to be fundamentally male: "There can be no further doubt that the real Other for the white man is and will continue to be the black man." As Homi Bhabha writes: "It is always in relation to the place of the Other that colonial desire is articulated" (Bhabha, this volume pp. 186–87). But Fanon's anguished musings on race and sexuality dis-close that "colonial desire" is not the same for men and women: "Since he is the master and more simply the male, the white man can allow himself the luxury of sleeping with many women. . . . But when a white woman accepts a black man there is automati-cally a romantic aspect. It is a giving, not a seizing" (1967a, 46). Leaving aside, for the moment, Fanon's complicity with the stereo-type of women as romantically rather than sexually inclined, as giving rather than taking, Fanon opens race to a problematic of sexuality that reveals far more intricate entanglements than a mere doubling of "the Otherness of the Self." The psychological Manicheanism of *Black Skin, White Masks* and the more political Manicheanism of *The Wretched of the Earth* are persistently inflected by gender in such a way as to radically disrupt the binary dialectic.

For Fanon, the envy of the black man takes the form of a fantasy of territorial displacement: "The fantasy of the native is precisely to occupy the master's place." This fantasy can be called a *politics of substitution*. Fanon knows, however, that the relation to the white woman is altogether different: "When my restless hands caress those white breasts, they grasp white civilization and dignity and make them mine" (1967a, 63). The white woman is seized, possessed, and taken hold of, not as an act of *substitution*, but as an act of *appropriation*. However, Fanon does not bring this critical distinction between a politics of substitution and a politics of appropriation into explicit elaboration as a theory of gender power.

As Bhabha astutely observes, Fanon's *Black Skin, White Masks* is inflected by a "palpable pressure of division and displacement"—though gender is a form of self-division that Bhabha himself fastidiously declines to explore (this volume p. 181). Bhabha would have us believe that "Fanon's use of the word 'man' usually connotes a phenomenological quality of humanness, inclusive of man and woman" (this volume p. 195). But this claim is not borne out by Fanon's texts. Potentially generic terms like "the Negro" or "the Native"—syntactically unmarked for gender—are almost everywhere immediately contextually marked as male: "Sometimes people wonder that the native, rather than giving his wife a dress, buys instead a transistor radio" (1967a, 81); "the Negro who wants to go to bed with a white woman" (1967a, 16); "the Negro who is viewed as a penis symbol" (1967a, 159). The generic category "native" does not include women; women are merely possessed by the (male) native as an appendage. "When the native is tortured, when his wife is killed or raped, he complains to no one" (1967a, 92).

For Fanon, colonized men inhabit "two places at once." If so, how many places do colonized women inhabit? Certainly, Bhabha's text is not one of them. Except for a cursory appearance in one paragraph, women haunt Bhabha's analysis as an elided shadow—deferred, displaced, and disremembered. Bhabha concludes his eloquent meditation on Fanon with the overarching question: "How can the human world live its difference? How can a human being live Other-wise?" (this volume p. 195). Yet immediately appended to his foreword appears a peculiar note. In it Bhabha announces, without apology, that the "crucial issue" of the woman of color "goes well beyond the scope" of his foreword. Yet its scope, as he himself insists, is bounded by nothing less than the question of humanity: "How can the human world live its difference? how can a human being live Other-wise?" Apparently, the question of the woman of color falls beyond the question of human difference, and Bhabha is content simply to "note the importance of the problem" and leave it at that. Bhabha's belated note on gender appears after his authorial signature, after the time and date of his essay. Women are thus effectively deferred to a nowhere land, beyond time and place, outside theory. If, indeed, "the state of emergency is also a state of emergence," the question remains whether the national state of emergency turns out to be a state of emergence for women at all (this volume p. 183).

To ask "the question of the subject" ("What does a man want? What does the black man want?"), while postponing a theory of gender, presumes that subjectivity itself is neutral with respect to gender (this volume pp. 188, 189). From the limbo of the male afterthought, however, gender returns to challenge the male question not as women's "lack," but as that excess that the masculine "Otherness" of the Self can neither admit nor fully elide. This presumption is perhaps nowhere more evident than in Fanon's remarkable meditations on the gendering of the national revolution.

At least two concepts of national agency shape Fanon's vision. His anticolonial project is split between a Hegelian vision of colonizer and colonized locked in a life-and-death conflict and an altogether more complex and unsteady view of agency. These paradigms slide discrepantly against each other throughout his work, giving rise to a number of internal fissures. These fissures appear most visibly in his analysis of gender as a category of social power.

On the one hand, Fanon draws on a Hegelian metaphysics of agency inherited, by and large, through Jean-Paul Sartre and the French academy. In this view, anticolonial nationalism irrupts violently and irrevocably into history as the logical counterpart to colonial power. This nationalism is, as Edward Said puts it, "cadenced and stressed from beginning to end with the accents and inflections of liberation" (1993, 89). It is a liberation, moreover, that is structurally guaranteed, immanent in the binary logic of the Manichean dialectic. This metaphysics, as Terry Eagleton nicely phrases it, "of the entry into full self-realization of a unitary subject known as the people" (1990, 28). Nonetheless, the privileged national agents are urban, male, vanguardist, and violent. The progressive nature of the violence is preordained and sanctioned by the structural logic of Hegelian progress.

This kind of nationalism can be called an anticipatory nationalism. Eagleton calls it nationalism "in the subjunctive mood," a premature utopianism that "grabs instinctively for a future, projecting itself by an act of will or imagination beyond the compromised political structures of the present" (1990, 25). Yet, ironically, anticipatory nationalism often claims legitimacy by appealing precisely to the august figure of inevitable progress inherited from the Western societies it seeks to dismantle.

Alongside this Manichean, mechanical nationalism, however, appears an altogether more open-ended and strategically difficult view of national agency. This nationalism stems not from the inexorable machinery of Hegelian dialectics but from the messy and disobliging circumstances of Fanon's own activism, as well as from the often dispiriting lessons of the anticolonial revolutions that preceded him. In this view, agency is multiple rather than unitary, unpredictable rather than immanent, bereft of dialectical guarantees and animated by an unsteady and nonlinear relation to time. There is no preordained rendezvous with victory, no single undivided national subject, no immanent historical logic. The national project must be laboriously and sometimes catastrophically invented, with unforeseen results. Time is dispersed and agency is heterogeneous. Here, in the unsteady, sliding interstices between conflicting national narratives, women's national agency makes its uncertain appearance.

In "Algeria Unveiled," Fanon ventriloquizes—only to refute—the long Western dream of colonial conquest as an erotics of ravishment. Under the hallucinations of empire, the Algerian woman is seen as the living flesh of the national body, unveiled and laid bare for the colonials' lascivious grip, revealing "piece by piece, the flesh of Algeria laid bare." (1967c, 42). In this remarkable essay, Fanon recognizes the colonial gendering of women as symbolic mediators, the boundary markers of an agon that is fundamentally male. The Algerian woman is "an intermediary between obscure forces and the group" (1967c, 37). "The young Algerian woman . . . establishes a link," he writes (1967c, 53).

Fanon understands brilliantly how colonialism inflicts itself as a domestication of the colony, a reordering of the labor and sexual economy of the people, so as to divert female power into colonial hands and disrupt the patriarchal power of colonized men. Fanon ventriloquizes colonial thinking: "If we want to destroy the structure of Algerian society, its capacity for resistance, we must first of all conquer the women" (1967c, 37–38). His insight here is that the dynamics of colonial power are fundamentally, though not solely, the dynamics of gender: It is the situation of women that was accordingly taken as the theme of action. Yet, in his work as a whole, Fanon fails to bring these insights into theoretical focus.

Long before Anderson, Fanon recognizes the inventedness of national community. He also recognizes the power of nationalism as a scopic politics, most visibly embodied in the power of sumptuary customs to fabricate a sense of national unity: "It is by their apparel that types of society first become known" (1967c, 35). Fanon perceives, moreover, that nationalism as a politics of visibility, implicates women and men in different ways. Because, for male nationalists, women serve as the visible markers of national homogeneity, they become subjected to especially vigilant and violent discipline. Hence the intense emotive politics of dress.

Yet a curious rupture opens in Fanon's text over the question of women's agency. At first, Fanon recognizes the historical meaning of the veil as open to the subtlest shifts and subversions. From the outset, colonials tried to grant Algerian women a traitorous agency, affecting to rescue them from the sadistic thrall of Algerian men. But, as Fanon knows, the colonial masquerade of giving women power by unveiling them was merely a ruse for achieving "a real power over the man" (1967c, 39). Mimicking the colonial masquerade, militant Algerian women deliberately began to unveil themselves. Believing their own ruse, colonials at first misread the unveiled Algerian women as pieces of "sound currency" circulating between the Kasbah and the white city, mistaking them for the visible coinage of cultural conversion (1967c, 42). For the *Fidai*, however, the militant woman was "his arsenal," a technique of counterinfiltration, duplicitously penetrating the body of the enemy with the armaments of death.

So eager is Fanon to deny the colonial rescue fantasy that he refuses to grant the veil any prior role at all in the gender dynamics of Algerian society. Having refused the colonial's desire to invest the veil with an essentialist meaning (the sign of women's servitude), he bends over backward to insist on the veil's semiotic innocence in Algerian society. The veil, Fanon writes, was no more than "a formerly inert element of the native cultural configuration" (1967c, 46). At once the veil loses its historic mutability and becomes a fixed, "inert" element in Algerian culture: "an undifferentiated element in a homogeneous whole" (1967c, 47). Fanon denies the "historic dynamism of the veil" and banishes its intricate history to a footnote from where, however, it displaces the main text with the insistent force of self-division and denial" (1967c, 53).

Fanon's thoughts on women's agency proceed through a series of contradictions. Where, for Fanon, does women's agency begin? He takes pains to point out that women's militancy does not precede the national revolution. Algerian women are not self-motivating agents, nor do they have prior histories or consciousness of revolt from which to draw. Their initiation in the revolution is learned, but it is not learned from other women or from other societies, nor is it transferred analogously from local feminist grievances. The revolutionary mission is "without apprenticeship without briefing" (1967c, 50). The Algerian woman learns her "revolutionary mission instinctively" (1967c, 50). This theory is not, however, a theory of feminist spontaneity, for women learn their militancy only at men's invitation. Theirs is a designated agency—

an agency by invitation only. Before the national uprising, women's agency was null, void, inert as the veil. Here Fanon colludes not only with the stereotype of women as bereft of historical motivation, but he also resorts, uncharacteristically, to a reproductive image of natural birthing: "It is an authentic birth in a pure state" (1967c, 50).

Why were women invited into the revolution? Fanon resorts immediately to a mechanistic determinism. The ferocity of the war was such, the urgency so great, that sheer structural necessity dictated the move: "The revolutionary wheels had assumed such proportions; the mechanism was running at a given rate. The machine would have to be complicated" (1967c, 48). Female militancy, in short, is simply a passive offspring of male agency and the structural necessity of the war. The problem of women's agency, so brilliantly raised as a question, is abruptly foreclosed.

Women's agency for Fanon is thus agency by designation. It makes its appearance not as a direct political relation to the revolution but as a mediated, domestic relation to a man: "At the beginning, it was the married women who were contacted. Later, widows or divorced women were designated" (1967c, 51). Women's first relation to the revolution is constituted as a domestic one. But domesticity, here, also constitutes a relation of possession. The militant was, in the beginning, obliged to keep "his woman" in "absolute ignorance" (1967c, 48). As designated agents, moreover, women do not commit themselves: "It is relatively easy to commit oneself. . . . The matter is a little more difficult when it involves designating someone" (1967c, 49). Fanon does not consider the possibility of women committing themselves to action. He thus manages women's agency by resorting to contradictory frames: the authentic, instinctive birth of nationalist fervor; the mechanical logic of revolutionary necessity; male designation. In this way, the possibility of a distinctive feminist agency is never broached.

Once he has contained women's militancy in this way, Fanon applauds women for their "exemplary constancy, self-mastery, and success" (1967c, 54). Nonetheless, his descriptions of women teem with instrumentalist similes and metaphors. Women are not women, they are "fish"; they are "the group's lighthouse and barometer," the *Fidai's* "woman-arsenal" (1967c, 54, 55). Most tellingly, Fanon resorts to a curiously eroticized image of militarized sexuality Carrying the men's pistols, guns, and grenades beneath her skirts, "the Algerian woman penetrates a little further into the flesh of the Revolution" (1967c, 54). Here, the Algerian woman is not a victim of rape but a masculinized rapist As if to contain the unmanning threat of armed women—in their dangerous crossings—Fanon masculinizes the female militant, turning her into a phallic substitute, detached from the male body but remaining, still, the man's "woman-arsenal." Most tellingly, however, Fanon describes the phallic woman as penetrating the flesh of the "revolution," not the flesh of the colonials. This odd image suggests an unbidden fear of emasculation, a dread that the arming of women might entail a fatal unmanning of Algerian men. A curious instability of gender power is here effected as the women are figured as masculinized and the male revolution is penetrated.

Fanon's vision of the political role of the Algerian family in the national uprising likewise proceeds through contradiction. Having brilliantly shown how the family constitutes the first ground of the colonial onslaught, Fanon seeks to reappropriate it as an arena of nationalist resistance. Yet the broader implications of the politicizing of family life are resolutely naturalized after the revolution. Having recognized that women "constituted for a long time the fundamental strength of the occupied," Fanon is reluctant to acknowledge any gender conflict or feminist grievance within the family prior to the anticolonial struggle or after the national revolution. (1967c, 66). Although, on the one hand, he admits that in "the Algerian family, the girl is always a notch behind the boy," he quickly insists that she is assigned to this position "without being humiliated or neglected" (1967c, 105). Although the men's words are "Law," women "voluntarily" submit themselves to "a form of existence limited in scope" (1967c, 66).

The revolution shakes the "old paternal assurance" so that the father no longer knows "how to keep his balance," and the woman "ceased to be a complement for man" (1967c, 109). It is telling, moreover, that in his analysis of the family, the category of mother does not exist. Women's liberation is credited entirely to national liberation and it is only with nationalism that women "enter into history." Prior to nationalism, women have no history, no resistance, no independent agency (1967c, 107). And since the national revolution automatically revolutionizes the family, gender conflict naturally vanishes after the revolution. Feminist agency, then, is contained by and subordinated to national agency, and the heterosexual family is preserved as the "truth" of society—its organic, authentic form. The family is revolutionalized, taken to a higher plane through a Hegelian vision of transcendence, but the rupturing force of gender is firmly foreclosed: "The family emerges strengthened from this ordeal" (1967c, 116). Women's militancy is contained within the postrevolutionary frame of the reformed, heterosexual family, as the natural image of national life.

In the postrevolutionary period, moreover, the tenacity of the father's "unchallengeable and massive authority" is not raised as one of the "pitfalls" of the national consciousness (1967c, 115). The Manichean dialectic—as generating an inherently resistant agency—does not, it seems, apply to gender. Deeply reluctant as he is to see women's agency apart from national agency, Fanon does not foresee the degree to which the Algerian National Liberation Front (FLN) will seek to co-opt and control women, subordinating them unequivocally once the revolution is won.

A feminist investigation of national difference might, by contrast, take into account the dynamic social and historical contexts of national struggles; their strategic mobilizing of popular forces; their myriad, varied trajectories; and their relation to other social institutions. We might do well to develop a more theoretically complex and strategically subtle genealogy of nationalisms.

12.

Interior Colonies:
Frantz Fanon and the
Politics of Identification

Diana Fuss

In this chapter I make two claims: first, that identification has a history—a colonial history; and second, that this colonial history poses serious challenges for contemporary recuperations of a politics of identification. I do not mean to imply that identification, a concept that receives its fullest elaboration in the discourse of psychoanalysis, cannot be successfully mobilized for a radical politics. I mean only to suggest that if we are to begin to understand both its political usages and its conceptual limitations, the notion of identification must be placed squarely within its other historical genealogies, including colonial imperialism. To assist me in the reading, I turn to one of the most important twentieth-century writers working at the intersection of anti-imperial politics and psychoanalytic theory, the practicing psychiatrist and revolutionary philosopher, Frantz Fanon. Psychoanalysis's interest in the problem of identification provides Fanon with a vocabulary and

Originally published in *Identification Papers: Readings on Psychoanalysis, Sexuality, and Culture,* by Diana Fuss (New York: Routledge, 1995), pp. 141–65. Reprinted with permission.

an intellectual framework in which to diagnose and to treat not only the psychological disorders produced in individuals by the violence of colonial domination but also the neurotic structure of colonialism itself. At the same time, Fanon's investigation of the dynamics of psychological alterity within the historical and political frame of colonialism suggests that identification is neither a historically universal concept nor a politically innocent one. A by-product of modernity, the psychoanalytic theory of identification takes shape within the larger cultural context of colonial expansion and imperial crisis.

IMPERIAL SUBJECTS

Contemporary theories of racial alterity and difference owe much to the rethinking of self-other relations that Fanon elaborates in his anticolorialist treatise, *Black Skin, White Masks* (1952). Most prominently, Edward Said's enormously influential theory of orientalism, which posits the Muslim "Orient" as a phobic projection of a distinctly Western imaginary (Said 1978, 1989), echoes elements of Fanon's own theory of colonial psychopathology, in which the black man is subjugated to the white man through a process of racial othering: "for not only must the black man be black; he must be black in relation to the white man" (Fanon 1967a, 110).[1] Assigned the role of embodying racial difference within a colonialist metaphorics of representation, the black man becomes for the white man the repository of his repressed fantasies, "the mainstay of his preoccupations and his desires" (1967a, 170). Under colonialism, Fanon contends, "the real Other for the white man is and will continue to be the black man" (1967a, 161). Yet significantly complicating this notion of "Black as Other" is a rather different reading of alterity in Fanon's work with potentially even greater import for an anticolonialist politics. In this second theory of white-black relations, Fanon implicitly disputes his own initial formulation of racial alterity and asks whether, in colonial regimes of representation, even otherness may be appropriated exclusively by white subjects. Fanon considers the possibility that colonialism may inflict its greatest psychical violence precisely by attempting to exclude blacks from the very self-other dynamic that makes subjectivity possible. This alternative theory of (non)alterity elaborated in *Black Skin, White Masks* does not so much call into question the first as uncover another, deeper, more insidious level of orientalism.

Fanon proposes that in the system of power-knowledge that upholds colonialism, it is the white man who lays claim to the category of the Other, the white man who monopolizes otherness to secure an illusion of unfettered access to subjectivity. Deploying the conventional psychoanalytic grammar of "the other" and "the Other" to distinguish between imaginary and symbolic difference, or between primary and secondary identification,[2] Fanon implies that the black man under colonial rule finds himself relegated to a position other than the Other. Colonialism works in part by policing the boundaries of cultural intelligibility, legislating and regulating which identities attain full cultural signification and which do not. For the black man, the implications of his exclusion from the cultural field of symbolization are immediate and devastating. If psychoanalysis is right to claim that "I is an Other," then otherness constitutes the very entry into subjectivity; subjectivity names the detour through the Other that provides access to a fictive sense of self.

Space operates as one of the chief signifiers of racial difference here: under colonial rule, freedom of movement (psychical and social) becomes a white prerogative. Forced to occupy, in a white racial phantasm, the static ontological space of the timeless "primitive," the black man is disenfranchised of his very subjectivity. Denied entry into the alterity that underwrites subjectivity, the black man, Fanon implies, is sealed instead into a "crushing objecthood." Black may be a protean imaginary other for white, but for itself it is a stationary "object"; objecthood, substituting for true alterity, blocks the migration through the Other necessary for subjectivity to take place. Through the violence of racial interpellation—"'Dirty nigger!' Or simply, 'Look, a Negro!'"—Fanon finds himself becoming neither an "I" nor a "not-I" but simply "an object in the midst of other objects": "the movements, the attitudes, the glances of the other fixed me there, in the sense in which a chemical solution is fixed by a dye" (1967a, 109). Stricken and immobilized by a white child's phobically charged cry, "Mama, see the Negro! I'm frightened!" Fanon's very body strains, fragments, and finally bursts apart: "I took myself off from my own presence, far indeed, and made myself an object. What else could it be for me but an amputation, an excision, a hemorrhage that spattered my whole body with black blood!" (1967a, 112). "Fixed" by the violence of the racist interpellation in an imaginary relation of fractured specularity, the black man, Fanon concludes, is "forever in combat with his own image" (1967a, 194). The black man (contra Lacan) begins and ends violently fragmented.

For the white man, the considerable cultural capital amassed by the *colonization of subjectivity* amounts to nothing less than the abrogation of universality. While the "black man must be black in relation to the white man," the converse does not hold true; the white man can be white without any relation to the black man because the sign "white" exempts itself from a dialectical logic of negativity. Consider Fanon's formula for "whiteness":

$$\frac{\text{White}}{\text{Ego different from the Other}}$$

(Fanon 1967a, 215)

Claiming for itself the exalted position of transcendental signifier, "white" is never a "not-black." As a self-identical, self-reproducing term, white draws its ideological power from its proclaimed transparency, from its self-elevation over the very category of "race."[3] "White" operates as its own Other, freed from any dependency upon the sign "Black" for its symbolic constitution. In contrast, "Black" functions, within a racist discourse, always diacritically, as the negative term in a Hegelian dialectic continuously incorporated and negated. Fanon articulates the process precisely: "The Negro is comparison" (1967a, 211).

The broad outlines of Fanon's theory of otherness are borrowed from Jean-Paul Sartre, whose use of the Hegelian dialectic in *Being and Nothingness* (1957) provides Fanon with a useful para-

digm for theorizing psychological alterity in specifically historical
and political terms. Sartre's thesis that it is the Other who founds
one's being, the Other who holds for the Self the "truth" of identity, becomes the theoretical basis for Fanon's repeated calls in
Black Skin, White Masks for an ethics of mutual identification, "a
world of reciprocal recognitions" (Fanon 1967a, 218).[4] Recently, the
category of the Other has achieved considerable prominence in
critical discussions of identity, offering a ready and useful short-
hand for signaling the production of cultural difference. Yet often
in reading this work I am struck by the inadequacy of the term to
do everything we ask of it. To invoke "the Other" as an ontological
or existentialist category paradoxically risks eliding the very range
and play of cultural differences that the designation is intended to
represent. Reliance upon the Other as a categorical imperative
often works to flatten rather than to accentuate difference.[5]

Moreover, the signifier "Other," in its applications, if not
always its theorizations, tends to disguise how there may be other
Others—subjects who do not quite fit into the rigid boundary definitions of (dis)similitude, or who indeed may be left out of the
Self/Other binary altogether. Fanon sees the Other for what it is:
an ideological construct designed to uphold and to consolidate
imperialist definitions of selfhood. Thus, in Fanon's estimation,
Sartre's theory of alterity fails on two counts. First, it fails to register how, in colonial history, not all others are the same: "Though
Sartre's speculations on the existence of the Other may be correct,"
Fanon argues, "their application to a black consciousness proves
fallacious. That is because the white man is not only The Other but
also the master" (Fanon 1967a, 138). Second, Sartre's deployment
of a Self/Other dialectic fails to see how *the Other who is master* is
firmly located in an economy of the Same. In a colonial dialectic,
based on a radical asymmetry of power, symbolic alterity operates
precisely as a privilege of the Self-Same.[6]

The problem originates with the Hegelian dialectic which, as
Robert Young has recently observed, is modeled upon Enlighten-
ment history. As a form of knowledge based upon incorporation,
Hegel's philosophical theory of self-other relations "simulates the

project of nineteenth-century imperialism . . . mimics at a conceptual level the geographical and economic absorption of the non-European world by the West" (Young 1990, 3). Both the existentialist and the psychoanalytic notions of otherness, which Fanon inherits from Sartre and Freud respectively, operate on the Hegelian principle of negation and incorporation. The colonial-imperial register of self-other relations is particularly striking in Freud's work, where the psychoanalytic formulation of identification can be seen to locate at the very level of the unconscious the imperialist act of assimilation that drives Europe's voracious colonialist appetite. Identification, in other words, is itself an imperial process, a form of violent appropriation in which the Other is deposed and assimilated into the lordly domain of Self. Through a psychical process of colonization, the imperial subject builds an Empire of the Same and installs at its center a tyrannical dictator, "His Majesty the Ego" (Freud 1908a).

What happens when imperial subjects become Imperial Subjects? When Otherness, and thus subjectivity, is claimed as a prerogative of the colonizer alone? For Fanon, the answer is clear: When subjectivity becomes the exclusive property of "the master," the colonizer can claim a sovereign right to personhood by purchasing interiority over and against the representation of the colonial other as pure exteriority. This is the elusive meaning of Fanon's enigmatic phrase "the *Umwelt* of Martinique" (Fanon 1967a, 37), one of many references in *Black Skin, White Masks* to Lacan's 1949 paper on the mirror stage, in which the function of the mirror is said "to establish a relation between the organism and its reality . . . between the *Innenwelt* and the *Umwelt*" (Lacan 1977, 23). But if Martinique is the *Umwelt* to Europe's *Innenwelt*, if the colonized is no more than a narcissistic self-reflection of the colonizer, then the latter's exclusive claim to "humanness" is seriously compromised, put into jeopardy by the very narcissism that paradoxically constructs the nonhuman in the Imperial Subject's own image. Moreover, by imposing upon the colonial other the burden of identification (the command to become a mimic Anglo-European), the Imperial Subject inadvertently places himself in the perilous position of object-object of the Other's aggressive, hostile, and rivalrous acts of incorporation.

It therefore becomes necessary for the colonizer to subject the colonial other to a double command: Be like me, don't be like me; be mimetically identical, be totally other. The colonial other is situated somewhere between difference and similitude, at the vanishing point of subjectivity. Of course, the same dialectic of difference and similitude constitutes the Imperial Subject as well. Any racial identity is organized through a play of identification and disidentification: "The Negro is not any more than the white man" (Fanon 1967a, 231). But "white" defines itself through a powerful and illusory *fantasy* of escaping the exclusionary practices of psychical identity formation. The colonizer projects what we might call identification's "alienation effect" onto the colonized who is enjoined to identify and to disidentify simultaneously with the same object, to assimilate but not to incorporate, to approximate but not to displace. Further, in attempting to claim alterity entirely as its own, the Imperial Subject imposes upon all others, as a condition of their subjugation, an injunction *to mime* alterity. The colonized are constrained to impersonate the image the colonizer offers them of themselves; they are commanded to imitate the colonizer's version of their essential difference. What, then, is the political utility of mimesis for the colonized, when mimesis operates as one of the very terms of their cultural and political dispossession under colonial imperialism?

In recent feminist theory, mimesis is most frequently understood in opposition to the category of masquerade: "Mimicry" (the deliberate and playful performance of a role) is offered as a counter and a corrective to "masquerade" (the unconscious assumption of a role).[7] The critical difference between masquerade and mimicry—between a nonironic imitation of a role and a parodic hyperbolization of that role—depends on the degree and readability of its excess. In this reading, mimicry resists and subverts dominant systems of representation by intentionally ironizing them. Postcolonial discourse theory understands mimicry in strikingly contrary terms, not as a tactic of dissent but as a condition of domination. In the

words of Homi Bhabha, "mimicry emerges as one of the most elusive and effective strategies of colonial power and knowledge."
Bhabha's theory of colonial mimicry, developed through a series of
important readings on Fanon's work, reminds us that it is precisely
through the figures of *"trompe l'oeil,* irony, mimicry, and repetition"
that the discourse of colonial imperialism exercises its authority
(Bhabha 1984, 126).[8] In this second reading, mimicry subtends
rather than disturbs dominant systems of representation; it operates as an emphatic instrument of political regulation, social discipline, and psychological depersonalization.

Yet despite their apparent incompatibility, these two notions of
mimesis cross, interact, and converge in ways that make it increasingly difficult to discriminate between a mimicry of subversion
and a mimicry of subjugation, or at least to know with any degree
of certainty their possible political effects. Bhabha makes it clear
that the ever-present possibility of slippage—from mimicry into
mockery, from performativity into parody—immediately dis-
credits colonialism's authorized versions of otherness and profoundly undermines the colonizer's elusive self-image to the point
where "the great tradition of European humanism seems capable
only of ironizing itself" (1984, 128). As narcissistic authority
evolves into paranoiac fear (Bhabha 1985, 78), the rents and divisions within colonialist narratives of domination become more visible. Not even the colonial production of the divided other—black
skin, white masks—leaves the colonizer's authority completely
intact: "In occupying two places at once . . . the depersonalized,
dislocated colonial subject can become an incalculable object, quite
literally, difficult to place. The demand of authority cannot unify
its messages nor simply identify its subjects" (Bhabha 1986a, xxii).
Bhabha's point, simply put, is that the production of mimic others
can prove to be disruptive in ways colonial discourse does not
intend and cannot possibly control.

If the mimicry of subjugation can provide unexpected opportunities for resistance and disruption, the mimicry of subversion
can find itself reinforcing conventional power relations rather than
eroding them. This is the conclusion of several recent studies on a

form of racial cross-identification that Fanon does not discuss in
Black Skin, White Masks, namely the subject position of white skin,
black masks, or whites in blackface.[9] In a reading of racial fetishism
and the homoerotic imaginary, Kobena Mercer asks: "what is
going on when whites assimilate and introject the degraded and
devalorized signifiers of racial otherness into the cultural construction of their own identity? If imitation implies identification,
in the psychoanalytic sense of the word, then what is it about
whiteness that makes the white subject want to be black?" (1992,
21). Kaja Silverman, in her analysis of Lawrence of Arabia, provides a possible answer with her theory of the double mimesis.
While, on the one hand, T. E. Lawrence's adoption of Arab dress
and custom promoted an unorthodox homoerotic identification
with Arab nationals, on the other hand, the very same cultural
impersonation masked a will to power, a desire to out-do the
Arabs in their "Arabness," an ambition to become more truly other
than the Other (Silverman 1989, 17–20). Gall Ching-Liang Low
expresses a similar concern when she speculates on whether, for
the colonial subject, "the primary attraction of the cross-cultural
dress is the promise of 'transgressive' pleasure without the penal-
ties of actual change" (Gall Ching-Liang Low 1989, 93). Keeping in
mind the power relations involved, there may be little if anything
subversive in cross-cultural impersonations that work in the service of colonial imperialism. When we take into account multiple
axes of difference that cross-cut, interfere with, and mutually constitute each other, the dream of a playful mimesis cannot be so
easily or immediately recuperated for a progressive politics. Given
the various and continually changing cultural coordinates that
locate identity at the site of both fantasy and power, one would
have to acknowledge, at the very least, that the same mimetic act
can be disruptive and reversionary at once.

Folded into one another, these two notions of mimicry together
suggest that context is decisive in registering the full range of political meanings one might attribute to even a single identification. The
deceptively simple details of who is imitating whom, and under
what conditions, stand as the most insistent, intricate, and indis-

pensable questions for a politics of mimesis. The project of evaluating the political effects of mimesis encounters further complications when we consider the ways in which "imitation repeatedly veers over into identification" (Silverman 1989, 19). Psychoanalytic theories of identification all seem to agree that "every imitation . . . is also an incorporation" (Lacoue-Labarthe and Luc-Nancy 1989, 208). In the next section I would like to examine at least one instance in Fanon's work where this premise does not appear to hold true, one scene of mimesis that draws its power from a certain *refusal* of identification. Tentatively unfastening impersonation from identification, I propose to demonstrate how mimesis might actually be deployed to counter a prescribed identification. When situated within the context of colonial politics, the psychoanalytic *assumption* that every conscious imitation conceals an unconscious identification needs to be carefully questioned, read for the signs of its own colonizing impulses.

IMPERSONATING IDENTIFICATION

The wearing of the veil throughout the period of the French occupation of Algeria provides Fanon with one of his most important examples of the role of mimesis in the psychopathology of colonial relations. In the opening essay of *A Dying Colonialism*, entitled "Algeria Unveiled," Fanon examines the mutable and contradictory cultural meanings attributed to Arab women's dress, what he suggestively denotes as "the historic dynamism of the veil" (1967c, 63). For the European occupiers, the veil functions as an exotic signifier, invested with all the properties of a sexual fetish. Faced with a veiled Algerian woman, Fanon writes, the European is consumed with a desire to see, a desire that, in colonialism's highly sexualized economy of looking, also operates as an urge for violent possession:

> Every new Algerian woman unveiled announced to the occupier an Algerian society whose systems of defense were in the process of dislocation, open and breached. Every veil that fell, every body that became liberated from the traditional embrace of the

haïk, every face that offered itself to the bold and impatient glance of the occupier, was a negative expression of the fact that Algeria was beginning to deny herself and was accepting the rape of the colonizer. (Fanon 1967c, 42)

The colonialist desire to unveil the Algerian woman is given special urgency by the capability of the veil to block the look of the Other while permitting the woman herself to assume the privilege of the Imperial Subject—to see without being seen (Fanon 1967c, 44). Fanon reads the French colonial political program of "unveiling" as an attempt to strip all Algerians of their national, cultural, and religious identity by reducing the Algerian woman to a sexual representation more readily assimilated to white European ideals of womanhood. In direct opposition to the signification of the veil for the French colonialists, the veil comes to function for the colonized as a visible sign of Algerian nationalist identity and a symbol of resistance to imperial penetration and colonial domination. Each attempt to Europeanize the Algerian woman is countered by a reinvestment of the veil with national import. Even more importantly for Fanon, the wearing of the veil operates as one of the most visible and dramatic indices to the historical emergence of women's political agency: "the Algerian women who had long since dropped the veil once again donned the *haïk*, thus affirming that it was not true that woman liberated herself at the invitation of France and of General de Gaulle" (Fanon 1967c, 62).

Yet as Mervat Hatem reminds us, revolutionary calls for the reassumption of the veil may have quite other motivations during times of severe economic hardship brought on by the colonial wars: The veil, and the exclusion of women from the public sphere that it signifies, upholds a traditional sexual division of labor and preserves for men increasingly scarce jobs in the workplace (1993, 31).[10] Within a single discourse the veil can thus signify doubly, as a mode of defying colonialism and as a means of ensuring patriarchal privilege.[11] Conversely, the veil can carry a similar meaning across seemingly antithetical discourses: In the discourse of colonial imperialism and in the discourse of national resistance, the veiled Algerian woman stands in metonymically for the nation. In both instances, the woman's body is the contested ideological battleground, over-burdened and saturated with meaning. It is the woman who circu-lates as a fetish—both the site of a receding, endangered national identity and the guarantor of its continued visibility. In Fanon's "Algeria Unveiled," the wearer of the veil *becomes* a veil, the inscrutable face of a nation struggling to maintain its cultural invio-lability. A fetishistic logic of displacement operates in Fanon's own text, as the veiled Algerian woman comes to bear the burden of rep- · resenting national identity in the absence of nation.

Fanon extends this logic of fetishization to include the unveiled Algerian woman as well. His argument rests on a paradox of unveiling: If some Algerian women during the war have begun to dress in European clothes, this act of cultural cross-dressing is tes-timony not to the success of the relentless European attempts at psychological conversion and deculturation but to their failure; these women, enlisted by the FLN, unveil themselves only in order to better disguise themselves. "Passing" as European, Algerian women can move freely through the European quarters of the city, carrying concealed guns, grenades, ammunition, money, papers, and even explosives. For Fanon, this kind of national passing in the service of revolutionary activity is never a question of imitation:

> It must be borne in mind that the committed Algerian woman learns both her role as "a woman alone in the street" and her rev-olutionary mission instinctively. The Algerian woman is not a secret agent. It is without apprenticeship, without briefing, without fuss, that she goes out into the street with three grenades in her handbag or the activity report of an area in her bodice. She does not have a sensation of playing a role she has read about ever so many times in novels, or seen in motion pictures. There is not that coefficient of play, of imitation, almost always present in this form of action when we are dealing with a Western woman. What we have here is not the bringing to light of a character known and frequented a thousand times in imagination or in sto-ries. It is an authentic birth in a pure state, without preliminary instruction. There is no character to imitate. On the contrary,

there is an intense dramatization, a continuity between the woman and the revolutionary. (Fanon 1967c, 50)

Fanon's insistence upon the nonmimetic character of the Algerian woman's national cross-dressing poses a number of questions for a politics of mimesis. What does it mean to say that this woman "learns" her role "instinctively," without apprenticeship and without example? Can one imitate without an object or a model to impersonate? Can there be impersonation without imitation, or role-playing without a role to play? In one sense, yes. Theories of the masquerade remind us that there is no model behind the imitation, no genuine femininity beneath the performance, no original before the copy.[12] But Fanon's insistence that the Algerian woman's European impersonation is "an authentic birth in a pure state" presumes not that femininity is itself a cultural production or the masquerade, but that masquerade is a natural function of femininity. It assumes that if the Algerian woman in her performance as "European" expertly dissimulates, she does so naturally, without "that coefficient or play, of imitation" that characterizes Western women. Fanon's retrieval of an essentialist discourse of black femininity to explain the paradox of the unveiled Algerian woman's nonmimetic imitation appears motivated by a desire to refuse any possibility of cultural contamination between the imitator and her subject, the colonized and the colonizer, the Algerian and the European. But is it possible to separate so completely the imitation from what it imitates? Is it possible for the mimicking subject to inhabit fully a performative role while still remaining largely outside it? Where, in other words, in a politics of imitation can one locate the politics?

Following the mimicry/masquerade distinction, we might be tempted to conclude that the revolutionary agent that Fanon describes, the Algerian woman "radically transformed into a European woman, poised and unconstrained, whom no one would suspect" (Fanon 1967c, 57), engages in a form of mimicry but not masquerade. Her "transformation" involves the deliberate taking up of a cultural role for political ends rather than the unconscious "bringing to light of a character known and frequented a thousand times in imagination or in stories." However, the success of this particular mimetic act depends not upon excess but equivalency, not upon mimicry's distance from masquerade but upon its approximation to it. "Algeria Unveiled" dramatizes a form of mimesis that takes masquerade as its object; the political strategy described is more like that of miming *masquerade*. To avoid inspection by the French soldiers, the unveiled Algerian woman, by impersonating the sartorial masquerade of white European femininity, submits herself to another kind of examination: "The soldiers, the French patrols, smile to her as she passes, compliments on her looks are heard here and there, but no one suspects that her suitcases contain the automatic pistol which will presently mow down four or five members of one of the patrols" (Fanon 1967c, 58). To do its work, this form of tactical mimesis must be perceived by its colonialist target as feminine masquerade (where both "feminine"and "masquerade" signify "European"), and the masquerade, in turn, as evidence of another Algerian woman "saved," another victory of Europeanization, another piece of "the flesh of Algeria laid bare" (Fanon 1967c, 42).

It might be more accurate to say, then, that imitation is very much at issue in Fanon's example of the Algerian woman unveiled, but that not all forms of imitation are identifications. The importance of Fanon's reading of this particular scene can be registered elsewhere, in its attempt to install a wedge between identification and imitation, in its suggestion that not every imitative act harbors a secret or unconscious identification. Indeed, to read uncritically the Algerian woman's *dramatization* as an act of *identification* risks trivializing the role that political necessity plays in this performance and minimizing the trauma of the historical event that occasions it. Fanon implies that some imitations may only disguise themselves as identifications. But, it could be objected, in so doing might the act of mimesis actually produce the very identification it seeks to disavow? Identification, after all, is an unconscious operation that repeatedly resists our attempts to govern and to control it. Did the opportunity to dress in European clothes permit some Algerian women to engage in cross-national, cross-racial, cross-class, and cross-cultural identifications with white bourgeois European women? Perhaps. (Although there is no simple way of knowing anything about the fantasies, desires, and identifications of the women in the FLN from Fanon's admittedly opaque texts: elsewhere Fanon claims to "know nothing" about the woman of color [1967a, 179–80]). But the point to be registered is that while imitation may either institute or gratify an unconscious identification, it can and does frequently exceed the logic of that identification. Put another way, identification with the Other is neither a necessary precondition nor an inevitable outcome of imitation. For Fanon it is politically imperative to insist upon an instrumental difference between imitation and identification, because it is precisely politics that emerges in the dislocated space between them.[13]

It is because the French colonialists did not understand the difference between identification and imitation that their own deployment of a politics of mimesis failed as spectacularly as the Algerians' succeeded. In *The Wretched of the Earth* Fanon discusses the colonialist practice of interning leading Algerian male intellectuals and submitting them to prolonged sessions of brainwashing, a strategy designed "to attack from the inside those elements which constitute national consciousness" (1968, 286). The details Fanon provides of the "pathology of torture" show how this particular form of psychological abuse aspires to nothing less than the *forcible realignment of identifications* achieved through a program of strictly monitored imitations. During the psychological "conversion" process, the intellectual is ordered to "play the part" of collaborator; his waking hours are spent in continuous intellectual disputation, arguing the merits of French colonization and the evils of Algerian nationalism; he is never left alone, for solitude is considered a rebellious act, and he must do all his thinking aloud, since silence is strictly forbidden (1968, 286–87).

Ultimately, the native intellectual's life depends upon his ability to imitate the Other perfectly, without a trace of parody; it depends, in short, upon his ability to mime without the perception of mimicry. Once again, mimicry must pass as masquerade if the subject who performs the impersonation is to survive to tell the tale. This type of torture is perhaps only the most extreme form of what Bhabha has described as the primary mode of subjectification under colonial domination: "a grotesque mimicry or 'doubling' that threatens to split the soul" (Bhabha 1983b, 27). Yet this violent attempt to produce an identification (what psychoanalysis calls an "identification with the aggressor") fails "to split the soul," and it fails because imitation alone is not sufficient to produce an identification. Those interned subjects released after "successful completion" of the conversion program, Fanon tells us, all returned to their communities and took up, once again, their respective roles in Algeria's struggle for national liberation.

This is not to say, however, that the male revolutionaries Fanon describes in *The Wretched of the Earth*, forced to imitate the ideology, speech, and mannerisms of their European captors, were not left unscarred by the process. Indeed, as early as *Black Skin, White Masks*, Fanon is concerned with the profoundly debilitating psychological effects of colonial mimesis on all black men who must labor under the brutal colonial injunction to become (in Bhabha's eloquent turn of phrase) "almost the same but not white" (1984, 130). For the black man, mimesis is a by-product of the colonial encounter, a pathology created by the material conditions of imperial domination, a psychological "complex" that at all points must be refused and resisted.[14] If we compare Fanon's discussion of black men in *Black Skin, White Masks* to his later discussion of black women in "Algeria Unveiled," we detect a dubious gender incongruity structuring Fanon's theory of colonial mimicry: whereas colonial mimicry for black men is alienating and depersonalizing, for black women it is natural and instinctive. In Fanon's view, black women are essentially mimics and black men are essentially not. Fanon's analysis of colonial mimesis repeatedly runs aground on the question of sexual difference. What are the implications of Fanon's sex/gender essentialisms for his project to decolonize sexuality?

DECOLONIZING SEXUALITY

Fanon's disquieting discussions of not only femininity but homo-sexuality—inextricably linked in Fanon as they are in Freud—have received little if any attention from his critical commentators. Passages in Fanon's corpus articulating ardent disidentifications from black and white women and from white gay men (for Fanon, homosexuality is culturally white) are routinely passed over, dismissed as embarrassing, baffling, unimportant, unenlightened, or perhaps simply politically risky. In this section I turn specifically to Fanon's theory of "the sexual perversions" for several reasons. First, these difficult passages tell us something important about Fanon's own sexual identifications as they are shaped within and against a colonial discourse of sexuality that appropriates masculinity as the exclusive prerogative of white male colonizers while relegating black male sexuality to the culturally abjected, pathologized space of femininity, degeneracy, and castration. Second, Fanon's remarks on homosexuality, while failing to challenge some of Freud's most conventional and dangerous typologies of sexuality, simultaneously question, at least implicitly, the ethnological component of psychoanalysis that has long equated "the homo-sexual" with "the primitive."[15] Finally, Fanon's theory of racialized sexualities under colonialism helps point us in the direction of interrogating the ethnocentrism of the very category of "sexuality." Along the way, I hope to avoid the problem of oversimplification—either hastily dismissing Fanon's notions of sexuality as theoretically suspect, or uncritically recuperating them as historically overdetermined—by employing a double reading strategy. The most appropriate methodology for reading the politics of sexual identifications may be to theorize and to historicize at once, to follow what I take, in fact, to be Fanon's own reading strategy elaborated more fully in later works like The Wretched of the Earth.

Fanon's theory of the sexual perversions appears within a broader discussion of the problem of Negrophobia in chapter 6 of Black Skin, White Masks. "The Negro and Psychopathology" takes as

its central focus fantasies by white subjects in which black men perform the role of "phobogenic object[s]" (Fanon 1967a, 151). Following closely Angelo Hesnard's definition of phobia as "a neurosis characterized by the anxious fear of an object,"[16] Fanon widens
the field of the clinical disorder by explaining that the phobic object
need not be present in actuality but need only exist as a possibility
in the mind of the subject (Fanon 1967a, 154). In a reading of the
fantasy "A Negro is raping me" (the chapter's central example of
Negrophobia), Fanon identifies the phobia as a disguised expression of sexual desire: "when a woman lives the fantasy of rape by a
Negro, it is in some way the fulfillment of a private dream, of an
inner wish. . . . [I]t is the woman who rapes herself" (1967a, 179).
How can it be said that the Negrophobic woman rapes herself? Like
Freud's hysteric,[17] Fanon's phobic can apparently occupy in fantasy
two or more positions at once. Through a cross-gendered and cross-
racial identification, the white Negrophobic woman usurps the
position she herself has assigned to the black man and plays the
role not only of victim but of aggressor: "I wish the Negro would
rip me open as I would have ripped a woman open" (Fanon 1967a,
179). For Fanon, the white woman's fantasy "A Negro is raping
me" is ultimately an expression of either a violent lesbian desire or
a wish for self-mutilation, with narcissism ultimately blurring the
distinction between them. Even more questionable, the desire to be
a rapist is posited as the basis of the desire to be raped, a
masochistic identification that Fanon unproblematically takes as
one of the defining psychopathologies of white femininity. It is,
however, important to recall at this juncture that Fanon constructs
his reading of this particular fantasy during a period when fabricated charges of rape were used as powerful colonial instruments
of fear and intimidation against black men. Fanon's deeply troubling comments on white women and rape are formulated within a
historical context in which the phobically charged stereotype of the
violent, lawless, and oversexed Negro puts all black men at perpetual risk. What we might call Fanon's myth of white women's
rape fantasies is offered as a counternarrative to "the myth of the
black rapist" (see Davis 1981).

Ultimately, what may be most worrisome about the treatment of interracial rape in *Black Skin, White Masks* is not what Fanon says about white women and black men but what he *does not* say about black women and white men. As Mary Ann Doane notes in her reading of Fanon's analysis of rape and miscegenation,

> Fanon asks few (if any) questions about the white man's psycho-sexuality in his violent confrontation with the black woman—fewer still about how one might describe black female subjectivity in the face of such violence. In the historical scenario conjoining rape and lynching, the emotional charge attached to miscegenation, its representational intensity, are channeled onto the figure of the white woman, effectively erasing the black woman's historical role.

According to Doane, rape itself undergoes a certain displacement—"from the white man's prerogative as master/colonizer to the white woman's fears/desires in relation to the black male" (Doane 1991, 222). What disappears in Fanon's act of displacement is any analysis of the production and institutionalization of a violent imperial masculinity necessary to keep the social structure of colonial domination firmly in place. What drops out is a recognition of how sexual violence is imbricated in an entire economic and political system in which the rape of black women by white settlers (or "colons") works to establish and to maintain what is, in effect, a slave economy.[18] What is missing, finally, is any serious discussion of black women's subjectivity under colonial rule: "Those who grant our conclusions on the psychosexuality of the white woman may ask what we have to say about the woman of color. I know nothing about her" (Fanon 1967a, 179-80).[19]

If, in Fanon's theory of Negrophobia, the white woman who fears the black man really desires him, then so apparently does the phobic white man: "the Negrophobic woman is in fact nothing but a putative sexual partner—just as the Negrophobic man is a repressed homosexual" (Fanon 1967a, 156). For Fanon, the root pathogenic cause of Negrophobia is sexual perversion—a perversion of sexual object-choice for men and sexual behavior for women ("All the Negrophobic women I have known had abnormal sex lives. . . . [T]here was also an element of perversion, the persistence of infantile formations: God knows how they made love! It must be terrifying" [1967a, 158]). In both instances, perversion is represented specifically as a *white* pathology. There are no homosexuals in Martinique, Fanon speculates, because the Oedipus complex remains, in every sense, foreign to the Antilles: "Like it or not, the Oedipus complex is far from coming into being among Negroes" (Fanon 1967a, 152). Fanon insists that while Martinique may have its "godmothers," male transvestites in the Antilles nonetheless lead "normal sex lives" and "can take a punch like any he-man" (Fanon 1967a, 180). For white men homosexuality is a pathological condition; for black men it is "a means to a livelihood," a by-product of colonialism in which black men from the colonies are forced into homosexual prostitution in the metropole in order to survive economically.

The most serious problem with Fanon's theory of the sexual perversions is the pivotal role assigned to homosexuality in the cultural construction of racism. All of the psychical components Fanon identifies as central to the "hate complexes" are identical to those he posits as constitutive of same-sex desire: "fault, guilt, refusal of guilt, paranoia—one is back in homosexual territory" (Fanon 1967a, 183). It is not entirely clear which of these two "complexes" (racism or homosexuality) Fanon believes to be the pathological trigger for the other; more certain is the sleight of hand in which "homosexuality" is inserted into a violent cultural equation where "homophobia" properly belongs. As Lee Edelman has pointed out, homosexuality and homophobia are made to change places with one another in a falsely syllogistic logic: "Homophobia allows a certain figural logic to the pseudo-algebraic 'proof' that asserts: where it is 'given' that white racism equals castration and 'given' that homosexuality equals castration, then it is proper to conclude that white racism equals (or expresses through displacement) homosexuality and, by the same token, in a reversal of devastating import for lesbians and gay men of color, homosexuality equals white racism" (Edelman 1993, 55). If racism is articulated with homosexuality instead of homophobia, where are antiracist lesbians and gay men, of all colors, to position themselves in relation to same-sex desire? Fanon's theory of sexuality offers little to anyone committed to both an anti-imperialist and an antihomophobic politics.

Yet, like Fanon's theory of white femininity, his complicated reading of homosexuality needs to be framed historically, placed within the prism of the particular colonial history that shapes and legislates it. Fanon's concern with the economics of sexual exchange between colonizer and colonized is not entirely without warrant; prostitution was indeed one of the few occupations open to black immigrants in colonial France. The point needs to be made that colonialism's insatiable desire for exotic black bodies, its institutionalization of a system of sexual exploitation that focused largely on black women, was extended to include many black men as well. Moreover, Fanon's effort to call into question the universality of the Oedipus complex may constitute what is most revolutionary about his theoretical work, a political intervention into classical psychoanalysis of enormous import for later theorists of race and sexuality. Responding to an allusion by Lacan to the "abundance" of the Oedipus complex, Fanon shows instead the limitations of Oedipus, or rather the ideological role Oedipus plays *as a limit in* the enculturating sweep of colonial expansionism. Prone to see Oedipus everywhere they look, Western ethnologists are impelled to find their own psychosexual pathologies duplicated in their objects of study (Fanon 1967a, 152). Under colonialism, Oedipus is nothing if not self-reproducing.

Taking their cue in part from Fanon, two French theorists of the metropole, Gilles Deleuze and Felix Guattari, unmask oedipality as a form of colonization turned inside out: "Oedipus is always colonization pursued by other means, it is the interior colony, and . . . even here at home, where we Europeans are concerned, it is our intimate colonial relation."[20] Deleuze's and Guattari's *Anti-Oedipus*, originally published in the early 1970s during the watershed period of publications on Fanon's work,[21] is as much a polemic against the psychology of colonization as it is a demystification of the imperial politics of oedipalization, and indeed the great insight of this wildly ambitious book is its demonstration of how the historical emergence of both colonization and oedipaliza- tion participate in a double ideological operation where each serves effectively to conceal the political function and purpose of the other. "Even in the case of worthy Oedipus," pronounces *Anti- Oedipus*, "it was already a matter of 'politics'" (1983, 98).

Fanon's insistence that there is no homosexuality in the Antilles may convey a more trenchant meaning than the one he in fact intended: If by "homosexuality" one understands the cultur- ally specific social formations of same-sex desire as they are artic- ulated in the West, then indeed homosexuality is foreign to the Antilles. Is it really possible to speak of "homosexuality," or for that matter "heterosexuality" or "bisexuality," as universal, global formations? Can one generalize from the particular forms sexu- ality takes under Western capitalism to sexuality *as such*? What kinds of colonizations do such discursive translations perform on "other" traditions of sexual differences? It is especially important, confronted by these problems, to focus attention on the ethnocen- trism of the epistemological categories themselves—European identity categories that seem to me wholly inadequate to describe the many different consolidations, permutations, and transforma- tions of what the West has come to understand, itself in myriad and contradictory fashion, under the sign "sexuality."

Fanon's disavowal and repudiation of "homosexuality" take on special meaning in light of the parallel that psychoanalysis draws between "perversion" and "primitivity." This is not by any means to say that Fanon's work is free of the specter of homophobia. When Fanon confesses, "I have never been able, without revulsion, to hear a man say of another man: 'He is so sensual!'" (Fanon 1967a, 201), the very form of the enunciation obeys the terms of Fanon's own earlier definition of phobia as "terror mixed with sexual revul- sion" (Fanon 1967, 155). However, Fanon's disidentification can be read as another kind of refusal as well, an implicit rejection of the "primitive = invert" equation that marks the confluence of evolu- tionary anthropology and sexology and their combined influence on early twentieth-century psychoanalysis.

Inversion, Freud comments in *Three Essays on the Theory of Sexuality*, "is remarkably widespread among many savage and primitive races . . . ; and, even amongst the civilized peoples of Europe, climate and race exercise the most powerful influence on the prevalence of inversion and upon the attitude adopted towards it" (Freud 1963, 7:139).[22] In these curious lines linking inversion to race and climatology, Freud has in mind the influential theory of the "Sotadic Zone" developed in the final volume of Richard Burton's *The Arabian Nights* (1885). Burton's Sotadic Zone, a global mapping of inversion according to certain latitudes and longitudes, covers all the shores of the Mediterranean, including North Africa, and extends as far as the South Sea Islands and the New World.[23] While Burton describes his sexual topography as "geographical and climactic, not racial," he nonetheless finds the incidence of "Le Vice" to be highest among the Turks ("a race of born pederasts" [232]), the Chinese ("the chosen people of debauchery" [238]), and the North American Indians ("sodomites" and "cannibals" [240]). The sexologist Havelock Ellis, following Burton, also finds a "special proclivity to homosexuality . . . among certain races and in certain regions" (Ellis and Symonds 1897, 22). For Burton and Ellis, the category "race" encompasses more than simply skin color; for these writers "race" operates as a somewhat more elastic term folded into the category of nation ("the British race"), species ("the human race"), and even gender ("the male or female race"). Not insignificantly for the present reading of racialized sexualities, fin-de-siècle sexology routinely refers to "the third sex" as a separate race or species. In both Ellis's and Burton's discourse of Empire, Algeria is singled out as the most dangerous—because the most sexually infectious—of the Sotadic Zones. Like a kind of venereal disease threatening the moral health of an empire, homosexuality is said to be "contracted in Algeria" by members of the French Foreign Legion, "spread" through entire military regiments, and finally transmitted to the civilian population (see Ellis and Symonds 1897, 10; Burton 1885, 251). Through what we might call an *epidemiology of sexuality*, colonial discourse represents places like North Africa as breeding grounds for immorality and vice, thereby inverting and disguising the real trauma of colonial imperialism: the introduction of highly infectious and devastatingly lethal European diseases into the colonies.

Fanon's theory of the sexual perversions can thus be more fully understood as an impassioned response to popular colonialist theories of race and sexuality. Fanon's resolutely masculine self-identifications, articulated through the abjectification of femininity and homosexuality, take shape over and against colonialism's castrating representations of black male sexuality. Unfortunately, Fanon does not think beyond the presuppositions of colonial discourse to examine how colonial domination itself works partially through the social institutionalization of misogyny and homophobia. Fanon's otherwise powerful critique of the scene of colonial representation does not fundamentally question the many sexualized determinations of that scene. In each of Fanon's works, including "Algeria Unveiled," the colonial encounter is staged within exclusively masculine parameters; the colonial other remains an undifferentiated, homogenized male, and subjectivity is ultimately claimed for men alone. When the politics of sexual difference is in question, Fanon's theory of identification risks presenting itself as simply another "theory of the 'subject' [that] has always been appropriated by the 'masculine'" (Irigaray 1985, 133–46).

IDENTIFICATION IN TRANSLATION

It is important to remember, when discussing the complicated subject of Fanon's own personal identifications, that he was a practicing clinician whose theoretical and cultural work was informed and shaped by an entire institutional, professional, and political apparatus located in the space of violent colonial struggle. The complexity of Fanon's heterogeneous subject position—an Antillean-born, French-educated physician practicing psychiatry in North Africa—helps to frame one of the most startling contradictions of his clinical practice. As a psychiatrist Fanon treated all types of patients during the early years of the Algerian war: During the daytime he worked with French soldiers suffering psychological breakdowns as a result of their daily torture of suspected Algerian nationals; at night he treated the victims of these tortures, often restoring them to health only to see them returned once again to the brutality of a French police interrogation (McCullogh 1983, 1).

Not surprisingly, Fanon's attitudes toward psychiatry reflected the deep ambivalences of his own changing political affiliations and personal identifications. As a member of the FLN and eventually one of its most important international spokesmen, Fanon warned against colonialist appropriations of the psychoanalytic "cure" as a convenient method of cultural socialization, a means of adjusting members of the colonial population to their political condition of social alienation. At the same time, as a doctor from the metropole, Fanon continued throughout his life to promote psychoanalysis as one of the most powerful instruments available to combat those mental pathologies that are "the direct product of oppression" (1968, 251). Introduced into Algeria in 1932, the psychiatric hospital ironically became for Fanon a site of active resistance to the violence of the colonialist enterprise that instituted such Western-style institutions in the first place.

When Fanon was appointed in the fall of 1953 director of the Hospital at Blida-Joinville, the largest psychiatric hospital in Algeria, there were eight psychiatrists and 2,500 beds for a national population of 8.5 million Muslims and 1.5 million Europeans (Gendzier 1973, 73). Disproportionate to their numbers, over half of Fanon's patients were white Europeans, the rest black Algerians; Fanon ministered to both. However, Fanon's sessions with his European and Algerian patients were marked by a radical disparity, for the French-speaking Fanon spoke neither Arabic nor Kabyle and could not communicate with his Muslim patients without the mediation of a translator.[24]

There are two immediate points to be made on the subject of the translator in Fanon's clinical practice. The first is what is added to the analytic process: a heightened awareness of language as an embattled site of historical struggle and social contestation. Fanon's complete reliance upon translators to converse with his Muslim patients is nothing if not a powerful reminder, to both doctor and patient, of the immediate political context in which the therapeutic dialogue struggles to take place. The daily translations of Arabic and Kabyle into French could not avoid reproducing, within the space of the clinical treatment, the very structure of the colonial relation. The second is what is lost in this translation: quite simply, the analysand's own speech, the speaking unconscious. What ultimately escapes Fanon are the slips and reversals, the substitutions and mispronunciations, in short, the free associations that provide the analyst with his most important interpretive material, the traces and eruptions of the patient's unconscious into language. Strictly speaking, the speech Fanon analyzes in the sessions with his Muslim patients is the translator's, not the patient's, a situation that impossibly confuses the analytic process and urgently poses the question of whether a therapeutic model constructed in one language or culture can be so easily or uncritically *translated* into another.

Fanon's essay "The North African Syndrome," published in the February 1952 issue of *L'esprit*, gives us some indication of the formidable problems posed by the use of a translator in colonial medicine. The following scene dramatizes, with wry humor, a routine medical examination between a French doctor and a North African patient:

> [The patient] tells about *his pain*. Which becomes increasingly his own. He now talks about it volubly. He takes hold of it in space and puts it before the doctor's nose. He takes it, touches it with his ten fingers, develops it, exposes it. It grows as one watches it. He gathers it over the whole surface of his body and after fifteen minutes of gestured explanations the interpreter . . . translates for us: he says he has a belly-ache. (Fanon 1967b, 5).

Fanon later faced very similar difficulties in his psychiatric practice at Blida, where the problem of language comprehension was further exacerbated by the tendency of analysis to base itself almost exclusively upon dialogue, upon close attention to the intonations and equivocations of language, language that indeed must be said to be completely and inescapably culturally inflected.

Fanon's own clinical writings provide us with little clue to the presence of a third party interpreter in the psychiatric sessions with his Algerian patients; all traces of this fundamental disturbance in the actual scene of analysis are entirely erased from the written case histories. Who were these translators without whom Fanon could not do his work? Fanon's translators at Blida were the hospital's male nurses, educated Algerian men who, under colonial rule, were denied the opportunity to pursue advanced medical degrees. It was this group of male nurses whom Fanon counted as his closest supporters in the battle to institute a series of controversial hospital reforms; it was the Algerian nurses and not the European staff who possessed the appropriate language skills necessary for running a multilingual hospital; and it was the nurses to whom Fanon dictated his case notes, the nurses who, in some instances, actually *wrote* the case histories that were later edited by Fanon (Gendzier 1973, 77; Geismar 1969, 83). Unlike Freud, then, who had the luxury of a private practice that selectively treated exclusively middle-class patients, Fanon's professional sessions were conducted in a large psychiatric state hospital and were dependent upon the intensive labor of a whole team of invisible workers that administered to the needs of many hundreds of patients a day. This cadre of nurse-translators may be only the most visible sign of an institution that in both purpose and design continued to bear the stamp of a colonial import.

Ultimately, the use of a translator in his clinical work may provide the most powerful testimony of all to Fanon's hypothesis that to be exiled from language is to be dispossessed of one's very subjectivity.[25] Where Fanon begins his investigation of cross-racial identifications in *Black Skin, White Masks* with a chapter called "The Negro and Language," he does so to emphasize the importance of speech to the assumption of subjectivity: "to speak is to exist absolutely for the other" (Fanon 1967a, 17). Moreover, "to speak a language is to take on a world, a culture. The Antilles Negro who wants to be white will be the whiter as he gains greater mastery of the cultural tool that language is" (Fanon 1967a, 38). Racial difference operates in this context as a linguistic construct bounded and defined by opportunities of class and education. Fanon recognizes that his facility with the French language accords him what he calls "honorary citizenship" as a white man (Fanon 1967a, 38). He also recognizes that this citizenship is never more than "honorary," insofar as a racialist discourse of immutable biological difference ceaselessly works to "seal" the white man in his "whiteness" and the black man in his "blackness" (Fanon 1967a, 9). To his white European patients, Fanon is ineluctably black—"the Negro doctor" (Fanon 1967a, 117). To his black Algerian patients, Fanon is white: a French-educated, upper-middle-class professional who cannot speak the language. Identifying with both groups but accepted by neither, Fanon's shifting and contradictory subject positions keep identity perpetually at bay. It is precisely identity that is suspended or deferred by the work of identification, identity that remains in a state of internal exile. Put another way, Fanon's own identifications are in constant translation, caught in a system of cultural relays that make the assumption of racial identity both necessary and impossible.[26]

In light of his own ambivalent identifications, Fanon's attempt to perform a sociohistorical analysis of the process of psychical incorporation takes on singular political importance. Interestingly, the question of the politicality of Fanon's psychoanalytic theory is a contentious, even divisive issue for his biographers. Irene Gendzier's important biography of Fanon notes that although Fanon was aware of a connection between psychiatry and politics, he nonetheless "abandoned" the one in his quest for the other (Gendzier 1973, 64). Gendzier expresses the view held by many readers of Fanon's life and work that it was necessary for Fanon, after the publication of his first book, *Black Skin, White Masks*, to repudiate "psychoanalysis" to access "politics." Jock McCullogh's carefully researched study of Fanon's often overlooked clinical writings makes the counterargument that "there is no epistemological or methodological break between Fanon's earlier and later works" and that indeed "all of Fanon's works form part of a single theoretical construct" (McCullogh 1983, 3). The critical debate over the relation between Fanon's psychiatric training and his political education—posed in the oppositional terms of dramatic break or seamless continuity—obscures the critical fault lines upon which Fanon's own work is based, for Fanon himself was interested precisely in the linkages and fissures, the contradictions and complications, the translations and transformations of the theory-politics relation. I have tried to explore in this essay the way in which, in Fanon's thinking, the psychical and the political are hinged together on the point of identification. I am reminded of the concluding line of Philippe Lacoue-Labarthe's study of mimesis: "why would the problem of identification not be, in general, the essential problem of the political?" (Lacoue-Labarthe 1989, 300).

Fanon's own politics takes the multifarious form of an extended investigation of the psychopathology of colonialism that not only describes imperial practices but also, where sexual differences are concerned, problematically enacts them. When addressing the politics of sexual identifications, Fanon fails to register fully the significance of the founding premise of his own theory of colonial relations, which holds that the political is located within the psychical as a powerful shaping force. I take this working premise to be one of Fanon's most important contributions to political thought—the critical notion that *the psychical operates precisely as a political formation*. Fanon's work also draws our attention to the historical and social conditions of identification. It reminds us that identification is never outside or prior to politics, that identification is always inscribed within a certain history: Identification names not only the history of the subject but the subject in history. What Fanon gives us, in the end, is a politics that does not oppose the psychical but fundamentally presupposes it.

NOTES

1. Later in this chapter I discuss more fully Fanon's problematic use of the masculine as both the point of departure and the final referent for a new theory of the subject. Suffice it to say here that Fanon's powerful anticolonial polemics remain completely caught up in the masculinist presuppositions of the discourse they seek to displace.

2. In Lacanian terms, these two concepts can be distinguished in at least three ways: first, the other (small o) denotes a specular relation to an Imaginary rival, while the Other (capital O) designates a linguistic relation to a Symbolic interlocutor; second, the other depends upon a narcissistic relation, while the Other marks the locus of intersubjectivity; and third, the other is produced as an effect of primary identification in which the subject recognizes itself in its own image, while the Other is constructed as an effect of secondary identification in which the subject shifts its point of address to another speaking subject. For a much fuller discussion of the psychoanalytic definition of alterity, see Marie-Claire Boons-Grafé's entry on "Other/other" in Wright 1992.

3. In "Race Under Representation," David Lloyd emphasizes the explicitly metaphoric pretenses of a white mythology: "this Subject becomes representative in consequence of being able to take anyone's place, of occupying any place, of a pure exchangeability" (1991, 70). Deconstructing the category *white* therefore involves making visible its founding metaphorics and ideology of invisibility. For more on the culturally constructed category of whiteness, see Toni Morrison (1992), Richard Dyer (1988, 44–64), Jane M. Gaines (1992, 24–39), Elizabeth Abel (1993, 470–498), and Kobena Mercer (1987, 33–54).

4. To avoid terminological confusion, let me note that the "Other" for Sartre refers to a specular, dyadic order similar to Lacan's idea of the Imaginary. Sartre's "Other" thus corresponds roughly to Lacan's "other," the other of the mirror stage. Fanon takes his theory of "recognition" from the section on "Lordship and Bondage" in Hegel's *The Phenomenology of Mind*.

5. Eve Kosofsky Sedgwick has recently made a very similar point about the colloquial use of the term "Other": "the trope of the Other . . . must a priori fail to do justice to the complex activity, creativity, and engagement of those whom it figures simply as relegated objects" (1993, 147).

6. I should clarify here that Fanon's profound discomfort with Sartre's endorsement of négritude in *Orphée Noir* (1963) is provoked not by Sartre's use of the dialectic per se, but by the specific place that négritude is made to occupy within it. Sartre's dialectic of thesis (white racism), antithesis (négritude), and synthesis (humanism) assigns "black" to the role of negation in what is essentially, for Fanon, a dialectic of racial assimilationism. See Jean-Paul Sartre, *Orphée Noir*. The works of Aimé Césaire, Léopold Senghor, and Léon Damas, featured in the négritude anthology prefaced by *Orphée Noir*, provide Fanon with an alterna-

tive philosophical and political position from which to critique Sartre's controversial introduction.

7. This theory of subversive mimicry finds its most extended treatment in the work of Luce Irigaray (1985). Carole-Anne Tyler (1996) offers a careful and thorough critique of the problems with Irigaray's mimicry/masquerade distinction as it falters on the twin grounds of intention and reception.

8. Bhabha, whose work centers on investigating the place of fantasy and desire in the exercise of colonial power, is one of the first cultural theorists to think through the ambivalences of identification in terms of its inscription in colonial history.

9. One instance where Fanon does talk about this phenomenon is in a brief footnote where he lists a series of cultural impersonations in which white "admiration" for black culture masks a hidden identification: "white 'hot-jazz' orchestras, white blues and spiritual singers, white authors writing novels in which the Negro proclaims his grievances, whites in blackface" (1967a, 177).

10. Julie Peteet speaks of the "remarkable flexibility" of a symbol like the veil whose use can be "both calculated and creative": "The same veil that symbolized a militant, female activism now is used to circumscribe women's presence in the workplace and confine them to the home" (1993, 52). Both Merrat Hatem and Peteet interrogate women's semiotic role as bearers of culture. Hatem notes that "while men were expected to interact with their changing environment, women were relegated to the task of being the conservators of the traditional culture" (1993, 43). Peteet points out that this is true whether women symbolize progress or tradition; either way, they are still considered repositories of "authentic culture" (1993, 60). See also Juliette Minces (1978, 159–71). For more on the figure of the veil, see Fatima Mernissi (1987), Malek Alloula (1986), and Lama Abu Odeh, (1993, 26–37). Odeh, discussing the veil in a contemporary context, observes that many Muslim women typically wear Western clothes under their veils, further complicating the question of sartorial impersonation and cultural resignification.

11. For a more extended treatment of this theme, see Jeffrey Louis Decker (1990). See John Mowitt's investigation of Fanon's fetishistic investment in the category of nation (1992). For an interesting reading of the etymological link between fetish and masquerade, see Charles Bernheimer (1993, 62–83).

12. Joan Riviere (1986, 35–44), Stephen Heath (1986), and Mary Ann Doane (1991, 17–43).

13. Fanon does not get away from the problem of intentionality here; indeed, Fanon's point is that politics necessarily resides in intentionality. Fanon's strategy is to reconstruct the possibility of agency that colonialism vitiates, and he does this by locating "politics" in the space where imitation exceeds identification.

14. The clearest statement of Fanon's view that identification itself is a pathological condition produced by the colonial relation comes in *Black Skin, White Masks*, where Fanon suggests, again using Sartrean terms, that "as long as the black man is among his own, he will have no occasion . . . to experience his being through others" (1967a, 109). For Fanon it is not the case that unconscious racial identifications create the colonial drive for assimilation, but rather that colonial dominations produce the phenomenon of racial identification. No identification without colonization.

15. A significant body of work already exists on the role nineteenth-century racial models of the Jew play in shaping Freud's work. See, for example, Jay Geller (1992, 427–44; 1994, 180–210); Daniel Boyarin (1994a and b, 17–41). Most recently, Sander Gilman (1993) argues for understanding Freud's theory of femininity as an anxious displacement of dominant racial representations of the male Jewish body. Something rather similar may be going on in Fanon's passages on femininity and homosexuality, where the popular colonialist caricature of the black man as castrated and sexually degenerate is seamlessly transposed onto women and gay men. In this section I briefly discuss Fanon's complicated negotiations of colonial representations of black sexuality–racial epistemologies in which Freud is inevitably implicated. For Fanon, the problem of anti-Semitism and racism are not unrelated. Fanon in fact models his investigation of negrophobia in *Black Skin, White Masks* on Sartre's study *Anti-Semite and Jew*, adapting Sartre's claim that "it is the anti-Semite who makes the Jew" into his own formulation on racism, "it is the racist who creates his inferior" (Fanon 1967a, 93). The representational history of Jews as "the Negroes of Europe" (cited in Gilman 1993, 20) provides the basis of a powerful and ambivalent identification for Fanon with the figure of the male Jewish intellectual. For Fanon's comparisons in *Black Skin, White Masks* of the Jew and the Negro, the anti-Semite and the Negrophobe, see especially 87–93, 115–16, 157–66, and 180–83.

16. The original citation is from Angelo Louis Marie Hesnard's *L'univers morbide de la faute* (Paris: Presses Universitaires de France, 1949), 37.

17. I refer to Freud's favorite example of hysteria: the woman who plays both parts of a seduction at once, tearing her dress off with one

hand ("as a man") and pressing it to her body with the other ("as a woman"). See Freud 1908b and 1909.

18. For just such a careful analysis of the racialized class field of sexuality, see, for example, M. Jacqui Alexander (1991, 133–52). Chandra Talpade Mohanty also analyzes how "racialized sexual violence has emerged as an important paradigm or trope of colonial rule" (1991, 17).

19. Fanon immediately undermines this disclaimer by extending the myth of rape fantasy to black women, asserting in the very next line that light-skinned Antillean women also have fantasies of rape, masochistic wish fantasies in which the role of aggressor is played by black men of darker skin color than their own. While Fanon sympathizes with black men who are constrained under colonial domination to identify with white men, his comments on black women's identification with white women are comparatively harsh and unsympathetic. See Fanon's reading of Mayotte Capecia's autobiographical book, *Je suis Martiniquaise*, in chapter 2 of *Black Skin, White Masks*. For a more extended analysis of Fanon's dismissal of Capecia's book, see Gwen Bergner (1995).

20. After all, "the revolutionary is the first to have the right to say: 'Oedipus!' Never heard of it" (Deleuze and Guattari 1983, 96).

21. In addition to Gendzier's biography, several other critical studies on Fanon appeared in the early 1970s, including those by Pierre Bouvier, David Caute, Phillippe Lucas, Jack Woddis, Renate Zahar, and Peter Geismar.

22. Most of what Freud has to say on race can be found in his anthropological work, where Gustave Le Bon's use of the phrase "racial unconscious" as a synonym for "archaic" or "primitive" is revised and expanded by Freud to include his theory of repression. For Freud's most extended treatment of the subject of race, see Freud (1913). For the influence of Darwin on Freud's theory of race, see Edwin R. Wallace (1983), and Lucille B. Ritvo (1990). Freud's *Group Psychology and the Analysis of the Ego* (originally published in 1921) provides us with a psychoanalytic theory of racism that may not be without interest in the context of the present chapter: "Closely related races keep one another at arm's length; the South German cannot endure the North German, the Englishman casts every kind of aspersion upon the Scot, the Spaniard despises the Portuguese. We are no longer astonished that greater differences should lead to an almost insuperable repugnance, such as the Gallic people feel for the German, the Aryan for the Semite, and the white races for the coloured," (Freud 1963, 18:101). See also Gilman (1993).

23. Burton writes: "There exists what I shall call a 'Sotadic Zone,' bounded westwards by the northern shores of the Mediterranean (N. Lat. 43 degrees) and by the Southern (N. Lat. 30 degrees). Thus the depth would be 780 to 800 miles including meridional France, the Iberian Peninsula, Italy and Greece, with the coast-regions of Africa from Morocco to Egypt" (1885, 206). See Burton's "Terminal Essay" for the full coordinates of the Sotadic Zone, too lengthy to be cited here.

24. There is considerable disagreement over the extent of Fanon's language skills and its consequences for his professional work, a dispute that in the level of its intensity underscores how very high are the stakes involved. Fanon's most sympathetic biographer, Peter Geismar, claims that by the end of 1956, several years after arriving in Algeria, Fanon could "understand most of what his patients were telling him" (1971, 86). Irene Gendzier provides a sharply differing account, describing Fanon's efforts to learn Arabic as "stillborn" and personally anguishing (1973, 77). For Albert Memmi, Fanon's refusal to learn the language of the patients he was treating constituted nothing less than a "psychiatric scandal" (Memmi 1971, 5).

25. Walter Benjamin's "The Task of the Translator" takes as its thesis the useful notion that any language is a place of exile, that "all translation is only a somewhat provisional way of coming to terms with the foreignness of languages" (1969, 75). Benjamin's interest in translation, however, lies in the "suprahistorical kinship of languages" or "the relatedness of two languages, apart from historical considerations" (74). The theoretical move to banish history from the realm of translation operates to conceal, and ultimately to preserve, a colonizing impulse at work in translation; Benjamin's "great motif of integrating many tongues into one true language" (77) represents an imperialist dream, a fantasy of linguistic incorporation and cultural assimilation. If it is impossible to read translation outside the history of colonial imperialism, then it may also be the case that colonial imperialism operates as a particular kind of translation. In the roundtable discussion on translation included in Derrida's *The Ear of the Other*, Eugene Vance poses the question in its simplest rhetorical form: "Isn't the colonization of the New World basically a form of translation?" (Derrida 1985, 137). For more on the imperial history of translation, see Arnold Krupat (1992, 193–200).

26. Complicating matters further is the question of Fanon as object of identification. In "Critical Fanonism," Henry Louis Gates Jr. (see chapter 9, this volume) demonstrates how Fanon is inevitably a repository for his

critic's projective identifications: "If Said made of Fanon an advocate of post-postmodern counternarratives of liberation; if [Abdul] JanMohamed made of Fanon a Manichean theorist of colonialism as absolute negation, and if Bhabha cloned, from Fanon's theoria, another Third World post-structuralist, [Benita] Parry's Fanon . . . turns out to confirm her own rather optimistic vision of literature and social action" (this volume, p. 260). To this list I would have to add my own identification with Fanon the psychoanalytic theorist and university teacher.

13.

Fanon's Feminist Consciousness and Algerian Women's Liberation: Colonialism, Nationalism, and Fundamentalism

T. Denean Sharpley-Whiting

*I made up my mind to fight for my country's independence . . . Why?
. . . Because our cause is just. Because, come what may, we shall achieve it.*

Djamila Boupacha

The Angel and the Man work for unity; Satan and the Woman for division.

Algerian Proverb

The unveiled Algerian woman, who assumed an increasingly important place in revolutionary action . . . discovered the exalting realm of responsibility.

Fanon

"This war," Frantz Fanon wrote in the July 1959 preface to *A Dying Colonialism*, "has mobilized the whole population, has driven them to draw upon their entire resources and their most hidden resources"

A version of this article appears in Sharpley-Whiting, *Frantz Fanon: Conflicts and Feminisms* (Lanham, Md.: Rowman & Littlefield, 1997). Reprinted with permission of the publisher and the author.

(23). The veiled and cloistered Algerian woman could certainly be counted among those resources most hidden. She was the axis upon and around which the colonizing mission and anticolonial resistance oftentimes spun. Within the pages of Fanon's analysis of the dialectical relationship between the colonized and the colonizer in *A Dying Colonialism*, the Algerian woman equally becomes a centrifugal force. It is equally within two essays of this political manifesto, "Algeria Unveiled" and "The Algerian Family," that Frantz Fanon can be situated among the twentieth century's most progressive male modernist thinkers on the interlocking nexus of ethnicity, gender, and sexuality; that Fanon, in relating lucidly the liberation praxis of Algerian women, evinces a profeminist consciousness.

Before undertaking an examination of the feminist dimensions in "Algeria Unveiled" and "The Algerian Family," let us first take up some feminists' readings of Fanon's very positions on women's liberation during the Algerian liberation struggle as well as analyses of the regressive status of women since national independence. Among Fanon's critics on the subject is Marie-Aimée Helie-Lucas, an Algerian feminist-activist and founding member of the Network of Women Living Under Muslim Laws, which assists Muslim women living under oppressive Islamic laws.[1] As feminist philosopher Linda Bell rightly suggests, we cannot simply accept and dismiss Helie-Lucas's challenge to Fanon's sociological and historigraphical study as just another point of view (Bell 1993, 59). Bell continues, "Male assumptions of objectivity have been a camouflage covering male dominance and hiding the way male interests and desires are imposed on females" (59). What are those hidden interests and desires proposed in general by Bell, yet clearly at issue in Helie-Lucas's reading of Fanon?

Featured in this anthology (chapter 10), Helie-Lucas's essay, "Women, Nationalism, and Religion in the Algerian Liberation Struggle" argues that Fanon's books have shaped mythologies surrounding Algerian women as freedom fighters equal to their male counterparts:

The image that the outside world has formed of women in the

Algerian liberation struggle is shaped by Frantz Fanon's books, a very widely distributed film called *The Battle of Algiers*, and the true story of a few national heroines. From these sources, the Algerian woman appears as a freedom fighter who carried arms against French colonialism and its army, a "terrorist" who planted bombs in the city during the Battle of Algiers, who was equal to men in the struggle and who shared decision-making both at the political and at the military levels. (this volume p. 271)

Helie-Lucas's criticism is multilayered. Using freedom fighter Djamila Amranes's *La Femme Algérienne et la Guerre de Libération Nationale (1954–62)* to support her discussion of inequities and Fanon's "mythmaking," she emphasizes the ways that gender hierarchies persisted in the percentage of tasks parceled out to women along traditional gender roles during the liberation struggle, the erasure of women's contributions in the archival records, (i.e., in the registry of the Veteran's Ministry), the relegation of women and their performed tasks to that of "helpers" of men "fighting for the cause" rather than freedom fighters, and the continued subordination of women in the postcolony.

While the revolutionary phase of the war occasioned transformations in sexual relations and women's status, under the "new" Algerian government that transformative component dissipated, stopped short, in revolutionizing the patriarchal nature of Algerian society's institutions and customs and dismantling the discriminatory practices meted out against women in the public spheres of employment and education and within the family. Shortly after national independence was gained, women were, for the most part, shuttled back into the kitchen under the secular, nationalist military government of the National Liberation Front (FLN). And since the 1989 decline in popularity of the FLN, due to its failed economic programs, its repressive Western-backed military junta government, and the rising appeal of the Islamic Salvation Front (FIS), Algerian women have been forcibly enveloped in the *haïk* (veil). "So much," Helie-Lucas writes, "for Fanon's and others' myth of the Algerian woman liberated along with her country" (1990, 107).

Women's liberation and nationalism, whether in the form of
the FLN's patriarchal secular nationalism in Algeria, or conservative and fundamentalist nationalism, appear to be irreconcilable,
leading many Arab feminists to point to nationalism as among one
of the primary oppressive factors impacting women's daily lives
and to sound the call for a postnationalist feminism. The crux of
the nationalist/women's liberation polemic is rooted in the fact
that traditional gender relations and the regulation of gender is
critical to conservative and fundamentalist nationalist ideology in
Algeria and other Islamist countries. Even the secular nationalism
of the FLN has, as Mai Ghousoub relates, "reclaimed many of the
most patriarchal values of Islamic traditionalism as integral to
Arab cultural identity" (cited in Accad 1990, 14). Moreover, the
language used to articulate Algerian national identity and culture
was and continues to be highly feminized. The land, "nation-
state," culture, and the woman are merged, conflated. Culture and
identity are imagined as uniquely transmitted through women.
The Algerian woman becomes the symbolic repository for group
identity (Kandiyoti 1988, 376–91). Hence, in order to protect and
preserve the nation, the family, which is the foundation of patriarchal culture, the woman must be sheltered from the immorality
and corruptions of modernity, that is, the West. The land, like the
female body, must be policed, protected from rape, Western feminisms, and other intrusions. Algerian nationalist discourse and
ideology lock women into "tradition," and thereby deprive them
of the citizenship rights enjoyed by their male compatriots.[2] The
discourse becomes, according to Helie-Lucas, recycled, reinvented,
and reinterpreted ad infinitum to suit the needs of the nation-state
in its various evolutionary and developmental phases. The more
threatened the Algerian nation-state, the more conservative, or traditionalist, rising to the level of fundamentalist, the nationalist discourse and its systemic mechanisms become. Women are at once
the custodians of national identity and culture, and the wards of
the nation-state, central to the preservation of the state, and relegated to the margins of the body politic.

Helie-Lucas notes:

[S]ince there was "no humble task in the revolution" we did not dispute the roles we had. . . .The overall task of women during liberation is seen as symbolic. Faced with colonization the people have to build a national identity based on their own values, traditions, religion, language, and culture. Women bear the heavy burden of safeguarding this threatened identity. And this burden exacts it price. . . . Women are supposed to raise sons in the faith and traditional moral standards and to teach the language of the forefathers. Women should be bound by tradition, while men had some access to modernity. (this volume pp. 274–75)

Confronted with the potential destruction of their local culture and customs by the French colonial and imperialist project, Algeria turned virulently inward with particularly regressive gendered ramifications. This turning inward has reproduced in our postmodern times, a "kind of 'siege mentality' in which stripping Arab women of their rights has become well justified and condoned as a protective act" (Kandiyoti 1988, 385).

As educators, nurses, nurturers, mothers, liaison agents, as veiled and unveiled freedom fighters, women's roles during the revolution were refashioned and molded in the simultaneous service of the "higher" goals of the struggle—national liberation—and within a narrow, antifeminist political discourse. As Egyptian feminist Nawal el-Saadawi insists, women were "used by the revolution as tools, as cheap labor, cheap fighters—to die first and be liberated last!" (cited in Tohidi 1991, 260; also see Nawal el-Saadawi 1980).

The working plans for Algerian liberation did not particularly identify women's emancipation as one of its aims. Many Middle Eastern feminist thinkers, activists, and writers such as Helie-Lucas, Mervat Hatem, Deniz Kandiyoti, Evelyne Accad, Nayereh Tohidi, and Nawal el-Saadawi maintain that women assumed national liberation meant the destruction of oppressive forces from without *and* within Algerian society; that it was, in effect, inclusive of women's liberation from Algerian patriarchal oppression. Women's liberationist dimensions were manifested through women's collective participation in national struggle. Their feminism "was not however, autonomous, but bound to the signifying network of the national context which produced it." (Kandiyoti 1988, 380). Common to Third World women and other women of color, their feminism was and is importantly tied to anti-imperialist, antiracist, anticolonialist, and anticapitalist struggles (see Mahmoud 1986, 3). However, as Iranian feminist Nayereh Tohidi writes in hindsight, women must demand that their liberation, their needs, and specific oppressions be clearly addressed and incorporated into nationalist liberation movements from the outset (Tohidi 1991, 287). Since those measures were not proactively taken, Algerian women's various innovative strategies of resistance during the national liberation struggle were turned against them, appropriated by the post-colonial nationalist Algerian nation-state, and used to police feminine conduct and conformity.

The veil is emblematic of such an usurpation of Algerian women's methods of resistance; it was used during the revolution, and, since the 1990 massive victory of the FIS in the legislative body of Algerian governance,[3] continues to be used as a means of turning back the clock on the socially transformative potential the revolution offered. Helie-Lucas explores the uses and abuses of Algerian women with respect to the veil:

Although there is no doubt that veiling women is a measure for control and oppression, it became for a time a symbol of national resistance to the French. During the war, French officials had insisted that Algerian women should be freed from the oppression of the veil. French army trucks had transported village women to urban areas. There the women were forced to unveil publicly thereby proving their renunciation of outworn traditions. Both Algerian men and women resented this symbolic rape. In addition to its symbolic role, the veil was supported to have a practical function. Fanon praised the revolutionary virtue of the veil—it allowed urban women freedom fighters to escape the controls of the French army. . . . How, therefore could we take up the issue of the veil as oppressive to women without betraying both *nation* and *revolution*? . . . The FLN (the National Liberation Front) encouraged such an attitude that emphasised women's modesty and could also be labelled "fighting for the Cause." (this volume pp. 275–76)

The complexity involved in the Algerian woman's decision to wear the *haïk* is indisputable. Islamist traditions demanded a rigid separation of the sexes, and the veil served this purpose in traditionalist Algeria. Even though the Koran (24:30–31) demanded modesty from both sexes, the veil came to be identified exclusively as a mandate for women, and signified modesty and adherence to the traditions of Islam. The veil was rarely worn by practicing Muslim Algerian women in the rural areas where a great deal of the fighting took place. And Kabyle women never donned the *haïk*. Prior to 1957, the veil had been abandoned by the women in the city. Notwithstanding this virtual abandonment, there were women who continued to wear the veil. The public unveiling of Algerian women to the battle hymn *"Vive l'Algérie française!"* prompted Algerian women to redon the veil. Even women who had long stopped wearing the veil once again enveloped themselves in the *haïk*.[4] Yet one cannot overlook the coercive element manifested in this "voluntary" decision. As Helie-Lucas reasons, "How *could* women resist wearing the *haïk* without betraying both nation and revolution?"

Further, as Mervat Hatem suggests, "Besides frustrating colonial designs, it was not clear what concrete benefits women derived from being defenders of tradition" (1993, 45). But as demonstrated by the French campaign of unveiling, not all women were struggling to be rid of the veil at that historic moment. And in parts of the contemporary Muslim world, there are still a great many women who voluntarily don the veil.

The appeal of conservatism and fundamentalism today and their mandates to veil women and return them to their place are as much structured around attempts to regulate women's bodies as they are symptomatic of post-colonial economic, political, and social disarray; structural maladjustments aggravated by Western imperialist powers and the International Monetary Fund (IMF); the modernization of the family; disillusionment due to the failure of socialism; and rising youth unemployment. In Algeria specifically, there were riots in October 1988 as a result of this post-colonial disarray. Algeria's economy is literally fueled by a dependence on its petrochemical exports such as oil. In the 1980s, the plummeting global price of oil seriously impacted its national revenues (St. John 1996, 5). The veil as perceived by fundamentalist and conservative Islamist groups symbolizes adherence to traditional values; it comforts and appeals to those weary and fearful of the rigors of modernity and female sexuality; and it signals a return to tradition as a cure to postmodern *malaise* (see Mernissi, 1987; 1989; 1992).

In her book, *Both Right and Left Handed: Arab Women Talk About Their Lives* (1991), Syrian feminist Bouthaina Shabaan chronicles stories of women whose decision to wear the *hijab* provides them access to certain public spaces and authority denied secular women. Turkish feminist Deniz Kandiyoti observes that there is a "patriarchal bargain" between women like Egyptians Zainab al-Ghazali and Safinaz Kazim, and the men who endeavor to return women and men to their "rightful" places. And this bartering has helped to maintain social, economic, and political structures that at the very least strengthen male hegemony (Kandiyoti 1988).

And so it would appear inevitable that Frantz Fanon, with his discussion of the revolutionary uses of the veil in *A Dying Colonialism* would run into conflicts with contemporary Algerian feminists. Helie-Lucas has, however, simplified Fanon's analysis of the veil, Algerian women's liberation, and the family during the Algerian liberation struggle.

As the war for independence progressed, the means of combat strategy mutated. When Algerian women unveiled themselves, acting as *assimilées*, Fanon praised the "revolutionary virtue" of this strategy. Indeed, as the epigraph from Fanon attests, it was the "unveiled Algerian woman" who assumed an increasing importance in revolutionary action. But more than this, Fanon saw that the veil, like the radio described in "This Is the Voice of Algeria," was no longer a static cultural symbol; it too could be transformed, modified under revolutionary circumstances. During the doffing and donning commanded by the revolution, the veil ceased to function as an inert traditional symbol. When the French discovered this ruse and began publicly and forcibly unveiling women in the streets, symbolically raping the women as both Fanon and Helie-Lucas assert, the Algerians' methods of combat again mutated, and in effect, regressed. Fanon writes at length on the subject:

> Removed and reassumed again and again, the veil has been manipulated, transformed into a technique of camouflage, into a means of struggle. The virtual taboo character assumed by the veil in the colonial situation disappeared almost entirely during the course of the liberating struggle. Even Algerian women not actively integrated into the struggle formed the habit of abandoning the veil. It is true that under certain conditions, especially from 1957 on, the veil reappeared. . . . The adversary now knew . . . French colonialism, on the occasion of May 13th, reenacted its old campaign of Westernizing the Algerian woman. . . . Before this new offensive old reactions reappeared. . . . Algerian women who had long since dropped the veil once again donned the *haïk*, thus affirming that it was not true that the woman liberated herself at the invitation of France and General de Gaulle. Behind these psychological reactions, beneath this immediate and almost unanimous response, we again see the overall attitude of rejection of the values of the occupier, even if these *values be objectively worth choosing.* . . . In organizing the famous cavalcade of May 13th, colonialism obliged Algerian society to go back to methods of struggle already outmoded. In a certain sense, the different ceremonies have caused a turning back, a regression. (1967c, 62–63, my emphasis)

Fanon notes that this particular value of the occupier, the removal of the veil, may be worth choosing, but that the occupier's drive to save, to convert violently, the savages "in spite of themselves" forced the redonning of the veil (1967c, 63). The fact that France focused a significant amount of their energies on the veil and the Algerian woman as the last vestige of resistance served merely to "strengthen the traditional patterns of behavior" (1967c, 49).

Given Fanon's views on human freedom, it is interesting to find analyses of his work on Algerian women and the veil as constituting a denial of female oppression by Algerian men, a pro-male cultural supremacist bias, and a camouflage for male desires and interests.[5] But what is particularly unsettling is Helie-Lucas's assertion that Fanon maintains that the "Algerian woman was liberated along with her country." Fanon identifies women's liberation with national liberation (1967c, 107). Indeed, he spoke of the transformation of value systems and sexual and familial relations that silenced and rendered woman the complement of man (1967c, 109). The Algerian woman "developed her personality and discovered the exalting realm of responsibility" (1967c, 107). This realm of responsibility did not make her the symbolic repository for group identity, nor did she become the body through which language and customs are passed; she assumed an individual responsibility for herself and her actions denied by traditional Islamist laws, yet challenged, overturned, during the course of revolutionary struggle. At that moment in Algerian history, Fanon saw many Algerian women liberated from time-honored traditions of silence, invisibility, and sequestration.

That the veil is being used in contemporary Algeria and other Muslim countries as a tool of repression and justification for the murder of women (see St. John 1996) by the outlawed FIS and other fundamentalists and traditionalists factions, that the "threat" of the Occident and modernity is consistently recalled in order to circumscribe women's behavior and deny their access to the true fruits of citizenship described by el-Saadawi, Helie-Lucas, Mernissi, et al. represents one of the many "Pitfalls" or "Misadventures of National Consciousness":

> History teaches us clearly that the battle against colonialism does not run straight away along the lines of nationalism. . . . It so happens that the unpreparedness of the educated classes, the lack of practical links between them and the masses of the people, their laziness, and let it be said, their cowardice at the decisive moment of the struggle will give rise to tragic mishaps. National consciousness, instead of being the all-embracing crystallization

of the innermost hopes of the whole people, instead of being the immediate and most obvious result of the mobilization of the people, will be in any case only an empty shell. . . . A government that calls itself a national government ought to take responsibility for the totality of the nation . . . it must guard against the danger of perpetuating the feudal tradition which holds sacred the masculine element over the feminine. Women will have exactly the same place as men, not in the clauses of the constitution but in the life of everyday: in the factory, at school, and in the parliament (Fanon, 1967c, 148, 201–202).

The innermost hopes of the whole people have not been embraced in Algeria. Women's particular interests, their liberation, was subjugated to the "common good" of the nation, embodied in the particular interests of Algerian patriarchy. Helie-Lucas reveals that nationalism, religion, and socialism helped to elaborate and legislate antiwomen state policies (this volume p. 278). Embroiled on the one hand in Algeria's anti-imperialist stance, and on the other, in a patriarchal social structure and fabric, Algerian women continue to bear the brunt of politically conservative social and ideological maneuvers.

Fanon, who died before seeing the evolution of the independent Algeria, witnessed a transformation in the Algerian family and the status of Algerian women during the war. As feminists write in hindsight concerning the shortcomings of the architecture of the Algerian liberation struggle, it is clear that Fanon was at worst optimistic ("Mankind, I Believe in You," 1967a, 7) in assuming that the path toward the liberation of Algerian women opened by the women's organized and collective participation in the revolution would continue to evolve, be embraced by all, and form the basis of the new Algeria.

In contemporary Algeria the rise of fundamentalism, reactionary antiwoman policies, and family codes in keeping with the Sharia, which condones stoning (women) for adultery and the haïk, is undeniably narrowly tied to those transformations. Those transformations, occurring at the moment when women entered into the fighting phase of the revolution, spurred the century's long legacy of Algerian women's activism into a collective feminist consciousness and provided the momentum to continue the organized fight for contemporary Algerian women's liberation.[6]

In light of Helie-Lucas's important criticisms of Fanon on the question of gender, the veil, and oppression, we now turn our concern to the question of Fanon's commitment to women's liberation as discussed within the very pages that Helie-Lucas challenges, querying, in effect: "Does Fanon's analysis of Algerian women, the veil, and the family represent a profeminist consciousness, that is, a belief in 'woman's right to life as a free woman and as a complete social being'? Or does it merely reinscribe conventional gender roles and camouflage male interests?"[7]

"ALGERIA UNVEILED"

"Algeria Unveiled" goes a long way in explaining the intricacies and developments of the Franco-Algerian war. Not only does Fanon offer insights into the insurrectional role of the women but exposes the fundamental flaws of Western liberal strategies from the 1930s onward to unveil the Algerian woman and thereby colonize and unveil Algeria— the nation—to remove Islamic darkness and savagery and replace it with the light of Western ideas and idealism. From a quasi-sociological point of departure, Fanon attempts to explain the "hows" and "whys," the evolution, of the Algerian woman's integral role in the liberation struggle.

In France's application of liberal democratic ideals, bordering on paternalism fueled by cultural imperialism, racialism, and economics, the male would come to be perceived as an interference in the Algerian woman's individuality. And while Fanon recognized and clearly advocated Algerian women's right to exist as free and autonomous beings, he equally realized that the Algerians, men and women alike, had to come to this realization on their own terms; that the occupier, in attempting to violently and clandestinely prevent the Algerian man from interfering with the Algerian woman's cultivation of her subjectivity, equally violated the liberal principles of noninterference; and finally that those terms would be realized through their collective participation in revolutionary struggle which inevitably transforms the lives and histories of individuals, communities, and countries.

In effect, group culture and tradition are generally signified by dress. And, in the Arab world, the veil worn by women suffices generally to characterize Arab society to the foreigner (Fanon 1967c, 35). While a culture or society may be essentially patriarchal and patrilineal in structure and in its doling out and denying of equitable gender roles, the essence of the culture and land, whether it be in the United States of America and "her" citizens or France and "her" colonies, assumes peculiarly feminized dimensions. While feminized language was and is deployed by Algerian nationalist rhetoricians, this same language and thought pattern were assumed by the French in 1954. Algeria was envisioned as having a "feminine" cultural essence. To secularize, to unveil the women, would mean to secularize Algeria proper. Hence, as much as the veil represented cultural symbology, it equally reflected for the French occupier the status of Algerian women—repressed, hidden, and cloistered by an omnipresent and oppressive Arab patriarchy. Following the principles of a skewed Millsian liberalism (see Souffrant 1996), the French sought simultaneously to liberate the Algerian woman from the veil and destroy the structure of Algerian society. In doing right by the Algerian women, the French would be doing right for themselves. The formula, "Let's win over the women and the rest will follow," based on research from Western sociological pundits became colonial policy (Fanon 1967c, 37).

Liberating the women, unveiling the women, would also represent a disrobing of the Algerian man, a usurping of his power over the women, and thus, Algeria. It was hoped that the unveiled women would, like tilled, fertile soil, facilitate the sowing of Western colonial seeds throughout Algeria: "Converting the woman, winning her over to the foreign values, wrenching her free from her status, was at the same time achieving a real power over the man and attaining a practical, effective means of destructuring Algerian culture" (Fanon 1967c, 39).

In French efforts to save the women from the brutish Algerian men, a multitude of strategies were deployed, most notably one involving French women, advocates of women's liberation through colonialization:

> Mutual aid societies and societies to promote solidarity with Algerian women sprang up in great number . . . in the course of which droves of social workers and women directing charitable works descended on the Arab quarters. The indigent and famished women were the first to be besieged. Every kilo of semolina distributed was accompanied by a dose of indignation against the veil and cloister. The indignation was followed up by practical advice. Algerian women were invited to play "a functional, capital role" in the transformation of their lot. They were pressed to say no to a centuries-old subjection. (Fanon 1967c, 38)

Notwithstanding the fact that Algerian men were equally indigent and famished, Algerian patriarchy and its "arcane" and "archaic" cultural traditions of cloister and the veil were posited as the primary cause of the women's wretched existences. Colonialism, on the other hand, as espoused by the French missionary women, with its explicit political doctrine bent on cultural destruction and exploitation, was transformed into a liberatory women's movement.

Fanon reveals the hypocrisy of these "colonialist" feminists; he points to the reality of the unequal distribution of *intragender* power as well as the complicity and benefits derived from the expropriation of resources, raw materials, and labor to colonialist women at the mere cost of Algerian cultural identity.

The case of Suzanne Massu, a colonialist feminist and wife of General Jacques Massu, an agent of the French military who ordered and defended the torture of thousands of Muslim Algerians and participated in the Battle of Algiers, is worth mentioning here as an illustrative example. In 1958, Suzanne Massu established Le Mouvement de Solidarité Féminine. The movement purported to "be an action of deeply humane and fraternal social order . . . for friendship between the women of the two communities" (see Massu 1972). It was not an attempt to "provoke any kind of revolutionary change from tradition."[8] Suzanne and Jacques Massu further adopted two Muslim children, one boy and girl, "as a symbol of the integration [they] were planning" (Massu 1972, 114). The largesse of these two colonialists was duly repaid, for the young girl, Malika, delivered a speech that can only be characterized as colonialist's propaganda to a crowd of 30,000 of her Muslim Algerian compatriots: "I wish with all my heart that Algeria remain French" (Massu 1972, 288–89).

As much as the donning of the veil and cloister are decried as antiwoman, Fanon relates that the rending of the veil has particularly sexualizing, indeed violently sexual, antiwoman implications for the Algerian woman in the male colonialist imagination. Replete with metaphors of flesh laid bear and rape, Fanon taps into the European male unconscious with a psychiatric evaluation of stereotypes and dream content. What he unveils is the hypocrisy of the male colonizer's desire to unveil/liberate the woman only to imprison her in stereotypes that render her violable, more ripe for rape:

> The rape of the Algerian woman in the dream of a European is always preceded by a rending of the veil. We here witness a double deflowering. . . . The European's aggressiveness will express itself likewise in contemplation of the Algerian woman's morality. Her timidity and her reserve are transformed. . . . [T]he Algerian woman becomes hypocritical, perverse, and even a veritable nymphomaniac. (Fanon 1967c, 46)

For as much as the Algerian woman is described as the "demonetized" object of the Algerian man, she is instantaneously objectified, degraded, in the European male psyche at the moment of her unveiling, her liberation, her entering into "subjectivity." The occupier wrongly assumed that the Algerian woman exercised absolutely no will; she was importantly envisioned as "inert," "a dehumanized object"—a puppet whose strings were pulled by Algerian male puppeteers (Fanon 1967c, 36). They equally erroneously estimated that she had no identity, and certainly not one rooted in any aspect of Algerian customs and traditions. In the course of the intensified struggle over the women and the veil, the colonized reacted violently. "To the colonialist offensive against the veil, the colonized opposes the cult of the veil" (Fanon 1967c, 47). As the war progressed to Clausewitzian total war, the Algerians drew upon their entire arsenal, inclusive of the women. And it is at this moment that Algeria entered into veritable revolutionary warfare.

BODY POLITICS: REVOLUTIONARY WOMEN, REVOLUTIONARY WAR

Fanon's discussion of the Algerian woman thus far entails his recounting of the factors and events that led to her participation in aspects of the liberation struggle that would require her to step outside the binding ties of tradition, and create a woman-outside-of-herself. She was always involved in the war as a nurse, typist, seamstress—in various traditional gender roles—via the occupier's use of her as a symbol of oppression, as well as the Frenchman's real and imaginative raping of the woman. Yet different forms of combat were introduced in 1955 as a result of the occupier's relentlessness in making the woman so visible and integral to their colonial enterprise.[9] The decision to involve women was wholly, as Fanon acknowledges, entrusted to the males.[10] The male's *extending* of the privilege to join the struggle for Algerian independence does not mitigate the fact that women agitated and volunteered to participate in the fight for decolonization. The first women revolutionaries were married women whose husbands were militants; later, divorced and widowed women, then young, unmarried women joined the ranks. With the swelling of the numbers of women volunteers from various age categories and marital statuses, the roles of the women multiplied, ranging from nurses to mountain guides to liaison agents responsible for carrying money, messages, fuel, arms, identity cards, and medicine. Fanon writes that a "moral obligation and a strength of character that were altogether exceptional would therefore be required of the women" (1967c, 48). Unlike the Algerian male freedom fighter, rape and death was certain for the captured Algerian woman revolutionary. Revolutionary warfare and violence are tragic; lives are lost, but freedom is gained. For Fanon, there is continuity between the woman and the revolutionary. She rises directly to the level of tragedy, as her death is certain (1967c, 49–50).

There were no training camps, extensive preparation, or characters from novels or plays to emulate for the Algerian woman. When either pared down (to appear as an assimilated Algerian) or swelled (carrying various essentials under the *haïk*), the Algerian woman had to appear at ease in the European streets. Yet, for the woman who has never wandered the streets alone and without her veil for fear of punishment; ostracism; public, familial, and personal humiliation, the experience is at once daunting and liberatory. She had to appear confident with easy strides, overcome all timidity and awkwardness. She had to relearn her body and invent new dimensions and muscular control (1967c, 59). Hips freed, legs bared, the body, unleashed from the "disciplining," "tempering," "isolating" *haïk*, was naturally in conflict with itself (1967c, 59). After years of sequestration and draping in the layers of the veil, she was in the most profound sense bare, naked. In reinventing her corporeal pattern for the revolutionary struggle, she refamiliarizes herself with her own bodily schema, creates a completeness by reestablishing her body in a new and "totally revolutionary fashion" (1967c, 59). There is, Fanon writes, a "new dialectic of the body of the revolutionary Algerian woman and the world" (1967c, 59). Abandoned for the revolutionary cause, the veil would again be taken up in the course of struggle. Algeria's willingness to change, accept new ways of fighting colonialism, created a space where the Algerian woman could and did change. She was and could no longer be characterized as an "inert object," but as a woman of action. This liberatory path, now opened, could lead to the creation of a new woman.

"THE ALGERIAN FAMILY"

Fanon opens his analyses of the Algerian family with references again to the centrality of the Algerian woman. Her transformation "could not have occurred without having profound repercussions" on the Algerian family (1967c, 59). The war for national liberation has had significantly positive consequences for Algerian women, feeding their collective and organized political consciousness and radicalism; it equally challenged the concept of the nuclear "patriarchal" family with the killing of fathers and brothers and through the participation of women as revolutionary actors and agents of freedom.

However, for Fanon, traditional ideas and modes of behavior are ineffective, counterrevolutionary, and must be abandoned during revolutionary warfare. And as contemporary events in the aftermath of national independence continue to unfold, tradition proves equally confining in the face of postmodernity and feminist consciousness.

Fanon divides the essay on the Algerian family into several sections, addressing various familial relations and traditional rules governing those relations. In each section, "The Son and Father," "The Couple," "The Daughter and Father," "The Brothers," "Feminine Society," and "Marriage and Divorce," he outlines the transformations in and of relationships occasioned by the revolution and the futility of adhering to and enforcing centuries-old traditions during and even after the struggle, specifically in the case of the young Algerian woman.

In the section, "The Daughter and Father," the revolutionary theorist provides insight into the structure of the traditional father-daughter relationship and girls'/women's place in prerevolutionary Algerian society. "In the Algerian family," he observes, "the girl is always one notch behind the boy." He continues: "[T]he male . . . enjoys an almost lordly status. The birth of the boy is greeted with greater enthusiasm than that of the girl. . . . The girl has no opportunity, all things considered, to develop her personality or to take any initiative" (1967c, 105–106). Clearly aware of the hierarchical nature of gender relations, Fanon reveals how women are marginalized in the household and treated as "minors." The facility with which divorce can be granted to the male "imposes the weight of an almost obsessional fear on the Algerian woman of being sent back to her family" (1967c, 106). The young girl adopts her mother's attitude of acquiescence and obedience to male authority. At the moment she reaches puberty, she, a "childwoman," is married off (1967c, 106). While still considered a "minor" in married life, she nonetheless receives a semblance of authority as head of her own domestic space in her husband's household. Unlike the modern Western model for female development, characterized by childhood, puberty, and marriage, Fanon states that the Algerian knows only two stages: childhood-puberty and marriage (1967c, 107).[11] In this analysis, Fanon is careful to explain that illiteracy, poverty, and unemployment in Algeria, exacerbated by colonialism, leave the child-woman no other options (1967c, 107).

The fight for national liberation forced the abandonment of many of these traditional modes of behavior and customs. The revolutionary war paved the way for the woman-as-revolutionary agent to liberate herself from the veil, to relearn her body and develop her personality. Let us again cite Fanon at length:

> This woman, who . . . would carry grenades or submachine-gun chargers, this woman who tomorrow would be outraged, violated, tortured, *could not* put herself back into her former state of mind and relive her behavior of the past; this woman who was writing the heroic pages of Algerian history was, in doing so, bursting the bounds of the narrow world in which she had lived . . . and was at the same time participating in the destruction of colonialism and in the birth of a new woman. . . . The woman-for-marriage progressively disappeared, and gave way to the woman-for-action. . . . The men's words were no longer law. The women were no longer silent. . . . The woman ceased to be a complement for man. *She literally forged a new place for herself by her sheer strength.* (1967c, 107–109, my emphasis)

That Fanon recognized the Algerian woman's right to exist as an autonomous and complete social being is clear. That he acknowledged her marginalization is equally clear. She was an actor, an agent, in trying to bring about the freedom of Algeria and her own liberation. The father could no longer question the woman-revolutionary's right to speak, nor her morality when at the maquis, or revolutionary outpost, for months, weeks, or days on end. She no longer bowed her head when speaking to the patriarch. Women began to agitate for the right to choose their own partners. More importantly, Algerian women began to forge their place in history; to rewrite the historical record; to refuse to be silent, invisible, and obsequious. They were creating a new woman and a new womanhood to which other Algerian women, the "Feminine Society" could look and emulate. These women could not go back to their silent existences. And it is this literal forging of themselves into history, into traditionally "forbidden quarters" of work, school, and public spaces, that has helped to give rise to contemporary fundamentalist activities.

THE WRITING OF ALGERIAN
FEMININE HISTORY

Throughout his writings on Algerian feminine society and the Algerian liberation struggle, Fanon resists the notion that women should be mere "replacement parts for men," for "revolutionary war is not a war of men" (1967c, 48). Hence its benefits, namely liberation, should not uniquely extend to men. Generally depicted as *fatmas*, doe-eyed, inactive, and voiceless in historiographic records and texts, Algerian women's contribution to the national liberation struggle is often forgotten, diminished in contemporary cultural memory, in the French archival records of the war, and in the archives of the Algerian Ministry of Veterans.

Contemporary feminist writers, like Algerian Assia Djebar, Fadela M'Rabet, and Djamila Amranes, have undertaken the task of rewriting history and the historical record to give voice and presence to Algerian women. The surface of this feminist project, however, was merely scratched in July 1959 with the writing of *A Dying Colonialism*. "Algeria," Fanon insists, "is not a womanless society" (1967c, 67). And women must have a place in the writing of the history of the "new" Algeria. It is not simply the women who carry grenades, the nurses, the sub-machine-gun charger carriers, nor the liaison agents whose voices, stories, and struggles should be heard and written, but "the woman in the city, in the *djebel*, in the enemy administration; the prostitute and the information she obtains; the women in prison, under torture, facing death, before the courts. All these chapter headings, after the material has been sifted, will reveal an incalculable number of facts essential for the history of the national struggle" (1967c, 60, n. 15).

Unlike the Ministry of Veterans in its attempt to deny women's roles in the revolution and thus their access to jobs and retirement benefits in the postcolony, every role and every woman who participated in the national independence struggle is acknowledged in *A Dying Colonialism* as revolutionary, as a fighter for an independent Algeria and feminine collective. As a revolutionary thinker, theorist, and participant in the Algerian revolutionary war, Fanon's writing is, if nothing else, a testament to women's resistance to oppression from within and without. While Fanon's writing on Algerian women may provide the stuff for contemporary mythmaking, his writing is not the least bit mythical. To proclaim such is to dismiss the experiential nature of Fanon's writings, what he witnessed and interpreted. It is clear that he did not intend nor did he believe that his work represented the definitive, complete historical picture of the Algerian national struggle when he wrote that "after all the material has been sifted, . . . an incalculable number of facts essential for the history of the national struggle" will be revealed. The research of Amranes, Helie-Lucas, M'Rabet's *La Femme Algérienne*, and Djebar's novels and films disclose a number of important facts and contradictions.

That women fought, died, and helped to bring about a free Algeria should be duly noted. That a male writer chooses to chronicle women's activism demonstrates an awareness of the importance of women and their contributions at historical moments and to historical movements. It represents equally a resistance to what feminist critics have long pointed to as the patriarchal tendency to exclude women from history. Algerian women entered themselves into history. History was importantly made by the women. Fanon has merely related Algerian women's resistance in a way that can be remembered, recalled, and corrected by women in their present quests for self-actualization.

As of late, Fanon has been put into a lurch of sorts, the clichéd "damned if you do, damned if you don't." In writing about Algerian women, he has been accused of reinscribing silence, male privilege, and ventriloquism.[12] If in 1959, he had written of the Algerian revolution without a word on the women, he would have been accused of sexism; as he has written of the subject, he now stands accused of mythmaking with a sexist/conservative subtext.

In our rethinking of Fanon in contemporary culture and feminist resistance politics, it certainly does not serve our interests to inscribe "myths" onto Fanon's thought at the very moment when we are claiming to unpack his "myths." An ethics of feminist criticism should allow one to critically engage and expose flaws in Fanon's writings and versions of history without aggressive misreadings and textual revisionism.

It is possible, as Henry Louis Gates observed of Homi Bhabha, that one "wants Fanon to be even better than he is" (Gates, this volume p. 255). Yet, in all earnestness, there are many feminist critics who refuse to acknowledge and put to use the best of Frantz Fanon.

NOTES

1. Barbara Burris (1973, 322–357) also takes Fanon to task in her discussion of "National" Culture as the Dominant Male Culture. Burris's premise is that Fanon is pro–male cultural supremacy. Her reading is flawed on the most fundamental levels as she begins by insisting that Fanon and not the French identified the veil as an Algerian cultural artifact. Her analyses then spiral out into a cascade of misreadings. She appears at odds with Fanon primarily because of his "hatred" of European colonizers. She goes on to maintain that Fanon does not recognize female oppression.

National culture *has* unfortunately in Algeria turned out to be pro-male supremacy. But Fanon certainly would not condone such a view of national culture or the struggle for independence as we will reveal and as his son attests in Isaac Julien's "Frantz Fanon; Black Skin White Mask" and Algerian feminist-writer-activist Assia Djebar remarks in *Le blanc de l'Algérie*. Burris's other charges in this essay are marred by her "common oppression" rhetoric and her attempts to deny white women's privilege in an antiblack culture. It is apparent that her reading of *A Dying Colonialism* stopped at "Algeria Unveiled."

2. Here I want to stress that there are feminists who believe that nationalism and feminism can be reconciled if the discussion of sexuality is opened (see Accad 1990). There are even feminist nationalists who argue that feminism can change the "masculinist face" of nationalism (see West 1996). There are then differences between nationalist discourses. There are modernists, conservatives, and fundamentalists. The secular nationalism of the FLN, however, has failed in Algeria because it consistently reinscribes sexist and misogynist practices with the monetary support of the West.

3. Although the FIS won the municipal elections by a landslide (850 municipalities out of 1500), with 54 percent of the popular vote and only 28 percent for the incumbent FLN, through gerrymandering the Western-backed government expanded the parliament in order to favor the FLN. Violence resulted because of this manipulation of the electoral process. The FIS declared a holy war on the secular government. The FIS has been outlawed since 1992. For more, see Peter St. John (1996).

4. Tohidi explains this phenomena in Iran. Women who deemed the *hajib* as unprogressive voluntarily wore the veil as a form of solidarity against a common enemy, the U.S.–backed Shah of Iran.

5. See the essays by Anne McClintock and Diana Fuss in this volume. Fuss unpacks the textual layers of "Algeria Unveiled" specifically within a poststructuralist framework of mimicry. She equally refers to Fanon's misogyny on the question of Mayotte Capécia. What is troubling about the article is that it attempts to read Fanon psychoanalytically in spite of his own renunciation of psychoanalysis as unable to understand the neurosis of the black in particular. Moreover, Fuss situates Fanon's decolonizing medicine in *The Wretched of the Earth* within the psychoanalytic discourse of *analysand*, etc., when Fanon was not a psychoanalyst but a psychiatrist. He did not practice psychoanalysis. Equally troubling is the erasure of ethnic specificity in her projection of a "black" identity on Algerians in an

attempt to create continuity between the psychoanalysis taken up in *Black Skin, White Mask* and the psychiatry in *The Wretched of the Earth* and the textual metaphors in *A Dying Colonialism*. This is of course one of the problems with poststructuralist feminism, as noted by Teresa Ebert (1996). It "substitutes a politics of representation for radical social transformation." It consists of "poststructuralist assumptions about linguistic play, difference, and the priority of discourse."

McClintock's work on "Fanon and Gender Agency" is a complex and insightful read of the shortcomings and contradictions of "Algeria Unveiled" and "The Algerian Family" with respect to women's agency. McClintock and Helie-Lucas are at two extremes of the spectrum. While McClintock insists that Fanon wholly denies women's agency, Helie-Lucas maintains that Fanon, in his celebration of women's agency, inflates it to such an extent that it masked the reality of gender inequity. There is of course a middle ground, which I hope to open up. McClintock questions where the agency begins for the women in Fanon's text. Fanon's writing, for McClintock, denies feminist resistance prior to the national revolution and equally ties that resistance into male militancy. Fanon did not mention the longstanding resistance of Arab women to patriarchal oppression, but he certainly did not suggest that women's resistance was filtered through men's militancy. There were various stages of women's involvement in the struggle. Fanon interprets every action of the women as militant. Algerian women were always active in the struggle; it was *the women*, as Fanon and Helie-Lucas write, who decided to redon the *haïk* because of the French's campaign of unveiling, of rape. Fanon does not deny the historic dynamism of the veil. He states that the veil functioned to separate the sexes. Helie-Lucas's elaboration of designated agency theory and disjointed citings of Fanon to prove this theory are too numerous to cite. While McClintock integrates a good deal of Fanon's other work into her feminist theorizing, suffice it to say that her critique of *A Dying Colonialism* selectively cites Fanon and in doing so distorts his analysis. For more on Capécia, see Sharpley-Whiting (1997) and Sharpley-Whiting in Gordon et al. (1996).

6. See Enloe 1989. For a comparative view of fundamentalism, the family, modernization, and women see Accad's, Gilliam's, and Tohidi's essays in *Third World Women and Politics of Feminisms* (Bloomington: Indiana University Press, 1991); see F. Azari (1983); E. Sansarian (1982).

7. See Patricia McFadden's "Women and Liberation" cited in *Out of the Kumbla*, (Trenton, N.J.: Africa World Press, 1990), xii–xiii.

8. Massu 1972, 103–104. Contrary to Suzanne Massu's claims, Le Mouvement clandestinely acted to convert Algerian women, represented by the fact that many members burned their veils during the Battle of Algiers. See 96–97, 102 of her *Le Torrent et la Digue*.

9. At the Tenth Berkshires Conference on the History of Women, Indian feminist Tanika Sarkar also discussed how the British made Indian women critical to their colonial campaigns and versions of history.

10. Burris takes offense at the fact that men made this final decision to involve the women. The situation was clearly no different in the United Staes. Women agitated in order to join the fighting ranks of the U.S. military. Fanon applauds the males for such a decision because the fight for decolonization is just as much women's fight. Moreover, through revolutionary struggle, the status of the women would be changed to sister and comrade in arms—at least that is what he believed. More importantly, Fanon insisted that the women should not be regarded as replacement products/subordinates to/for the men.

11. It is particularly the modern model. As late as the nineteenth century, French men were allowed to take child-women, that is, pubescent teenaged brides.

12. See Rajanna Khanna's unpublished paper, "The Fourth Cinema" on the film *The Battle of Algiers*, which she maintains borrowed heavily from Fanon's *A Dying Colonialism*. Saadi Yacef, however, a member of the FLN/ALN who was critical to the Battle of Algiers, informed much of Pontecorvo's rendition. Yacef stars in the film as himself.

14.

Challenging the Social Order: Women's Liberation in Contemporary Algeria

Zouligha

THE FAMILY CODE AND VIOLENCE AGAINST WOMEN

Today's Family Code is the latest version of an old legislative project which has come to the forefront at various times in independent Algeria's history. From the start, this project obscured the ideological assault against women. It was in 1984 that it was finally passed into law. At that moment women mobilized and demonstrated against it. Today, the government plans to introduce a few amendments to it. These amendments promise a few small openings for women, which may help them to escape some of the impossible situations they face, specifically, in relation to divorce. The old code had seven clauses; a new one would be added permitting a woman to ask for divorce on the grounds of incompatibility.

How can one explain a very authoritarian regime proposing these amendments? First of all, since independence we have had nothing but authoritarian regimes. The laws regarding women are

Interview conducted by Charles Reeves and John Marcotte, July 27, 1998.

posed in terms of their obligations not their rights. In the code there is only one article which permits women to keep the property they had when they got married. It is the only article in the code which says: "the woman has the right to. . .". All the other articles, whether on marriage or divorce, say: "the woman must, the woman must, the woman must . . .". It is clear to me that these amendments are not the result of any relation of forces in society, they are above all a concession by the government to the pressures of foreign powers such as the United States and France. They are part of the need for an image of openness. That is the spirit in which this is being done.

From 1980 until the start of the war [between the Islamists and the government]—and it is war—the whole campaign of the Islamists was directed against women. Until 1990, we had preaching and propaganda against women. One could almost say that the program of the FIS (Islamic Salvation Front) was nothing but a series of points and invectives, all directed against women. Almost nothing else. Everything that was wrong was the women's fault! There was receptive ground for this kind of speech. Let's not forget that since 1962, mass schooling had completely changed the situation of women in Algeria. Women began to fill the public space but this was not sufficient to change the relation of forces with male power and to get people involved in the women's struggle. Even on the political terrain this struggle is very recent. At the time of the last election campaign the so-called democratic parties got involved. They talked about the abrogation of the Family Code and of an equal status for women. But there was very little debate. Women were hardly involved in political life.

It may appear contradictory that women were occupying more and more of the social arena. In the decade of the 1980s, because of the violence of the Islamist campaign against women, feminists had ended up internalizing the idea that we should not impose ourselves too much, "we should not push too much." At the same time, one already felt that women were present, that despite the physical, moral, and social violence, there was a will to affirm ourselves. The men were accepting—out of necessity—the fact that women were starting to nibble at their turf, their public space. It was then, at that moment, that the Islamists became most violent. It was then that they branded all women Western, denouncing women in public places. One must underline that from 1985 to 1990, the first violent acts were ones openly directed against women. And no one said a word. In 1985 leaflets were distributed which condemned all women who did not wear the regulation Islamic dress code. It was not just a matter of wearing the veil; you had to hide your face, you had to wear gloves. In the South, they went so far as to physically attack some women and burn their houses. Violent actions were organized against female students. There were several demonstrations by women but few political parties supported us. The media ignored us. That's when women got scared.

Since then, a lot has changed. Ironically, the fact that the Islamist movements organized themselves against women brought about the appearance of militant women among them! Islamic women have organized themselves and are visible. They can organize demonstrations when they want to. Since 1989, an association of Islamic women, *El Irchad arv El Islah*, has counterdemonstrated in the streets against our demonstrations. The first big change then is that the Islamist women have organized politically. Today, there are women active in the "maquis." They have become combatants. We also know that in the course of the latest massacres in the Algiers region, it was the women of the armed groups who came to reconnoiter, who chose the families to be massacred, who directed the executions. While this is not a positive evolution, women's engagement in the Islamist groups has forced even the most rigid Islamists, and the ones most hateful against women, to let them occupy the space and be active in the same manner. Certainly it is not a question of praising this fact, but of pointing it out and seeing what it means. These are very authoritarian organizations and when there is a decision to be made it is always the same person who makes it. At that level there are no women. The militant Islamist women come mostly from the poorest layers of the population, while the chiefs of the movement are mostly from the wealthier and more educated classes. But when the Islamist girls and women started to be political they did it in the same way we did, and that has given them a status which has nothing to do with that of the women in the FLN during the war of independence.

THE WOMEN'S ASSOCIATIONS
AND WOMEN'S LIBERATION TODAY

Our association is in Algiers and is called the Association for the Emancipation of Women. It was created in 1989, when associations were first recognized by the state. In the beginning the association was formed by feminists who had been organizing video clubs since 1985. We were semiclandestine and the activity of the video clubs enabled us to meet and organize discussions around films. There were also women involved who came from the union movement. In 1989, all these women came together to form the association. Our objective was to work on the two fronts which seemed most important: consciousness and the law including the Family Code. Starting in 1989, we started to create circles, to organize discussions on the condition of women. We organized little theater pieces, we did propaganda. Among the members of the association were students who would come to study in Algiers, and when their studies were finished they would return to their towns. We set up a legal service for women who had no way to defend themselves. On the national level we also organized several women's encounters.

For two years, when the terror was greatest, we had to stop functioning. First, because we often lived and worked in dangerous neighborhoods, neighborhoods in which we were always closely watched and were known. We had demonstrated with uncovered faces and the Islamists had filmed us. We had to protect ourselves. Second, because any public political meeting had to be conducted under military protection and we did not accept this. We could not support the military.

Today, all of the women's associations have aged. Very few youth join us, you can count them on one hand. This is despite the fact that we believe the women's movement has to be younger and that girls have to become interested in it. The new generation has many problems in school, in the family, at work. Today the principal preoccupation of young women is to get married in order to have a social status as a protection. This is a society in which an unmarried woman is given no recognition. Socially she is considered as someone poor, vulnerable, incomplete. On the other hand, there is a preoccupation with women having their own income which can be seen in the changing attitude of the man to the woman. Ten or fifteen years ago, men preferred a woman who stayed home and took care of them. Today life is so hard economically that men look first of all for a job. That has even become a value: The capacity of the woman to have an income now forms part of the dowry. In the same way, in the family, a woman cannot impose herself, have her space, as small as that may be, if she doesn't work. Certainly there is a desire to affirm yourself. This includes women of the poor classes, who work in the informal economy, at home. These women have changed the relations at the heart of the couple: They have a responsibility and bring an income into the home, just as much as the man. In many cases it is even inverse, as unemployment grows faster and faster among men. In two years there have been 200,000 lay-offs in the public sector, and it continues. Suddenly, it is the women who make the families survive and have more force to defend themselves.

This is an unconscious movement, which is taking place in Algeria just as in any society where women acquire a certain financial autonomy. Relations of power at the heart of the family change. When I say unconscious I also mean there is an adaptation, that there is no movement toward liberation, toward a fundamental change. The actual changes take place at the cost of increased exploitation of women. The attitude of the men who lived through the independence movement and the years of the FLN in the 1950s is also changing. They did nothing to modify the condition of women, and have often been carriers of antiwoman rhetoric, of the traditional practices and mentalities. Today, they are fathers and, by force of circumstance, they are obliged to change their views about women, because their daughters suffer under the Family Code, who find themselves thrown out in the street if their husband decides to get divorced. Right now the percentage of divorces is around 30 percent or more.

This question of divorced women is very important. If a woman earns a salary, she can try to find new housing. This is not a given because rents are very high. For the woman who doesn't work it is terrible. Before, the divorced woman was automatically taken back into the family. The old law counted on that tradition. In the old Family Code, housing goes to the husband, with the unspoken understanding that the wife returns to her family. Care of the children, on the other hand, goes to the woman. Today, due to the general impoverishment of the society, this return of the divorced woman to her family is in many cases not possible. So, many end up in the street with their children with no means of subsistence. This is a totally new phenomenon in Algerian society. Some live by begging, others find little jobs, do cleaning, sell food in the street, or else end up in prostitution. They are strictly on their own. It is only insofar as they can bring in an income that their families will take them back. This misery upsets everything, especially in a country where the masculine identity rests on the honor of men to protect "their women." It gives very starkly the impression of a society that is falling apart.

Prostitution has been increasing rapidly, from the cities to the smallest villages. They are women who are divorced or widows, their husbands killed in the war, on one side or the other. They prostitute themselves in front of the whole village, everyone knows. There had always been some isolated cases, "fallen women" as they said, but now prostitution has developed to the point where people don't justify it, but understand, and shut their eyes to it. There, too, traditional morality is being called into question. When dozens of girls from nine to sixteen years old have been kidnapped and raped by members of the armed groups, where do you set the barriers of morality? And what of the young men who are raped by the Emir [guerrilla leader] when they join the "maquis"? The eyewitness accounts are numerous. There are so many horrors that in comparison the problem of prostitution passes as one more form of survival. How do you invoke references to a morality which no longer has any relation to the reality of peoples' lives?

THE CHILDREN OF THE CRISIS

I teach in a high school. In 1984–85, the Islamist teachers would keep up a constant barrage of propaganda in class against the women students saying they must wear the veil. A lot of young girls acceded and started to use it. Today, hardly 10 percent of the girls in my school wear the veil. You feel they don't believe in it. And now the regime forbids the teachers from intervening on this subject. Of course the government and the Islamists are equally repressive. So now you realize a lot of the kids wore the veil only because of the pressure from the teachers. And yet this is in an area where Islamist activism is very strong. When I came to this school in the 1980s, I walked into the teachers' room and I was the only woman without a veil. I instinctively recoiled. I became afraid. All at once I felt, "I am in an Islamic country, I am in Iran." I forced myself to remain strong. I had friends telling me, "You just don't understand the situation." At that moment I told myself if I have to wear the veil to avoid being killed I will. But I resisted, and it passed. Today, if one wears the veil it is not due to fear, nor because it is imposed. Taking into account all that has happened, the religious have devalued themselves in the eyes of many women, for whom only habit remains. They tell us, "Had we known we would never have worn the veil. But now it is difficult to take it off. I've worn it for so many years, if I take it off I feel as if I was going out naked."

My school is mixed, boys and girls, but there is not really any mixing. In the schoolyard a few mixed groups sometimes form, but very rarely. Of course, the boys have girlfriends, the girls have boyfriends, there are little crushes, they send each other little love notes, they are like any adolescents in the world. But in class they refuse to sit together. And outside, as soon as they are outside the high school walls, they don't know each other: The boys go one way, the girls the other.

In school it is very difficult to talk about what is going on, about the massacres. Why? Because on one side are the children whose fathers have been deported, who have brothers in the Islamist armed groups, others who have had family members assassinated. On the other side are the children whose fathers and brothers are in the police, in the army, in the parallel police created by the government. It is very divided. This makes for a heavy silence, in which each is afraid of the other. One day there was a massacre in the area and three of our students were killed. We did not even stop working. We cried in some corner and kept going. The students were traumatized, some didn't come to class, they stayed locked up at home. It was impossible to mourn. That is what is so dramatic about life in Algeria today: We cannot talk, everything is repressed, we keep everything inside, we don't express ourselves. It is a sick society. We did not stop for a single hour just to mourn, to express our grief. You have kids who have seen their parents, their close family killed. And they're sitting there in front of you. As far as school work these students no longer do anything, of course they have no motivation left, they are lost, they are just there.

We did a survey in class of future occupations. Ninety percent said they want to be in the police, the army, or the security services. It is for a sense of security but it is also an expression of the desire for revenge which these students have. One told me, "I want to be in the police to wipe 'them' out." That is another aspect of this repression. No one names the armed groups, the Islamists. But just by their vocabulary you can tell with whom you are dealing. Someone who is a partisan of the Islamists will call them "the brothers" or "the moudjahedeen." Someone who is opposed will call them "them." Others who don't take sides, are afraid, use the expression "them" for everyone. Everyone is terrorized and no one talks about it. It was only from the moment that people started to arm themselves that tongues started to loosen. It was only then that people started to say, "We are armed, if 'they' come we will defend ourselves." Last year, at the time of the biggest massacres, people also began to talk. How was it possible, that babies, women, the elderly are murdered? It was too much barbarism, the people were so revolted they reacted, including those who had been active militants in the FIS. I have coworkers who are members of the FIS who have denounced the massacres, even if they always start by putting emphasis on the complicity of the state.

The young people who join this armed struggle have no other alternative, nothing left to lose. It is in that sense that they go to the "maquis" to revalorize themselves, to gain a certain recognition in their own eyes. They feel stronger. They gain an authority they cannot have in society but it is also a very risky bet, almost suicidal. On the other hand, as I said earlier, something has changed in the man-woman relation. I found what I consider an important aspect of this in the course of a discussion with some women colleagues who are rather traditional, who don't aspire to emancipation. These massacres bring out the impotence of the men to protect; they cannot assume the "traditional" role they have given themselves. Their image as protectors of women no longer exists. The women say, "It's true they can't do anything, and they are afraid just like us." The myth of the man who is not afraid, who is strong, who can guarantee safety, is completely debunked, and is disappearing. The women say it openly. Today, from nine o'clock at night onward, it is the woman who opens the door when someone knocks. This goes totally against the tradition that the master of the house, the head of the family, is the man. It is not for the woman to open the door. But when it appears dangerous it is the woman who goes out first, because according to tradition you cannot attack the woman; she is not who is looked for. Also, if the woman opens the door, one must not cross the threshold. That attitude permitted women to assume the role of protector of the family, including of the man, which has enormously changed relations. However, recently this, too, has changed. Terrorism now itself ignores Islamic traditions. In fact, in the name of struggling for the respect of traditions, all traditions are completely overturned. Everything is upset. And what is terrifying is that this is not going in any good direction. It is a society completely disoriented, there are no points of reference left. People have lost all points of reference in relation to traditions and religious values. The only new values are those of consumer goods, of money.

The youth are emptied out and dragged into the logic of revenge. They don't even see a perspective of moving elsewhere. In the 1980s, any kid on the street would tell you, "Me, I'm going to go to France." Thus they would translate the aspirations of the entire society, to escape, to try their life elsewhere. You don't hear this any more. My students have never expressed the desire, or even mentioned the possibility, of going abroad. They know it is closed off, they know they don't even have the possibility of leaving. If one leaves, it is to the "maquis." Today the life expectancy in the "maquis" is two years and the average age of the members of the armed groups is going down. At the start it was men in their thirties or older. They say that today the majority are young boys, eighteen or nineteen years old.

THE MASSACRES

The youth find themselves face to face with each other, on one side armed by the government, on the other by the Islamist movement. They share the same history, follow the same course, and live the same misery. It would be in their interest to have the same enemy, but no. Brothers in their social situation, each has chosen his camp and they find themselves confronting each other as enemies. There are also those who are mobilized by a desire for revenge. It is not at all rational nor organized in a political manner. In all this barbarism there is vengeance and a settling of scores. Others find themselves in the armed groups by force of circumstance. They have not chosen their situation. By chance they end up in one camp or the other. That is why all of this is very complex, and why the actual events of the massacres appear incomprehensible. There are people who are killed by old accomplices, those they aided and supported for years.

Since 1995, most often it is the families of Islamist sympathizers and the families of those in the "maquis" who have been victims of massacres. In general, these are families who are close to the FIS and not the GIA (*Groupes Islamiques Armée*), the GIA being the most radical representative of the armed Islamist movement. There are many massacres in the zones where there was great sympathy for the FIS. This is not contradictory, it is rather the expression of sharp divergences within the Islamist movement. On top of that are added the irrational factors I mentioned before. In principle these are families who had nothing to fear from terrorism, since they were part of the logistical support, seeing as they had sons and daughters in the "maquis." The members of the armed groups come down to the village with lists of those to be kidnapped or massacred. These massacres are often carried out by groups of youth. One knows that there are people from the village among them, who wear masks so they will not be recognized. On the other hand, in all the massacres there is always the same eyewitness account: Those who massacre insult and blaspheme. This leaves people confused, since those who fight in the name of a religious ideal are not supposed to carry on this way. They no longer recognize themselves in these groups said to be Islamist. In one massacre I heard of, one of the Islamists from the armed group hid some children to protect them from the massacre. That means that behavior changes even within an armed group. If some of the combatants seem so sure, others are asking questions. Therefore it is an error to say they are all barbarians and should all be killed. Finally, one other aspect which has been confirmed by many eyewitness accounts: They are looters. Their objective is not only to massacre people, they also come to take all they find, and often that is not much, obviously, as these villages are very poor. These are people who sometimes barely have anything to eat. The armed groups loot everything they have, even blankets and mattresses. The villagers are left confused: "How can it be?" they say, "Such and such a family was massacred, and yet their son is in the 'maquis' . . .". So the easy solution is to say: It's the police. Other accounts say that the alert was given and the police did nothing. Which is also true. Today we see that as soon as the people are armed and fight back, the armed groups go away. That is to say they are not guerrillas who would be ready to fight to the death to accomplish their ends. They operate only on sure ground. As soon as there is resistance they leave.

THE WOMEN'S ASSOCIATION TODAY

Today the government does not permit street demonstrations—
except for those organized in its favor or which they can use to
their advantage, such as the recent ones this summer (1998)
against the Arabization law which had an anti-Arab Berber nationalist content. It has to be underlined that the regime regularly uses
the demonstrations on March 8, International Women's Day, as
propaganda against the Islamists. In the same way it has, since the
1980s, used the women's movement as a passageway between the
modernist forces and the conservatives as part of its image of
openness. We prefer to organize debates in the homes of young
people. Any public meeting brings with it the presence ("protection") of the police and the army and you appear publicly as an
ally of the ruling power. On top of that you have to invite political
personalities who are close to the regime, who have participated in
a regime which has denied us for decades. That is the price you
pay for their "protection." We refuse to join such activities. Even if
we face the Islamists, we have no intention of finding ourselves
with our enemies of yesterday and today. We must continue to
battle for the abrogation of the Family Code and struggle for better
conditions of life and work for women. These are concrete things
that women are living through. We also organize debates on the
code, since women actually aren't very familiar with it. They know
there is injustice but they don't make the connection to the text.
The only problem is that we don't have a hall and to rent a space
in Algeria is very expensive: about 2,000 francs compared to a
monthly salary of 800 francs. We survive from the membership
dues, we have no other funds. There are other little associations
elsewhere in the country that we are trying to link up with. Lately
we started another area of work, which is the struggle of young
girls. When children are removed from school it is the girls who
are affected first. They are removed both for economic reasons and
because there are villages and neighborhoods where the schools
have been destroyed. Then, there are also the displaced families:

There is a big exodus of people after the massacres. These are people who have lost everything, their belongings, their jobs, their home. They have installed themselves in shantytowns around the big cities of the north, often where they have family. To go to school the children of these shantytowns are often obliged to travel very far and they have no money for transportation, nor for books, nor for shoes. In such a situation the family must make a choice and of course they favor the boys. To add to this, these neighborhoods become reserves of child labor, exploited in the new informal economy that is developing.

In our association we think we are living at a turning point: It is possible to succeed or it is possible to fail. We think this is a crucial time to get involved in these struggles which are going on against the Islamists and against the government power at one and the same time. The women's associations who limited themselves to the struggle against the Islamists ended up allying themselves with the state power. During that same time the state passed all sorts of liberal economic reforms which threw the Algerian people into total misery. It is not Islamism which aggravated the situation. It is the state power which, using the excuse of Islamism, has impoverished the people and made the situation even worse than before, dramatically so. The state of public health is enormously degraded, birthing takes place in abysmal conditions. The state power has withdrawn from the social terrain. As they themselves say, there is the "useful" Algeria, and "the other," and Algerian women are receiving a lot more blows than the men. It is a turning point precisely because the population in general, and the women in particular, are starting to become conscious that the perpetuation of this war between the Islamists and the government is only in the interests of the powers that be.

IV. Fanon's Quest for a New Humanism

15.

Fanon and the FLN: Dialectics of Organization and the Algerian Revolution

Lou Turner

BY WAY OF INTRODUCTION

The North African experience of Frantz Fanon may be said to have begun in 1944 when, as a raw recruit in the Free French Army in North Africa he observed that racism in the French military was more than matched by the French colonialists in Algeria and Morocco. Fanon often referred to the behavior of the First French Army in North Africa during World War II when fighting French propaganda about Algerian terrorism. Whatever *Black Skin, White Masks* is supposed to have disclosed of the existential dilemma Fanon encountered as a black intellectual in postwar France, one need only recall the radicalization of African-American servicemen during their tours of duty in Vietnam in the 1960s and 1970s to recognize Fanon's war experience as a source of his radicalism. It no doubt seemed an unsettling irony to the young Fanon (barely nineteen years of age) that the "war of liberation" in which France was violently engaged to expel the Axis powers from North Africa was, too, an idea that had occurred to the Algerians chafing under French colonialism. This was certainly the attitude of returning Algerian soldiers like Ahmed Ben Bella.

That the French war of national resistance should be taken by Algerians as a model is not surprising. Veterans of World War II like Ben Bella and Fanon viewed the Algerian Revolution as a natural outcome of their war experience. Nonetheless, new historical prerogatives, expressed by a new generation of national militants in an emergent "Third World," generated centrifugal forces within the liberation front that left it, after 1959, a deeply fractious and factionalized organization at war with itself. The first five years of the Algerian "war of liberation," 1954 to 1959, that is, the period from Fanon's arrival in Algeria (which was actually in October or November 1953), and the beginning of the revolution on All Saints Day, November 1, 1954, to the year he published his studies in *A Dying Colonialism*, represented the most radical period of the Front de Libération Nationale (FLN).

Frantz Fanon matured as a political thinker in this first crucial period of the Algerian Revolution. Critical to Fanon's development was his relationship to the political figures, tendencies, and policies of the FLN. While there has been some analysis of this relationship, particularly in the works of Peter Geismar and Irene Gendzier, the approach has not been sufficiently critical of FLN organizational development vis-à-vis the violent and often contradictory unfolding of the Algerian Revolution. This seems an odd lapse given the fact that Fanon's last testament, *The Wretched of the Earth*, represents such a thoroughgoing critique of the organizational insufficiencies of the anticolonial political elite. If anything, the tendency of scholars has been to assume an uncritical posture toward the FLN and accord it legitimacy by virtue of it being the incipient government of independent Algeria.[1]

Getting to the bottom of Fanon's relationship to the FLN, the radical nationalist organization he joined in 1956, involves first unraveling the internal politics of this very divided political and military party, and where helpful, taking into account its ideological antecedents insofar as they continued to resonate or resurface in the political life of the Front. It involves, crucially, discerning the dialectical criteria Fanon found indispensable to making national self-determination "an indispensable condition for the existence of men and women who are truly liberated, in other words who are truly masters of all the material means which make possible the radical transformation of society" (Fanon 1968, 310). That is to say, it involves how to turn nationalism into "a consciousness of social and political needs, in other words, into humanism" (Fanon 1968, 204). Fanon's concern with this dialectic motivated his original preoccupation with the so-called Woman Question, as well as with problems of organization. The dialectic of turning nationalism into socialism also distinguished the political-theoretical perspectives of Fanon's closet intellectual comrades-in-arms, especially the one considered Fanon's "mentor," the Kabyle revolutionary Abane Ramdane, the leading intellectual figure in the first period of the revolution.

CONCERNING FANON AND "THE BATTLE OF ALGIERS"

In his 1956 letter of resignation as Médecin-Chef de Service à l'Hôpital Psychiatrique de Blida-Joinville to the newly appointed Socialist Resident Minister and governor-general of Algeria Robert Lacoste, Fanon referred to the recently begun July 5th strike. Lacoste had already, on March 8, called for military and economic provisions to check the insurgency in Algeria. And by March 13, the French National Assembly had granted "extraordinary powers" to the Socialist head of state, Guy Mollet, to deal with the "Algerian situation."

Fanon wrote his letter of resignation not only under the impact of such developments, but as a result of the intensification of his own involvement in the FLN underground in Algiers and its surrounding suburbs. Blida, where Fanon lived and worked, was one such suburb where FLN militants operated, and, in Fanon's case, where they could turn for aid and refuge from non-Algerian sympathizers. Of the six *wilayas*, or political-military districts into which the FLN divided Algeria, *wilaya* IV, covering Algiers and its surrounding areas, was administered by the Kabyle revolutionary Ramdane Abane. Fanon's relationship to Abane would be his single most important intellectual link to the leadership circles of the FLN. Whatever he may have meant by his statement, recorded by Simone de Beauvoir when he spent an evening with her and Jean-Paul Sartre in Rome the summer of 1961, "I have two deaths on my conscience which I will not forgive myself for: that of Abane and that of Lumumba" (Gendzier 1973, 199), it is certain that Fanon was greatly troubled by the deadly contradictions within the FLN, especially as he had had his own near fatal brush with them.[2] Abane had been killed in 1958 by his political rivals in the FLN. Despite denials by FLN officials that Fanon knew or had been close to Abane, we have it on the authority of Fanon's wife, Josie Dublé, that Abane was among the people whom Fanon gave refuge at Blida, and one of Fanon's biographers and close friends from the period, an Italian Left scholar Giovanni Pirelli, who claimed Abane was "a great friend and model of Fanon" (Gendzier 1973, 251).[3]

In any case, the call up of an additional 50,000 French reservists for active duty in Algeria; Lacoste's placing radical eastern Algeria under martial law; the French razing of the village of Ouled Djerrah near Algiers; and the sealing off and siege of the Kasbah, culminating in the Battle of Algiers, expressed in no uncertain terms the violent maintenance of French colonialism, all in the single month of May 1956.

By November, France had invaded Egypt with Britain, in response to Nasser's nationalization of the Suez Canal, with a view toward cutting off the FLN's arms supply. This slowed the arms supplies that Ben Bella was charged with procuring through his base in Cairo, weakening his organizational position in the FLN leadership, but also greatly reducing the flow of arms into the Algerian interior. Instead, what arms the FLN managed to procure for the ALN (*Armée de Libération Nationale*) only reached the periphery and accumulated in the hands of the exterior military forces along the Moroccan and Tunisian frontiers. While only a temporary set-back for Ben Bella, the far-reaching effect of the disruption of the arms flow to the interior was to increase the power of the exterior military forces in the factional conflicts within the FLN. So poorly equipped were the interior forces that Fanon floated the idea of opening a third supply route through the sub-Saharan south, particularly through Mali. Fanon's field notebook, posthumously published in *Toward the African Revolution*, was written while on the reconnaissance mission through Mali to organize such a supply route in the summer of 1960.

Both Geismar and Gendzier contend that Fanon reconciled himself to the changed political reality in the FLN following Abane's death in 1958 and the ascension of the ALN leadership over the political wing of the FLN that Abane had led, and to which Fanon was close. Fanon's supposed reconciliation, however, does not explain two things. First, Fanon's southern strategy meant the introduction of black troops from sub-Saharan Africa to reinforce the nearly defeated interior forces. And second, although Fanon undertook the reconnaissance mission himself, and lined up both commitments from sub-Saharan African leaders and demonstrated the feasibility of a southern strategy, the ALN command rejected it. This rejection spelled the end of Abane's perspective of returning the direction of the liberation struggle to the interior where it was being waged. It suspended as well Abane's notion that the liberation struggle should be fought over the political and social issues of the new Algerian society to come, and not over the diplomatic and military concerns that would best expedite arriving at a negotiated settlement, and which leave the masses cheated at the end of the day. These, of course, were some of the principal concerns Fanon would take up in *The Wretched of the Earth*.

So, instead of Fanon having reached a reconciliation with the exterior military command, it is more likely that his efforts to open a southern front represented the last attempt by a partisan of Abane's interior/political faction to return the direction of the revolution to its mass base inside Algeria. (As we shall see, though Fanon had powerful allies in the FLN leadership sponsoring his southern mission, more powerful opponents in the ALN trumped his proposal to open a sub-Saharan front to the Algerian Revolution.) Fanon's writing, in *A Dying Colonialism*, on the revolutionary transformation of the Algerian woman, the Algerian family, and role of "Radio Free Algeria" as an instrument of mass propaganda and agitation,[4] all point to this as the governing idea in his vision of revolution.

His view of the role of the French Left in relation to the FLN was also consistent with Abane's. Francis Jeanson, an active FLN sympathizer who arranged Fanon's passage into exile in Tunisia from Algeria, had written the preface to the first French edition of *Black Skin, White Masks* and the postface to the second edition. That Fanon's relationship to Jeanson goes back to his university days in France, Jeanson being the first one Fanon wanted to read the manuscript of *Black Skin*, suggests that there was more deliberation involved in his decision to enter the Algerian scene than previously recognized. Pierre Chaulet along with his wife and sister Anne-Marie, considered the first French radicals to join the FLN, were part of what the dissident Algerian writer Mohammed Lebjaoui called the Mandouze group. Professor André Mandouze, who headed a group of French radical intellectuals sympathetic to the FLN, arranged for Fanon to lecture at the University of Algiers. Chaulet was Fanon's contact with the FLN in Blida, and arranged interviews between Abane and Jeanson and Jeanson's wife, Colette, for an important book (*L'Algérie Hors la Loi*) they were writing on the Algerian situation. Chaulet also came to Tunis to work on *El Moudjahid* with Fanon. Chaulet's influence on Fanon though significant politically was perhaps most crucial organizationally. It was probably Chaulet who brought Fanon into the FLN as one of those non-Algerian intellectuals prepared to become more active in the revolution (Gendzier 1973, 141).

Fanon first wrote for the Moroccan-based newspaper *Résistance Algérienne*, and in the summer of 1958 after the reorganization of the FLN press began to write for and became one of the editors of *El Moudjahid*. Gendzier notes that Fanon only wrote on external or international, not internal organizational, affairs when he wrote for *Moudjahid*. His decision to write *The Wretched of the Earth* represented his turning inward to critically examine the dialectic of an organization like the FLN and its relation to the revolution.

Strangely enough, this view of *The Wretched of the Earth* is borne

out by Irene Gendzier's moralizing judgment of Fanon's commitment to his theory of violence in that work. It is Fanon's organizational relationship to arguably the most revolutionary event of the
Algerian liberation struggle—the Battle of Algiers—that Gendzier
assesses to measure Fanon's theoretical commitments to the revolution. In the penultimate chapter of her critical study of Fanon in
which she sums up Fanon's influence on the Algerian Revolution,
Gendzier writes:

> *In the summer of 1956, some months after he had come to Tunis,* and
> hence long enough to have learned something about the issues
> and personalities involved in the Tunisian capital, the Soummam
> Valley conference took place. (Gendzier 1973, 250, emphasis
> added)

This follows Gendzier's claim that according to Josie Fanon's
chronology Fanon left Algeria in 1956, not January 1957, as other
accounts attest. Fanon's reference to the July 5th strike in his 1956
letter of resignation as chief resident at Blida-Joinville, and the
letter of expulsion he received in January 1957, would certainly
suggest that there is little basis for Gendzier's claim.

One page later, she inveighs against Fanon's theory of violence, which she equates with terrorism instead of the spontaneity
of mass revolt that Fanon clearly had in mind in *The Wretched*:

> His Algerian colleagues reproach him, at least in retrospect, for
> his excesses in this direction. *Fanon was not in Algeria in any case,*
> *when the Battle of Algiers was being fought.* If he had anything to say
> on the subject, it was *safely* said to friends and militants *far away*
> *from the scene of battle.* (1968, 251–52, emphasis added)

What highlights Gendzier's anxious rush to pass moral judgment
on Fanon's theoretical commitments on the basis of a misplaced
concreteness regarding his supposed absence from or presence at
any practical involvement in the Battle of Algiers is Gendzier's own
earlier account of Fanon's whereabouts from mid-1956 to early
1957. She writes, on page 131, that "the city of Algiers became the

target of direct action, and *from December 1956* [*sic*] until the fall of 1957 the period of the Battle of Algiers was on [emphasis added]." Earlier, on page 98, she had acknowledged that "In January 1957 Fanon's letter of resignation was answered by a letter of expulsion from the office of the Resident Minister. *Within two days Fanon and his close associates, especially the male nurses at Blida, left* [emphasis added]." Apparently, the discrepancy concerning the time that Fanon left Blida comes in an article Josie Fanon wrote in 1963 in which she states that they left Algeria in 1956 (Gendzier 1973, 140).[5]

Renate Zahar maintains that the FLN's underground operations were "discovered in late 1956" (Zahar 1974, xi). The Battle of Algiers, which began in September 1956, not December, as Gendzier claims, had already gotten underway. The proximity of Blida, only thirty miles southwest of Algiers, meant that it would come under the security dragnet of the French military. Fanon was expelled from Algeria January 28, 1957, and after a brief, secret sojourn in Paris, arrived in Tunis. Abane Ramdane and the CCE (*Comité de Coordination et d'Exécution*) formed after the Soummam Congress, the summer of 1956, were forced to flee Algeria into exile in Tunis by May 1957.

If, as Gendzier correctly contends, Fanon's treatment of the question of violence is not the "principal contribution" of *The Wretched of the Earth*, why then her moralizing judgment as if it were, and why the further vulgarization of his views: "His conviction that it was only through violence that international opinion could be affected would have led him to endorse urban terrorism" (1973, 251)?[6]

The position of those militants within the FLN associated with Abane, and closest to Fanon's thinking is reduced by Gendzier to nothing more than mass mobilizations around strikes complemented by urban terrorism.[7] Having reduced the views Abane and Fanon held in common to terrorism in which the Algerian people figure as no more than an inert mass, unaware of their own force until the party awakens and directs it, Gendzier then places Fanon in Tunis far removed from the culmination of the mass mobilizations and strikes in the Battle of Algiers. The truth is that so important did Abane and Fanon hold the principle of being grounded in the Algerian mass struggle that only at the last moment did they make the decision to flee the country. So opposed were they to the politics of compromise and negotiated settlement espoused by the Abbas wing of the FLN,[8] and so opposed were they to raising the ALN above the mass struggle inside Algeria, that Abane labored within the FLN leadership to concentrate the political direction of the revolution into the hands of the interior political wing of the Front. So again, why Gendzier's reduction of Fanon's views of the dialectics of organization and the revolutionary mass movement as if they were summed up in the loaded term *terrorism*?

Any chance we have of getting to the bottom of this question entails scrupulously tracing the dialectics of organization and national liberation as it unfolded from the summer of 1956 when Abane convened the pivotal Soummam Congress to reorganize the FLN, to the summer of 1960 when Fanon, on a reconnaissance mission through Mali, was engaged in the final effort by a partisan of the Abane faction to redirect the political course of the revolution back to the organizational principles of Soummam.

CONCERNING RAMDANE ABANE, SOUMMAM, AND THE "ABSENCE OF IDEOLOGY"

The Soummam Valley Congress, convened August 20, 1956, was the political and organizational high point of the FLN. Ramdane Abane, the leading figure of the congress and one of the few leaders in the Front not limited by a narrow nationalism of either religion or region, was, more than anyone else, responsible for setting the theoretical and political perspectives of the first five years of the revolution. Abane was, in fact, the architect of the Battle of Algiers. And as we saw earlier, he was pivotal to Fanon's relationship to the radical intellectual leadership of the FLN and the radical French intellectual circles who actively sympathized with the FLN.

Two key issues were articulated in the deliberations and program of the congress which would impact Fanon's later thinking. The first concerns the question of national minorities, e.g.,

Algerian Jews, Kabyles, and the Europeans who desired citizenship in an independent, secular Algeria. The second issue revolved around the organizational relationship of the political to the military cadre and command structures. On both of these questions Fanon's affinities lay with Abane.

Approximately fifty delegates and two hundred militants attended the Soummam Congress planned by Abane and the leadership of the interior.[9] It created the FLN's first political institution, the CNRA (*Conseil National de la Révolution Algérienne*), a legislative body to deliberate FLN general decisions. The CNRA was comprised of seventeen full and seventeen deputy members, representing a plurality of political views. The congress also created the *Comité de Coordination et d'Exécution* (CCE) made up of five members, including Abane, who was in charge of organization, as the executive committee charged with the day-to-day operations of the FLN. This reorganization distributed power in the FLN according to Abane's notion of collegial or collective leadership. In his study of the FLN, Henry Jackson explains that

> the internal leaders succeeded in gathering authority among themselves simply because they were the only FLN chiefs then on the battlefield. In the context of war, decisions had to be made rapidly, and therefore time worked to the advantage of the internal leaders. (Jackson 1977, 37)

The FLN divided Algeria into six *wilayas*, or military districts, each under military leadership, with political cadre serving in a more or less advisory capacity. Soummam definitively changed that arrangement by raising the political cadre to leadership status equal with, if not elevated above, the military leadership of the *wilaya*. The areas designated as *wilayas* were (1) the Aures mountains, (2) North Constantine, (3) Kabylia, (4) Algiers, (5) Oran, and (6) the Sahara region. As political head of *wilaya* IV, Algiers, and serving under the military leadership of Belkacem Krim, Abane was strategically positioned within radical intellectual circles to develop the international, secular, democratic perspectives that became the hallmark of the Soummam program and the FLN, and which persisted even after his death.

Jackson critically evaluates the Soummam Congress as having articulated a program and perspectives for independence but not for postindependence Algeria. In his view, the tensions between the external and internal leadership foreclosed any possibility of spelling out the latter. Indeed, as important a point of departure as Soummam was from past political formations in Algeria, Jackson contends it was nevertheless stymied by the problem of

> whether to proceed with the emphasis on military strategy or whether to risk the dissolution of the whole movement by trying to reach agreement on the consolidation of political institutions and definition of ideology. In the end, the FLN leaders opted for the military solution, and this choice sealed the wartime destiny of the FLN. (Jackson 1997, 43)

The crisis in FLN-governed Algeria today is haunted by the specter of this retreat from defining the ideological ground of the revolution. In fact, Jackson's critical view of the ideological weakness of the congress places Fanon's critique of the same phenomenon in a new light. While engaged in the most practical of tasks—the reconnaissance mission in Mali—Fanon wrote the following in his fieldbook in the summer of 1960:

> Colonialism and its derivatives do not, as a matter of fact, constitute the present enemies of Africa. In a short time this continent will be liberated. For my part, the deeper I enter into the cultures and the political circles the surer I am that the great danger that threatens Africa is the absence of ideology. (Fanon 1967b, 186)

After Abane's death the ideological void would be filled by Arab nationalist and Islamicist tendencies. By the time of the 1961 Evian Congress, the Soummam perspectives on a future secular Algerian state had been overthrown and replaced with ones calling for an "Arab-Moslem" state. It is not likely, however, that Fanon had

Soummam and Abane in mind in the summer of 1960, which problematizes Jackson's criticism.

Along with Abane, Belkacem Krim (later vice-president of the provisional government and the FLN leader who delivered the official eulogy at Fanon's funeral),[10] Yussuf Ben Khedda, and Saad Dahlab were the leading radical Left figures at Soummam, who along with another radical, Mohammed Ben M'hidi, made up the CCE. All agreed that the revolution should proceed along the lines of a mass movement which popular consultative assemblies elected in the *wilayas* were to mobilize. The leftist political leadership also supported the participation of non-Algerians in the revolution, and envisioned postindependence Algeria as a secular, democratic republic. Organizational developments at Soummam were thus the first indication of a fundamental change in the ideological direction of the revolution and the FLN. The five-member CCE, the group responsible for the day-to-day operations of the revolution, was dominated by leaders who identified with Abane's perspectives. In the spring of 1957, when four of the five were forced to flee Algeria for Tunis, Abane's ideological nucleus became vulnerable. No longer able to operate in the interior, the CCE radicals found their position weakened in the larger CNRA body. It is likely that these were the revolutionaries in the party Fanon wrote about in *The Wretched*, who find themselves isolated after independence by the nationalist bourgeoisie and their political representatives in the party. What became the provisional government in exile, in 1958, certainly provided him sufficient opportunity to witness during the revolution what he would theorize in *The Wretched* as postindependence phenomena.

Gendzier's chronological error in locating Fanon's whereabouts in the period of the Battle of Algiers is, as we saw earlier, recapitulated when she locates Fanon in relation to the Soummam Congress. The same error that made Fanon peripheral to the Battle of Algiers isolates him from the major organizational development of the FLN.

Just before the Soummam Congress, Mollet, France's newly elected Socialist premier, had gone to Algeria to discuss a negotiated peace with Algerian leaders. He promised justice and fair treatment only after the rebels laid down their arms as the condition for any discussion of national independence. The Mollet negotiations were an initiative taken by the reformist wing of the FLN led by Ferhat Abbas and vigorously opposed by Abane. Soummam was in part called as a repudiation of such conciliatory policies. Mollet's deployment of 200,000 additional troops to Algeria, bringing the occupying troop strength up to 400,000, following his return to France, effectively undermined the reformist leaders in the FLN. The tactical importance of holding the congress in the occupied Soummam Valley, two days after the arrival of the additional 200,000 French troops, not only outmaneuvered the reformist forces within the FLN but the external leaders like Ben Bella based in Cairo. So tenuous was Mollet's position at home in the face of a growing strike wave and youth opposition to conscription, however, that France's troop reinforcements in Algeria had to come from West Germany and West Africa.

For his part, Lacoste had in May placed eastern Algeria under a state of martial law. French troops on May 22 destroyed the village of Ouled Djerrah near Algiers in retaliation for the ambush of seventeen French soldiers by the ALN. By the end of the month the French military sealed off and began searching the Kasbah in a hunt for FLN arms and equipment. This was the prelude to the Battle of Algiers that was to erupt in September, and intensified the underground activities around Blida.

Lacoste had not only presented the FLN with a military challenge, but with an ideological one, which the Soummam perspectives aimed to answer. Dismissing the FLN as nothing more than a terrorist organization, Lacoste issued the following polemic:

> It has been said and reiterated that every conflict is, basically, a conflict of ideologies. But contrary to what may happen in other places, and even if behind them the disturbing Communist propaganda and the conquering passion of Islam may be discerned, our adversaries of today, the terrorists, the rebels, have no ideology other than the wish to evict France from Algeria.

In this "internal" conflict which they want to transform into
an "external" conflict, they have no valid theory or framework.
They are trying to make up for the absence of any political doctrine by a real racism (which the unconscionable action of certain
Frenchmen has, unfortunately, sometimes encouraged). They are
seeking to justify, on the grounds of religious kinship, the inad-
missible interference of foreigners.

Against this absence of ideology, we can offer not any particular political ideology but that which the present crisis may rein-
vigorate, the "national" ideology, the love of France. (Quoted in
Gendzier 1973, 130).

Lacoste's ideological challenge revolved around three questions: (1) despite either the rebels' so-called Communist propaganda or their conquering passion of Islam, their actual lack of an
ideology reduced the FLN to nothing more than terrorists; (2) the
lack of political doctrine and resorting to violence represented
racism in reverse; and (3) "foreign" support from other North
African countries, especially Nasser's Egypt, was an attempt to
turn an internal conflict into an external one, on the grounds of
"religious kinship." Now, it isn't that Lacoste's appraisal of the
FLN should be taken as anything more than French imperialist
propaganda. Nevertheless, being the social democrat that he was,
Lacoste wasn't unmindful of the challenges the FLN faced in legit-
imating its claim of being the sole representative of the Algerian
people; in gaining support within France among the Left; in
achieving solidarity with other Third World nations; and in distinguishing itself as a movement for total national self-determination
vis-à-vis the reformist tendencies within the FLN who represented
the political aspirations of the national bourgeoisie desiring a
negotiated neocolonial settlement.

If Lacoste represented the ideological challenge that lay before
the FLN, the Soummam Declaration was the movement's answer.
On the basis of the declaration, the FLN took the position that aid
be sought from Europe, and that the party develop contacts with
French liberals. The declaration read: "The Algerian Revolution

does not have as its goal to 'throw in the sea' Algerians of European origin, but to destroy the inhuman colonial yoke" (Gendzier 1973, 175). Denying that the revolution was either a civil war or a religious war, the declaration claimed that "The Algerian Revolution wishes to conquer national independence in order to establish a democratic and social republic guaranteeing true equality to all citizens of the same country, without discrimination." The revolution, it declared, aimed to bring about "the rebirth of the Algerian state in the form of a democratic and social Republic and not the restoration of an obsolete monarchy or theocracy." This was aimed at counteracting the caricature of national independence projected by French ideologues like Lacoste.

Paraphrasing the Soummam Declaration, Fanon wrote on the Jewish question in *A Dying Colonialism* that "Jewish intellectuals have spontaneously demonstrated their support of the Algerian cause, whether in the democratic and traditionally anticolonialist parties or in the liberal groups. Even today, the Jewish lawyers and doctors who in the camps or in prison share the fate of millions of Algerians attest to the multiracial reality of the Algerian nation" (Gendzier 1973, 181). "What Fanon excerpted from the Soummam statement on the Jews," observes Gendzier, "was the request that they join the Revolution and reclaim their Algerian nationality along with other Algerians" (Gendzier 1973, 181).

Finally, the separation of political ideology from revolutionary violence, which Lacoste polemicized made the FLN no more than terrorists, was the crucial question the congress sought to answer. Military operations and revolutionary violence had to come under political direction, and the FLN as an organization had to be restructured toward that end. This took the form of reconstituting the role of the ALN in the interior and the exterior military forces along the Moroccan and Tunisian borders, on the one hand, while concentrating responsibility for the direction of the revolution in the hands of the leftist political leadership of the interior on the other.

All of these questions, except the last one, were openly addressed by Fanon in his articles for *El Moudjahid* and in *A Dying Colonialism*. The last question on the multisided relationship of the party to the army and politics to revolutionary violence was addressed in *The Wretched of the Earth*. Abane and the first CCE having fled Algeria in May 1957, Fanon was struck and disappointed by the CNRA's election of the new CCE when it met in Cairo in August-September 1957. Narrow nationalist tendencies associated with the army were beginning to assert themselves and vie for direction of the revolution. Gendzier recounts the outcome of the month-long Cairo meeting of the CNRA:

> Differences over the size of the CCE and its effectiveness in Algeria, to which Dahlab, Ramdane [Abane], and Ben Khedda believed it ought to return, broke out in a serious manner. In Cairo, the CNRA members faced with the proposal of these three men rejected them "apparently fearing that these three were becoming too powerful. They voted instead for the formation of a large and more functionally specific CCE of nine members. Two of the radical politicians from the previous CCE, Ben Khedda and Dahlab, were eliminated in what one described as 'circumstances full of intrigue' and the other a 'minor coup d'état.'"
>
> [William] Quandt quotes Dahlab's observations on the changing character of the new executive as reflecting the "elimination of the politicians by the *militaires* who saw themselves as the real 'combatants.'" The substitution of the military for the politicians, in this instance, revealed the growing importance of the military leaders of the interior. The Soummam decision not to allow the military to dominate the political had been superseded. (Gendzier 1973, 252).

At the next CNRA conference a year later the Provisional Government of the Algerian Republic (GPRA) was formed to replace the expanded second CCE. With Abane murdered earlier in the year (February 1958),[11] the last radical Left figure had been eliminated from the CCE. The army foreclosed any possibility of returning the direction of the revolution to the interior political wing, and thus to the mass movement. Following the formation of the second CCE, that is, after the "coup," a military coordinating committee called COM (*Commandant des Opérations Militaires*) was formed. The COM stationed itself in two peripheral areas, Oujda in Morocco and Ghardimaou in Tunisia. The latter is significant as the encampment where Fanon gave the three lectures to ALN cadre in 1961 that would become the basis of *The Wretched of the Earth*.

According to Gendzier, tensions between the leadership of the interior and exterior military forces were resolved through the creation of an Etat Major Général. It so happens that the president for most of Algeria's independent existence, Colonel Houari Boumedienne, controlled this supreme military command. It was with the blessings of the Etat Major that Fanon undertook the reconnaissance mission to investigate opening a southern supply route into the Algerian interior.[12] It was also Boumedienne and the Etat Major who made the decision not to go forward with Fanon's recommendations for opening a southern front through sub-Sahara Africa.

Joan Gillespie, writing on the Soummam perspectives of Abane, noted that despite being forced to flee Algeria (the interior) due to the intensification of the Battle of Algiers, when the CCE met at Tunis and formally in Cairo at the second CNRA conference, Abane continued to argue that the direction of the revolution had to come from the mass movement of the interior. This did not negate the necessity of military and guerrilla forms of engagement given the nature of the French occupation. For Abane, however, the mass movement of the Algerian people themselves was the soul and substance of the revolution, and the manifest new "reality of the nation." As organizer of the two general strikes that led to the Battle of Algiers, Abane comprehended the dialectics of revolution that made the organizational initiatives and policies of the FLN and ALN possible. His insistence that the mass movement dictate the political direction of military strategy, and not the other way around, also brought him into conflict with his fellow Kabyle, Belkacem Krim, who was the interior military leader for whom Abane originally served as political advisor.

At Soummam, the interior military leadership relegated control of the military campaign to itself to the exclusion of the exterior military leadership, while Abane successfully argued that overall leadership of the revolution be invested in the political leadership of the interior, thereby subordinating the role of the political leadership of the exterior. This reorganization was no mere power play. Abane had proven that the mass movement was the essence of the revolution through the mass insurrectionary strikes that culminated in the Battle of Algiers. Fanon, for his part, would demonstrate in *A Dying Colonialism* the new "reality of the nation" that the mass struggle had brought forth. Further plans for the mass strikes that Abane and his comrades organized and which led to the Battle of Algiers came out of the deliberations at Soummam, establishing the political struggle of the masses over the military campaigns in either the countryside or along the borders, and in opposition to the reformist politicians calling for a negotiated settlement.

However, once the Battle of Algiers, and the repression brought on in response to another "insurrectional strike" called after the Battle of Algiers, forced the interior leadership into exile, the tables had turned. When the CCE regrouped in Tunis, Krim was ready to entertain a military solution for a revolutionary problem. This is when the split between Krim and Abane occurred. By the second CNRA congress in Cairo, the interior military leadership was moving to a rapprochement with its exterior military counterpart. The organizational implications of this reconciliation were indeed dire: the military was widely suspected of the murder of Abane, with Krim the prime suspect. In Tunis and in Cairo, Abane passionately argued for the Soummam perspective that the direction of the revolution come from the mass struggle inside Algeria, and that political, not military, perspectives determine the course of the revolution.

There was, in other words, more than a question of organizational hegemony involved in Abane's perspectives for the Algerian Revolution; there was instead a question of the theoretical comprehension of the dialectic of the revolution's development and social deepening. Moreover, if, as Pirelli, the only Fanon biographer who was himself close to the FLN and the Algerian Revolution at the time, claims, Abane was both friend and model to Fanon

(Gendzier 1973, 283, n. 76), then Fanon's thinking on revolution and the party in *The Wretched of the Earth* lies not in an abstract belief in the spontaneity of the masses or in his supposed metaphysics of violence. Instead, the dialectic of a work like *The Wretched of the Earth* flows from the concrete and contradictory relations Fanon witnessed, and at many points participated in, between the organizational vicissitudes of the FLN, the theoretical perspectives of his revolutionary mentor Ramdane Abane, and the dialectics of the Algerian Revolution.

Behind the organizational machinations of the FLN after Soummam, which led to the murder of Abane, lay a metastasizing narrow nationalism whose debilitating effects on the Algerian Revolution Fanon uncompromisingly criticized in *The Wretched of the Earth*, a work that began with three lectures he gave to ALN cadre at Ghardimaou, in 1961. No doubt, it was the deadly consequences of these contradictory developments within the liberation movement that Fanon felt so painfully with the deaths of Abane and Lumumba. They were not only a consequence of the absence of ideology in the leadership circles of the national liberation parties, they marked the separation of the political party from the masses' struggles in which Ramdane Abane had labored so arduously to ground the FLN.

"THE LONG CRISIS BY WHICH A MULTIPLICITY BECOMES A UNITY": ORGANIZATION AND THE PITFALLS OF NATIONALISM

In one of two articles he wrote for *El Moudjahid* in September 1957, while the August-September 1957 congress of the CNRA was in session, Fanon's caricature of French rumors about FLN discord sounded strangely prescient:

> Quarrels are said to be on the point of breaking out within the FLN. The military are reportedly trying to take over the control of the movement. There is talk of a very tough fight between

extremists and moderates and of the Kabyles being ready to perpetuate a *coup d'état*. On top of all this, a showdown among the
colonels is supposed to be imminent. (Fanon 1967b, 61)

A second article he wrote in September 1957, while the Battle of
Algiers was in its last stages, suggests his further involvement in
FLN organizational debates. Like the previous one, this article, too,
is on a topic that does not appear initially to involve organizational
questions within the FLN. It addresses the issue of the French use
of torture. At the end of the piece, however, Fanon concludes,
"How can we modify our strategy and intensify our combat in
order that the national territory may be liberated at the earliest
possible moment? Any other consideration is radically foreign to
us" (Fanon 1967b, 72).

At the time he wrote this article, the CNRA had expanded the
CCE, mostly with military leaders, and was in the process of
reversing the perspectives of the Soummam Declaration. Fanon's
question—"How can we modify our strategy and intensify our
combat?"—is written at the very moment when the strategy of the
Soummam Congress was being modified by the Cairo Congress.
The question of intensifying the struggle is also significant, inasmuch as the Battle of Algiers is winding down (actually ending in
October 1957), and Abane planned to intensify the struggle with a
call for another general strike. It is quite conceivable then that the
intensification of the struggle Fanon had in mind was not only an
implicit reference to the Battle of Algiers and Abane's plans for a
fresh round of strikes, but an oblique reference in support of
Abane's perspectives against the *militaires*. In this organizational
context, Fanon's meaning is less opaque: only the mass struggle
can liberate the "national territory . . . at the earliest possible
moment," and "Any other consideration [i.e., those being proposed in Cairo by the *militaire*] is radically foreign to us."
    The older generation of leaders of the exterior like Ben Bella
who did have an international perspective (e.g., Ben Bella wrote
the introduction to Nelson Mandela's *No Easy Walk to Freedom*),

nevertheless, resorted to narrow nationalist appeals to win the support of a younger generation of army leaders and militants who entered the FLN after 1954. These young military leaders did not see in Abane's perspectives and the Soummam Declaration a new stage in the political direction of the revolution as much as a threat to the nationalism that brought them into the movement. Lacking political education about the new social reality that the Algerian masses were bringing into existence, these young militants were allowed to believe that Arab nationalism was the only legitimate claim of the Algerian revolution. It was this growing narrow nationalism within the ranks of FLN that Fanon addressed in his lectures in Ghardimaou.

When the GPRA was formed in September 1958, it included two formerly excluded members of the Soummam CCE, Ben Khedda and Dahlab. Although the provisional government now included these Left nationalist intellectuals formerly associated with Abane, the moderate Ferhat Abbas initially headed the GPRA. In August 1961 Ben Khedda and Dahlab became President and foreign minister of the provisional government, respectively, with Krim as vice-president. The latitude with which Fanon moved within the FLN and the positions and missions he was assigned were a result of the good offices of these former colleagues of Abane. Under the old CCE that came out of Soummam, Ben Khedda had headed propaganda work and Saad Dahlab had been in charge of foreign relations. Fanon's position on the editorial board of *El Moudjahid* and as the FLN's representative in Africa can be credited to these men. Ben Khedda headed the Algiers Autonomous Zone at the time of the Battle of Algiers when Fanon came in contact with him.

Ben Khedda and Abane Ramdane were the ideological heirs of the radical intellectuals in the Central Committee of the Messalist MTLD (Movement for the Triumph of Democratic Liberties), formed in 1946 by Hadj Ben Ahmed Messali, considered the founder of Algerian nationalism, and a figure who was active in the Communist Party in Lenin's time. Opposed to the "cult of personality" leadership style encouraged by Messali, Hussein Ait

Ahmed, one of the intellectual leaders of the Central Committee and, later, a founder of the FLN, argued that the MTLD should follow neither the Communists nor the reformists. Instead, Ait Ahmed and the committee argued that "the revolutionary must... descend from the pedestal of his theory to root himself in concrete life, in order to draw upon it and to verify there his principles of action" (Gillespie 1961, 80).[13] Ait Ahmed was the Kabyle mentor to Abane, and in the Kabyle tradition of the *djemma*, or Berber assemblies, favored collective leadership, and a democratic, secular state. The personalization of power in the hands of a single charismatic leader like Messali was now challenged, though not fully surpassed. As Fanon was to observe in *The Wretched of the Earth*, the leader at this stage serves as a screen for the national bourgeoisie to solidify its class prerogatives.

It so happens that the alienation of the nationalist leadership from the mass struggle, and the new reality of the nation that it engenders, ironically, leads to the idealization of a "lost" cultural heritage by the nationalist party and bourgeoisie. This idealization of the national culture assumes the character of a dogma when, inside the national movement with its living proletarian and peasant culture, there arises a new national politics and national consciousness to challenge the old nationalism. However, unless this new national consciousness becomes the basis for new historical organizational imperatives to transform society and new theoretical developments aimed at re-envisioning the "reality of the nation," the new not only signals the end of the old nationalist stage but the beginning of the end of its own social existence. Herein lies the "pitfalls of national consciousness" Fanon spent so much time critically evaluating in *The Wretched of the Earth*. "In fact, there must be an idea of man and of the future of humanity," he writes (203). Otherwise, "if nationalism is not made explicit, if it is not enriched and deepened by a very rapid transformation into a consciousness of social and political needs, in other words into humanism, it leads up a blind alley" (204).

This was no abstract *pronunciamento* on Fanon's part. For as early as his July 1956 letter of resignation in which he referred to the July 5th general strike that Abane had organized, the FLN saw in it "the popular character of the national revolution, expressed by the full participation of all social classes . . . intellectuals, workers, students, peasants alike" (Gillespie 1961, 131). Although space does not permit me here to go into the history of Algerian nationalism, the conflict between the idea of collective leadership and the organizational practice of "cult of personality" was a phenomenon Fanon also devoted much space to in *The Wretched of the Earth*. In this regard, too, Fanon understood that the struggle for national self-determination had to be independent of both Cold War superpower blocs. In this, he recognized that the struggle in the FLN over organizational hegemony was not only an expression of the class antagonisms in Algerian society but involved larger global forces.

From the MTLD, a group of young, working class militants broke away to form the CRUA (Comité Révolutionaire pour l'Unité et l'Action) in early 1954, among them Ait Ahmed, Ben Bella, Ben M'Hidi, Mohammed Khider, and Belkacem Krim. It was this group, at a clandestine meeting in Algiers, October 10, that made the decision to initiate some thirty synchronized attacks on French military and police installations on November 1, 1954, inaugurating the Algerian Revolution. On the eve of the insurrection, which involved some two to three thousand militants armed only with hunting rifles and small arms, the CRUA was transformed into the FLN and ALN. The original nine militants of the CRUA were seconded by such men as Abane (Kabylia), and Dahlab and Ben Khedda (Algiers). This leadership arrangement lasted until August 1956.

From the outset, the CRUA/FLN believed that only action could reconcile all of the quarreling factions and forge organizational unity. Indeed, revolution was defined by the CRUA militants as "the long crisis by which a multiplicity becomes a unity" (Gillespie 1971, 96). This overestimation of the role of revolutionary action, too, is found in Abane's and Fanon's thought. However, differences in the way in which action was to be interpreted, and under whose direction, surfaced in the FLN over military versus mass action, and military versus political leadership. Moreover, the Centralist (i.e., Central Committee) intellectual heritage concerning the need for theory, and going beyond national to social and economic liberation, also defined political differences in the FLN.

The notion of forging organizational unity through action was a recurrent theme and pitfall throughout the course of modern Algerian political history. In the second chapter of *The Wretched of the Earth* on the question of spontaneity and organization, Fanon critically examines political attempts to mystify revolutionary action, either that of the masses or that of the party, as a means of forging organizational unity.

Abane had also sought an indigenous Algerian road to revolution independent of either the Soviet bloc or Nasser, whereas Ben Bella and the CRUA subscribed to Nasserism both in the form of their organization and in their ideological appropriation of Nasser's "philosophy of faith" with its thinly disguised Bonapartist reliance on military initiatives.[14] The work of the Soummam Congress to draw up new perspectives for the FLN and the revolution represented as well Abane's attempt to break the FLN away from Nasserism. Soummam meant that now that action, both of armed militants and mass insurrectionary strikes, made organizational unity of Algeria's disparate nationalist tendencies possible, a new basis for the FLN could finally be theorized. In Abane's view, and Fanon's as well, the new organizational basis of the FLN was not the Nasserite military, but the movement from below of oppressed Algerian society. Abane saw that it was not the nationalists who stirred the people to united action, but the movement among the masses of "suffering Algeria" that stirred the nationalists to organizational unity and to defining their own indigenous theoretical perspectives. Tragically, Abane discovered, too late, as history would have it, the meaning of Lenin's aphorism: "Practice does not erase differences but enlivens them" (Dunayevskaya 1989, 8).

While Soummam represented a definitive but short-lived break from Nasserism, it theorized that in tandem with this new mass basis for carrying out the revolution would also come the strategic shortening of the conflict. That the organizational and ideological machinations within the FLN were expressions of the class divisions in Algerian society was not lost on Fanon. The Algerian peasantry had since the end of World War II sustained prolonged colonial repression under the French. Where the cities had prevented full-scale regulation of the Algerian population, even during the most intense periods of the Battle of Algiers, the countryside saw the implementation of the same population control tactics the French had used in Vietnam. In spite of this, or perhaps because of it, the peasant movement remained fluid. In fact, when the mass movement was periodically checked in the cities, the Algerian peasantry remained in motion throughout the revolution. After the death of Abane, the FLN radicals closest to the peasantry were the political cadre of the interior army, the very ones to whom Fanon delivered his 1961 lectures that were to become *The Wretched of the Earth*. Peter Geismar contends that the reason Fanon made three excursions to the Ghardimaou encampment to lecture on the pitfalls that follow a successful struggle for national liberation was Fanon's concern by 1961 "that a Moslem bourgeoisie would replace the European settlers without any real restructuring of Algerian society" (Geismar 1971, 179).

The serious turn that Fanon takes toward the peasantry, which is evident from the difference in subject matter found in *A Dying Colonialism* and *The Wretched of the Earth*, occurred after 1958.[15] Without a significant urban mass movement after 1957, bourgeois nationalist forces began to take over political control of the FLN. In other words, with the urban mass movement checked and with the peasantry having military but not political representation in the FLN, the bourgeois nationalists in league with the colonels assumed control of the FLN and the provisional government.

It is clear too that the fate of the external delegation in Cairo, Ben Bella and Co., went the way of Nasser's fortunes. Nasser's preoccupation with the Suez crisis and the subsequent drop in military supplies to the FLN were thus other factors that conditioned the estrangement of the interior from the exterior. The internal political situations in Tunisia and Morocco also influenced the FLN's internal politics. Tunisian President Bourguiba's reformist

"independence by stages," which was the basis of Tunisia's negotiated independence from France in 1956, was castigated by Ben
Bella. However, while Ben Bella and his associates could afford to
sound militant and critical of Morocco and Tunisia while under the
umbrella of Nasser, FLN militants based in Tunis had to adjust to
the political reality of a quite different situation when the defeat of
the more radical Neo-Destour party signaled the ascension of
Bourguiba.[16]

Fanon's demarcation of the first five years of the Algerian Revolution into pre- and post-1955–56 addressed the strategic as well
as theoretic content of these organizational conflicts. "Colonialism," he writes in A Dying Colonialism, a work published one
year after the murder of Abane and which must be viewed as
directed as much (if not more) to the FLN as to a French audience,

> shuts its eyes to the real facts of the problem. It imagines that our
> power is measured by the number of our heavy machine guns.
> This was true in the first months of 1955. It is no longer true
> today. First of all, because other elements have their weight in the
> scales of history. Next, because machine guns and cannons are no
> longer the weapons of the colonialist alone. . . . [T]he power of
> the Algerian Revolution henceforth resides in the radical muta-
> tion that the Algerian has undergone. (1967c, 31–32)[17]

The period from the beginning of the revolution to 1955–56 had
been directed by the Cairo "Club of Nine" as the external delegation was called. Abane's rise to political power in the FLN dates
from 1955, when the mass struggle began to intensify through the
mobilization of mass strikes, culminating in the Battle of Algiers
and the Soummam Congress in 1956.

In A Dying Colonialism, which he had originally intended to
title "The Reality of the Nation," Fanon was calling upon his comrades to once again recognize, in 1959, the primacy of the mass
movement over the military campaign. For all intents and purposes, the ALN military campaign had been shut down by
France's military operations, elevating the importance of the polit-

ical struggle. The coming to power of General Charles de Gaulle as head of the Fifth Republic in June 1958, and his shift to a more calculated political strategy in dealing with the insurrection through reforms and referenda aimed at enfranchising, and thus assimilating, Algerians placed the struggle on a different footing.

BIRTH OF A NEW DIALECTIC: WOMAN AS REVOLUTIONARY

The challenge of de Gaulle brought home the real significance of Ramdane Abane's Soummam perspectives and Fanon's concretization of them in *A Dying Colonialism*. The first announcement of the constitutional referendum of September 28 was made by de Gaulle during his tour of France's overseas territories in August. The referendum meant that every French colony, with the exception of Algeria, would have the opportunity to vote on remaining under neocolonial rule within the French Community. (Only small Guinea voted a resounding "No!") The effect of the referendum was to isolate the Algerian Revolution. De Gaulle scheduled Algeria to vote in a separate referendum on a new Algerian Constitution, not independence, under a single electoral college that was expanded to include women for the first time. This precipitated the FLN announcement, nine days before the September 28 referendum and simultaneously from Cairo, Tunis, and Rabat, that it had formed a provisional government.

The Algerian constitutional referendum was but the first of several elections and reforms de Gaulle extended to Algerian women. Writing in *A Dying Colonialism* Fanon noted that "the colonial strategy of destructuring Algerian society very quickly came to assign a prominent place to the Algerian woman" (1967c, 46). The provisional government called on the Algerian population to boycott the referendum. The complicating factor in this call was it ostensibly denied universal suffrage to Algerian women. After the first referendum on the Constitution, three more were held in November; then finally a referendum to decide Algerian independence was held. Through colonialist election-rigging and the FLN boycott, the results appeared, on the surface, predictable. Joan Gillespie offers a more telling view of the results, however:

> The results of the battle of the referendum: 96.5% "yes," 3.5% "no." This percentage refers to the division of valid votes; it does not tell the whole story. Of 4,335,009 registered voters, 3,445,060 cast ballots, of which 3,416,088 were valid: 3,299,908 voted "yes," 115,791 voted "no." From the registration figures, which no doubt includes virtually all eligible colons and French soldiers, it is clear that many Muslims, perhaps as many as 1,000,000, avoided registration, even though French soldiers personally visited many villages to obtain names of voters. These nonregistrants included not only the rebel forces, but Muslims most opposed to the French regime. The figures also indicate that almost 1,000,000 of those registered did not vote; the vast majority of these and, of course, of those who voted "no" were probably Muslims. Thus over 2,000,000 Muslims, almost half the adult population, managed to show its opposition to the French colonial regime in some way. (Gillespie 1961, 166)

With SAS, the psychological and propaganda division of the French military, heading up "the colonial strategy of destructuring Algerian society," with the capitulation of Muslim religious leaders who, at the behest of the French authorities, admonished women in their congregation to vote, with opportunist Muslim political leaders trying to appear as a "third force," with the French army taking the names of those who registered as a method of isolating FLN sympathizers, and finally, with the FLN calling for a boycott of the election, the Algerian masses still managed to show its opposition to de Gaulle's political strategy of cooptation and assimilation. Indeed, it was the need to decipher the meaning embedded in these events which impelled Fanon to take off three weeks in early 1959 to write *A Dying Colonialism*. In other words, as against the reality of an assimilated Algeria that de Gaulle was trying to conjure up through a hastily concocted reform program, and as against the unpreparedness of the FLN to recognize the political maturity of the Algerian masses, Fanon rushed into print with a work that disclosed the new "reality of the nation" that had now become manifest in the national consciousness of the most oppressed quarters of the population.

The revolutionary transformation of the Algerian woman was the central motivation behind Fanon's writing *A Dying Colonialism*. In the struggle of the colonized and colonizer, the apparent inertia of certain elements of the native's culture comes to life. Which doesn't mean that Fanon uncritically accepted the behavior, customs, and culture of the colonized as "progressive." On the contrary, he recognized that "The colonialist's relentlessness, his methods of struggle were bound to give rise to reactionary forms of behavior on the part of the colonized" (1967c, 46). Or, as he was later to state in *The Wretched of the Earth*: "The struggle for freedom does not give back to the national culture its former value and shape" (1968, 245–46). The *haïk*, or Algerian veil, is "given new life" due to the colonialist's "deliberately aggressive intentions, whereas formerly it was a dead element of the Algerian cultural stock—dead because stabilized, without any progressive change in form or color" (Fanon 1967c, 46). Thus, "In an initial phase, it is the action, the plans of the occupier that determine the centers of resistance around which a people's will to survive becomes organized" (Fanon 1967c, 47).

The first chapter in *A Dying Colonialism* is not only sequentially but is consequentially primary in Fanon's mapping of the new "reality of the nation." It is precisely here, in the discussion of cultural domination and the artifacts of gender subjugation, that the question of violence arises unexpectedly. Fanon emphasizes that the culture of the colonized is fabricated from without by agents of the colonial regime, and that the violent reaction of the colonized is against the object of the colonizer's attention. This impels the colonizer's further attempt to "modify" the behavior of the colonized, indeed, to modify the very identity of the colonized because it has become the object of the latter's resistance. It is the new emphasis the colonized give to their culture, or rather to its transformation, which makes its appearance as a cultural reality coexisting in the form of conflict and latent warfare. This conflict of two worlds produces an atmosphere of social insecurity that signals a revolution in both worlds. The new content that infuses the culture of the colonized comes from this revolution, upsetting its own traditional, patriarchal arrangements and customs.

Fanon illustrates this in reviewing the position the FLN was forced to adopt in face of the profound changes that Algerian women were undergoing regarding their place in traditional society. Despite the failure of the FLN to include these changes in its program, though, Fanon contends that through the "practice of the Revolution the people have understood that the problems are resolved in the very movement that raises them" (Fanon 1967c, 48). He again refers to the transitional year 1955, maintaining that "Until 1955, the combat was waged exclusively by the men" (1967c, 47). In arguing that the very conception of the combat had to be modified, Fanon is re-emphasizing the changes in the revolution's direction inaugurated by Abane and articulated in the Soummam Declaration, which devoted a section to the role of women in the revolution. The urgency to make the revolution total, Fanon argues, meant recognizing the new subjective element in the struggle women represented. In terms which recall his university studies of Hegel's *Phenomenology of Spirit* and the German philosopher's treatment of Sophocles' tragic drama *Antigone*, Fanon claims that the participation of Algerian women was so new and original a phenomenon that their historic emergence represented both "an authentic birth in a pure state, without preliminary instruction, [and] an intense dramatization, a continuity between the woman and the revolutionary [that] rises to the level of tragedy" (1967c, 50)

The "considerable number of taboos" (Fanon 1967c, 51) that the colonized must overcome in undertaking action against the violent maintenance of colonial oppression brings to mind Antigone's tragic challenge to the official taboos of the state in her liberatory act in defense of the memory of her brother. In Hegel, as in Fanon, there is a "continuity between the woman and the revolutionary." At the source of the "continuity between the woman and the revolutionary" lies a deep and abiding social memory of the Algerian woman's revolutionary opposition to nineteenth-century colonial and earlier precolonial patriarchy, that is, a social memory of *woman as revolutionary*.[18] The Soummam Declaration referred to the participation of women in every insurrection against French domination since the beginning of French colonialism in 1830.

Perhaps it is not accidental then that Fanon's theory of violence should begin here, in his discussion of the Algerian woman as revolutionary, considering her engagement in "fighting two colonialisms" (see Urdang 1979). Fanon finds in the Algerian woman's unveiling of herself and retrieval of her body and mind from the "two colonialisms" of Muslim and Western patriarchy a new dialectic of the body and the world (Fanon 1967c, 59).

In locating the question of violence in the revolutionary transformation of the Algerian woman, Fanon has returned to the philosophic investigations of the Hegelian master-slave dialectic he began in *Black Skin, White Masks*. There, his testing of the Hegelian dialectic with the additive of race, while disclosing deeper revolutionary impulses than those manifested on the basis of a simple class reading of Hegel, revealed that the black (male) slave also manifested qualities which did not get beyond the self-limiting desire of merely wanting to substitute himself for the master.[19] The Algerian Revolution, particularly Fanon's discovery that the transformation of the Algerian woman represented its most revolutionary impulses, showed him just how "total and absolute" (Fanon 1967b, 72) the revolutionary Reason of a new "reality of the nation" had to be. His deepening the master-slave dialectic, this time, not only according to class and race prerogatives but inseparable from its "feminine ferment," intimated that Fanon would have considered the "new dialectic" of *woman as revolutionary* the turning point in the transcendence of the contradictions of the master-slave dialectic he confronted in *Black Skin*, simply because it (the new dialectic) constitutes "the innermost and most objective moment of Life and Spirit, by which a subject is personal and free." (Hegel 1969, 836).[20]

Fanon's claims for the revolutionary character of the Algerian woman have been assailed from many quarters,[21] the most common argument being that after the revolution she was once again forced back under the veil. The fact that today's Algerian woman continues to be the "object" of struggle among Islamic fundamentalists, the government, and Algerian progressives, especially feminists, on the one hand, and has become a regular target of murderous reprisals by fundamentalists (and many suspect the government) wishing to place her under strict Muslim law, on the other, suggests that reports of the Algerian woman's retreat from resistance are surely premature.

Once Fanon's theoretical work is estranged from the dialectics of organization, as Fanon confronted them within the objective propulsion of his times, his critics, ironically, begin to express the same incomprehension of the dialectics of the Algerian Revolution found within the leadership circles of the FLN. Thus, far from the philosophic content of Fanon's views on the Algerian woman having no relevance beyond either the programmatic aims of the FLN, or alternatively, postcolonial discourses regarding representations of the veil that Fanon supposedly did not comprehend, his writings on the Algerian woman as revolutionary represent his concretization of the dialectical investigations he had published in *Black Skin, White Masks* the year before he entered revolutionary Algeria, and into new adventures of the dialectic.

NOTES

1. In the new introduction to the 1985 edition of her 1973 "critical study" of Fanon, Irene Gendzier, devoted much of her space to discussing the importance of this, in turn, "regretting" not "further clarifying" Fanon's relation to various political tendencies in the FLN, or acknowledging that her "decreased" attention to the details of the history of the Algerian movement was a result of it being a "difficult assignment." "Had my emphasis been less on the experiences of the man and more on the evolution of the movement," admits Gendzier, "a richer map of both would have emerged, and some of the pitfalls in the FLN's self-image could have been more properly addressed" (Gendzier 1985, xi).

2. In 1959, the jeep in which Fanon was riding along the Moroccan-

Algerian border was blown up, in circumstances, Geismar tells us, that remain unclear. Because he worked in FLN clinics along the Moroccan and Tunisian frontiers, it is likely that he was either en route to or returning from one of the clinics when his jeep exploded, fracturing twelve spinal vertebrae and leaving the lower half of his body almost totally paralyzed. It was rumored that the "circumstances" surrounding this incident involved the same kind of fratricidal assassination attempt that killed Abane a year earlier.

3. Oddly enough, the Panaf Great Lives volume on Fanon is so narrowly Third Worldist in its ideological orientation that although it has the merit of recognizing the relationship between Fanon and the radical wing of the FLN which organized the crucial 1956 Soummam Congress and publishes extracts from the proceedings of the congress, it never once mentions Ramdane Abane, the FLN leader most responsible for organizing the congress. It seems that whereas Panaf is sharp in its critique of reformist forces within the FLN like the bourgeois politician Ferhat Abbas, it is less willing to wade into the murky waters of organizational fratricide among the nonreformist forces in the FLN who may have been responsible for the murder of Ramdane Abane.

4. See Nigel Gibson's perceptive examination of Fanon's treatment of the role of the Radio Free Algeria, "Jammin' the Airwaves and Tuning into the Revolution: The Dialectics of Radio in *L' An V de la révolution algérienne*," in *Fanon: A Critical Reader* (Gibson 1996).

5. From Gendzier's vague summary of the "number of clarifications and corrections" Josie Fanon provided her regarding Gendzier's treatment of facts and events, it is not clear that her conflicting references to Fanon's departure from Algeria has been clarified. On the contrary, Gendzier indicates in her new introduction (1985) that only "minor changes" were made to her work. Because she issues one of the most damning accusations at Fanon "concerning violence," based on when he left Algiers and the timing of the Battle of Algiers, clarifying such a contradiction surely constitutes more than a "minor change." See new introduction, 1985, x; xix, n. 12.

6. Illustrative of Abane's conception of basing FLN propaganda on the truth, Fanon candidly dealt with the difficulties of enforcing organizational discipline in cases where militants gave in to violent excesses. As against the overworked notion that Fanon was an "apostle of violence" (a notion recapitulated by Gendzier), consider the following from *A Dying Colonialism*:

Because we want a democratic and a renovated Algeria, because
we believe one cannot rise and liberate oneself in one area and
sink in another, we condemn, with pain in our hearts, those
brothers who have flung themselves into revolutionary action
with almost physiological brutality that centuries of oppression
give rise to and feed. (Fanon 1967c, 25)

7. Once again, Gendzier's new introduction to the 1985 edition of
her book is revealing. From the "classification" she borrows from "one
former militant" (Mohammed Harbi), who characterized Fanon as
belonging "to those aligned with the urban, jacobin, centralizing element
associated with Ramdane [Abane]," it's evident that Gendzier, perhaps
unknowingly, has identified herself with one of the anti-Fanon/Abane
faction of the original FLN. Harbi was a "socialist advisor" to Ben Bella.

Edward Behr, a liberal historian of the Algerian revolution, is also
reductionist in his characterization of the FLN as "urban terrorists."
However, his account has the merit of at least giving us a description of
the revolutionary process that is quite at odds with what the designation
"terrorist" conjures up in our imagination today. The avowed aim of the
FLN and of the leaders of the "Zone autonome d'Alger"

was to bring the city of Algiers to its knees by indiscriminate terrorism [sic], and they very nearly succeeded. The Algiers Kasbah
was a superb natural hiding place; despite French claims that at
no time were more than 4,500 Algerians directly concerned with
terrorism (out of a total population of 450,000), it seems certain
that the terrorists benefited from the complicity of a huge
majority of the Moslem population, as well as from the aid of a
small number of Europeans. Among those arrested and convicted for having taken part in terrorist activity during this
period were employees of the Algiers gas and electricity services;
postmen and post office clerks; students, doctors, tradesmen,
custom officials, even Moslem police officers and a prominent
"bachaga", the Bachaga Boutaleb, whose nationalist sympathies
overcame his basically pro-French sentiments. Practically no
Moslem representative of Algiers society was lacking, from the
most humble welders and dockers to the wealthy members of
tiny Algiers Moslem "bourgeoisie" and including that well-
known element of Kasbah society, the pimps and petty racke-
teers. (Behr 1961, 114–15)

8. The complex relationship of Abane and Abbas must be considered in the context of World War developments in Algerian nationalism. According to Joan Gillespie,

> In December 1942 Ferhat Abbas and a number of other prominent Algerian elected representatives presented a series of demands. . . . The proclamation of the Manifesto of the Algerian People of 10 February 1943 was a cardinal step in the development of Algerian nationalism. . . . The Manifesto . . . called for the application of the right of self-determination, and for a constitution for Algeria guaranteeing the absolute liberty and equality of all inhabitants without distinction of race or creed. . . . The Manifesto ends with the declaration that the Muslims could not wait until the end of the war for needed reforms.
>
> This document, bitter and sometimes revolutionary in tone, was signed by Ferhat Abbas, Dr. Bendjelloul and other prominent Muslims of more conservative views. It represents the most serious condemnation of the French regime in Algeria made up to that date by moderates and Westernized intellectuals who had previously hoped for full participation in French cultural life. (Gillespie 1961, 53–54)

The similarities between the Manifesto and Abane's Soummam Declaration are striking. Abbas's role in the creation of the Manifesto clarifies Abane's efforts to have Abbas participate in the FLN in 1956, despite others' dismissal of him as "reformist." Abane understood that Algerian nationalism didn't simply spring up with his adversary, Ben Bella. He therefore sought a continuity with Algerian nationalism by bringing all progressive nationalist tendencies into the Soummam conference. The Manifesto, later called the Additif, has also called for a North African federation among Algeria, Morocco, and Tunis.

9. Supposedly, due to a series of misunderstandings regarding the date of the congress, the leaders of the exterior, most notably Ben Bella, did not attend the Soummam Congress. The major figures in the FLN leadership constituted an exile leadership that usually held its organizational conferences abroad in Arab or European countries. Soummam was the only such conference held on Algerian soil which the French had pronounced pacified territory during the revolution.

10. In October 1970, Belkacem Krim was murdered in a Frankfurt

hotel; the year before he had been convicted of "treason and conspiring to assassinate top leaders of the country" (Gendzier 1973, 238).

11. There is some discrepancy over the date of Abane's murder. Alistair Horne gives December 26, 1957, as the date (1977, 133). This seems a little early. The Battle of Algiers only winds down in October 1957, and Abane was preparing to call for another general strike. Moreover, the Cairo conference is held in September. Gillespie (1961, 99–100), Gendzier (1973, 197), and Renate Zahar (1974, xii), relying on Giovanni Pirelli, all give early 1958 as the date of Abane Ramdane's murder.

12. The Meurice-Challe Line, an electrified line and minefield that the French constructed in 1957 along the Algeria-Tunisia border and guarded by 40,000 troops, severed the exterior military forces from the interior military campaign. This effectively cut off the interior from fresh arms supplies. According to Edward Behr,

> Once the arms were in Tunisia or Morocco the problem remained that of bringing them into Algeria and of distributing them fairly. It was obvious that the *Wilaya* commanders nearest the Tunisian or Moroccan borders were better placed to receive fresh arms consignments than *Wilaya* commanders in the centre of Algeria, and the reluctance of the "frontier" *Wilaya* commanders to allow consignments through and their tendency to increase their own reserves at the expense of the *Wilayas* of the centre led to bitter recriminations. (Thus, for a year and a half after the rebellion began, the Wilaya number 3 [Kabylia] was still mainly armed with shotguns while FLN units in the Oranais and Constantinois areas were far better equipped.) (Behr 1961, 109).

13. Gillespie writes that "In defending itself against Messali's charges the expelled Central Committee stated:

> The conflict had as its cause the questions of leadership and methods. . . . [Messali] was against theoretical work looking to the establishment of a precise doctrine which would permit the carrying out of the struggle on more and more scientific rational bases, because he was afraid of being by-passed.

This nationalism now too favored by the Centralists above the 'adventurism' of Messali, was founded neither upon race nor upon religion but was essentially the 'will to struggle for the political, economic, social and cultural liberation of the Algerian people'" (1961, 86).

14. The pull of Nasserism was often more pragmatic than ideological, according to Gillespie:

> In Cairo, a number of politicians . . . , jockeying for position and hoping perhaps to offset the preponderance of the "military" clique around Ben Bella, signed a "Protocol of General Union" on January 11, 1955. It proclaimed Algeria to be "Arab and Moslem," an integral part of the Arab Maghrib, itself a part of the "Arab fatherland." (1961, 185)

No doubt, Kabyle leaders like Krim, Dahlab, Ben Khedda, and Abane hearing of this were even more motivated to establish the secular, democratic basis of the future Algerian state articulated in the Soummam Declaration. A rather different view is offered in September 1955, by an unidentified FLN leader (perhaps Abane):

> [Our] political training is uniquely based on the national ideology. We are, above all, Algerians. Certainly, Islam cannot flourish under colonialism; for me, this may be one more reason to act. But we do not ask our members if they are Muslim. We have perhaps atheists. We would accept a Jew, a Protestant, a Catholic provided that he has decided to struggle for the National Liberation. (Gillespie 1961, 124–25)

As we saw earlier, it was precisely these tensions Lacoste aimed to exploit.

15. Outside of the difference in subject matter of the two works, the more profound philosophic difference between them was a consequence of the contradictory developments within the FLN and Africa's liberation struggles Fanon witnessed in the last two years of his life. In the fifth year of the Algerian Revolution, he could assert confidently that *A Dying Colonialism*

> shall show that the form and the content of national existence already exist in Algeria and that there can be no turning back. While in many colonial countries it is the independence acquired by a party that progressively informs the diffuse national consciousness of the people, in Algeria it is the national consciousness . . . that make[s] it inevitable that the people must take its destiny into its own hands. (1967c, 28)

The Wretched of the Earth, however, is a troubled presentiment of the crisis already befalling this new "reality of the nation" as a result of the ideological and organizational contradictions within the party and leadership circles of the independence movements. Which is why we may have taken too literally Geismar's claim that the idea for a book on the Algerian Revolution Fanon originally had in mind had changed by March 1961 to one which was to be "a more general study of Third World upheaval" (1971, 179). We may have, in other words, overlooked the fact that Fanon's critical evaluation of the Algerian Revolution was still at the conceptual center of *The Wretched of the Earth.*

16. Perhaps this, and the fact that he was Ben Bella's "chief adviser on socialism" (Humbaraci 1966, 85), explains Mohammed Harbi's recent slander in Isaac Julien's cinematic gloss on Fanon, "Black Skin, White Mask," that Fanon was associated with conservative tendencies in the FLN. The political cadre of the ALN that Fanon lectured to on the pitfalls of postindependence development at Ghardimaou were the very same intellectuals Arslan Humbaraci believed were the only group prepared to work out the problems of Algerian society after the revolution. According to Joan Gillespie, upon finding himself isolated in Tunis in 1957, Abane began to work on the economic questions that Algeria would face after the revolution. In a quite interesting twist, it may have been Abane and Fanon's concerns about postindependence Algeria and both men's theoretical efforts to map the terrain of future pitfalls, as well as provide economic and organizational blueprints, that found their way into Ben Bella's famous 1962 Tripoli Program coauthored by Mohammed Yahyia and Harbi. Gendzier describes the Tripoli Program as embodying "nothing less than a programmatic definition of the Algerian Revolution and its objectives" (1973, 242). She also writes that Fanon's brother, Joby, "recalled conversations that took place in Fanon's Tunis home, . . . where the subjects discussed were subsequently to become part of the Tripoli program" (1973, 242). Due to his own studies of agrarian problems in the Antilles, Joby Fanon was already conversant with the issues of agrarian development that preoccupied Fanon and Abane. In fact, as far back as Fanon's involvement with Aimé Césaire's 1946–47 failed electoral campaign in Martinique, Joby had pointed out to Frantz the weaknesses of Césaire's campaign as its failure to reach the agrarian masses in the countryside. See Geismar's reference to Joby Fanon's article on agrarian reform, "Autonomie et économie des Antilles" (1971, 41–42, note).

17. Fanon's confidence in this revolutionary transformation of the

Algerian, especially the deepest strata of Algerian society which he brings to life in *A Dying Colonialism*, was not misplaced. At the conclusion of the revolution, when civil war broke out between ALN units from several *wilayas*, as Boumedienne prepared to march into Algiers, Humbaraci describes the following scene:

> Then suddenly the civil war came to an abrupt halt. Not as the result of political action or any change of heart on the part of Boumedienne (who proceeded to enter Algiers as planned), but because the people of Algiers, among them women bearing children in their arms, threw themselves between the fighting men (the armed bands of Algiers-*Wilaya* IV, Kabyle units of *Wilaya* III and the [very Islamicized] Saharan forces of *Wilaya* VI locked in a fratricidal struggle in Algeria). "We want bread. We don't want war", they shouted. "*Baraket, Sabla s'nine, baraket*—Enough, seven years of it, enough!" The ALN officers, ashamed, grounded their troops' arms. When the Political Bureau, victorious at last, appeared on the balcony of the Forum . . . there were only a couple of thousand Algerians to applaud them. Independence found the Algerian people cruelly wounded and sick at heart. (1966, 79–80)

18. This is indicative of Raya Dunayevskaya's discovery of Marx's concept of the "feminine ferment" in history, mythology, and in revolution. "Marx held that the Greek goddesses on Olympus were not just statues, but expressed myths of past glories that may, in fact, have reflected a previous stage, and/or expressed a desire for a very different future" (Dunayevskaya 1996, 201).

19. For a discussion of Fanon's earlier treatment of Hegel's master-slave dialectic in *Black Skin*, see my essay "On the Difference between the Hegelian and Fanonian Dialectic of Lordship and Bondage," in *Fanon: A Critical Reader* (Turner 1996).

20. I have in mind here Raya Dunayevskaya's reading of this formulation in the Absolute Idea chapter of Hegel's *Science of Logic*. See Dunayevskaya 1989, 33.

21. T. Denean Sharpley-Whiting's recent work, *Frantz Fanon: Conflicts and Feminisms*, which is the only full-length treatment of this crucial category in Fanon's thought, succeeds in avoiding this pitfall, in large part because she does not separate Fanon from his time, nor crucially from the dialectics of revolution.

16.

Radical Mutations: Fanon's Untidy Dialectic of History

Nigel Gibson

Comrades, let us flee this motionless movement where gradually the dialectic is changing into the logic equilibrium. Let us reconsider the question of mankind. . . . For Europe, for ourselves, and for humanity, comrades, we must turn over a new leaf, we must work out new concepts, and try to set afoot a new man.   Fanon

THE SUBJECT/OBJECT DIALECTIC

It is rigorously false to pretend and to believe that this decolonization is the fruit of an objective dialectic *which more or less rapidly assumed the appearance of an absolutely inevitable mechanism.*   Fanon

Frantz Fanon is perhaps best remembered for his powerful descriptions of, and prescriptions for, a violent engagement with colonialism whose Manichean logic, derived from "belonging or not belonging to a certain race, a given species" (1968, 40), inexorably determines an individual's social position. To read *The Wretched of the Earth* is to receive an unforgettable instruction in a lexicon of dehumanization—the "reptilian motions . . . the stink of the native quarter . . . of breeding swarms . . . of hysterical masses . . . those distended bodies . . . that laziness stretched out in the sun . . . that vegetative rhythm of life" (1968, 42–43). It is furthermore supposed that characterizing the colonized and colonizer as two different species, who subsist in a relationship of *mutual Manichean exclusivity*, Fanon's contention that the settler and native inhabit opposed categories, "not in the service of a higher unity [but] obedient to the rules of pure Aristotelian logic" (1968, 38) should lay to rest any notion of dialectics in his work. Yet understanding Fanon requires that we recognize "the difference between the settler's logic and the *apparently similar* logic of the colonized," as Robert Bernasconi has pointed out, contending, too, "there is the Aristotelian logic of the colonizer and, on the other hand, the dialectical logic that responds to it. It is through the dialectic that the new humanism avoids reduplicating the logic of the old humanism" (1996, 118). The response and the new humanism, what Fanon calls an original idea, is absolute for Fanon. Unlike Aristotle's absolute, Fanon's does not lie in metaphysics but in "the replacing of certain 'species' of men by another 'species' of men" within the historical context of decolonization.

How might we understand a dialectic that is not a synthesis but an "absolute" opposition? Can we do this by recalling the notion of the fragmented subject, who has experienced the shattering of everything that is solid and secure, a characteristic of the bondsman in Hegel's master/slave dialectic that Fanon considers directly in *Black Skin, White Masks*? My aim is not to reiterate Fanon's philosophic pedigree, nor simply to separate Hegel from vulgar Hegelianism,[1] but to investigate the way Fanon negotiates and reconfigures self-alienation (in an Hegelian sense),[2] through a dialectic of negativity. Further, I want to suggest that these reconfigurations could have much to say not only about the value of Hegel's dialectic in an age dominated by poststructuralism but also begin to criticize the caricature of dialectic (which is equated with imperialism, racism, and communism) in postcolonial studies.

Hegel's absolutes end in syntheses whereas like Marx, Fanon's absolute ends in "total *diremptions*—absolute, irreconcilable contradictions" (Dunayevskaya 1988, 93) which are at the heart of the program of "complete disorder" put forward by decolonization. Whether Fanon's direct relationship to Hegel can be fully sustained (see Turner 1989, 1996; Sekyi-Otu 1996) depends on a different conception of the Hegelian dialectic than the one usually offered—one that views the dialectic as *movement* through absolute, irreconcilable contradictions. In contrast to a static, inert Manicheanism, I want to emphasize both the unstable, critical, and creative moment of negativity and transcendence in Fanon's thought.

Such a conceptualization of dialectical negativity puts in question the apparent parallelism between Fanon's description of the static colonial/racial Manicheanism and his description of the creativity and movement of national liberation. In other words, the difference between the colonial period—where "the settler makes history . . . , is the absolute beginning . . . [and] is the unceasing cause" (1968, 51)—and the period of national liberation—where "the 'thing' which has been colonized" becomes an historical protagonist (to use Gramsci's term)—turns on fleshing out the meaning of a dialectic of revolution in Fanon's thought.

This is not to undermine Fanon's powerful description of colonial reality and the thinking it embodies, nor to deny that the native *takes over* this way of thinking and uses it against the colonizers. However, that very appropriation, the very wish to "take over" the place of the colonialists is not simply a substitution. Rather it marks the historical moment when the native begins to be released from the crushing objecthood of totalitarian colonial reality and disrupts the spatial ordering central to the colonial regime. It is this historical movement, namely national liberation, its drama and unfolding, including negotiating its misadventures, overcoming its contradictions and making the process intelligible—i.e., giving it a direction—that preoccupies Fanon in *The Wretched of the Earth*.

Decolonization is an historical *process*, not an historical inevitability: "It is rigorously false," Fanon argues in a 1960 article on African liberation, "to pretend and to believe that this decolonization is the fruit of an *objective dialectic*" (Fanon 1967b, 170). And at the very point in *The Wretched of the Earth* that Fanon speaks of decolonization as a "program of complete disorder" he adds:

that is to say that it cannot be understood, it cannot become intelligible nor clear to itself except in the exact measure that we discern the movements which give it *historical form and content*.
(1968, 36, my emphasis)

Out of the timeless spatial vortex of colonial Manicheanism, with
its lines of force keeping everything in place, "the thing becomes
man during the same process by which it frees itself" (1968, 36–37).
Far from a simple substitution of one species for another, the very
process of substitution indicates the transition from Manichean to
dialectical logic where the "will to liberty is expressed in terms of
time and space" (1968, 240). Such a process of dialectical movement is purposefully directed toward a fully realized liberation.
The movement from colonial to post-colonial society is also a move
away from the dominance of the spatial. Whereas Fanon's survey
of colonial spacing in "Concerning Violence" recapitulated the
ordering of Césaire's Martinique described in the opening of
Cahier d'un retour au pays natal, Fanon's vision of a society liberated
from colonialism is embedded in his description of colonial com-
partmentalization.

> If we examine closely this system of compartments, we will at
> least be able to reveal the lines of force it implies. This approach
> to the colonial world, its ordering and its geographical layout,
> will allow us to mark out the lines on which a decolonized
> society will be reorganized. (1968, 38)

Decolonization involves more than eradicating the lines of force—
the police station, barracks, and border check points—that keep the
zones apart. Rather, Fanon echoes Marx's call to make the revolution "permanent."[3] Continuous revolution—a continuously
unfolding dialectic and constant criticism, as Marx put it—is central
to what Fanon means by "transform[ing] the national revolution
into a social revolution" (1967c, 169). Fanon's reference to the revolution's "form and content" and his insistence that the creation of
new subjectivities are not the result of "supernatural powers" but
are born in the revolutionary process, are reminiscent of Marx's

Eighteenth Brumaire, which Fanon had quoted approvingly in *Black Skin, White Masks*: The revolution, Marx wrote, "cannot begin with itself before it has stripped itself of all superstitions concerning the past"; it must find its "own content" rather than "drug [itself] against [its] own content." It was the content "exceeding the form," as Marx put it, that Fanon uncovered in the Algerian revolution.

To find an appropriate content, to transcend the colonial vortex, requires investigating the subjective side of the subject/object dialectic, namely how subjectivity becomes objectivity through revolutionary praxis, or as he put it in his "Letter to the Resident Minister," "a subjective attitude in *organized* contradiction with reality" (1968b, 53). Such a dialectic appears in Fanon's profound re-telling, in chapter 2 of *The Wretched of the Earth*, of the *lived experience* of anti-colonial political activity. Fanon offers more than a mere empirical account. Under the pressure of his analysis, the activities described disclose an experience that "explodes the old colonial truths and reveals unexpected facets which bring out new meanings and pinpoints the contradictions camouflaged by these facts" (Fanon 1968, 147). Spontaneous activity reaches for a self-understanding not restricted by Manicheanism. In its unfolding as a self-referential absolute, "the rebellion gives proof of its rational basis" (Fanon 1968, 146). This "rational basis" indicates a path beyond a postmodernist appreciation of Fanon's insights about Manicheanism which takes seriously his claims as a revolutionary theoretician.

Fanon's invocation to action is more than a rhetorical fillip to conclude his analysis of the racial Manicheanism of the colonial condition. It is often lamented that Fanon's claims about "The Revolution" creating the "new person" are naive, and even a dangerously utopian addenda to his explication of colonial relations (see Memmi 1971). These caveats, however, betray a banal understanding of the place of activity, and especially the notion of violence in Fanon's thought. Like Marx's analysis of proletarian revolution in *The Eighteenth Brumaire*, Fanon's painstaking working out of the revolution conceives the "new person," not as a miraculous creation immediately begot by violent activity, but as a product of a constant movement and principled criticism. Such criticism is not a priori. The disappearance of the colonized and the appearance of a new humanity "is prefigured in the objectives and methods of the conflict" (Fanon 1968, 197). Such objectives, while certainly historical, are neither simple reflections of spontaneous activity nor pre-existing aims. Neither content with praising the movement's strengths or criticizing its weaknesses, this prefiguration is a fruit of the hard labor of a social movement's "tarrying with the negative."

Given the dismal and frequently horrific consequences of revolution that this century has seen, such claims for the redemptive power of revolution to transform life for the better may seem little more than dreams of another era. Nevertheless, to misrepresent Fanon as a cultural conservative upholding the "traditional"[4]—the common conclusion when Fanon is viewed as an advocate of Manicheanism—is a willful distortion since Fanon sees culture as an effect of the relations of power. Thus the revolution will undermine the material/ideological basis of "traditional" culture. Just as he proclaims in *A Dying Colonialism* that the Algerian revolution has proved the truth of "the thesis that men change at the same time that they change the world" (Fanon 1967b, 30), he insists that national liberation will create radical changes in culture.

In the following, I consider Fanon's immanent dialectic in his essays on medicine and on the radio in *A Dying Colonialism*.[5] Unlike *The Wretched of the Earth*, which was written with the context of the counterrevolution in the revolution (not only from the nationalist middle class but also from within the "revolutionary" organization itself[6]) in mind, *A Dying Colonialism* focuses on the tremendous changes which Fanon calls "the radical mutations" that result in and from the process of revolution. This realization of radical mutation, grounded in the political experimentation of the revolution has a metaphysical and an ontological significance for Fanon [see 1968b, 24]). What Fanon theorizes as a radical mutation occurs at the intersection of spontaneity and organization. By "organization," I mean both as a reference to the framework and epistemic structures of intellectual communication and exchange, as well as the resources the people draw on as they reflect on their revolutionary experiences. In other words, the "strength of spontaneity" not only refers to mass activity but also the meaning brought by the intellectual, namely a Fanon, who helps those in the rebellion reach beyond themselves to the type of "essential" self-understanding he describes in *The Wretched of the Earth*: It is "the *essence* of the fight which explodes old colonial truths and reveals unexpected facets, which bring about new meanings" (Fanon 1968, 147, my emphasis).

Some political implications of this dialectic of knowledge, action, and experience emerge when Fanon, neither an advocate of the introduction of modern techniques nor an antimodernist, gives us another view of "the essence of the fight" and the production of "new meanings." The changing attitude to medicine and the radio show how, in the heat of the battle, these techniques can be "taken over," used, and comprehended in totally different ways—"stripping them of their superstitions."

FROM MANICHEANISM TO DIALECTICS

Because it is a systematic negation of the other person and a furious determination to deny the other person all attributes of humanity, colonialism forces the people it dominates to ask themselves the question constantly: "In reality, who am I?"   Fanon

Antibiotic Attitudes

The colonized exerts a considerable effort to keep away from the colonial world.   Fanon

In Fanon's schematic mapping of anticolonial activity—which in effect imitates the two modes of logic under consideration here, the Manichean and the dialectical—the organization of the first resistance is *determined* by the colonizer. That is to say the actions of the occupier "determine the centers around which a people's will to survive becomes organized" (Fanon 1967c, 47). From various cultural constellations of discontents, a "whole universe of resistances" develops "to justify the rejection of the occupier's presence" (Fanon

1967c, 93). These protests represent an obstinate allegiance to the "traditional," not because of any inherent value in the "traditional," but because the "traditional" had offered a refuge from colonial predations—a form of repudiation of, or resistance to, the colonizer who has been bent on destroying those "traditions." Fanon calls this negativity a "defense mechanism." Such resistances were characteristic of the whole period of colonialism in Algeria up to 1954.

The native's hostile reaction to everything French is characteristic of this Manichean stance, at first glance reminiscent of Hegel's description of the skeptical consciousness in *The Phenomenology* which enjoys being contentious for its own sake, which says B to the other's A and A to the other's B. But the natives' reaction to everything French may not be in their own interests. The native rejects values even if they might "be objectively worth choosing" (1967c, 62), only because they are the values of the occupier. This tendency to stand against anything colonialism introduces simply because it is colonial, and to appraise all the colonizer's contributions in a pejorative way, is in fact an expression of the native's absolutism described by Fanon in his essay on "Medicine and Colonialism."

We would think that any society would unreservedly welcome knowledge or discovery of methods to ease pain and promote health. But rather than recognizing advanced medical technology as an improvement, the colonized view such technology as "proof of the extension of the occupier's hold on the country." The native's reaction, like Hegel's skeptic, might seem childish but it is rooted very much in reality.[7] In the colonial world, the colonial doctor very often is associated with the army, and is thus *correctly* perceived as part of a system that functions as a policeman. In this atmosphere there is real difficulty in being "objective." There is no objective truth.

Aided by our "healthy" skepticism of the medical establishment, medicine in the West is characterized by our trust and goodwill. The Hippocratic oath is taken seriously, and there is a whole series of checks to enforce a medical ethics. In the colonies the "truth objectively expressed is constantly vitiated by the lie of the colonial situation" (1967c, 128), and the attitude to Western medicine (the medicine of the settler) is entirely different. Because "the

doctor and the patient belonging to two irreconcilable species"
(Bulhan 1985, 96), the discussion between them is completely at
odds. The patient entering the doctor's officer is tense and rigid:

> The *doctors* say: "The pain in their case is protopathic, poorly dif-
> ferentiated, diffuse as in an animal; it is a general malaise rather
> than a localized pain."
>   The *patient* says: "They ask me what was wrong with me, as
> if I was the doctor; they think they're smart and they aren't even
> able to tell where I feel pain. . . ."
>   The doctors say: "Those people are rough and unmannerly."
>   The patients say: "I don't trust them. . . . I know how to get
> into your hospital, but I don't know how I'll get out—*if* I get out."
> (Fanon 1967c, 127)

Because everything is modified by the colonial system, there can
be no neutral standpoint from which to distinguish the objective
from the attitudinal. In the colonial set-up, the idea of what is true
is constructed by a Manichean interpretation. For the native,
saying "no" to the French "yes" can be the only truth. It is an
absolutely intransigent attitude that provides no room for any
qualification. The absolute here is Manichean with any qualification or compromise constituting error, a concession to the colonial
world. "[E]very qualification is perceived by the occupier as an
invitation to perpetuate the oppression, as a confession of congenital impotence." Any agreement with the colonizing society signals
an acceptance, a signal willingness to assimilate.

In the colonial situation where the subjugation of the colonized
body is particularly marked, medicine takes on additional import.
The native reacts in an "undifferentiated, categorical way" (Fanon
1967c, 122), because swallowing the pill constitutes a feeling of
infection by the colonial power. In short, colonialism has entered
the body, has invaded the internal organs, has compromised the
native's natural autoimmunity making the antibiotic nothing but
an extension of colonial power.

One need not be a native in a colonial society to experience the
subjugations that are promoted via Western medicine, but in colo-

nial society its objectification and dehumanization are absolute. The fatalism exhibited by the "father's apparent refusal, for example, to admit that he owes his life to the colonizer's operation must be studied in two lights," argues Fanon:

> [T]he colonized person . . . in underdeveloped countries, or the disinherited in all parts of the world, perceives life not as a flowering or development of essential productiveness, but as a permanent struggle against an omnipresent death. This ever-menacing death is experienced as endemic famine, underemployment, a high death rate, an inferiority complex, and the absence of any hope for the future. All this gnawing at the existence of the colonized tends to make of life something resembling an incomplete death. (1967c, 128)

In the context of a living death the *raison d'être* of colonial Manicheanism is complete: "acts of refusal or rejection of the medical treatment are not refusal of life, but a greater passivity before that close and contagious death" (1967c, 128).

It is not surprising that the French medical service could not be separated from French colonialism. Doctors, schoolteachers, and engineers are literally little different from policemen, parachutists, and army commandos, and are all to be dismissed in "one lump." Because colonialism is a total system it must be totally rejected. There is no need for nuance. Medicine is part of the disciplinary system, introduced into Algeria at the same time as "racialism and humiliation," and finds its most dehumanized character in monitoring the pain of the tortured during the war of liberation: "[D]octors, attached to various torture centers, intervene after every session to put the tortured back into condition for new sessions" (1967c, 138). This is an extreme example of a colonial medical enterprise whose project is the dehumanization of the native. Degraded, polluted, and diseased, the native is the object of medical practices, which under colonial regimes are means of political and social domination. The practical concern of hygiene is part of the project of "taming the 'native' work force," as John and Jean Comaroff put it (1992, 216), underwriting the spatial divisions of the colonial city:

[P]ublic health was to serve in the discipline of black populations whose ambiguous physicality was a source of wealth and danger.... [A]n obsession with infectious disease . . . shaped national policies and practice of racial segregation, especially in growing cities. (Comaroff and Comaroff 1992, 229)[8]

The native's attitude to sanitary improvements "as fresh proof of the extension of the occupier's hold on the country" expressed a reality. Yet we also face an ambiguity. What to do in the face of a medical crisis? What happens if my son has meningitis? In this case, Fanon suggests that "traditional" medicines won't do,[9] but at the same time the treatment by the European doctors is an insult. Face to face with the two worlds, the patient becomes a "battle-ground for different and opposed forces" (1967c, 131), for the parent passionately wants to cure the meningitis. Fanon maintains that the colonized "obscurely realizes" the effectiveness of peni-cillin, but for political, psychological, social reasons, he must at the same time give "traditional" medicine its due. The limited validity given to Western medicine must be curbed by an "application of a preparation or the visit to a saint" (1967c, 131). In chapter 2 of *The Wretched* Fanon argued that the colonial system is also in the busi-ness of interpolating the native within certain "traditions." In the medical context we find the native's common sense use of the "tra-ditional" healer expresses not only custom, or even a remedy to Western medicine, but also that the "traditional" healer make a living. What is at stake is not simply a choice between two modes of healing but two social systems: colonial and precolonial. For Fanon, the sensibility of the "native" to the healer's need to make a living recalls precolonial attitudes. The native does not thought-lessly embrace "traditions," nor are "traditions" static. The ways of being, on the contrary, reflect real social relations. Fanon warns:

It is necessary to analyze patiently and lucidly, each one of the reactions of the colonized, and every time we do not understand, we must tell ourselves that we are in the heart of the drama—that of the impossibility of finding a meeting ground in any colonial situation. (1967c, 125)

Because relations with the "traditional" healer have immediate psychological and political ramifications, even if the colonized understands the advantages of a modern drug like penicillin, they will have to continue to pay tribute to "traditional" remedies (1967c, 130–31). To shun the "traditional" healer would be to risk ostracism from the social group. In fact, intellectual qualification is a sign of disloyalty. The Manichean attitude reflects the way things really are and are of a different order than a simple division between "tradition" and "modernity" dominant in Western sociology in the 1950s. There is no room for discussion or choice. Despite its rhetoric about "individualism," colonialism always dismisses the colonized as a homogenized mass. The native's distrust of the rhetoric of the individual follows suit. It is us and them. This is why treating the "individual" case of meningitis with Western medicine, for example, has to be immediately remedied by a visit to the "traditional" healer.

This defensive, intransigent, and clandestine resistance to colonial society is characteristic of the dominant period of colonial rule, a period that attempts to break up the economy and cultural life of the people and reproduces a Manichean culture and distorts, disfigures, and invents "traditions." Even when the native understands the nuances of the situation, colonialism's "perverted logic" always comes into play:

> Colonialism is not satisfied merely with holding a people in its grip and emptying the native's brain of all form and content. By a kind of perverted logic, it turns to the past of the oppressed people, and distorts, disfigures, and destroys it. (Fanon 1968, 210)

As the native moves from "desperate refusal" to active revolt, the habits of Manicheanism are undermined. With decolonization there is an opportunity for radically new behavior in both public and private life, a chance for cultural regeneration and creation where positive concepts of self-determination, not contingent upon the colonial status quo, are generated. "The shock that broke the chains of colonialism," Fanon claims, "has moderated exclusive attitudes, reduced extreme positions, made certain arbitrary views obsolete" (Fanon 1967c, 139).

Whereas the first stage of anticolonial resistance expresses the contradictory interrelation of "tradition" and resistance, the second stage expresses the breaking up of this interrelation. With decolonization culture becomes reinvigorated as a *fighting culture*, transforming subjectivity as the struggle for the new way of life and the native's daily "ways of life" become one and the same. Rather than valorize "tradition," a fighting culture seeks to forge totally new relations between people. The fight for liberation, Fanon declares, "sets culture moving and opens to it the doors of creation." This struggle is dialectical. It is also foreshadowed in changes in culture before the "fighting stage." New forms and themes that represent the summoning" of a people for a "precise purpose":

> [The struggle] does not give back to the national culture its former values and shapes; this struggle which aims at a fundamentally different set of relations between men cannot leave intact either the form or content of the people's culture. (Fanon 1968, 243)

Exemplified by the issue of medicine, new techniques, formerly shunned by the Algerian people, were adopted during the "course of the fight" (Fanon 1967c, 126). The "mechanical sense of detachment and mistrust" of everything associated with the colonial regime began to weaken. Such change marks a dialectical progression where something once eschewed as part of the colonial system becomes consciously appropriated by the colonized for use in their struggle. The colonized move toward a fighting culture where "everything becomes possible" (Fanon 1967c, 145).

What kind of open-ended dialectic are we talking about here, where everything seems possible? Indeed, the notion of appropriating and "taking over" modern techniques does not mean that the movement is now indebted to the colonial system. Fanon's earlier description of the absolute divide of colonial Manicheanism is not vitiated. The fact that medical techniques can be "taken over" as an element of how "everything becomes possible" is an internal dialectic of decolonization. The mental and real strategies of the native are no longer hemmed in by Manichean logic. But this does not warrant a newly uncritical attitude toward modern technologies. Rather than focusing on how "Western medical science [is] part of the oppressive system," Fanon is at pains to describe the mutation of attitudes among the colonized. Fanon is not arguing that medicine is "neutral," but science can be depoliticized: "science depoliticized, science in the service of man, is often non-existent in the colonies" (1967c, 140). The point was to make it existent and to put it into the "service" of the people. This is what happened during the revolutionary struggle. Still the actions of the occupier determined the colonized reactions, but the colonizers' actions now aided a confrontation with old attitudes to Western medicine.

During the war, the embargo on antibiotics and tetanus vaccination, ether, and alcohol, which created a terrible health problem for the liberation army, had to be tackled creatively. In the context of the national movement the fight against death took on a totally new meaning as the "people have abandoned their old passivity" (1967c, 142). Algerian doctors who had previously been considered ambassadors for the colonizing system became "reintegrated into the group," and the restriction of the availability of drugs brought sympathetic whites, who could acquire medicines, into the struggle. In the utopian atmosphere, Fanon argues, the Algerian doctor "sleeping on the ground with the men and women of the *mechatas*, living the drama of the people . . . became part of the Algerian body" (1967c, 142). The antibiotic was stripped of its negative associations and the "most modern forms of technology" were assimilated "at an extraordinary rate" (1967c, 145). It was a remarkably creative and dynamic atmosphere that approached the prevention of disease in entirely new ways. With the undermining of the pervasive power of colonial rule, the old Manichean attitudes began to dissipate. Attitudes to hospitals, mentioned earlier, completely changed with the number of "native" patients increasing fivefold (1967c, 143n).

Perhaps we have become too jaded, too Manichean, to believe these changes in attitude. Fanon's description of medicine and the colonial situation in many ways can be applied to the postcolonial situation. However, the more important issue here is whether Fanon's writing on medicine adequately expresses the breakup of Manichean thinking. We will find in his writing on the radio a more concrete indicator of radical changes as the radio has a direct utility in forming the new reality of the nation and the development of a new social consciousness.

Wiring Participatory Democracy

The identification of the voice of the Revolution with the fundamental truth of the nation has opened up limitless horizons.   Fanon

During the war of independence, the radio assumed a vital role especially as a means of mediation between the liberation army and the people: the radio could reach everybody. Through listening to radio broadcasts, those not directly involved in the armed struggle could identify with the liberation movement and feel they were part of the emerging nation. Radio, however, was a Western commodity alien to the indigenous culture and had been stubbornly resisted by the Algerian people. For it to become an important medium in the revolutionary struggle required a dramatic change in native attitudes; and this change provides a fascinating example of a dialectic of revolution and the leap from Manicheanism.

A colonial import, the radio had previously functioned as a link to "civilization" and "culture" for the settlers and helped them achieve a sense of community; it was an invention, Fanon argues, that "strengthen[ed their] certainty in the historic continuity of the conquest." Until 1945, the radio represented the French in Algeria— the news of France, the music of Paris. Radio was a reminder of the reality of colonial power. As a technical instrument of the dominant society it protected the Europeans against "Arabization."

The radio as a "technique in the hands of the occupier . . . [was] a symbol of French presence . . ." (Fanon 1967c, 72–73), and, as a "bearer of [the French] language," the radio existed in colonial society in "accordance with a well-defined statute":

Before 1954, the receiving instrument, the radiophonic technique of long-distance communication of thought, was not a neutral object. . . . [S]witching on the radio meant giving asylum to the occupier's words; it meant allowing the colonizer's language to filter into the heart of the house. . . . Having a radio meant accepting being besieged *from within* by the colonizer. (Fanon 1967c, 92, my emphasis)

Fanon notes that from the colonialist's point of view, a view mirrored in positivist sociology, the native's resistance to the radio was a reactionary reflex based on feudal traditions and religious and patriarchal hierarchies which perceived in such technology a threat to the stability and the "traditional types of sociability." Discounting this interpretation, Fanon argues that the initial resistance can only be understood from the point of view of the anticolonial movement, and that the extent of the "radical transformation" among the colonized can only be understood from the point of view of the resistance to colonial rule (Fanon 1968, 224).

The rejection of the radio expressed the resistance among the colonized to the extension of the colonialists' "sensorial powers." Moreover, there was no reason for the colonized to listen to the French broadcasts because, under colonialism, Algerian society "never participate[d] in this world of signs" (Fanon 1967c, 73). The fact that *Radio Alger* was "Frenchmen speaking to Frenchmen" about things French should sufficiently explain the native's indifference or hostility. How Fanon accounts for this change involves his theory of "radical mutation" taking place among those who were not directly involved in the fighting. Can its transformation be simply explained by its utility in the radio's reporting of day-to-day events of the liberation struggle?

Because the mass of people couldn't read the press, they had been "relatively uninvolved in the struggle" (Fanon 1967c, 82); consequently, there was a tendency during the early period of the anticolonial war to overestimate the movement's successes (an overestimation also addressed by Fanon in his critique of spontaneity).

The radio provided the vehicle for a new sense of objectivity.

With *La Voix de l'Algérie Combattante* (The Voice of Fighting Algeria) a change occurred and "in less than twenty days the entire stock of radio sets was bought up" (Fanon 1967c, 82–83). It brought into being the historical protagonist living with the revolution:

> Since 1956 the purchase of a radio in Algeria has meant, not the adoption of a modern technique for getting news, but the obtaining of access to the only means of *entering into communication with the Revolution, of living with it.* (Fanon 1967c, 83, my emphasis)

A technology formerly accounted as totally alien was now arrested from the "occupier's arsenal" and served as the "primary means of resisting" the psychological and military pressures of the colonialists. As a means of communicating with the revolution, the radio acted as an organizer, unifying the nation. It brought together all the "fragments and splinters," fitting together the "scattered acts" of rebellion "into a vast epic." The radio helped organize the resistance into a national and political idea:

> We have seen the rapid and dialectical progression of the new national requirements. . . . Algerian society made an autonomous decision to embrace the new technique and tune itself in on the new signalling systems brought into being by the Revolution. (Fanon 1967c, 84)

The radio became a power for sedition: "Establishing contact with the official voice of the Revolution became *as important* for the people as acquiring weapons or munitions for the National Army" (Fanon 1967c, 85n). Listening to *La Voix* attained a status comparable to helping the armed militants, of partaking indirectly in armed fight, of "experiencing" liberation:

> The Algerian who wanted to live up to the Revolution had at last the possibility of hearing an official voice, the voice of the combatants explain the combat to him, tell him the story of the Liberation on the march, and incorporate it into the nation's new life. . . . Having a radio meant seriously going to war. (Fanon 1967c, 85)

When the French jammed *La Voix*, it responded by rebroadcasting from a second station. A new form of struggle, the battle of the airwaves, began: "The listener involved in the battle of the waves, had to figure out the tactics of the enemy, and in an almost *physical way* circumvent the strategy of the enemy" (Fanon 1967c, 85). Rather than mere passive listeners, the radio drew the listeners into a collective battle, turning the dial, searching for *La Voix*, brought the native closer to the real fight of the revolution and to the feeling that he or she was part of it.

The radio, as an organizer, became an important medium for the expression of a new democratic society. Fanon describes a room full of people with one person glued to the radio searching for news as it shifts along the radio's dial; everyone is listening to the static trying to comprehend what is being said. At the end of the broadcast, the audience asks about a specific battle that had been mentioned in the French press which the "interpreter" had not heard *La Voix* mention:

> But by common consent, after an exchange of views, it would be decided that the Voice had in fact spoken of these events. . . . A real task of reconstruction would then begin. Everyone would participate, and the real battles of yesterday and the day before would be re-fought in accordance with the deep aspirations and unshakable faith of the group. The listener would compensate for the fragmentary nature of the news by an *autonomous creation of information*. (Fanon 1967c, 86)

Here we have an example of a "radical mutation" in the consciousness of the oppressed who have now entered history and become authors in its invention. Everyone could participate in the reconstruction and invention of the nation.

Jammed by the French, those who had listened to static all day would insist, after some debate, that they had heard *La Voix* speak of certain engagements. The idea of truth now took on a different character as it was invented in a social and revolutionly democratic context: In this collectivity, truth becomes subjective and subjectivity acquires a dimension of truth. Fanon saw it as the "practice of freedom" taking place in "the structure of the people," not merely truth in reaction to colonialism. In this context, it is not the actual sounds of *La Voix*, but the people's collective interpretation that represents the creative moment. The listeners' invention involves a productive dialogue, imparting meaning both to the fragments of information and to the nascent national consciousness; this dialogue is an engagement that prefigures a possible democratic form for the new society.[10] The language here alludes to Freud's interpretation of dreams. The static appears like a dream "fragment" found in waking life. But the emphasis here is conscious, deliberated decision-making with eyes on the future rather than on the past. That is why Fanon also thinks that the radio will have "an exceptional importance in the country's building phase" (Fanon 1967c, 97).

The very act of listening to the radio denoted a new relationship between organization, epitomized by the "choppy, broken voice," and the audience which, mediated by the militant, epitomized the "structure of the people." The militant's authority shifted: Instead of somewhat dictatorially telling the listener what was going on and what it all meant, the militant now listened to the people (to the audience which had now become audible) and accepted "by common consent [and] . . . after an exchange of views" the "reconstruction" of events by those in the room (Fanon 1967c, 86). Because of its directly democratic form, this organizational context did not stifle creative energies but encouraged them. The "imagining" of concrete battles, together with an "inner perception" of the nation which now "materialized in an irrefutable way," fostered the development of a historical protagonist. The shift from the hysteric's *hearing voices* to the revolutionary subject's hearing *La Voix* represented part of the real, not hallucinated, disintegration of colonialism. Fanon declares almost too triumphantly that, under these conditions, "claiming to have heard the Voice of Fighting Algeria was, in a certain sense, distorting the truth." But it meant making a choice between two lies, the "enemy's congenital lie and the people's own lie, which suddenly acquired a *dimension of truth*" (Fanon 1967c, 87, my emphasis). Such a choice expressed a dialectical transcendence of Manicheanism insofar as it proves to itself that it can grasp and manipulate its own ends against colonialism, but it is still an alienated consciousness. Moreover, the process of interpreting static and reconstructing fragments emphasized the importance of the group's "own working existence," as Marx put it when speaking of the Paris Commune. The people here take the creation of the nation into their own hands; they realize that the future lies with them, not with some "authority" telling them what to think. Further, the French radio jamming inadvertently mobilized the people's energies by demanding a more active imagination; it abetted a dialectical progression which helped liberate the people from *La Voix* as a "directive" and transformed its role into one of mediation in the democratic process.

Additionally, the search for *La Voix* across the wavelengths introduced the native to other voices and "other prospects." In place of the Manichean monologue of the colonial radio, having a radio gave access to a whole range of views (not only those of *La Voix*) communicated in different languages and expressing the multicultural richness of the anticolonial absolute.

The colonial world was "destructured" (to use Fanon's term) and in its place *La Voix* helped create a "fundamental change in the people," a change that "out of nothing brought the nation to life and endowed every citizen with a new status" (Fanon 1967c, 96).

The radio becomes an empty medium. It is in one sense "nothing," for it is not the radio, nor even the broadcast, but the creative subjective dialectic in response to the French jamming of the broadcast—its organization seen in the dialogue involved in interpreting the static—that creates national consciousness.

The "radical mutation" of the native's consciousness that brought about a complete change in attitude toward the radio was, Fanon argues, "not a back and forth" or "an ambivalence but rather . . . a dialectical progression," and a "transformation into opposite" that brought about a "radical change in valence"(1967c, 89n). Furthermore, the native's attitude to the French language underwent such a significant change that it also became "an instrument of liberation."

While one might challenge the native's "mutation" vis-à-vis the radio as little more than a pragmatic adaptation to a rather "neutral" technology, the changed experience of language, while perhaps more limited, is harder to dismiss as it involves a "structure" fundamental to consciousness and experience. In *Black Skin, White Masks*, Fanon viewed language as integral to a dialectic of recognition. In a Hegelian sense, language and recognition presuppose each other: "to speak is to exist absolutely for the other" (Fanon 1967a, 17) and to possess a language assumes a culture and a world expressed by that language. If language is the way in which man "possesses the world" and "take[s] on the world" (Fanon 1967a, 18, 38), in the colonial situation it is intimately connected with non-recognition: "Every people in whose soul an inferiority complex has been created by the death and burial of its local cultural originality—finds itself face to face with the language of the civilizing nation" (Fanon 1967a, 18). Civilization is expressed either in the language of orders,[10] or through an identification with an "official" language which is a *means* of advancement within the white world.

In "This is the Voice of Algeria," Fanon argues that it was, paradoxically, the radio broadcasts in French that "liberate[d] the enemy language from its historic meanings" (Fanon 1967c, 89).[11] The language of order, threat, and insult was transformed into its "antithesis" and thus "lost its accursed character, revealing itself to be capable also of transmitting, for the benefit of the nation, the messages of truth that the latter awaited." At the same time, the use of French in revolutionary radio broadcasts encouraged the spread of the French language among the colonized who had resisted its sway.

Before 1954, French was a sign of the influence of the occupier, with "ontological implications within Algerian society" (Fanon 1967c, 91). French was the language of oppression, Arabic the language of choice in the nationalist movement. But the revolution "stripped the Arabic language of its sacred character" while it removed the negative connotations associated with the French language.[12]

Just as Fanon rejects the sociologists' interpretation of the native's initial resistance to the radio, so, too, he rejects a cultural politics based on language. In contrast to the native's silent resistance to the "master's orders" conveyed in French (1967a, 19), French, now a language of *La Voix*, becomes a language of discussion. "The Voice's" new universalism and ability to unite the nation's "fragments" was further manifested in its multilingual transmission (*La Voix* was broadcast in Arabic, Kabyle, and French) and attested to the "multi-racial reality of the Algerian nation" (1967c, 157). French became one among many languages and lost its accursed character:

> The broadcasting in French of the programs of *Fighting Algeria* was to liberate the enemy language from its historic meanings. The same message transmitted in three languages unified the experience and gave it a universal dimension. (1967c, 89)

To conclude, listening to the radio contributed to the "mutation" in the people's consciousness because it reflected and assisted their desire to be involved in a dialogue: "Every Algerian felt himself to be called upon and wanted to become a reverberating element of the vast network of meanings born of the liberating combat" (Fanon 1967c, 94). These ontological and metaphysical changes challenged the "sclerosis" of the FLN leadership (see Fanon 1967c, 66). The existence of *La Voix* helped liberate the masses from the Manichean viewpoint. It resonated beyond the program of the FLN, providing a much richer context in which a new democratic society could be prefigured. In this, the radio is not identical to attitudes toward medicine. The radio had a direct utility in forming the new reality of the nation, whereas medicine, or attitudes to it, is a sociological *indicator* of the radical mutation of Algerian consciousness—the transformation of national into social consciousness. The radio represents more. With the radio, the ambiguity between "Western" and "traditional," which was expressed by attitudes toward medicine, is transcended. The radio provides the basis for a reinvigoration of the type of democracy found in pre-capitalist village assemblies where decisions are arrived at by "common consent" and are only established themselves through general acceptance. It is worth noting that Fanon's own rethinking of Marx's conceptualization of precapitalism also jibes with Marx's own consideration of new roads to revolution in the 1880s (see Shanin 1983 and Dunayevskaya 1991).

Finally, what becomes important is not the radio itself, not even the ways in which as an authority it aided the liberation of the people, but the collective form of discussion it represents. One could take this further along a postmodern route attaching all meaning to the static. Certainly it was the interpretation of the static, not the radio broadcast itself, that was the creative act. In the hands of the nationalists, La Voix brought Algerians into the political debate as junior partners. Like other national radio stations La Voix sought to establish itself as the national auhority and to create a master narrative. But it did not alone encourage dialogue. Modern talk radio which appears dialogic expresses a political disempowerment of people. In other words, radio helps legitimize political, religious, or cultural views simply through the broadcast. The broadcasts might challenge the ruling authorities and ruling ideologies but their form is not democratic or nonhierarchical.

Fanon's conception of the liberating space created by the static plays with liminality but it is grounded in reality. Meaning is not created out of nothing, but from below in the very rich context of a revolutionary situation.* But this loses the social context and in fact is close to Fanon's conception of the "hysteric" who acts on voices, blows up the local police station, and declares victory (Fanon 1967c, 79). He adds that the difference between the hysteria of the dominant group and that of the colonized was that "the colonizer always translated his subjective states into acts, real and multiple murders" (Fanon 1967c, 79). He then proposes a study to "deal with these different problems, arising out of the struggle for liberation . . . directly based on psychopathology." Unfortunately, apart from the case studies in the final chapter of *The Wretched of the Earth*, Fanon never wrote such a study. In terms of the new

---

*Fanon's description of the group listening to the radio also suggestively prefigures the theorization of "small media," like cassette tapes. Outside the controls on the media established by the state censor, and reproduced cheaply, tapes have become popular for Islamic and Christian sects in Africa.

meanings attached to the radio, Fanon sees a parallel between the victim of hallucinations who creates "friendly voices" to ward off "hearing voices," and the "disintegration of the colonial system." This transformation into opposite is the process by which "the radio voices become protective, and friendly, a "protective organ against anxiety" (1967c, 89). The people who claim that they have heard *La Voix* represent a revolutionary reason. This conscious (as opposed to unconscious) action is not reducible to representational statutory rule being erected by the dominant faction in the FLN but represents instead something different, a process of rule established by common consent.

KNOWLEDGE, IDEOLOGY, ORGANIZATION

A Postmodern Fanon?

> *Leave this Europe where they are never done talking of Man but murder him everywhere. . . . Today we are present at the stasis of Europe. Comrades, let us flee from this motionless movement.* Fanon

Having put forward some ways of understanding the transition from Manicheanism to dialectic in his discourse on liberation, I now want to turn and assess Homi Bhabha's challenge that the more subversive Fanon is not found in dialectical transcendence but in the explorations of the gaps created by shifting and crossing Manichean boundaries.

Homi Bhabha claims *against* Fanon, or in Fanon's better interest, that "in his more analytic mode Fanon can impede the exploration of these ambivalent, uncertain questions." Fanon's need for closure, Bhabha continues, is occasioned by the situation in which he writes, which demanded "more immediate identifications." We, perhaps, should know better. Rather than a need for closure conditioned by immediacy, I believe that Fanon's "untidy" dialectic, especially as it relates to questions of organization, provides a quite different area of exploration.

Is the characterization of Fanon as the last global theorist or a postmodernist *avant la lettre* (Gates, chapter 9 this volume) simply a matter of taste? Fanon's narrative of progress in *The Wretched of the Earth* where the "revolution is everything, all else is bilge," to echo Rosa Luxemburg, would seem blasphemous to postmodern orthodoxy, which equates revolution with totalitarianism. Nonetheless, Fanon commands the awed attention of postmodernists, who find compelling such works as *Black Skin, White Masks*, because it (i.e., *Black Skin*) conveys both the incoherent, fragmented, character of the self and the idea of politics as an invented performativity. Indeed, the young Fanon appreciated "style" as constitutive of "the greatness of a man" (Geismar 1970, 11). The importance of local performance and style over content, in short an aestheticism—such is the essence of a postmodern politics and sensibility (see Ankersmit 1997)—makes suspicious any gesture of totality (including the discourses of "national liberation"). Postmodernism, instead, privileges a multitude of local narratives and exalts incoherent and fragmented political dramas. Nothing lies beyond or behind the local, there is no essential power structure, no grand event, only the political day-to-day. It is the "scattered acts of rebellion," and the "splinters and fragments," not their collection into a "vast epic" (to refer to the previous section) that appeals. Bhabha echoes this bias in his essay "Day by Day," when he talks of the distinction in Fanon's "Spontaneity: Its Strength and Weakness," "between what he calls 'the historical law,' and his sense of the performance of the politics of the day-to-day" (Bhabha 1996, 188). The "law" of "transcendence" marginalizes the splintered and fragmented politics of the day to day. In this vein, the political party, or the nation, suppresses difference and marginalizes the very, almost carnivalesque, elements of anticolonial rebellion that Fanon uncovered, channelling dissent into "rational" discourse. There is a truth to this but taken to its logic conclusion, such an "anarchist" critique can lead almost anywhere, celebrating ethnicities, nativism, retrograde ideas—any resistance for its own sake.

I think Paul Gilroy (1990) is right to consider the modernist/postmodernist rupture as another passing phase in Western thought. At the moment when there are attempts in Africa to reconstruct a narrative of emancipation, it is particularly ironic that postmodern critics have pronounced its impossibility. Why should postmodernism, a Western product which eschews universals, be applicable to Africa?

Paradoxically, post-colonial Africa, the Africa that, as Fanon warns, is the result of a failed decolonization, is intimately connected up with postmodernism. Despite the hybrid appearance of the premodern with modernity, Africa never became "modern" in the sociological sense (leaving aside its skewed white form in Apartheid). Africa's insertion into global capitalism which, in the past, had been mediated by Western slavers, military, and colonial business ventures, is now mediated by its nationalist "bourgeoisie," who are not, Fanon argues, a modernizing bourgeoisie. In the postmodern sense the native bourgeoisie took on the "style" and trappings of the capitalist class without ever becoming involved in production (this mimicry, as Bhabha correctly implies, is an effective strategy of neocolonial power [see Bhabha 1984]). Accumulation of capital came not through profits from production but the rent of space—the native bourgeoisie, that kleptocratic caste as Fanon puts it, is in the business of asset stripping and then banking the proceeds in personal accounts. Rent is paid by multinational corporations for the right to set up a "Western compound" and effectively rule over large tracts of land, now outside the control of the nation state, to extract "natural" resources like oil, diamonds, or gold, at terrible environmental and human cost. Even in oil-rich Nigeria, technical staff is flown in from Europe. Indigenous labor is merely menial. Shell Oil's destruction of the Ogoni Delta, with the aid of the police and the military, achieved world renown because of the murder of Ken Saro Wiwa and others, but this is the tip of the iceberg.[13] In Africa, capitalism rehashes the "rosy dawn" of its primitive accumulation over and over again with the native "middleman" playing a familiar role. Yet despite the postmodernist's insight into Africa's present it erases Africa's real multifaceted anticolonial struggles and closes off the historical context of Africa's present predicament. Africa is still playing out the problematic of decolonization.

Fanon's critique of colonial hegemony remains a cogent perspective on post-colonial Africa. His "rational" examination in *The Wretched* of the apparently irrationality of "tribal" dance in colonial society, for example, perceptively differentiates between "traditions" which are genuinely anticolonial and those which act to dissipate anticolonial action. For example, Fanon interprets the social character of "tribal" dance, which exhibits a certain permissiveness under the watchful eye of the chiefs, as a "huge effort of a community to exorcise itself, to liberate itself, to explain itself" (Fanon 1968, 58). In contrast to the zonal limits of colonialism, the dance seems to defy limits. It is a liminal phase characterized by the suspension of "normal" behavior. For the postmodernist, its transgression of boundaries and the disintegration of the personality is to be celebrated. But this limitless freedom is a pseudofreedom: a symbolic and controlled release that returns peace and calm to the village and changes nothing. Fanon's critique is an historical one; "tradition" which had been important to the maintenance of indigenous society had offered initial resistance to colonialism, but now in a different phase the dispossession of personality simply mirrors the dispossession of space: The world belongs to someone else. Far from subversive, Fanon argues, such permitted freedom actually helps preserve colonial society. For Fanon, this controlled release and sublimation of violence "turns into a void." This is not simply a result of collaboration, though that is certainly a facet, but, more importantly, expresses the fact that the type of resistance offered is no longer valuable.

"Ancestral leaders" are neither automatically resisters or collaborators. "They do not offer . . . any stiffer resistance to the logic of cooption," opines Jean-François Bayart, and have in fact "contributed to the production of inequality" (Bayart 1989, 188). Rather than celebrate ancestors, and other-worldly powers, which had certainly been an earlier rallying point,[14] Fanon champions cultural expressions representing action that promote the native's ability to strike a blow against colonial violence. Such action could include the "Mau Mau" revolt in Kenya. Fanon's concern was to unmask ideologies that led to political passivity in the face of colonialism.

In a psychoanalytic fashion he argued that the embrace of other-worldly powers exhausted the native, channelling frustrations inward rather than toward their "real" source, the colonial regime.

Ideology, Organization, Humanism

> *To put Africa in motion, to co-operate in its organization, in its regrouping, behind revolutionary principles. To participate in the ordered movement of a continent—this was really the work I had chosen.*   Fanon

One expression of the power of Fanon's dialectic emerges when we consider the question of organization. Not surprisingly, Fanon recognizes that the importation of the Western party model merely constitutes a "fetish of organization." In the colonial context the limitations of the spontaneous, decentered, fragmented, anticolonial movement are answered by raising dialogue to a principle. The dialogic basis of the Fanonian concept of organization aims to break down the "brutality of thought" inherent in anticolonial movements: A brutality based on pragmatic decisions and lazy Manichean thinking that resists "shades of meaning." The transition from Manichean to dialectic is reflected in changes in organizational form, from one that suppresses difference for the sake of unity to one encouraging open-ended dialogue. Such a dialectic is not based on a regurgitating a liberal humanist conception of the subject. On the contrary, the subject is the result of the experiences of "radical mutation"—the social and democratic processes of becoming historical protagonists as we considered earlier.

Fanon's conception of national liberation is already a counter-narrative (Said 1988) for two reasons. First, it is not the narrative of orthodox nationalism, led by the nationalist bourgeoisie, but of the marginalized nationalist militant, an alternative nationalist intelligentsia, and the common people, all of whom are outside mainstream urban nationalist discourse. Second, while organizational centralization is necessary to prevent the degeneration of national consciousness into a series of regional or "tribal" favoritisms, it is not its guarantee. Fanon recommends that a radical decentralization take place as soon as possible. In other words, one expression of the dialectic of organization is that the "local" is reintroduced into a single dialectic of organization and national cum social consciousness as the corrective to the centralizing pull of nationalist orthodoxy. However, decentralization alone is not a principle, and alone it can lead to factionalism. In the Algerian context, the "decentralized" and militarized *wilayas* proved to be problematic because they were beyond control of a politics. Decentralization, in the context of what happens after revolution, is given content by the importance Fanon places on "political education" or the articulation of ideology and the ways in which national consciousness is deepened by a "new humanism."

Fanon's awakening to the vital role of "political education" brings about a fundamental shift in his thought which has been underestimated by Fanon's critics. By pointing to the centrality of ideology, Fanon marks a new theoretical divide among nationalist thinkers:

> Colonialism and its derivatives do not, as a matter of fact, constitute the present enemies of Africa. . . . For my part the deeper I enter into the culture and political circles the surer I am that the great danger that threatens Africa is the absence of ideology. (Fanon 1967b, 186)

It is not that there are no ideologies; there are plenty of "morbid symptoms" to choose from, as Gramsci once put it, but all are retrogressive. The problem is the lack of a revolutionary ideology or theory that is grounded in the aspirations of the anticolonial social movements and that articulates a vision for the future. "Ideology" is needed to counteract both the hollow rhetoric of the nationalist middle class and the romanticizing, and potentially retrograde, nativist ideology, which appeals to belief systems such as religion. The problem of the lack of ideology is expressed in the failure to convert the opening created by decolonization into a moment of change—into a genuine revolutionary moment.

For Fanon, ideology at first means explaining the long-term

objectives of the fight. It is not merely a question of strategy. Nor is this "enlightening of consciousness" to be imposed or imparted from the outside; it is rather "organic,"[15] a process that occurs through the dialogue about the aftermath of colonial rule and it brings into being a new relationship between the party militants and the people:

> All this taking stock of the situation, this enlightening of con-sciousness, and this advance in the knowledge of the histories of societies are only possible within the framework of an organiza-tion and inside the structure of the people. (Fanon 1968, 143)

This enlightenment, "inside the structure of the people," faces the consequences of "primitive Manicheanism." For one thing, the "truth" that the native inherently and intuitively expresses has a limit, not the least because his perceptions have for so long been influenced and conditioned by the Manichean structure. The remedy, therefore, cannot simply involve substituting for "false consciousness" the enlightenment of the party; one cannot appeal to absolutes of truth and falsehood that a straightforward inver-sion of racial Manicheanism would correct. Instead, Fanon focuses on the development of consciousness and knowledge in relation to postcolonial exigencies: "Exploitation can wear a black face" and, conversely, certain whites not only do not support the colonial regime but are prepared to fight for the people's self-determina-tion: "The people must also give up their too-simple conception of their overlord," Fanon declares, "in their weary road toward rational knowledge" (Fanon 1968, 145). Further, the settler "is not simply the man who must be killed" (Fanon 1968, 146).

Immediate violence, which had brought things to a head, now must be controlled. The greatest barrier to the development of rev-olutionary consciousness is the *quid pro quo* of simply answering colonial brutality with anticolonial brutality. The "political edu-cator," qua "social group" introduces "shades of meaning," bat-tling those in the organization whose underestimation of the people's reasoning capabilities leads them to believe that qualifi-cation brings confusion. Those involved in spontaneous activity

Gibson: Radical Mutations

search for meaning. For Fanon, political education encourages the people to reflect on their own experiences, to think for themselves. It recognizes like Lenin (and in contrast to Ché, who famously said the revolution could succeed without theory), that there can be no successful revolution without revolutionary theory, and at the same time almost in an anti-Leninist sense that there is "absolutely no strategically privileged position" (Fanon 1968, 135). In the Gramscian sense of war of position, there is no decisive battle, but the persistent enlightening of consciousness, of an articulation of a new humanism. In contrast to his earlier insistence on liberation without transition, Fanon envisioned a longer process of education. Such education required the deepening of democratic procedures, enforcing accountability.

The intellectual's job is to convince the people that the future depends on them. As Marx insisted, the "educators must be educated"; here, the political educator receives instruction in the "school of the people." Political education is crucial in the struggle for emancipation; without such education the movement can fail to appreciate the novelty and revolutionary character of its aims; the people might give over their freedom to some other organization, leader, or ideology. "Education for liberation" strives to effect a fundamental change in the native's consciousness and self-knowledge; confronting the "internalized" oppressor and the belief of their own ineptitude, ignorance, and fear.[16] Moreover, it is not simply "education for . . .". Political education takes its point of departure as an attempt to articulate the experience and creativity of the masses on the move by entering into the contradictory processes of their development and raising these contradictions to knowledge. Promoting, in other words, ways to get beyond Manichean thinking which are already intimated in the mass movement's activities. The practice of this consciousness of contradiction equals a self-knowledge and self-confidence, a cognition and recognition of the masses' self-determination. The new relationships between theory and practice developed in the dialogue represent a new type of politics which prefigures the structure of the intended new society. Fanon calls it a new type of politics *"living inside of history"*:

> These politics are national, revolutionary and social and these
> new facts . . . are the essence of the fight which explodes old colo-
> nial truths and reveals unexpected facets, which bring about new
> meanings and pinpoint the contradictions camouflaged by these
> facts. (Fanon 1968, 147, my emphasis)

However, the *native's* drive to achieve a fuller self-understanding
and the organization's ability to reveal new meanings are
impeded, Fanon maintains, by the "laziness" of those intellectuals
who persist in a Manichean analysis when more apposite "shades
of meaning" are needed.

An important turning point of Fanon's *The Wretched of the Earth*
occurs in his description of the movement's challenge to the intellectual. In "The Pitfalls of National Consciousness" Fanon confronts the "problem of the absence of ideology," calling it an historical lesson (1968, 148). This problem is apparent in "Spontaneity: Its Strength and Weakness," where he contrasts a small
group of revolutionaries with the dominant "legal" nationalist
party. Fanon emphasizes how this small group contributes vitally
to the development of an organization capable of articulating
"new meanings" inherent in spontaneous activity. On the other
hand, the intellectual is vitally problematic in the process.

VERTIGINOUS INTELLECTUALS

*In other words, we are forever pursued by our actions. Their ordering,
their circumstances, and their motivation may perfectly well come to be
profoundly modified a posteriori. This is merely one of the snares that
history and its various influences sets for us. But can we escape
becoming dizzy? And who can affirm that vertigo does not haunt the
whole of existence?*
                                                              Fanon

The radical intellectual occupies a central but problematical place
in Fanon's dialectic of organization. In the embryonic organization
forged between the urban militant and the rural masses, intellectuals play an important role "explod[ing] the old colonial truths"
and "bring[ing] out new meanings" inherent in the radical muta-

tions experienced in the anticolonial movement (Fanon 1968, 147). But their scripts are not ready-made. Gramsci explains this problem very well:

> The philosophy of praxis is consciousness full of contradictions in which the philosopher himself, understood both individually and as an entire social group, not merely grasps the contradictions but posits himself as an element of the contradiction and elevates this element to a principle of knowledge and therefore of action. (1971, 405)

Far from a simple identity with the people, Fanon argues that it is only by realizing "the extent of the intellectual's estrangement from [the people]" that the intellectual can posit "himself as an element of the contradiction" (Fanon 1968, 226). In the colonial setup, with the addictive of race, the process of estrangement has added complications. Schooled under colonialism, the intellectuals have undergone traumas, as detailed in *Black Skin, White Masks*. Made intellectual by the colonial system, Fanon wants them to eschew their elitism but doesn't see any use in their renouncing their education in a search for some lost authenticity. Instead, the intellectual has to put those skills "in the hands of the people."

To make this work, Fanon appeals to their honesty and virtue to recognize their "duty" to the "national cause," though he knows full well how few are willing to relinquish their class privilege and become "willing slaves of the people." Whereas the militants expelled by the nationalist organization largely hail from the socioeconomic fringes of urban colonial society (they "are often unskilled workers, seasonal laborers" [1968, 125]), the "honest" intellectuals come from the small native elite.[17] This group's disdain for the emerging wheeling-and-dealing "middle men" is often a product of moral upbringing:

> The personal situation of these men (breadwinners of large families) or their background (hard struggles and a strictly moral upbringing) explains their manifest contempt for profiteers and schemers. (1968, 177)

But Fanon's earlier description of the nationalist bourgeoisie's "own nature" goes further in explaining a "material" basis for the honest intellectual's "manifest contempt": "Under the colonial system, a middle class which accumulates capital is an impossible phenomena" (1968, 150). In other words, colonialism prevents the middle class from becoming truly bourgeois (and thus they give up very little of their own nature by becoming part of the "structure of the people"). This middle class is therefore relatively free to discover where its "real" interests lie. The appeal to "the national cause" has a material grounding, or more precisely its *lack* provides the basis on which the middle class is able to give up its pseudobourgeois nature. This rootlessness is the intellectual's real nature. In "Colonial War and Mental Disorders" (1968, 249–310), Fanon analyzes the native intellectual's alienation as an effect of colonial rule, which in extreme cases is experienced as "vertigo." Such a feeling of rootlessness was exacerbated by the extensive use of torture by the French during the war of liberation.

Unlike the nonintellectual, the intellectual, when arrested, is first asked to collaborate with the military intelligence in a reasoned dialogue.[18] It is a dialogue that presupposes a gulf between the native intellectual and nonintellectual: A "we" against the "poor mistaken" *fellaghas* (1968, 287). In contrast to the peasant's Manichean consciousness, which knows that every relationship between colonizer and colonized is one of falsity, the intellectual's cognition is less certain and more subtle. The result of the intellectual's experience of interrogation is an "inability to distinguish between true and false" (1968, 285). The intellectual experiences a melting of all that once seemed solid.

Fanon's critical (self-)interest in this group of "honest" intellectuals was first articulated in *Black Skin, White Masks*, where he spoke of the small number of intellectuals who could fully explore the negativity of Césaire's négritude. Such an exploration, split between moods of hope and despair, could easily prove "deadly," as Suzanne Césaire put it, but could also create a radical change in the psyche of the individual (S. Césaire 1978). In the revolutionary context of Algeria, this "race of angels," as Fanon describes them in *The*

Wretched of the Earth, comes to occupy a "zone of occult instability." Though this latter notion has been cited as evidence of Fanon's pre-figurative postmodernism, the proper context of the quotation reveals that Fanon is addressing the radical mutation intellectuals undergo when they enter the liberating zone of the revolution. Unlike the colonial zoning, this revolutionary zone doesn't merely transgress but breaks up old boundaries and old ways of thinking. Without the organizational space (where the intellectual and the people can meet on a new equal footing "inside the structure of the people"), the intellectual *is* decentered, rootless, unsure of what is true and false. Simply identifying with the people's culture, without a concern for political developments, can easily become "opportunist" or, worse, retrograde. Put another way, the vertiginous intellectual simply mirrors the opposition between modernity and tradition propagated by the modernization school of social science. In a Manichean rather than dialectical fashion, the intellectual moves from embracing metropolitan "modernity" to mouthing a nativism:

> These people forget that the forms of thought and what it feeds on, together with modern techniques of information, language, and dress have dialectically reorganized the people's intelligences and that the constant principles which acted as safeguards during the colonial period are now undergoing extremely radical changes. (Fanon 1968, 225)

Contrary to the nationalist organization's elitism, the new organizational consciousness that Fanon heralds is a product of the *experience* of those in the small illegal party as they make contact and develop a working relationship with the rural masses. It is this party that those few "honest intellectuals" join; it is this party that serves as the basis for truly revolutionary ideology. Fanon's claim that *The Wretched of the Earth* is directed to his African comrades, not to the West, should be taken seriously. Certainly chapters 3 and 4, "The Pitfalls of National Consciousness," and "On National Culture," are pointedly addressed to that small group of committed "honest intellectuals"; they are also critiques of a Pan-Africanist bootstrap ideology which says no to foreign ideology but hounds the peasantry to work harder, to make "colossal efforts" for the nation (Fanon 1968, 154–55). In today's post–Cold War Africa, such discourse, encouraged by "free market" rhetoric, once again thrives.

Though Fanon never directly defines "ideology," for him it is clearly analogous to a vision of the future and a promotion of the people's self-reliance and creative potential while not simply mirroring what the people think. For Fanon, the philosophy of a new humanism had nothing to do with academic discourse about humanism. Intellectual responsibility meant critically engaging other ideologies as well as articulating the objective movement of liberation and theorizing its leadership. The problem of an explicit philosophical grounding for ideology still needs to be tackled. In the conclusion to *The Wretched of the Earth*, it is articulated as a "new humanism" whose pedigree includes a radical critique of the liberal humanist tradition and rethinking of Marx's idea of revolution. Fanon's humanism in *The Wretched of the Earth* is much sharper than in *Black Skin, White Masks*, which at times seems to rely on ethical abstractions. In *The Wretched of the Earth*, the need to have "an idea of man and of the future society" is quickly connected to the need to decentralize political organization "in the extreme," thus bringing full circle the dialectic of spontaneity and organization. The "dialectical leap" (1968, 198) is based on decision-making in democratic form and conceptualized within the Fanonian organization. Far from constituting an a priori universal, the dialectic of individual and national self-determination is not a remote prospect but a constantly developing process, figured in immediate social relations and given meaning in the organizational interrelationship between the intellectual and the mass movement. Fanon's humanism is a revolutionary-practical-critical humanism expressed through the individual's experience in building up a nation. Sense and meaning are made of experience in the organization, in the "zone" where the three elements—the masses, the militants, and the intellectuals—meet and where Fanon's philosophy of liberation is made real. That is why the degeneration of the organization marks the degeneration of the nation. Fanon's example of building a bridge is a metaphor for building bridges between the organization and the "people": If it does not "enrich the awareness of those who work on it, then the bridge ought not to be built" (Fanon 1968, 200–201). The most "urgent task" in the intellectuals' "building up" of the nation is "the discovery and encouragement of universalizing values" (1968, 247).

NOTES

1. See G. A. Kelly for a discussion of the internal and external dialectic in Hegel's *Lordship and Bondage*. Fanon's engagement with Hegel, I believe, is not simply filtered through Alexandre Kojéve. Lacan, however, was one of the auditors of Kojéve's famous lectures on Hegel.

2. On this also see Marcien Towa, *Essai sur la problématique philosophique dans l'Afrique actuelle* (1979).

3. It shouldn't be forgotten that *Black Skin, White Masks* was published one hundred years after *The Eighteenth Brumaire*. Fanon's journey to France in 1948 not only coincided with a series of militant strikes and the beginnings of a series of hundred year anniversary celebrations of Marx's work. Fanon was in Lyon during the hundredth anniversary of the 1848 Revolutions which actually began in Lyon.

4. I am using quotation marks around the term to indicate my awareness of the ongoing debate about it. Tradition has generally been thought of in Manichean or at least binary terms: tradition and modernity. Scholars have become critical of the term, stressing both its invented character (see Eric Hobsbawn and Terence Ranger, *Invention of Tradition* [Cambridge, 1983]) and the ways in which traditions, rather than static, are changing processes. Nevertheless such processes depend on a degree of autonomy. In the context of the extreme violence of Colonial Algeria, Fanon argues that the native's indigenous culture has broken down, become rigid and inert (to use Fanon's language).

"[T]raditions need autonomy," writes Jan Vansina:

> The peoples who carry them must have the power of self-determination. A tradition is maimed when autonomy is lost. Given its capacity to accept, reject, or modify innovation, a tradition will not be overwhelmed by another major tradition as long as its carriers still retain enough liberty of choice. (*Paths in the Rainforests: Toward a History of Political Tradition in Equatorial Africa* [Madison: University of Wisconsin Press, 1990], p. 259)

Thus, when considering "tradition" in Fanon's writing we have to understand that Fanon is not simply echoing the sociology of the modernization school but emphasizing the loss of "liberty of choice" and the maiming of traditions.

5. This title of the American edition, published in 1965, is a little misleading. The book is a study not so much of a dying colonial culture as of the coming to be of a new national Algerian culture, and could be named "Studies in a Fighting Culture." It was originally published as *L'An cinq de la révolution Algérienne*, a title, no doubt, with echoes of the French revolution.

6. The counterrevolution within the revolution had been intimated by the murder of his friend and comrade Abane Ramdane by forces inside the Algerian FLN. Fanon still had Abane's death on his conscience when he told Simone de Beauvoir shortly after Lumumba's murder that he had felt responsible because he had not "forced them [Abane and Lumumba] to follow his advice" (de Beauvoir 1992, 595).

7. Fanon argues that the native doctor, who might have overcome the "traditional prejudice" of hospitals, would still feel incredibly guilty at hospitalizing a patient. This was not because of his attachment to traditional medicine, but owing to the "group mentality."

8. Presumed to be the carriers of disease, single women living in towns became synonymous with transgression and disorder.

9. We might consider other types of healing, but when it comes to a life and death situation, the diagnosis we choose (is what is considered the best) is the highest technology. It is very difficult in this situation to take the "risk" of alternative medicine (even if allopathic cures are as problematic).

10. As Ngugi Wa Th'iongo puts it, "The night of the sword and bullet was followed by the chalk and the blackboard. The physical violence of the battlefield was followed by the psychological violence of the classroom." Ngugi explains that "education" included physical violence; anyone speaking the local language at school was subject to punishment. "Economic and political control," he adds, "can never be complete or effective without mental control" (1985, 109–27).

11. In *Black Skin, White Masks*, Fanon writes, "I make it a point always to talk to the so-called *bicot* in normal French, and I have always been understood. They answer me as well as their varying means permit; but I will not allow myself to resort to paternalistic 'understanding' [which he calls elsewhere "pidgin" and "childlike" speech]" (Fanon 1967a, 33).

12. Fanon is speaking not of official "proper" French but colloquial French.

13. Saro-Wiwa's detention diary, *A Month and a Day*, proves Fanon's analysis of the post-independence state and its coercive elites: "The Ogoni were consigned to political slavery at the hands of the new black colonialists wearing the mask of Nigerianism" (1996, 186). In contrast to the "Nigerian masquerade," Saro-Wiwa posits the importance of the "minds of Nigerians" and shows his amazement with the political maturity of the Ogoni youth who already understand the nature of their oppression.

14. Like the 1905 Maji Maji rebellion in German East Africa (Tanzania) which was articulated within the millenian discourse of a prophetic movement and found its strength on the borders far from the colonial administrative centers of power (not in the postmodern sense of the border as the hybrid space of resistence but as a space that had, in fact, not yet been subject to the full effects of colonial rule).

15. Farrington, who translates *parti organique* as "living party," emphasizes the "free flow of ideas" as ongoing (1968, 170). Sekyi-Otu is also right to emphasize the Gramscian character of "organic" in this context (1996, 148).

16. One is reminded how Steve Biko considered "fear" a weapon of the oppressor that needed to be confronted ideationally by black consciousness.

17. In 1954, 686 muslims matriculated from the University of Algiers. By that year about 90 percent of Algerians were illiterate. Before colonalism the Algerian literacy rate was higher than the French. One consequence of colonialism was the destruction of the indigenous educational system.

18. The techniques of torture on the nonintellectual are directly physical. Physical violence is used to "put the native in his place." There is no doubt that the physical experience of national liberation is countered in a physical way.

Bibliography

Abel, Elizabeth. 1993. "Black Writing, White Reading: Race and the Politics of Feminist Interpretation." *Critical Inquiry* 19, no. 3 (Spring): 470–98.

Accad, Evelyne. 1990. *Sexuality and War*. New York: New York University Press.

Achebe, Chinua. 1967. *A Man of the People*. New York: Anchor Books.

Adorno, Theodor. 1973; 1948. *Philosophie der neuen Musik* (Philosophy of Modern Music), translated by Anne G. Mitchell. New York: Seabury.

Ageron, Charles-Roberts. 1991. *Modern Algeria: A History from 1830 to the Present*. London: C. Hurst & Co.

Alexander, M. Jacqui. 1991. "Redrafting Morality: The Postcolonial State and the Sexual Offences Bill of Trinidad and Tobago." In *Third World Women and the Politics of Feminism*, edited by Chandra Talpade Mohanty, Ann Russo, and Lourdes Torres. Bloomington: Indiana University Press.

Ali, Bahir Hadj. 1965. "Some Lessons of the Liberation Struggle in Algeria." *World Marxist Review* (January).

Allen, Chris. 1995. "Understanding African Politics." *Review of African Political Economy*, no. 65: 301–302.

Alloula, Malek. 1986. *The Colonial Harem*, translated by Myma Godzich and Wlad Godzich. Minneapolis: University of Minnesota Press.

447

Amrane, Djamila. 1980. *La Femme Algérienne et la Guerre de Libération Nationale (1954–62).* Algeria: Actes due Colloque d'Oran.

Ankersmit, R. R. 1997. *Aesthetic Politics: Political Philosophy beyond Fact and Volume.* Stanford, Calif.: Stanford University Press.

Appiah, K. Anthony. 1988. "Out of Africa: Topologies of Nativism," *Yale Journal of Criticism* 1–2: 153–78.

———. 1991. "Tolerable Falsehoods, Agency and the Interests of Theory." In *Some Consequences of Theory* edited by Jonathan Arac and Barbara Johnson. Baltimore: John Hopkins University Press.

"A Propos des damnés de la terre." 1962. *Esprit*, 30, part 2 (September).

Apter, David. 1972. *Ghana in Transition*, 2d ed. Princeton, N.J.: Princeton University Press.

Armah, Ayi Kwei. 1988. *The Beautiful Ones Are Not Yet Born.* London: Heinneman.

Arnold, A. James. 1981. *Modernism and Négritude: The Poetry and Poetics of Aimé Césaire.* Cambridge, Mass: Harvard University Press.

Azari, F. 1983. *Women of Iran: The Conflict with Fundamentalist Islam.* London: Ithaca Press.

Baldwin, James. 1961. "Princes and Powers." In *Nobody Knows My Name.* New York: Vintage.

Barnard, Roger. 1968. "Frantz Fanon." *New Society* (January 4).

Bates, Robert H. 1981. *Markets and States in Tropical Africa.* Berkeley: University of California Press.

Baudrillard, Jean. 1983. *Simulations,* translated by Paul Foss et al. New York.

Bayart, Jean-François. 1989. *L'État en Afrique. La politique du ventre.* (Translation, 1993. *State in Africa: The Politics of the Belly.*) London: Longman.

Beckman, Bjorn. 1989. "Whose Democracy? Bourgeois or Popular Democracy," 45/46 *Review of African Political Economy.*

Behr, Edward. 1961. *The Algerian Problem.* London: Hodder & Stroughton.

Bell, Linda. 1993. *Rethinking Ethics in the Midst of Violence: A Feminist Approach to Freedom.* Lanham, Md.: Rowman & Littlefield Publishers.

Benhourya, Tahar. 1980. *Économie de l'Algérie.* Paris: Maspero.

Benjamin, Walter. 1969. "Theses on the Philosophy of History." In *Illuminations,* edited by Hannah Arendt, translated by Harry Zohn. New York: Schocken Books.

Benson, Mary, ed. 1976. *The Sun Will Rise.* London: International Defense and Aid Fund for Southern Africa.

Bergner, Gwen. 1995. "Who Is That Masked Woman? Or, the Role of Gender in Fanon's *Black Skin, White Masks.*" *PMLA* 110, no. 1.

Bernasconi, Robert. 1996. "Casting the Slough: Fanon's New Humanism for a New Humanity." In *Fanon: A Critical Reader,* edited by Lewis Gordon et al. New York: Blackwell.

Bernheimer, Charles. 1993. "Fetishism and Decadence: Salome's Severed Heads." In *Fetishism as Cultural Discourse,* edited by Emily Apter and William Pietz. Ithaca and London: Cornell University Press.

Bhabha, Homi K. 1983a. "Difference, Discrimination, and the Discourse of Colonialism." In *The Politics of Theory,* edited by Francis Barker. Colchester: University of Essex.

———. 1983b. "The Other Question." *Screen* 24 (November–December).

———. 1984. "Of Mimicry and Man: The Ambivalence of Colonial Discourse." *October* 28 (Spring).

———. 1985. "Sly Civility." *October* (Winter).

———. 1986a. "Remembering Fanon," Foreword to *Black Skin, White Masks* by Frantz Fanon. London and Sydney: Pluto Press; a version of this foreword can be found in "Interrogating Identity: The Postcolonial Prerogative." In *Anatomy of Racism,* edited by David Theo Goldberg, Minneapolis: University of Minnesota Press, 1990, as well as in this volume.

———. 1986b. "Signs Taken for Wonders: Questions of Ambivalence and Authority under a Tree Outside Delhi, May 1817." In *"Race," Writing, and Difference,* edited by Henry Louis Gates Jr. Chicago: University of Chicago Press.

———. 1991. " 'Race,' Time, and the Revision of Modernity." *Oxford Literary Review* 13, no. 1–2: 193–219.

———. 1996. "Day by Day . . . with Frantz Fanon." In *The Fact of Blackness,* edited by Alan Read. Seattle, Wa.: Bay Press.

Bhatnagar, Rashmi. 1986. "Uses and Limits of Foucault: A Study of the Theme of Origins in Edward Said's *Orientalism.*" *Social Scientist* 158: 3–22.

Bjornson, Richard. 1991. *The African Quest for Freedom and Identity: Cameroonian Writing and the National Experience.* Bloomington: Indiana University Press.

Boehmer, Elleke. 1991. "Transfiguring Body into Narrative in Post-Colonial Writing." Unpublished paper.

Bondy, François. 1966. "The Black Rousseau." *New York Review of Books* 31 (March).

Bourdieu, Pierre. 1958. *Sociologie de L'Algérie.* (English translation *The Algerians,* 1962, by Alan C. M. Ross.) Boston: Beacon Press.

Bouvier, Pierre. 1971. *Fanon.* Paris: Éditions Universitaires.

Boyarin, Daniel. 1994a. "Freud's Baby, Fliess's Maybe: Homophobia, Antisemitism, and the Invention of Oedipus," *GLQ* 2, no. 1.

———. 1994b. "Épater L'embourgeoisement: Freud, Gender, and the (De)colonized Psyche." *Diacritics* 24, no. 1 (Spring): 17–46.

Brace, Richard and Joan. 1965. *Algerian Voices*. Princeton, N.J.: Van Nostrand.

Bulhan, H. A. 1981a. "Psychological Research in Africa: Genesis and Function." *Race and Class* 23, no. 1: 25–41.

———. 1981b. "Psychological Research in Africa: Genesis and Function. *Race and Class* 20: 3.

———. 1985. *Frantz Fanon and the Psychology of Oppression*. New York: Plenum Press.

Burris, Barbara. "The Fourth World Manifesto." In *Radical Feminism*. New York: Quadrangle Books.

Burton, Richard E. 1885. *The Book of a Thousand Nights and a Night*, vol. 10. London: The Burton Club.

Cabral, Amilcar. 1974. "National Liberation and Culture." *Transition* 45.

———. 1980. *Unity and Struggle: Speeches and Writings*, translated by Michael Wolfers. New York: Monthly Review.

Caute, David. 1970. *Fanon*. London: Fontana.

Césaire, Aimé. 1972. *Discourse on Colonialism*, translated by James Pinkham. New York: Monthly Review.

———. 1983. *Collected Poetry*, translated, with an introduction by Clayton Eshelman and Annette Smith. Berkeley: University of California Press.

Césaire, Suzanne. 1978 [1943]. "1943: le surréalisme et nous." In *Tropiques II*. Paris: Éditions Jean Michel Place.

Chatterjee, Partha. 1986. *Nationalist Thought and the Colonial World: A Derivative Discourse?* Minneapolis: University of Minnesota Press.

Cherif, Mohammed. 1966. "Frantz Fanon and the African Revolution." *Présence Africaine* 58.

Clark, John. 1991. *Democratizing Development—The Role of Voluntary Organizations*. London: Earthscan Publications.

Clifford, James. 1988. *The Predicament of Culture: Twentieth Century Ethnography, Literature, and Art*. Cambridge, Mass.: Harvard University Press.

Cocks, Joan. 1995. "On Nationalism: Frantz Fanon, Rosa Luxemburg, and Hannah Arendt." In *Reading the Canon: Feminist Interpretations of Hannah Arendt*, edited by Anne Norton and Bonnie Honig. University Park: Pennsylvania State University Press.

Comaroff, John, and Jean Comaroff. 1992. *Ethnography and the Historical Imagination*. Boulder, Colo.: Westview.

Dash, Michael. 1973. "Marvellous Realism: The Way Out of Négritude." *Caribbean Studies* 13, no. 4: 57–70.

Davidson, Basil. 1978. *Let Freedom Come: Africa in Modern History*. Boston: Little, Brown.

Davies, Ioan. 1966. *African Trade Unions*. London: Penguin Books.

Davis, Angela. 1981. "Rape, Racism, and the Myth of the Black Rapist." In *Women, Race, and Class*. New York: Random House.

de Beauvoir, Simone. 1963. *La force des choses*. Paris: Gallimard.

———. 1965. *Force of Circumstance*. Translated by Richard Howard. New York: G. P. Putnam and Sons.

Decker, Jeffrey Louis. 1990. "Terrorism (Un)veiled: Frantz Fanon and the Women of Algiers." *Cultural Critique* (Winter): 177–95.

de Kadt, Emanuel, ed. 1972. *Patterns of Foreign Influence in the Caribbean*. New York: Published for the Royal Institute of International Affairs by Oxford University Press.

Deleuze, Gilles, and Felix Guattari. 1983. *Anti-Oedipus: Capitalism and Schizophrenia*, translated by Robert Hurley, Mark Seem, and Helen R. Lane. Minneapolis: University of Minneapolis Press. Originally published as *L'Anti-Oedipe*. Paris: Les Editions de Minuit, 1972.

Denis, Manule Maldonado. 1967. "Frantz Fanon (1924–61) y el pensamiento anticolonialistia contemoráneo." In *Revista de Ciencias Sociales*. Rio Piedras: Inter-American University of Puerto Rico.

Depestre, René. 1976. "Problems of Identity for the Black Man in the Caribbean." In *Carifesta Forum*, edited by John Hearne. Kingston, Jamaica.

Derrida, Jacques. 1985. *The Ear of the Other: Otobiography, Transference, Translation*, edited by Christie V. McDonald, translated by Peggy Kamuf. New York: Schocken Books.

Dhadha, Mustafah. 1993. *Warriors at Work: How Guinea Was Really Set Free*. Boulder: University of Colorado Press.

Diamond, L., J. J. Linz, and S. M. Lipset. 1988. *Democracy in Developing Countries*. Vol. 2: *Africa*. Boulder, Colo.: Lynne Reinner.

Diawara, Manthia. 1990–91. "The Nature of Mother in *Dreaming Rivers*." *Third Text* 13: 73–84.

———. 1991. "Englishness and Blackness: Cricket as a Discourse on Colonialism." *Callaloo* 13, no. 4: 830–44.

Dieng, Amady Ali. 1967. "Les damnés de la terre et les problemes D'Afrique noire." *Présence Africaine* 57.

Djebar, Assia. 1985. *Fantasia: An Algerian Cavalcade.* London: Picador.

Doane, Mary Ann. 1991. *Femmes Fatales: Feminism, Film Theory, Psycho-analysis.* New York: Routledge.

Dollimore, Jonathan. 1991. *Sexual Dissidence: Literatures, Histories, Theo-ries.* Oxford: Oxford University Press.

Domenach, Jean-Marie. 1962. "Les damnés de la terre," *Espirit*, 21, part 1.

Dumont, Rene. 1966. *False Start in Africa.* London: Sphere Books.

Dunayevskaya, Raya. 1977. *Sexism, Politics, and Revolution in Mao's China.* (Women's Liberation, News and Letters, Detroit, reprinted in R. Dunayevskaya, 1996, *Women's Liberation and the Dialectics of Revolu-tion*). Detroit: Wayne State University Press.

———. 1988 [1973]. *Philosophy and Revolution: From Marx to Mao and From Hegel to Sartre.* New York: Columbia University Press.

———. 1989. *The Philosophic Moment of Marxist-Humanism.* Chicago: News & Letters.

———. 1991. *Rosa Luxemburg, Women's Liberation, and Marx's Philosophy of Revolution.* Urbana: University of Illinois Press.

Dyer, Richard. 1988. "White." *Screen* 29: 4.

Dzhagarov. 1944. *Day Hospitalization and the Mentally Ill.* Moscow.

Eagleton, Terry. 1990. "Nationalism, Irony, and Commitment." In *Nation-alism, Colonialism, and Literature,* edited by Terry Eagleton et al. Min-neapolis: University of Minnesota Press.

Ebert, Teresa. 1996. *Ludic Feminism and After: Postmodernism, Desire, and Labor in Late Capitalism.* Ann Arbor: University of Michigan Press.

Edelman, Lee. 1993. *Homographesis: Essays in Gay Literary and Cultural Theory.* New York and London: Routledge.

el-Saadawi, Nawal. 1980. *The Hidden Face of Eve: Women in the Arab World.* London: Zed Press.

Elliot, Charles. 1987. "Some Aspects of Relations between the North and the South in the NGO Sector." *World Development* 15.

Ellis, Havelock, and John Addington Symonds. 1897. *Sexual Inversion.* London: Wilson and Macmillan. Reprinted 1975, New York: Arno Press.

Ellison, Ralph. 1967. "Some Questions and Some Answers." In *Shadow and Act.* New York: Random House.

Enloe, Cynthia. 1989. *Making Feminist Sense of Internationalist Politics.* London: Pandora.

Entelis, John. 1986. *Algeria: The Revolution Institutionalized.* Boulder, Colo: Westview Press.

Eshleman, Clayton, and Annette Smith. 1983. Introduction to *Césaire: Collected Poetry*. Berkeley: University of California Press.

Fanon, Frantz. 1967a. *Black Skin, White Masks*, translated by Charles Lam Markmann. New York: Grove.

———. 1967b. *Toward the African Revolution: Political Essays*, translated by Haakon Chevalier. New York: Grove.

——— 1967c. *Studies in a Dying Colonialism*, translated by Haakon Chevalier. New York: Monthly Review Press.

———. 1968. *The Wretched of the Earth*, translated by Constance Farrington. New York: Grove.

Fanon, F., and S. Asselah. 1957. "La Sociothérapie dans un service d'homme musulman, difficultés méthodique." *L'information Psychiatrique* 30, no. 9.

Fanon, F., and J. Azoulay. 1954. "La Socialthérapie dans un Service d'Homme Musulmans, Difficultés Méthodologique." *L'information Psychiatrique* 30, no. 9.

Fanon, Frantz, and C. Geronimi. 1959. "L'hospitalization de jour en psychiatrie, valeur, et limites. II. Considérations doctrinales." *La Tunisie Medicale* 38: 10.

Fanon, Frantz, and R. Lacaton. 1955. *Conduits d'aveu en Afrique de Nord*. Congrès des médicins aliénistes et neurologues de France et des pays de langue français. 53rd session, Nice, September 5–11.

Fanon, Frantz, and F. Sanchez. 1956. "Attitude de musulman maghrebin devant la folie." *Revue practique de psychologie de la vie sociale et d'hygiene mentale*. No. 1.

Feuchtwang, Stephan. 1985. "Fanon's Politics of Culture: The Colonial Situation and Its Extension." *Economy and Society* 14, no. 4: 450–73.

———. 1987. "Fanonian Spaces." *New Formations* 1 (Spring): 124–30.

Freire, Paulo. 1971. *Pedagogy of the Oppressed*. New York: Herder and Herder.

Freud, Sigmund. 1908a. "Creative Writers and Day-Dreaming." *Standard Edition* 9: 141–57

———. 1908b. "Hysterical Phantasies and Their Relation to Bisexuality." *Standard Edition* 9: 155–66.

———. 1909. "Some General Remarks on Hysterical Attacks." *Standard Edition* 9: 227–34.

———. 1913. "Totem and Taboo." *Standard Edition* 13: 1–162.

———. 1963. *The Standard Edition of the Complete Psychological Works of Sigmund Freud*, edited and translated by James Strachey. 24 vols. New York: Norton.

454 Bibliography

Friel, Brian. 1981. *Translations*. London: Faber & Faber.

Fuss, Diana. 1989. *Essentially Speaking: Feminism, Nature, and Difference*. London: Routledge.

Gaines, Jane M. 1992. "Competing Glances: Who Is Reading Robert Mapplethorpe's *Black Book*?" *New Formations* 16 (Spring): 24–39.

Gall, Ching-Liang Low. 1989. "White Skins/Black Masks: The Pleasures and Politics of Imperialism." *New Formations* 9 (Winter).

Gates, Henry Louis. 1990. "Afterword: Critical Remarks." In *The Anatomy of Racism*, edited by David Theo Goldberg. Minneapolis: University of Minnesota Press.

Gates, Henry Louis, ed. 1986. *"Race," Writing, and Difference*. Chicago: University of Chicago Press.

Geismar, Peter. 1969. "Frantz Fanon: Evolution of a Revolutionary." *Monthly Review* 21: 22–30.

———. 1971. *Frantz Fanon*. New York: Dial Press.

Geller, Jay. 1992. "A Glance at the Nose: The Inscription of Jewish Difference." *American Image* 49.

———. 1994. "Freud v. Freud: Freud's Reading of Daniel Paul Schreber's Denkwurdigkeiten Eines Nervenkranten." In *Reading Freud's Reading*, edited by Sander Gilman, Jutta Birmele, Jay Geller, and Valerie D. Greenberg. New York: New York University Press.

Gendzier, Irene. 1973. *Frantz Fanon: A Critical Study*. New York: Grove Press, Inc.; 2d. ed. with new introduction, 1985.

Ghe, Nghuyen. 1963. "Frantz Fanon et les problemes de l'independence." La Pensée 157 (February).

Gibson, Nigel. 1994. "Fanon's Humanism and the Second Independence in Africa." In *Africa, Human Rights, and the Global System*, edited by Eileen McCarthy-Arnolds, David R. Penna, and Debra Joy Cruz Sobrepena. Westport, Conn.: Greenwood Press.

———. 1996. "Jammin' the Airwaves and Tuning into the Revolution: The Dialectics of the Radio in *L' An V de la révolution algérienne*." In *Fanon: A Critical Reader*, edited by Lewis R. Gordon, T. Denean Sharpley-Whiting, and Renee T. White. Oxford: Blackwell.

———. 1999. "Fanon and/or Cultural Studies." In *Frantz Fanon: Critical Perspectives*, edited by Tony Alessandrini. New York: Routledge 1999.

———. In press. *Frantz Fanon: Key Critical Thinker*. Oxford: Polity Press.

Gillespie, Joan. 1961. *Algeria: Rebellion and Revolution*. London: Ernest Benn.

Gilman, Sander. 1993. *Freud, Race, and Gender*. Princeton, N.J.: Princeton University Press.

Gilroy, Paul. 1990. "One Nation under the Groove." In *Anatomy of Racism*, edited by David Theo Goldberg. Minneapolis: University of Minnesota Press.

Glissant, Edouard. 1981. *Le Discourse antillais*. Paris.

———. 1992. *Caribbean Discourse*. Charlottesville: University of Virginia Press.

Goldberg, David Theo, ed. 1990. *The Anatomy of Racism*. Minneapolis: University of Minnesota Press.

Gordon, David C. 1966. *The Passing of French Algeria*. London: Oxford University Press.

———. 1996a. *Fanon: A Critical Reader*. Oxford: Blackwell.

Gordon, Lewis. 1996b. *Fanon and the Crisis of European Man*. New York: Routledge.

Gordon, Lewis R., T. Denean Sharpley-Whiting, and Renee T. White, eds. 1996. *Fanon: A Critical Reader*. Oxford: Blackwell.

Gramsci, Antonio. 1971. *Prison Notebooks*. New York: International Publishers.

Grohs, J. R. 1968. "Frantz Fanon and the African Revolution." *Journal of Modern African Studies* (December).

Grosz, Elizabeth. 1990. "Judaism and Exile: The Ethics of Otherness." *New Formations* 12: 77–88.

Guha, Ranajit. 1989. "Dominance without Hegemony and Its Historiography." In *Sublatern Studies VI: Writings on South Asian History and Society*. Delhi: Oxford University Press.

Hall, Stuart. 1987. "Minimal Selves." In *The Real Me: Postmodern and Questions of Identity*. London: ICA documents 6.

———. 1988. "New Ethnicities." In *Black Film British Cinema*. London: ICA Documents 7.

———. 1990. "Cultural Identity and Diaspora." In *Identity, Community, Culture, Difference*, edited by J. Rutherford. London: Lawrence & Wishart.

Hansen, Emmanuel. 1977. *Frantz Fanon: Social and Political Thought*. Columbus: Ohio State University Press.

Harris, Wilson. 1974. *History, Fable, and Myth in the Caribbean and Guianas*. Georgetown, Guyana: Calaloux Publications.

Hatem, Mervat. 1993. "Toward the Development of Post-Islamist and Post-Nationalist Feminist Discourses in the Middle East." In *Arab Women: Old Boundaries, New Frontiers*, edited by Judith Tucker. Bloomington and Indianapolis: Indiana University Press.

Heath, Stephen. 1983. "Le Père Noel," *October*, no. 26.

————. 1986. "Joan Riviere and the Masquerade." In *Formations of Fantasy*, edited by Victor Burgin, James Donald, and Cora Kaplan. London and New York: Methuen.

Hegel, G. W. F. 1969. *Science of Logic*, translated by A. V. Miller. London: Allen & Unwin.

Hegel, G. W. F. 1977. *The Phenomenology of Mind*, translated by J. B. Baillie. New York: Humanities Press, Inc.

Helie, Damien. 1967. *L'Autogestion Industrielle*. Paris: Thesis.

Helie-Lucas, Marie-Aimée. 1990. "Women, Nationalism, and Religion in the Algerian Liberation Struggle." In *Opening the Gates: A Century of Arab Feminist Writings*. Bloomington: Indiana University Press. Reprinted in this volume.

Hobsbawn, Eric, and Terence Ranger. 1983. *Invention of Tradition*. Madison: University of Wisconsin Press.

Hodgkin, Thomas. 1957. *Nationalism in Colonial Africa*. New York: New York University Press.

Horne, Alistair. 1977. *A Savage War of Peace*. New York: Viking.

Humbaraci, Arslan. 1966. *Algeria: A Revolution That Failed*. New York: Praeger.

Hyams, Jacques. 1971. *Leopold Segar Senghor: An Intellectual Biography*. Edinburgh: University of Edinburgh Press.

Irele, Abiola. 1970. "The Theory of Négritude." In *Proceedings of the Seminar on Political Theory and Ideology in African Society*. Edinburgh: University of Edinburgh Press.

————. 1983. Introduction to Paulin Hountondji, *African Philosophy*, translated by Henri Evans and Jonathan Rée. Bloomington: Indiana University Press.

————. 1986. "Contemporary Thought in French Speaking Africa." In *The Legacies of Empire*, edited by Isaac James Mowoe and Richard Bjornson. Westport, Conn.: Greenwood.

Irigaray Luce. 1985. "Any Theory of the 'Subject' Has Always Been Appropriated by the 'Masculine.'" In *Speculum of the Other Woman*, translated by Gillian C. Gill. Ithaca, N.Y.: Cornell University Press.

Isaacs, Harold I. 1965. "Portrait of a Revolutionary." *Commentary* (July).

Jackson, Henry F. 1977. *The FLN in Algeria: Party Development in a Revolutionary Society*. Westport, Conn.: Greenwood Press.

JanMohamed, Abdul R. 1986. "The Economy of Manichean Allegory: The Function of Racial Difference in Colonialist Literature." In *"Race," Writing, and Difference*, edited by Henry Louis Gates. Chicago: University of Chicago Press.

Jeffries, Richard. 1992. "Dictator or Democrat?: Rawlings and the Process of Democratization in Ghana." Paper prepared for the African Studies Association of the U.K. Biennial Conference, University of Stirling, September.

Jinadu, Adele. 1986. *Fanon*. London: KPI.

Juminer, Bertene. "Homage to Frantz Fanon." 1962. *Présence Africaine* 12, no. 40.

Kandiyoti, Deniz. 1994. "Identity and Its Discontents: Women and the Nation." In *Colonial Discourse and Post-Colonial Theory: A Reader*. New York: Columbia University Press.

―――. 1989. "Bargaining with Patriarchy." *Gender and Society* 2, no. 3: 274–90.

Kesteloot, Lilyan. 1974. *Black Writers in French: A Literary History of Négritude*. Philadelphia: Temple University Press.

Kilson, Martin. 1966. *Political Change in a West African State*. Cambridge, Mass.: Harvard University Press.

Kitaj, R. B. 1989. *First Diasporist Manifesto*. London: Thames & Hudson.

Koundoura, Maria. 1989. "Naming Gayatri Spivak." *Stanford Humanities Review* 1, no. 1 (Spring): 84–97.

Kovatz, Edith. 1964. "Mariage et Cohésion Sociale Chez les Blancs Créoles de la Martinique." Unpublished Master's thesis, University of Montreal.

Krupat, Amold. 1992. *Ethnocriticism: Ethnography, History, Literature*. Berkeley and Los Angeles: University of California Press.

Lacan, Jacques. 1977a. *Écrits*, translated by Alan Sheridan. New York: W. W. Norton and Company.

―――. 1977b [1948]. "The Mirror Stage as Formative of the Function of the I as Revealed in Psychoanalytic Experience." In *Ecrits* translated by Alan Sheridan. New York: W. W. Norton and Company.

―――. 1981. *The Four Fundamental Concepts of Psychoanalysis*, translated by Alan Sheridan. New York: Norton.

Lacoue-Labarthe, Philippe. 1989. *Typology: Mimesis, Philosophy, Politics*, edited by Christopher Fynsk. Cambridge, Mass.: Harvard University Press.

Lacoue-Labarthe, Philippe, and Jean Luc-Nancy. 1989. "The Unconscious Is Structured Like an Affect" (Part I of "The Jewish People Do Not Dream"). *Stanford Literature Review* 6 (Fall).

Lambo, T. A. 1956. "Neuropsychiatric Observations in the Western Region of Nigeria." *British Medical Journal* 15.

Laremont, Ricardo. 1994. "Islam and the Politics of Resistance in Algeria, 1983–1992." Ph.D. diss., Yale University, New Haven, Conn.

Lazarus, Neil. 1990. *Resistance in Postcolonial African Fiction.* New Haven, Conn.: Yale University Press.

Leys, Colin. 1994. "Confronting the African Tragedy." *New Left Review,* no. 204: 33–47.

Lloyd, David. 1991. "Race under Representation." *The Oxford Literary Review* 13, nos. 1–2: 62–94.

Löwy, Michael. 1979. *Georg Lukács: From Romanticism to Bolshevism.* London: NLB.

Lucas, Phillippe. 1971. *Sociologie de Frantz Fanon.* Algeria: SNED, Société nationale d'édition et de diffusion.

Lukács, Georg. 1971a. *History and Class Consciousness.* Cambridge, Mass.: MIT Press.

———. 1971b. *Theory of the Novel.* Cambridge, Mass.: MIT Press.

Macpherson, C. B. 1966. *The Real World of Democracy.* Oxford: Oxford University Press.

Mahmoud, Fatima. 1986. "Women and Liberation: Fatima Babikar Mahmoud Talks to Patricia McFadden." *Journal of African Marxists* 8 (January): 7–23.

Malley, Robert. 1996. *The Call from Algeria: Third Worldism, Revolution, and the Turn to Islam.* Berkeley: University of California Press.

Marx, Karl. 1978 [1847]. *Communist Manifesto.* In *The Marx-Engels Reader,* 2d ed., edited by Robert C. Tucher. New York: W. W. Norton & Company.

Massu, Jacques. 1972. *Le Torrent et la Digue.* Paris: Plon.

McCullogh, Jock. 1983. *Black Soul, White Artifact: Fanon's Clinical Psychology and Social Theory.* Cambridge: Cambridge University Press.

McGann, Jerome. 1989. "The Third World of Criticism." In *Rethinking Historicism: Critical Readings in Romantic History,* edited by Marjorie Levinson et al. New York: Blackwell.

McRobbie, Angela. 1985. "Strategies of Vigilance: An Interview with Gayatri Spivak." *Block* 10.

Memmi, Albert. 1965. *The Colonizer and the Colonized,* translated by Howard Greenfield. New York: Orion Press.

———. 1968. "Frantz Fanon and the Notion of 'Deficiency.' " In *Dominated Man: Notes toward a Portrait,* translated by Eleanor Levieux. New York: Orion Press.

———. 1971. "Frozen by Death in the Image of Third World Prophet," *New York Times Book Review* (March 14).

Mercer, Kobena. 1986. "Racism and Transcultural Psychiatry." In *The Power of Psychiatry*, edited by Peter Miller and Nikolas Rose. Oxford: Polity Press.

———. 1987. "Black Hair/Style Politics." *New Formations* 3 (Winter).

———. 1990. "Black Art and the Burden of Representation." *Third Text* 10: 61–78.

———. 1992. "Skin Head Sex Thing: Racial Difference and the Homoerotic Imaginary." *New Formations* 16 (Spring).

Mernissi, Fatima. 1987. *Beyond the Veil: Male and Female Dynamics in Modern Muslim Society*. Bloomington: Indiana University Press.

———. 1989. *Doing Daily Battle: Interviews with Moroccan Women*. New Brunswick, N.J.: Rutgers University Press.

———. 1992. *Islam and Democracy: Fear of the Modern World*. Reading, Mass.: Addison-Wesley Publishing Co.

Messaoudi, *Unbowed: An Algerian Woman Confronts Islamic Fundamentalism*. Philadelphia: University of Pennsylvania Press.

Minces, Juliette. 1978. "Women in Algeria." In *Women in the Muslim World*, edited by Lois Beck and Nikki Keddie. Cambridge, Mass.: Harvard University Press.

Mohanty, Chandra Talpade. 1991. "Cartographies of Struggle: Third World Women and the Politics of Feminism." In *Third World Women and the Politics of Feminism*, edited by Chandra Talpade Mohanty, Ann Russo, and Lourdes Torres. Bloomington and Indianapolis: Indiana University Press.

Morrisson, Toni. 1992. *Playing in the Dark: Whiteness and the Literary Imagination*. Cambridge, Mass.: Harvard University Press.

Mowitt, John. 1992. "Algerian Nation: Fanon's Fetish." *Cultural Critique* 22 (Fall).

Mphahlele, Ezekiel. 1971. *Down Second Avenue*. Garden City, N.Y.: Doubleday.

Mrabet, Fadila. 1965. *Les Algériennes*. Paris: Maspero.

———. 1967. *La Femme Algérienne*. Paris: Maspero.

Mudimbe, V. Y. 1988. *The Invention of Africa: Gnosis, Philosophy, and the Order of Knowledge*. London: James Currey.

Murch, Arvin. 1971. *Black Frenchmen: The Political Integration of the French Antilles*. Cambridge: Schenkman.

Ngugi Wa Thiong'o. 1985. "The Language of African Literature." *New Left Review* #150. Reprinted as an appendix in Lou Turner and John Alan, *Frantz Fanon, Soweto, and American Black Thought*. Chicago: News and Letters, 1986.

———. 1986. *Decolonizing the Mind*. London: James Currey.

———. 1987. *Devil on the Cross*. London: Heinemann.

Nkrumah, Kwame. 1957. *Ghana: The Autobiography of Kwame Nkrumah* London: Thomas Nelson.

Odeh, Lama Abu. 1993. "Post-Colonial Feminism and the Veil: Thinking the Difference." *Feminist Review* 43 (Spring).

O'Hanlon, Rosalind. 1988. "Recovering the Subject: *Subaltern Studies* and Histories of Resistance in Colonial South Asia." *Modern Asian Studies* 22: 1.

———. 1989. "Cultures of Rule, Communities of Resistance: Gender, Discourse and Tradition in Recent South Asian Historiographies." *Social Analysis* 25.

Onwuanibe, Richard. 1983. *A Critique of Revolutionary Humanism: Frantz Fanon*. St. Louis: Warren Green.

Ousmane, Sembene. 1976. *Xala*. Chicago: Lawrence Hill.

Parry, Benita. 1987. "Problems in Current Theories of Colonial Discourse." *Oxford Literary Review* 9 (Winter).

Pease, Donald. 1991. "Toward a Sociology of Literary Knowledge: Greenblatt, Colonialism, and the New Historicism." In *Consequences of Theory*, edited by Barbara Johnson and Jonathan Arac. Baltimore: Johns Hopkins University Press.

Pêcheux, Michel. 1982. *Language, Semantics, and Ideology*, translated by Harbans Nagpal. New York: St. Martin's Press.

Peteet, Julie. 1993. "Authenticity and Gender: The Presentation of Culture." In *Arab Women: Old Boundaries, New Frontiers*, edited by Judith Tucker. Bloomington and Indianapolis: Indiana University Press.

Prince, R. 1967. "The Changing Picture of Depressive Syndromes in Africa." *Canadian Journal of African Studies* 1, no. 2: 177–92.

Quandt, William B. 1969. *Revolution and Political Leadership: Algeria 1954–1968*. Cambridge, Mass.: MIT Press.

Ravenhill, John. 1993. "A Second Decade of Adjustment." In *Hemmed In: Responses to Africa's Economic Decline*, edited by Thomas Callaghy and John Ravenhill. New York: Columbia University Press.

Ritvo, Lucille B. 1990. *Darwin's Influence on Freud: A Tale of Two Sciences*. New Haven, Conn.: Yale University Press.

Riviere, Joan. 1986. "Womanliness as a Masquerade." In *Formations of Fantasy*, edited by Victor Burgin, James Donald, and Cora Kaplan. London and New York: Methuen.

Roazen, Paul. 1974. *Freud and His Followers*. New York: New American Library.

BIBLIOGRAPHY   461

Rooney, Caroline. 1991. "Are We in the Company of Feminists?; A Preface for Bessie Head and Ama Ata Aidoo." In *Diverse Voices*, edited by Harriet Devine Jump. New York: St. Martin's Press.

Rose, Jacqueline. 1981. "The Imaginary." In *The Talking Cure*, edited by Colin MacCabe. London: Macmillan.

Ruedy, John. 1992. *Modern Algeria: The Origin and Development of a Nation*. Bloomington: Indiana University Press.

Said, Edward. 1978. *Orientalism*. New York: Vintage Books.

———. 1988. *Yeat and Decolonization*, reprinted in Jerry Eagleton et al., *Nationalism, Colonialism, and Literature*. Minneapolis: University of Minnesota Press.

———. 1989. "Representing the Colonized: Anthropology's Interlocutors." *Critical Inquiry* 15, no. 2 (Winter): 205–25.

———. 1993. *Culture and Imperialism*. New York: Knopf.

Sansarian, E. 1982. *The Women's Rights Movement in Iran: Mutiny, Appeasement, and Repression from 1900 to Khomeini*. New York: Praeger.

Saro-Wiwa, Ken. 1996. *A Month and a Day: A Detention Diary*. New York: Penguin Books.

Sartre, Jean-Paul. 1957. *Being and Nothingness*, translated by Hazel Barnes. London: Methuen.

———. 1963. *Orphée noir*. Preface to Anthologie de la nouvelle poésie negre et malgache. Paris: Presses Universitaires de France, 1948. (*Black Orpheus*, translated by S. W. Allen. [Paris: Présence Africaine]).

———. 1965. Introduction to Albert Memmi, *The Colonizer and Colonized*, translated by Howard Greenfield. New York: Monthly Review.

Sedgwick, Eve Kosofsky. 1993. *Tendencies*. Durham, N.C.: Duke University Press.

Seigel, J. E. 1968. "On Frantz Fanon." *American Scholar* (Winter).

Sekyi-Otu, Ato. 1996. *Fanon's Dialectic of Experience*. Cambridge, Mass.: Harvard University Press.

Serequeberhan, Tsenay. 1994. *The Hermeneutics of African Philosophy*. New York: Routledge.

Shaaban, Bothaina. 1991. *Both Right and Left Handed: Arab Women Talk about Their Lives*. Bloomington: Indiana University Press.

Shanin, Theodor. 1983. *Late Marx and the Russian Road*. London: Routledge and Kegan Paul.

Sharpley-Whiting, T. D. 1997. *Frantz Fanon, Conflicts & Feminisms*. Lanham, Md.: Rowman & Littlefield.

Shelley, F. 1995. "Africa, Postcolonialism, Fanon." *News & Letters* 40: 8.

462 Bibliography

Shohat, Ella. 1991. "Imagining Terra Incognita: The Disciplinary Gaze of Empire." *Public Culture* 3, no. 2: 41–70.

Silverman, Kaja. 1989. "White Skin, Brown Masks: The Double Mimesis, or With Lawrence in Arabia." *Differences* 1, no. 3 (Fall): 3–54.

Smith, Paul. 1988. *Discerning the Subject.* Minneapolis: University Minnesota Press.

Snead, James. 1988. "Black Independent Film." In *Black Film in British Cinema.* London: ICA documents, 7.

Sombart, Werner. 1948. "Capitalism." In *Encyclopedia of the Social Science.* New York: Macmillan.

Souffrant, Eddy. 1996. "To Conquer the Veil." In *Fanon: A Critical Reader,* edited by Lewis R. Gordon, T. D. Sharpley-Whiting, and Renee T. White. Oxford: Blackwell.

Soyinka, Wole. 1976. *Myth, Literature, and the African World.* Cambridge: University of Cambridge Press.

St. John, Peter. 1996. "Insurgency, Legitmacy, & Intervention in Algeria." *Commentary* 65 (January): 1–9.

Terdiman, Richard. 1985. *Discourse/Counter Discourse: The Theory and Practice of Symbolic Resistance in Nineteenth-Century France.* Ithaca, N.Y.: Cornell University Press.

Tohidi, Nayereh. 1991. "Gender and Islamic Fundamentalism." In *Third World Women and Politics of Feminism.* Bloomington: Indiana University Press.

Towa, Marcien. 1979. *Essai sur la problématique philosophique dans l'Afrique actuelle.* Yaoundé: Édition Clé.

Trinidad and Tobago, National Planning Commission. 1964–1968. *Draft Second Five Year Plan.*

Turner, Lou. 1989. "Frantz Fanon's Journey into Hegel's 'Night of the Absolute.' " *Quarterly Journal of Ideology* 13, no. 4: 47–63.

———. 1991. "The Marxist Humanist Legacy of Frantz Fanon." *News & Letters* 38, no. 10: 47–63.

———. 1996. "On the Difference between the Hegelian and Fanonian Dialectic of Lordship and Bondage." In *Fanon: A Critical Reader,* edited by Lewis R. Gordon, T. Denean Sharpley-Whiting, and Renee T. White. Oxford: Blackwell.

Turner, Lou, and John Alan. 1978, 1986. *Frantz Fanon, Soweto, and American Black Thought.* Chicago: News and Letters.

Tyler, Carole-Anne. 1996. *Female Impersonators.* New York and London: Routledge.

Urdang, Stephanie. 1979. *Fighting Two Colonialisms: Women in Guinea-Bissau*. New York: Monthly Review Press.

Vansina, Jan. 1990. *Paths in the Rainforests: Toward a History of Political Tradition in Equatorial Africa*. Madison: University of Wisconsin Press.

Wallace, Edwin R. 1983. *Freud and Anthropology*. New York: International Universities Press, Inc.

Wallerstein, Immanuel. 1979. "Fanon and the Revolutionary Class." In *Capitalist World Economy*. Cambridge: Cambridge University Press.

West. Lois A., ed. 1996. *Feminist Nationalism*. New York: Routledge.

Wiseman, John A. 1990. *Democracy in Black Africa: Survival and Renewal*. New York: Paragon House Publishers.

Woddis, Jack. 1972. *New Theories of Revolution*. New York: International Publishers.

Worsley, Peter. 1969. "Frantz Fanon: Evolution of a Revolutionary—Revolutionary Theories." *Monthly Review* 21 (May): 30–49.

Wright. Elizabeth. 1992. *Feminism and Psychoanalysis: A Critical Dictionary*. Oxford: Blackwell.

Young, Robert. 1990. *White Mythologies: Writing History and the West*. New York and London: Routledge.

Zahar, Renate. 1970. *L'Oeuvre de Frantz Fanon*. Paris: Maspero.

———. 1974. *Frantz Fanon: Colonialism and Alienation. Concerning Frantz Fanon's Political Theory*, translated by Willfied F. Feuser. New York: Monthly Review Press.

Zolberg, Aristide R. 1966. "Frantz Fanon: A Gospel for the Damned." *Encounter* 27, no. 5 (November).

About the Contributors

HUSSEIN ADAM is associate professor of political science and African American studies at Holy Cross College. He is the editor of *Mending Rips in the Sky: Options for Somali Communities in the 21st Century* and *Rethinking the Somali Political Experience.*

JOHN ALAN, a film maker and long-time activist in the civil rights and labor movements, writes the monthly Black/Red column for *News and Letters.*

HOMI K. BHABHA is professor of English and Chester D. Tripp Professor in the Humanities at the University of Chicago. He is author of *Location of Culture*, coauthor of *Anish Kapoor*, editor of *Nation and Narration*, and coeditor of *Negotiating Rapture: The Power of Art to Transform Lives.*

HUSSEIN ABDILIAH BULHAN is author of *Frantz Fanon and the Psychology of Oppression.* He is presently the president of BHM International, an international development consulting firm, and chairman of Black World Telecommunications, an organization which focuses on providing telecommunication services to black communities around the world. He recently established a nonprofit center in Hargeysa, Somaliland called the Center for Health and Development.

DIANA FUSS is associate professor of English at Princeton University. She is the author of two books, *Essentially Speaking* and *Identification Papers*, and the editor of *Inside Out* and *Human, All Too Human.* Her current book in progress, tentatively entitled "Interiors," focuses on the history and philosophy of the domestic interior.

HENRY LOUIS GATES JR. is W. E. B. Du Bois Professor of the Humanities at Harvard University and chair of the Department of Afro-American Studies. His selected works include *Thirteen Ways of Looking at a Black Man, The Future of the Race* (with Cornel West); *Colored People: A Memoir; Loose Canons:*

464

Notes on the Culture Wars; The Signifying Monkey; and *Figures in Black.* He has edited a number of books, including *The Dictionary of Global Culture,* and is co–general editor of *The Norton Anthology of African American Literature.*

NIGEL C. GIBSON is assistant director of the African Studies Institute at Columbia University where he also teaches. He has written a number of articles and book chapters on Frantz Fanon, including essays in *Fanon: A Critical Reader* and *Fanon: Critical Perspectives.* He is coeditor of two works in press, *Contested Terrains/Constructed Categories: Africa in Focus* with George C. Bond and *Adorno: A Critical Reader* with Andrew Rubin. He is currently completing a monograph on Fanon for Polity Press.

The late EMMANUEL HANSEN was the author of *Frantz Fanon: Social and Political Thought* and the editor of *Africa: Perspective on Peace* and *Development and State, Development and Politics in Ghana.* He was a founding editor of the *Journal of African Marxists.* During 1982–83 he served in the Rawlings Government and recorded his experiences and criticisms in the posthumously published *Ghana under Rawlings: Early Years.*

MARIE AIMÉE HELIE-LUCAS was born in Algiers and was active during the national liberation struggle. Trained as a sociologist and anthropologist, she taught for twelve years at the University of Algiers. She was a founding member of AAWORD, the Association of African Women for Research on Development and of the Action Committee which became the Network of Women Living Under Muslim Laws. She has compiled *Fatwahs against Women in Bangladesh* for Women Living under Muslim Laws and recently authored "L'internationalisme dans le mouvement des femmes comme modèle d'organization des nouveaux mouvement sociale."

TONY MARTIN is professor of African studies at Wellesley College. He has authored, compiled, or edited eleven books, including *Literary Garveyism: Garvey, Black Arts, and the Harlem Renaissance,* and the classic study of the Garvey Movement, *Race First: The Ideological and Organization Struggles of Marcus Garvey and the Universal Negro Improvement Association.* He is currently working on biographies of three Caribbean women—Amy Ashwood Garvey, Audrey Jeffers, and Trinidad's Kathleen Davis ("Auntie Kay"), and is also nearing completion of a study of European Jewish immigration into Trinidad in the 1930s.

ANNE MCCLINTOCK is currently visiting professor of English at New York University. She is author of *Imperial Leather: Race, Gender, and Sexuality,* and two monographs, *Simone de Beauvoir* and *Olive Schreiner*, and has edited a number of volumes, including *Dangerous Liaison: Gender, Nation and Poscolonial Perspectives*. Her latest work, *Skin Hunger: A Chronicle of the Sex Industry* (Jonathan Cape) will be published later this year.

BENITA PARRY is author of *India in the British Imagination 1880–1930, Delusions and Discoveries: Studies on India in the British Imagination*. She is coeditor of *Cultural Readings of Imperialism: Edward Said and the Gravity of History*.

EDWARD SAID is University Professor at Columbia. His books include *Beginnings; Orientalism; The Question of Palestine; Covering Islam; The World, the Text, and the Critic; After the Last Sky; Blaming the Victims; Culture and Imperialism*; and *The Politics of Dispossession*. His Wellek and Reith Lectures were published as, respectively, *Musical Elaborations* and *Representations of the Intellectual*. A book of essays, a memoir, and a study of opera are forthcoming.

T. DENEAN SHARPLEY-WHITING is associate professor of French and African American studies and acting chair of the Department of French at Purdue University. She is author of *Black Venus: Sexualized Savages, Primal Fears, and Primitive Narratives in French* and *Frantz Fanon: Conflicts & Feminisms*, and coeditor of *Spoils of War: Women of Color, Cultures*, and *Fanon: A Critical Reader*.

LOU TURNER, a colleague of the late Hegelian Marxist philosopher Raya Dunayevskaya, is managing editor of *News and Letters*, a Marxist-Humanist journal. He has published numerous articles on Marxist-Humanism, Frantz Fanon, and Hegelian dialectics. He teaches urban studies and social theory at North Central College, Naperville, Illinois.

ZOULIGHA is a feminist activist living, working, and struggling against the state, the military, and the Islamic fundamentalists in Algiers.